Livelihood and Sustainable Development in North East India

Edited by
Ram Krishna Mandal
A. Ibotombi Singh
Paritosh Chandra Dutta

CONCEPT PUBLISHING COMPANY PVT. LTD.
NEW DELHI-110059

ISBN-13: 978-93-86682-56-7

First Published 2019

Published and Printed by

Concept Since 1974

Concept Publishing Company Pvt. Ltd.
A/15-16, Commercial Block, Mohan Garden,
New Delhi-110059 (India)
T : 91 11 25351460, 91 11 25351794
E : publishing@conceptpub.com, *W*: www.conceptpub.com

Cataloging in Publication Data--Courtesy: D.K. Agencies (P) Ltd. <docinfo@dkagencies.com>

National Seminar on "Livelihood and Sustainable Development Strategies in North East States of India" (2013 : Itanagar, India)

Livelihood and sustainable development in North East India / edited by Ram Krishna Mandal, A. Ibotombi Singh, Paritosh Chandra Dutta.

pages cm

Papers presented at the National Seminar on "Livelihood and Sustainable Development Strategies in North East States of India" organized by the Department of Economics, Dera Natung Government College and sponsored by the University Grants Commission during 22-23 November, 2013.

Includes bibliographical references and index.

ISBN 9789386682567

1. Sustainable development--India, Northeastern--Congresses. 2. Women in economic development--India, Northeastern--Congresses. 3. India, Northeastern--Economic policy--Congresses. I. Mandal, Ramkrishna, 1966- editor. II. Ibotombi Singh, A., 1964- editor. III. Dutta, Paritosh Chandra, editor. IV. Dera Natung Government College (Itanagar, India). Department of Economics, organizer. V. India. University Grants Commission, sponsoring body. VI. Title.

LCC HC437.N57N38 2013 | DDC 338.9541 23

Dedicated
to
Anusree Krishna Mandal
Avinandan Krishna Mandal
A. Aena
and
Pikaso Pratik Dutta

Preface

Keeping in mind the importance of Livelihood and Sustainable Development Strategies in North East States of India, this National Seminar sponsored by UGC (NERO) was organised by the Department of Economics, Dera Natung Government College, Itanagar, to discuss and analyse the various issues, problems, challenges and strategies in context of Sustainable Development Strategies in view of Livelihood. The present volume is a collection of twenty eight papers contributed to the seminar by eminent scholars, academicians, policy-makers, bureaucrats and thinkers. The publication of this book will not have been possible unless the seminar is organised. In organising the seminar we have received supports and cooperation from different persons and institutions that we thankfully acknowledge. At the very outset we express our deep gratitude to Chief Guest, Dr. Tejum Padu, Joint Director, Directorate of Higher and Technical Education, Government of Arunachal Pradesh, Itangar, Guest of Honour, Mrs. Taba Yall Nabam, Councillor, Itanagar Municipality who kindly inaugurated the seminar and delivered their valuable inaugural speech. Mr. Tomar Ete, Principal, Dera Natung Government College, Itanagar extended a warm welcome to all the distinguished academicians, guests and other dignitaries, students and media persons.

We are also thankful to Prof. Amitava Mitra, Faculty of Social Sciences, Rajiv Gandhi University, for his kind presence and gracing the participants through his keynote addresse in the seminar. We feel obliged to our Vice-Principal, Mr. Sangja Khandu for his constant cooperation, encouragement and guidance in organising the seminar.

We would be falling in my duty if we do not extend my gratitude to our Principal, Mr. Tomar Ete for generating in us the interest to organise a seminar in the college. We are also thankful to the Chief Guest of the valedictory function, Dr. V.N. Sharma, Liaison Officer, Directorate of

Higher and Technical Education, Government of Arunachal Pradesh, Itangar, for the distribution of certificates to the participants. We are very much encouraged by the wide response from the scholars of different parts of India and abroad. We express a deep sense of gratitude to all the paper contributors in this volume.

We owe the debt of gratitude to all our colleagues especially Mrs. Suparna Bhattacharjee, Mrs. Madhuparna Bhattacharjee, Dr. A.K. Pandey, Mr. S.K. Sharma, Dr. R.B. Tripathy, Dr. B.L. Behera, UGC in-Charge, also to all our dear students especially of B.A. second and third year honours who shared with us all the troubles and pains in organising the seminar and made it successful.

We are also sincerely grateful to the Secretary, UGC (NERO) and the Deputy Secretary, UGC (NERO) for providing the financial assistance to hold the seminar in our college. We are also taking the opportunity to thank profusely to Concept Publishing Co. Pvt. Ltd., New Delhi, for publication this book.

Ram Krishna Mandal
A. Ibotombi Singh
Paritosh Chandra Dutta

Acknowledgements

The co-operation of Secretary, UGC (NERO) and the Deputy Secretary, UGC (NERO) for Financial Assistance for organising the National Seminar on "Livelihood and Sustainable Development Strategies in North East States of India".

Contents

Preface vii
Acknowledgements ix
List of Contributors xv
Introduction xix

SECTION-I
Livelihood Strategy and Sustainable Development

1. Livelihood Improvement of Hill Tribes Through Adaptive Aquacultural Approaches 3
Deepjyoti Baruah and *Aparna Baruah*

2. Fish Husbandry in Vast Expanse of Water: A Perspective Platform for Livelihood and Sustainability in Arunachal Pradesh 9
P. Nath, D.N. Das *and* S.C. Dey

3. NERIST in Development of Social Welfare and Economic Growth of the North Eastern Region Through CATRD 17
Debabrata Maji

4. Poverty and We: A Brief Preview 30
Swapnali Baruah

5. PRI in Sustaining Livelihood in Arunachal Pradesh 40
Bijay Raji

6. Strategies for Sustainable Socio-Economic Development in Arunachal Pradesh 46
Toku Chokio

7. Rubber Cultivation as Sustainable Livelihood in Arunachal Pradesh 60
Amum Tamuk

8. Educational Attainment for Changing Livelihood in Arunachal Pradesh — 68
Tumter Lollen

9. NGOs in Livelihood Strategies for Marginalised Differently Abled People: A Study on Atmanirbhar—Ek Challenge — 81
Dipakshi Das, Ira Das and *Namita Das*

SECTION-II
Tourism and Development

10. Problems and Prospects of Tourism: A Case Study of Kaziranga and Sibsagar in Assam — 93
Mithilesh Kumar Sinha and *Mriganka Saikia*

11. Tourism Development in Arunachal Pradesh: Opportunities and Challenges — 107
Wangda Gyatso Gyana

SECTION-III
Women Empowerment for Sustainable Society

12. Dipshikha Beneficiaries' Participation in Women Empowerment Activities — 129
M.S. Ali and *M.M. Islam*

13. Socio-Economic and Culture of the Backward Muslim Women in Basirhat Block-II of North 24 Parganas, in West Bengal, 2011-12 — 138
Kaniska Sarkar

14. Self-Help Groups on Socio-Economic Empowerment of the Rural Women: A Case Study of Cachar District, Assam — 149
Subhrabaran Das and *A. Pushpalata Singh*

15. Woman Empowerment through Self-Help Group: A Case Study of Women SHG in Kapili Development Block of Morigaon District of Assam — 161
Pankaj Saikia

16. Leadership Pattern in Lamps in Karbi Anglong District of Assam — 183
Beena Rongpipi and *Uttambir Basumatary*

17. Self-Help Groups in Development and Empowerment: With Special Reference to Assam — 199
Sanjay Kanti Das

18. Self-Help Groups: A Tool for Women Empowerment: A Case Study — 242
Smti Likha Kiran Kabak

19. Empowerment of Women and Socio-Economic Development of North Eastern Region of India — 253
Paritosh Chandra Dutta

20. Self-Help Groups: A Paradigm Shift of Women Empowerment — 266
Anusree Krishna Mandal

21. Women Education in Special Reference to Rural Areas of North East India — 284
Ritwika Rajendra

22. Status of Women and Their Role in Socio-Economic Development of Ilam District in Nepal — 298
Sudarshan Prasad Regmi

23. Empowerment of Indian Women in the 21st Century: A General Perspective — 320
V. Ramabrahmam

24. Constraints Faced by the Tribal (Santal) SHG Members in the Process of Empowerment — 328
Amitava Dutta and *Paulami Das*

25. Women Environment Interaction and Traditional Ecological Knowledge: Concerns in Mountain Region — 355
Bal Krishan Choudhary, Kaushik Majumder and *Badal Kumar Datta*

SECTION-IV
Entrepreneurship and Economic Development

26. Entrepreneurship: A Panacea to Socio-economic Problems of North Eastern Region — 373
Deep Jyoti Gurung

27. Trade and Economic Development through Look East Policy — 383
Archana Mandal

28. Economic Integration between India and ASEAN through North Eastern Region: Issues and Challenges — 408
Anjali Biswas

Index — 430

List of Contributors

Dr. A. Pushpalata Singh, Assistant Professor, Department of Economics, Cachar College, Silchar, Cachar, Assam. **Email:** *sigha.pushpu@yahoo.co.in*

Dr. Amitava Dutta, Assistant Professor, Integrated Rural Development and Management Faculty Centre, Ramakrishna Mission Vivekananda University, Ramakrishna Mission Ashrama, Narendrapur, Kolkata-700 103, West Bengal, **Email:** *adirdm@gmail.com*

Dr. Amum Tamuk, Assistant Professor, Department of Botany, D.N. Government College, Itanagar, Arunachal Pradesh.

Ms. Anjali Biswas, Research Assistant of ICSSR Sponsored Research Project under Dr. Ram Krishna Mandal, D.N. Government College, Itanagar-791 113, Arunachal Pradesh.

Anusree Krishna Mandal, Student of MBBS, Lady Elliott Hostel, NRS Medical College & Hospital, Kolkata-700 014, West Bengal. **Email:** *anuskrish95@gmail.com*

Ms. Aparna Baruah, College of Agriculture, Assam Agricultural University, Jorhat-785013, Assam.

Mrs. Archana Mandal, Assistant Teacher (PGT), Balupara Colony Nibedita Balika Vidyalaya, P.O.: Gopalganj-733 141, District Dakshin Dinajpur, West Bengal.

Prof. Badal Kumar Datta, Professor, Plant Diversity and Ecology Laboratory, Department of Botany, Tripura University, Suryamaninagar-799 022, Tripura.

Dr. Bal Krishan Choudhary, Assistant Professor, Department of Environment Science, Ambedkar College, Fatikroy, Unakoti, Tripura-799290.

Dr. Beena Rongpipi, Assistant Professor, Department of Commerce, Diphu Government College, Diphu, Karbi Anglong, Assam.

Dr. Bijay Raji, Assistant Professor in Political Science, D.N. Government College, Itanagar, Arunachal Pradesh. **Email:** *bijayrajitamin@gmail.com*

Prof. D. N. Das, Zoology Department, Rajiv Gandhi University, Arunachal Pradesh.

Mr. Debabrata Maji, North Eastern Regional Institute of Science and Technology, Nirjuli, P.O.: Itanagar-791 111, Arunachal Pradesh. **Email:** *dmaji2004@yahoo.co.in*

Mr. Deep Jyoti Gurung, Guest Faculty, Centre for Management Studies, NERIST, Arunachal Pradesh, C/o Head of Centre, Centre for Management Studies, North Eastern Regional Institute of Science & Technology, Nirjuli-791 109, Arunachal Pradesh. **Email:** *mrdjgurung@gmail.com.*

Mr. Deepjyoti Baruah, Livestock Research Station, Assam Agricultural University, Hekra-781127, Kamrup, Assam. **Email:** *deep_baruah@rediffmail.com*

Ms. Dipakshi Das, Guest Faculty, Department of Economics, Pragjyotish College, Guwahati-781 009, Assam. **Email:** *dipakshi2012@gmail.com*

Dr. Ira Das, Assistant Professor, Department of Economics, Pragjyotish College, Guwahati-781 009, Assam. **Email:** *iramirza15@gmail.com*

Dr. Kaniska Sarkar, Assistant Registrar, Jadavpur University, 4/2 Block-H, Jadavpur University, Main Campus, Kolkata-700 032, West Bengal. **Email:** *kani_ska@yahoo.co.in*

Dr. Kaushik Majumder, Senior Research Fellow, Plant Diversity and Ecology Laboratory, Department of Botany, Tripura University, Suryamaninagar, 799 022, Tripura.

Mrs. Likha Kiran Kabak, Deputy Director (Training & Research/PAMORD), SIRD, P.O. R.K. Mission-791 113, Itanagar, Arunachal Pradesh. **Email:** *likhakirank@yahoo.co.in*

Prof. M. Sekender Ali, Department of Agricultural Extension & Information System, Sher-e-Bangla Agricultural University, Dhaka-1207, Bangladesh. **Email:** *msa_sau@yahoo.com., Web: www.sekender.sau.edu.bd*

Prof. M.M. Islam, Department of Agricultural Extension & Information System Sher-e-Bangla Agricultural University, Dhaka-1207, Bangladesh.

Dr. Mithilesh Kumar Sinha, Professor, Department of Economics, Nagaland University, Nagaland. **Email:** *mithileshkumarsinha5gmail.com*

Dr. Mriganka Saikia, Assistant Professor, Dhing College, Dhing, Nagaon, Assam-782123. **Email:** *mrigankasaikia.dhing@gmail.com*

Dr. Namita Das, Associate Professor, Department of Economics, Pragjyotish College, Guwahati-781 009, Assam. **Email:** *saikianamita@yahoo.co.in*

Mr. P. Nath, Ex. Director of Fisheries, Government of Arunachal Pradesh, Presently, Resource Person, Management of Reservoir Fisheries, Damador Valley Corporation, Government of India.

Dr. Pankaj Saikia, Assistant Professor, Dhing College, Dhing, Nagaon-782123, Assam. **Email:** *pankajsk37@gmail.com*

Dr. Paritosh Chandra Dutta c/o. Ajanta Textiles, S.S. Paul Road, Dewanji Bozar, Silchar, Distt. Cachar-788 001, Assam. **Email:** *duttapc@yahoo.com*

Paulami Das, M.Sc. (Agriculture and Rural Development) Student, IRDM Faculty Centre, Ramakrishna Mission Vivekananda University, Ramakrishna Mission Ashrama, Narendrapur, Kolkata-700 103, West Bengal.

Dr. Ritwika Rajendra, Assistant Professor, Department of Social Work, Assam University, Silchar-788 011, Assam. **Email:** *ritwika.rajendra@gmail.com*

Prof. S.C. Dey, Ex-Prof. & Dean, Gauhati University (presently attached to Calcutta University as Visiting Professor). West Bengal.

Dr. Sanjay Kanti Das, Head, Department of Commerce, Lumding College, Lumding, Nagaon-782447, Assam. **Email:** *sanjay19711123@rediffmail.com*

Mr. Subhrabaran Das, Department of Economics, Assam University, Silchar-788 011, Assam. **Email:** *subhrabaran@hotmail.com*

Dr. Sudarshan Prasad Regmi, Ph.D., Livestock and Dairy Consultant, Nepal AG Tech., Kathmandu, Nepal, GPO Box No. 20728.
Email: *spregmi@gmail.com*

Dr. Swapnali Baruah, R.C.S. Main Road, Door No. 132/128, Nattrampalli (Post), Thirupattur (T.K.),Vellore (District), Tamil Nadu-635852.
Email: *bswapnali2016@gmail.com*

Dr. Toku Chokio, Assistant Professor of Economics, Department of Economics, Dera Natung Government College, Itanagar-791113, Arunachal Pradesh.
Email: *toku.chokio@gmail.com*

Dr. Tumter Lollen, Assistant Professor, Department of Geography, Dera Natung Government College, Itanagar, Arunachal Pradesh.
Email: *tumterlollen@rediffmail.com*

Dr. Uttambir Basumatary, Assistant Professor, Department of Commerce, Cachar College, Silchar, Cachar-788001, Assam.

Dr. V. Ramabrahmam, M.A., Ph.D., M.A., (Sociology), Assistant Professor, Department of History & Archaeology, Yogi Vemana University, Kadapa-516003, Y.S.R. District, Andhra Pradesh.

Dr. Wangda Gyatso Gyana, Assistant Professor of Commerce, J.N. College, Pasighat, East Siang District, Arunachal Pradesh.
Email: *wangda437@gmail.com*

Introduction

Ram Krishna Mandal

The NER Vision-2020 describes the North Eastern Region as "a rainbow country—extraordinarily diverse and colourful, mysterious when seen through parted clouds". Flanked by hills and with the mighty Brahmaputra River slashing a central path between its north and south, the North East India, potentially one of the richest geographical units of the country, consists of the States of Assam, Arunachal Pradesh (A.P.), Manipur, Meghalaya, Mizoram, Nagaland, Tripura and Sikkim with Assam comprising the heart. A.P. lies to its north and Sikkim a little away in the northwest bordering China and Bhutan. Bangladesh and Myanmar lie to its southwest and east. The torrential Brahmaputra deposits its rich alluvial silt along the banks of the plains of Assam. Tropical rain forest, rich in flora and fauna, spread their arms across A.P. into Assam. It is a land where tea is an industry, handicrafts—a major occupation. The western side of the NER is connected to the eastern part of the Indian subcontinent by a narrow land corridor, referred to as the Siliguri Neck or Chicken's Neck with an average width of 21 km to 40 km. The region reflects ecological and cultural contrasts between the hills and the plains; there are also significant elements of continuity. Available medieval and modern records indicate interdependence and interaction between the hills and plains. (The NER is one of the most bio-diverse regions in the world. The forest cover ownership varies with average 65 per cent is government owned, the village communities, individuals and chiefs own the rest. The economy of the region has got its definite identity due to its peculiar physical, economic and socio-cultural characteristics). This region covers an area of 2.62 lakh sq. km. It accounts for 7.9 per cent of total geographical area of the country. With a total population of 45,587,982 (2011 census), it accounts for 3.77 per cent of total population of India. About 98 per cent of border of the NER forms India's international boundaries (4,500 km). The region is known for its rich cultural tradition and history. Earliest mention of NER was made by the Chinese explorer, Chang Kien, in 100 BC and Huen Tsang, a Chinese traveller, visited the region in the 7th Century. Throughout its history the NER is known to have been an important physical and cultural bridge between India and Southeast Asia, a potential location for the domestication of several important plants, and is an important focus area for archaeology. The North Eastern Council (NEC) constituted in 1971 is the acting agency for the development of the region. The North Eastern Development Finance Corporation Ltd. (NEDFi) was incorporated on August 9, 1995 and the Ministry of Development of North Eastern Region (DoNER) was set up in September 2001. The altitude varies from almost sea-level to over 7000 metres above MSL (Mean Sea Level). The region's high rainfall averaging around 10,000 millimetres. During the entire British colonial period NER was ruled as a part of Bengal Province, consisted of Assam and the princely states of Manipur and Tripura. The state of Assam came into existence in 1874, Nagaland in 1963, Meghalaya in 1972, Arunachal Pradesh in 1975 and Mizoram in 1987, formed out of Assam. Manipur and Tripura remained as Union Territories between 1956 and 1972. Sikkim was integrated with NER in 2002. Shillong was capital of undivided Assam until formation of Meghalaya. The capital of Assam was then shifted to Dispur (Guwahati) and Shillong became the capital of Meghalaya. Over 68 per cent out of 45.59 million people of the region (31.17 million) live in the state of Assam alone with Sikkim lowest (6,07,688). The density of population varies from 17 per sq. km in A.P. to 397 per sq. km in Assam (density of population of country is 382, 2011 Census). The proportion of tribal population ranges from 19.3 per cent in Assam to 94.5 per cent in Mizoram. NER is largely rural with over 70 per cent of the population living in the country-side. It has over 160 Scheduled Tribes and over 400 other Sub-tribal communities and groups.

As per 2011 Census there are significant variations in the literacy rates among different states of the region with Assam 73.18 per cent (Females 67.27% and Males 78.81%), A.P. 66.95 per cent (Females 59.57% and Males 73.69%), Manipur 79.85 per cent (Females 73.17% and Males 86.49%), Meghalaya 75.48 per cent (Females 73.78% and Males 77.17%), Mizoram 91.58 per cent (Females 89.40% and Males 93.72%), Nagaland 80.11 per cent (Females 76.69% and Males 83.29%), Sikkim 82.20 per cent (Females 76.43% and Males 87.29%) and Tripura 87.75 per cent (Females 83.15% and Males 92.18%) comparing to the national average 74.04 per cent (Females 65.46% and Males 82.14%).

The region with over 220 ethnic groups and equal number of dialects makes it hugely diverse. The states of A.P., Meghalaya, Mizoram and Nagaland are predominantly inhabited by tribal people. There is a fair degree of diversity even within the tribal groups. People from Tibet, Burma (now Myanmar), Thailand, West Bengal and Bangladesh have migrated into the region at various periods of history. The basic information of NER is shown in Table 0.1.

Table 0.1: Basic Information of NER

Population	38,857,769 (2001) and 45,587,982 (2011)
Decennial growth	17.32
Area	262,230 km^2
Population density	148 /km^2
States	A.P., Assam, Manipur, Meghalaya, Mizoram, Nagaland, Sikkim, Tripura
Largest cities (2011)	Guwahati, Dimapur, Agartala, Shillong, Aizawl, Itanagar, Imphal, Gangtok
Religion	Christianity, Buddhism, Hinduism, Islam

Source: Census of India, 2011.

State-wise Basic Information of North Eastern States

The eight North Eastern States form a distinguishable group for its rich ethnic culture and prevalence of Tibeto-Burman language. These states have got influence of South-East Asian culture. The State-wise basic information of North Eastern States is shown in Table 0.2.

These states are home to many culturally diversified and linguistically different multi-ethnic tribes where four major religions of the world are followed by the inhabitants of the area. Arunachal Pradesh, Meghalaya, Mizoram, Nagaland and Sikkim states are the states where the population of Scheduled Tribes are in majority of proportion. The majority of general category people dwelt in Assam, Manipur and Tripura, which were princely states before Independence. And there are three states namely, Arunachal Pradesh, Nagaland and Mizoram where inner line permit system still exists. (The persistence of poverty in North East States of India is in stark contrast to its relatively high achievement in the social sectors as compared to the national average. However, this could be explained by considering that the region remained marginalised from the development activities that characterised mainstream, India. Poor connectivity with large markets and inhospitable geographical terrain add

Table 0.2: State-wise Basic Information of North Eastern States

States	*A. P.*	*Assam*	*Manipur*	*Meghalaya*	*Mizoram*	*Nagaland*	*Sikkim*	*Tripura*
Capital	Itanagar	Dispur	Imphal	Shillong	Aizawl	Kohima	Gangtok	Agartala
Largest city	Itanagar	Guwahati	Imphal	Shillong	Aizawl	Dimapur	Gangtok	Agartala
No. of districts	16	27	9	7	8	11	4	4
Date of establishment	20.2.1987	15.8.1947	21.1.1972	21.1.1972	20.2.1987	1.12.1963	16.5.1975	21.1.1972
Area sq. km.	83,743	78,550	22,347	22,720	21,081	16,579	7,096	10,491.69
Population (2011 Census)	1,382,611	31,169,272	2,721,756	2,964,007	1,091,014	1,980,602	6,07,688	3, 671, 032
Density of population	16.5 sq. km.	396.8 sq. km.	121.8 sq. km.	130.5 sq. km.	51.8 sq. km.	119 sq. km.	85.6 sq. km.	349.9 sq. km.
Literacy rate	66.95%	76.3%	79.85%	72.1%	89.9%	63.7%	76.6%	87.75%
Official language	English	Assamese; Bengali, Bodo	Meiteilon	*	English, Mizo	English	**	Bengali, Kokborok

Notes: * English, Garo, Hindi, Khasi and Pnar

** Bhutia, Gurung, Lepcha, Limbu, Mangar, Nepali, Newari, Rai, Sherpa, Sunwar and Tamang

Source: Census of India, 2011.

to the grievances of economic backwardness of this Himalayan region.) The region has high forest cover in comparison to other regions of the country. Forests are an important source of livelihood for the people of the states of North East India. Apart from the extraction of timber, fuel wood and bamboo, forests are also a source of herbs and plants that have been traditionally used as medicines. Moreover, the fact that forest is central to people's livelihoods is confirmed by the existence of many traditional forest based beliefs and folklores, which are mainly based on forests in the region.

The region is rich in human resources. However, most of the higher educational institutes are centrally located in the capitals of these states. There are few technical and vocational institutes in the region which led to migration of students to other parts of the country for pursuing higher education which causes a huge loss to state financial health and brain drain.

Land resources in North East States of India are constrained on account of demographic pressure (per capita availability) and activities that they can sustain as most of the states are hilly and mountainous terrain. Diversification in the pattern of land-use has to take into account both food security requirements and constraints imposed by the terrain. The limitations of terrace farming in terms of productivity, irrigation and the scope for extending cultivation highlight the constraints faced by farming for livelihood security. Under these conditions innovative practices in land management and horticulture and floriculture (including marketing and systems and linkages) can be identified as growth sectors.

The North East India is known for practices related to traditional medicines. These practices have a strong base in the socio-religious healing systems native to these states. The rich variety of plants and animals also help to sustain the system of traditional medicines. But very little attention has been given to the importance of protecting the intellectual property rights (IPRs) of indigenous peoples, whose traditional knowledge has often been the source of products introduced into the international market. Studies on the botanical resources of North East States of India in the past have placed little emphasis on the vast potential of studies on ethno-medico-botany particularly in the context of both the rich heritage of indigenous medical practices and the fast changing international regime on intellectual property rights. The 'bio-partnerships' for sustainable development is, therefore, very critical in this eastern Himalayan region. It is vital to develop bio-resources at the human level first since this will ensure, to a large extent, sustainable development of the other bio-resources. An emerging facet of biodiversity conservation is the medicinal and therapeutic value of plant and animal extracts. The rich possibilities of commercial exploitation of these resources could be assessed from the fact that herbal products are said to account for nearly half the medicines prescribed in the United States of America and this trend is likely to grow. The sustainability of the North East economy and society could be challenged in many critical dimensions. Scientific temper and awareness when infused into traditional practices can bring about a major transformation in the socio-economic profile of the villages of the region. This limited choice and the related constraints on development interventions as compared to the wide range of choices and techniques available to other States, need to be considered as the opportunity cost that North East States of India will have to forego. The benefits which would have otherwise accrued to the region need to be objectively assessed and provisions made accordingly for compensating the opportunities foregone. This is how a special category NE States need to be treated for, at least till it starts showing indications of self-reliance and sustainability. Therefore, recognition and assessment and compensation of these invisible costs are very critical for the sustenance of a strategic region like the North East States of India.

There is negligible presence of large scale industries and multinational companies due to poor infrastructure and market linkages in the region. The village and small scale industries and traditionally unorganised industries constitute a vital segment of the NE economies. This sector has not only continued to play an important role in fulfilment of socio-economic objectives but also provides an ample opportunity for self-employment of the unemployed youths. The expansion of this sector depends on a number of factors like procurement of raw-materials, availability of hydro-electric power, technical knowledge, creation of infrastructures and market linkages.

Globalization is commonly understood by the economists as a process of increasing economic integration among countries of the world which liberalizes all kinds of controls to facilitate free inter-flow of information, ideas of information, ideas, technologies, goods, services, capital, finance and people. The essence of globalization is connectivity through complete freedom of market mechanism. This requires the government to act as a facilitator but not as a regulator. It is argued that any form of intervention in the market by the government is bound to be inefficient. Hence, the free trade would decide on the resource allocation, utilisation and distribution in an efficient manner so that all players are better-off and none is worse-off. In the light of this reference, the NE states can be a player in the market integration of the South East Asian Countries through Look-East Policy of the Government of India.

In the light of the above discussion, it was proposed to organise a national seminar on the topic, "Livelihood and Sustainable Development Strategies of North East States of India" was organised on November 22-23, 2013, which would help in finding its design, efficiencies and implications to get all-round development in the underdeveloped region of North East States of India. It was hoped that this seminar would help in formulating a specific policy for livelihoods and sustainable development strategies of eastern Himalayas by the governments and other developmental agencies. Therefore, this volume was a collection of twenty eight papers presented in the seminar by the academicians from different parts of India and even one paper from Sher-e-Bangla Agricultural University, Dhaka, Bangladesh.

This book has been divided into four sections. Section-I concentrates itself for the discussion of Livelihood Strategies in context of Sustainable Development while Section-II deals only with Tourism and Development. Section-III focuses on Women Empowerment for Sustainable Society of different sections of people especially Women. Section-IV examines the performances of Entrepreneurship and Economic Development, and also investigates the potentialities of Trade in North East India with special emphasis on Look East Policy.

The Section-I discusses about the Livelihood Strategy and Sustainable Development consisting of nine chapters.

Mr. Deepjyoti Baruah and **Mrs. Aparna Baruah** on the theme "Livelihood Improvement of Hill Tribes Through Adaptive Aquacultural Approaches" have shown that mountain and hill regions of India have important natural resources that can contribute substantially to the economic development and the hill state of Arunachal Pradesh is no exception to that. With the growing importance of fishery as an economic activity, aquaculture is taking a firm root in the region and the people are presently looking forward to it as a means of additional income. The performance of each fish species in terms of growth, survival and contribution to total biomass were studied and analysed. The production figures indicate that culture of Chinese carps at this altitudinal regime can be suitably adopted and can contribute substantial income for the fishers of hill region.

Mr. P. Nath, Prof. D.N. Das and **Prof. S.C. Dey** in their study, "Fish Husbandry in Vast Expanse of Water: A Perspective Platform for Livelihood and Sustainability in Arunachal Pradesh" studied that urbanization is the sole hub not only for curbing Agricultural land but simultaneously destructing various other habitats. However, Industrialisation cannot be denied in context to economic growth as far as our country is concerned. Besides, climate change is another catastrophic ordeal *(The Telegraph*, 2013) awaiting us threatening the Mankind particularly in terms of food security as per reports from various corners. All the aforesaid warnings, calls for *in situ* and *ex situ* Conservation of our Nature Earth.

Mr. Debabrata Maji in his study, "NERIST in Development of Social Welfare and Economic Growth of the North Eastern Region Through CATRD" shows that North Eastern Regional Institute of Science and Technology (NERIST) provides non-formal vocational training to generate self-employment and establish micro-enterprise; technical support services to user group for propagation of appropriate and affordable technologies; technologies need analysis towards location specific HR development; Delivery system for appropriate technology, information dissemination through establishing a glaring house on low cost affordable technology within the campus through Centre for Appropriate Technology and Rural Development (CATRD). In this chapter attempt has been made to highlight the successes of social development activities through SHGs, Collaborative and convergence mode, Growth activities and Future development.

Dr. Swapnali Baruah in her study "Poverty and We: A Brief Preview" shows that although India has improved on poverty reduction, but the improvement is not satisfactory in rural India because the country is agro-based, the sector has not grown in the expected way. The number of suicide cases because of poverty has crossed 2000 in the year 2011. Government both at Union and State levels have taken number of plans and programmes to alleviate poverty in the course of time. But, success is not fruitful due to various shortcomings related to their implementation.

Dr. Bijay Raji in his study, "PRI in sustaining livelihood in Arunachal Pradesh" has searched that the possibilities of relative self-reliance through decentralized, democratic economics, which dramatically cut unsustainable transportation, empower people to be in control of their own lives need more attentions by the policy-makers. So, livelihood issue will empower people to be on control of their own lives, democratise market and provide a stable basis for wider socio-economic relations across communities and may reverse distress migration of villages into cities. So, the need is for more radical transformation and governance. The Forest Right Act and the Panchayat (Extension to Scheduled Areas) Act need to be implemented in letter and spirit in the tribal region and villages should be given land as an unconditional livelihood claim.

Mr. Toku Chokio in his study, "Strategies for Sustainable Socio-Economic Development in Arunachal Pradesh" finds out that Several Rural Development and Poverty Alleviation Programmes have been implemented by Government of India and the State Governments. While the objective of these programmes may be commendable, they are based on a belief that spending of money is in itself a necessary and sufficient condition for poverty alleviation. It has been the experience of many researchers that such programmes have not yielded the desired result. In Arunachal Pradesh, where tribal population is dominated, these programmes have also not faired well.

In her study, "Rubber Cultivation as Sustainable Livelihood in Arunachal Pradesh", **Mrs. Amum Tamuk** examines the possibilities of rubber cultivation which may bring sustainable livelihood as it is not dependent upon external support and its long term productivity can be maintained. Nine districts out of twenty districts in Arunachal Pradesh are identified for rubber cultivation. The State Government is also ready to give all types of incentives to the rubber cultivators. Rubber would be an alternative to end the destructive and low yielding *Jhum* Cultivation in the State.

Dr. Tumter Lollen in her study, "Educational Attainment for Changing Livelihood in Arunachal Pradesh" has tried to prove that education is a weapon which acts as an agent of social, economic, cultural and technological development in a society. The importance of education has long been realized in the national plans for development and therefore, a large proportion of governmental grants have been invested in educational sector. Arunachal Pradesh becomes an interesting case study for two reasons. First, its location in the North East of the country with hilly terrain which has kept the state in geographical and political isolation from the rest of the country. Second, while the percentage share of literate population in the state has been below the national average, the growth of literacy rate has been remarkable.

In their study, "NGOs in Livelihood Strategies for Marginalised Differently Abled People: A Study on *Atma Nirbhar-Ek* Challenge", **Ms. Dipakshi Das, Dr. Ira Das** and **Ms. Namita Das** explore on the activities through which the differently abled people earn their livelihood and the future plans of the NGOs, their successes, weaknesses, the obstacles that the organisation has to come across in achieving their target. There are very few NGOs in our country who are working in this direction and in this context *Atmanirbhar-Ek* Challenge is a reality instance which can pave the way to other NGOs to work for generating livelihood strategies for the differently abled people.

The Section-II devotes Tourism and Development which consists of two chapters.

Prof. Mithilesh Kumar Sinha and **Mr. Mriganka Saikia**, in their study, "Problems and Prospects of Tourism—A Case Study of Kaziranga and Sibsagar in Assam" have focused that Assam is the treasure house of valuable economic resources. The state has a rich cultural and ethnic heritage that can easily make it a tourist-spot. Tourism has the greatest potential for generating income and employment opportunities in our State. It is not only characterised by its rich flora and fauna, but it is also exceptionally rich in bio-diversity. Moreover, the wildlife sanctuaries at various places including Kaziranga of the state are attracting the tourists all over the world. The State Government though has taken some steps to improve the tourism sector yet it is at a very poor stage and has a long way to develop.

Wangda Gyatso Gyana in his study, "Tourism Development in Arunachal Pradesh: Opportunities and Challenges" showed that a huge amount of opportunities in tourism sector are looming large over the North East India including the state of Arunachal Pradesh. The number of international tourists having visited the region have risen to 58,920 in 2011 from 50,950 in 2010. In the process of developing state tourism, the natural environment must be protected by sensibly using, avoiding over exploitation of the resources, and minimising environmental pollution. Besides, it must be also taken care of that the rich and unique tribal socio-cultural fabric remains intact and is not influenced by any foreign culture. To meet the problem of inadequate accommodation, the locals can operate and offer home stay facility to the tourists. The State Government must work-out an exclusive and practical State Tourism Policy supplemented with procedural guidelines based on the local situations to promote tourism. The Government, both Central and State, must take more and more initiatives in the state tourism sector. The government must have sound planning and follow-up programmes. It must provide adequate incentives and schemes to motivate genuine entrepreneurs.

The Section-III examines the Women Empowerment for Sustainable Society consisting of fourteen chapters.

Prof. M. Sekender Ali and **Mr. M.M. Islam** in their study, "Dipshikha Beneficiaries' Participation in Women Empowerment Activities" have searched about Dipshikha beneficiaries' participation in women empowerment activities before and after involvement with Dipshikha, the rate of changes of Dipshikha beneficiaries' participation in women empowerment activities after involving with Dipshikha, and compared item-wise changes of participation in women empowerment activities. In case of item-wise participation, it was found that highest increase of participation in women empowerment was occurred in "ensuring equal importance for boys and girls in education" followed by "ensuring equal importance for male and female in decision-making", "ensure female freedom in income generating activities" and "participation female in buying and selling activities".

The study of **Mr. Kaniska Sarkar** in his study "Problems in the Context of Socio Economic and Culture of the Backward Muslim Women in Basirhat Block-II in North 24 Parganas" has focused that Muslim women who are backward in Basirhat Block-II, North 24 Parganas, West Bengal are very much deprived form their primary needs like education, economy, modesty, health, social status or social respect and women rights. This situation or scenario of the women is found from the earlier period of national freedom. From the childhood to old age life of these group of the people are suffering a lot. He has also shown different types of violation, deprivation or crime against women in this area with suitable statistical analysis.

Mr. Subhrabaran Das and **Mr. A. Pushpalata Singh,** in their study, "Role of Self-Help Groups on Socio-economic Empowerment of the Rural Women: A Case Study of Cachar District, Assam" have depicted the women's capabilities for empowering them to expand their choices as well as the surest route for their contribution to the economic growth and development of the nation. Empowerment requires the full participation of people in the formulation, implementation and evaluation of decisions determining the functioning and well-being of societies. This shows that the involvement of women in the development process is equally important as that of men and so their empowerment is a prime necessity. As Self-Help Groups (SHGs) are an effective tool to promote rural savings and gainful employment so it can transfer the real economic power in the hands of women and can considerably reduce their dependence on men.

Mr. Pankaj Saikia in his study, "Women Empowerment through Self-help Group: A Case Study of Women SHG in Kapili Development Block of Morigaon District of Assam" attempts to examine the empowerment of women through SHGs, which is one of the vital issues of development, especially for the poor, marginalised and vulnerable group. In most of the developing countries, gender inequality is a major obstacle to meeting the target of Millennium Development Goals. Achieving the goals will not be feasible without closing the gaps between women and men in terms of capacities, access to resources and opportunities.

The study of **Ms. Beena Rongpipi** and **Mr. Uttambir Basumatary** in their study "Leadership Pattern in LAMPS in Karbi Anglong District of Assam" deals with the tribal communities of Karbi Anglong in rural areas who are economically poor and social-backward. The leadership pattern and leaders of LAMPS (Large sized Multipurpose Co-operative Societies) play a crucial role in efficient management of tribal co-operatives, their social background, participation in community. These are measured with reference to the leaders' political awareness and participation, and political linkage with high-up leaders. On the other hand, because of state patronage some degree of political influence in co-operative is inevitable, thereby facilitating a group of leaders in using the society for their self-interest.

Mr. Sanjay Kanti Das on the theme "Self-Help Groups in Development and Empowerment with Special Reference to Assam" opines that Self-Help Group today has become a vehicle to pursue diverse developmental agendas and even for the profit motive. To avert such a situation, growth with quality has became the paramount agenda of today among different stakeholders, as there is an over reaching concern about the quality and sustainability of the SHG movement in India. An effort is made to make a quality assessment on functioning of the SHGs in three selected districts of Assam, *viz.* Nagaon, Dima Hasao and Karbi Anglong. Moreover, effort is also taken to study strengths, weaknesses, opportunities and threats (SWOT) of the sample respondents in micro-finance management.

Mrs. Likha Kiran Kabak try to find out in her study, "Self-Help Groups: A Tool for Women Empowerment : A Case Study" that women constitute nearly half of the population in India. But major percentage of women particularly of rural areas is poorer than men because of traditional social structure. To achieve the millennium development goal and to claim as developed country, it is mandatory that women are equally advanced and empowered. Gender equality and women empowerment are central to the achievement of different national developmental goals. Due to societal structured beliefs and norms, barriers in mobility and discrimination in education women are poorer than their counterparts. SHGs are assumed to play effective role in empowering women in economic, social and psychological dimensions. Her study examines how far SHGs can generate 'empowerment' of different dimension in women.

Dr. Paritosh Chandra Dutta in his study, "Empowerment of Women and Socio-Economic Development of North Eastern Region of India" has investigated that Empowerment is a process of increasing the capacity of an individual or a group of individuals to make choices and to transform those choices into desired actions and outcomes. Central to this process are actions which build both individual and collective assets and improve the efficiency and fairness of the organisational and institutional context that govern the use of these assets. The empowerment of women is one of the central issues in the process of development of countries all over the world. It is a process through which women gain greater control over resources—material, human and intellectual like knowledge, information, ideas and financial assets and control over decision-making at home as well as in the community, society and nation, and also gain 'power'. It is not be prudent on our part to restore the rights of the women belonging to the affluent section of the society only. The society should stop all kinds of gender based social injustice and create an atmosphere of equality where women can breath, freedom and justice in its true form.

Ms. Anusree Krishna Mandal in her study, "Self-Help Groups: A Paradigm Shift of Women Empowerment" depicts that power is exercised socially, economically and politically by one person over other person or over group of persons. Women usually falls under the powerless group which necessitates the programmes ensured empowerment of women. Power can be defined as the degree or assets fall into five broad categories: physical/material resources (like land, water, forests); human resources (people, their bodies, their labour and skills); intellectual resources (knowledge, information, ideas); social (social capital) and financial resources (money, access to money). Women are the nucleus of our civilization. They have different roles to play in the ever changing social set-up. A large number of schemes and programmes have been initiated for women's development, but it is not up to the expectation. It is found that SHG approaches are playing tremendous role to empower women because of its process oriented approach, member of the SHG are automatically becoming assertive after joining into the SHGs.

Mrs. Ritwika Rajendra in her study, "Women Education in Special Reference to Rural Areas of North East India" states that gender equality in terms of participation in, and attainment of, education has been achieved in most countries: girls have on average better grades and often outnumber boys among new college graduates. Gender gaps in performance are smaller than gender gaps in fields of tertiary study, Provision of education is key to the development of human resources. The women education in North East India presents a broad spectrum with gender biases leading to poor education and health of women and development constraints.

Sudarshan Prasad Regmi in his study, "Status of Women and Their Role in Socio-economic Development of Ilam District in Nepal" examines that the involvements of women in saving and credit cooperatives were substantial about 41.33 per cent of which had as high as 53.42 per cent. Similarly, they were attached to other organizations too; of about 14 per cent reported women directly participated to Governmental organization, 39.07 per cent and in non-governmental organization, 27.23 per cent. The facts and figures of Nepalese women in relation to the world has been revealed that women of Ilam District specially at rural area need specific attention regarding inputs in the field of education, agri-business, conflict resolution for more role in the society. Though they spend more on household work, which if capitalized would help promote livelihood of their family.

Dr. V. Ramabrahmam in his study, "Empowerment of Indian Women in the 21st Century: A General Perspective" finds out that the empowerment of women is located within the discourse and agenda of gender equality and is increasingly being taken in the agendas of international development organizations, perhaps more as a means to achieve gender equality than as an end in itself. Governmental organizations are formal agencies working for the empowerment of women. But, this work requires multidimensional approach and hence a large number of voluntary organizations/NGOs have gained increased attention in the field from grassroots level to national and international level.

Mr. Amitava Dutta and **Paulami Das** in their study, "A Study on Constraints Faced by the Tribal (Santal) SHGs Members in the Process of Empowerment" examines that tribal women in the process of empowerment faced several constraints which further deviated them from their empowerment. A lot of social evils and discriminations were still in practice for which it was very difficult for such women to be empowered through their effective participation in SHGs.

Bal Krishan Choudhary, Kaushik Majumder and **Badal Kumar Datta** in their study, "Women Environment Interaction and Traditional Ecological Knowledge: Concerns in Mountain Region" try to find out that sustainable development is our common need and is not possible without the empowerment of women and gender equity. They are most directly and differently affected than man by the environmental degradation, deforestation, pollution and environmental issues, so women becoming more concern about environmental problems. Women's low participation in the formulation, planning and execution of environmental policy is the main reason for delayed progress of women and environmental relationship. By involving women in environment decision-making at all levels, and looking the impact of development on women we can improve the women environment relationship in a sustainable manner. Traditional Ecological Knowledge (TEK) is outcome of long term trial and error practices.

The Section-IV examines the Entrepreneurship and Economic Development consisting of three chapters.

The study, "Entrepreneurship: A Panacea to Socio-Economic Problems of North Eastern Region" by **Mr. Deep Jyoti Gurung** has examined that North East India despite having immense bounty of nature still finds itself in the category of laggards as far as socio-economic development is concerned. Governmental organizations continue to be the main employment providers in North East India. Those who fail to get Government jobs are often found to be frustrated and also participating in anti-social activities. This source of providing employment is getting saturated as Governmental organizations have already attained maturity stage. If socio-economic development is to be sustained, North East India will have to look beyond this source and entrepreneurship will have to be explored that has the potential of turning people from job seekers to job providers.

Mrs. Archana Mandal in her study, "Trade and Economic Development through Look East Policy" illustrates the benefit of trade through Look East Policy (LEP), which is one of the latest buzzwords in the context of economic development of the North Eastern Region (NER) of India, even though the policy was initiated by the then Prime Minister, Narasimha Rao in 1991, i.e. about two and half decades ago. The policy was inaugurated in 1992 when Dr. Manmohan Singh was the Finance Minister. In the context of India's NER, its primary objective is said to take advantage of the new opportunities in trade and investment by improving socio-economic and political relationship with the neighbouring countries, though the major objective of India's LEP is stated to develop economic relationship with the ASEAN. The ASEAN countries too are looking towards Indian economy for trade and investment. It needs to be mentioned that in the recent decades, the East Asia has significantly increased its share of global GDP and trade. The centre of economic gravity in the world is now in East Asia. India's fortunes in trade and investment are now more linked with East Asia.

Ms. Anjali Biswas in her study "Economic Integration between India and ASEAN through North Eastern Region: Issues and Challenges" has tried to show that the Look East Policy (LEP) is one of the latest buzzwords in the context of economic development of the North Eastern Region (NER) of India through economic integration with the countries of the Association of South East Asian Nations (ASEAN). The LEP is a turning point in India's focus towards East Asia, South East Asia and the countries in the Pacific Region; although India's relationship with the countries of the Association of South East Asian Nations (ASEAN) is said to be central to the LEP, with Thailand occupying a central place.

SECTION-I

Livelihood Strategy and Sustainable Development

1

Livelihood Improvement of Hill Tribes Through Adaptive Aquacultural Approaches

Deepjyoti Baruah and *Aparna Baruah*

Introduction

The State of Arunachal Pradesh having an area of 83,743 sq.km. with a total population of 1,091,117 (2001 Census) is a mosaic of composite culture and tradition. A land inhabited by 28 major tribes and 110 sub-tribes, it is the 12th mega biodiversity region of the world and is the richest biotic province of Republic of India. The topography of the region varies from few metres from the sea level to Snow Line Mountains and has different kinds of agro-climatic zones. This area receives heavy rainfall during prolong rainy season from March to October resulting in vast and varied aquatic resources in the form of 2,000 km of rivers, 2,500 ha of wetlands and lakes, 1,250 ha of ponds and mini barrages and 2,925 ha of area suitable for paddy-*cum*-fish culture. The State is also home to rich fish fauna representing about 167 species including some coldwater species. But in spite of having vast aquatic resources and fish diversity, the region is yet to catch up with the rest of the country in developing its water resources for fisheries. Although fish production from the State has increased from 1.25 lakh tonnes during 1990-91, to 2.65 lakh tonnes during 2003-04, there still remains a good gap between the production and demand necessitating import of fish from other States like Andhra Pradesh, Bihar, and West Bengal. The per capita availability of fish in the state is low at 2.19 kg/yr against the national requirement of 11kg/yr.

The present investigation deals with successful attempts made on fish production by the rural tribe mass by applying appropriate Composite Carp Farming Technology fitting to natural environment and to create self-employment.

Materials and Methods

The study was conducted in Chug village situated at 1500 m asl and located 10 kms of Dirang Bazar in Dirang Block of West Kameng district, Arunachal Pradesh during 2008 to 2010. Twenty ponds were selected to demonstrate Chinese Carp Farming practiced in hill regions. Three species of Chinese carps, viz. silver carp (*Hypophthalmichthys molitrix*), grass carp (*Ctenopharyngodon idella*) and common carp (*Cyprinus carpio*) were stocked in combination with a density 3 fishes/m^2 and formulated supplementary diets with 2 different levels was provided under low temperature conditions. The performance of each fish species in terms of growth, survival and contribution to total biomass were studied and analysed.

Survey, PRA were conducted initially by the Dirang based Krishi Vigyan Kendra with a view to collect information on aquaculture activities in Chug village from the farmers, farm women, rural youth, *Gaon Burah* and Panchayat leaders.

Results and Discussion

Based on the data generated through survey conducted in the village on the status of the ponds and socio-economic conditions of the beneficiaries, it was found that fish culture in the region was neglected due to religious beliefs and the practice was considered as sin. Therefore, 20 numbers of used ponds were identified and the corresponding farmers were trained to motivate them to undertake composite fish farming with Chinese carps for income generation. Demonstration programmes were organised on feeding techniques, stocking procedure, liming and manuring techniques, water quality and hygiene management etc. Training and demonstration programmes were sponsored by National Fisheries Development Board, Hyderabad; Directorate of Coldwater Fisheries Research, Bhimtal and NABARD, Regional Office, Itanagar. Fish seeds and fish feeds were provided free of cost to the beneficiaries from the Kendra with the assistance from Department of Fisheries, Bomdila and Directorate of Coldwater Fisheries Research, Bhimtal.

The methods adopted by the farmers on Chinese Carp Farming can broadly be divided into three phases:

Pre-Stocking Management

(i) Drying of pond bottom until soil cracks followed by ploughing for eradication of undesired animals and removal of obnoxious gases from the bottom soil.

(ii) Manuring of pond with cow-dung prior to stocking as the basal dose for production of natural fish food organisms.
(iii) Liming of pond bottom 7 days after manuring and prior to stocking for correction of soil and water *p*H as well as pond disinfection.
(iv) Filling of pond with fresh and clean water.

Stocking Management

(i) *Stocking density:* As per the recommendations made by the Directorate of Coldwater Fisheries and Research (ICAR), Bhimtal fish seeds were stocked @ 3 nos./m^2.
(ii) *Stocking size:* Fish seeds of 60 mm size were procured from the neighbouring state Assam and were stocked.
(iii) *Species combination:* A proportion of 30 per cent Silver carp, 35 per cent Grass carp and 35 per cent Common carp were stocked.

Post-Stocking Management

The post-stocking pond management primarily involves the aspects of intermittent liming and fertilisation, supplementary feeding, water management and health care.

(i) Organic manure in the form of raw cow dung was applied every fortnightly. No inorganic fertilizers were used.
(ii) Supplementary feed at the rate of 3 per cent of the body weight of the stocked fish biomass per day. Grass carp were fed on terrestrial vegetation, fodder grasses and vegetable wastes.
(iii) Liming and manuring was done once in a month, 1-2 days after the application of organic manure.
(iv) Raking of pond bottom was done after liming, for proper mixing of lime and release of obnoxious gases.

The yield depends on growth rate and retrieval of the stocked fishes at harvest. The growth and survival of fishes are found directly correlated with water temperature, quality and quantity of supplementary feed provided, natural food available in ponds and the methodology followed by the operator. In the upland water of low thermal regime, the Chinese carps were found to have grown well as compared to the Indian major carps. Based on the demonstration results, it was observed that more biomass can be obtained by stocking fish seeds at the rate of 3 nos./m^2 in hill conditions as compared to 1 no./m^2. The growth of grass carp was

Table 1.1: Work Calendar for Chinese Carp Farming System in a Year

Period	*Work done*
February–March	Drying of pond bottom till soil cracks.
April	• Removal of unwanted materials from the pond. • Removal of marginal weeds. • Ploughing of pond bottom soil. • Manuring of pond bottom with raw cow-dung. • Liming of pond bottom. • Filling of pond with fresh stream water.
1st Week of May	• Stocking management. • Stocking of pond with Chinese carps.
May–October	• Culture period. • Post-stocking management.
1st Week of November	Harvesting of stocked fish.

Source: Sarma, *et al.* (2010): Performance of three pronged Chinese carp farming in mid Himalayas of West Kameng district, Arunachal Pradesh.

Table 1.2: Composite Carp Farming Technology and its Operational Calendar

Area of operation	*Chug village, Dirang (1500 m asl)*
Operational period	February–November
Nature of pond	Earthen
Pond size (average) and shape	600 m^2, rectangular
Pond depth	1.5 m
Source of water	Rain, stream
Fish species	Silver carp, Grass carp and Common carp
Stocking density	3 Nos./m^2
Stocking percentage	Silver carp (30%), Grass carp (35%) and Common carp (35%)
Fish size during stocking	60 mm
Feed	
(i) % of body weight	3%
(ii) Frequency	Daily
(iii) Items	Diet (1) for 30 per cent protein content: Mixture of maize crush, rice polish, wheat flour, vegetable oil, MOC, GNOC, Iodized salt, trace mineral mixture and vitamin mix. Diet (2) for 35 per cent protein content: Mixture of maize crush, vegetable oil, MOC, GNOC, Iodized salt, trace mineral mixture and vitamin mix.
(iv) Feed for Grass carp	Terrestrial grasses, vegetable wastes
Liming (in installments)	
(i) Dose	250 kg/ha/yr
(ii) Frequency	Fortnightly
Manuring (in installments)	
(i) Dose	10,000 kg/ha/yr
(ii) Frequency	Weekly

(Contd.)

Area of operation	*Chug village, Dirang (1500 m asl)*
Production (per 600m^2)	293 kg/600 m^2/ 6 months
Estimated expenditure	Rs. 33.00/ kg fish
Total income	Rs. 35,160.00 (Rs. 120.00/ kg fish)
Net income	Rs. 87.00/ kg fish

Source: Punniah, *et al.* (2000): Fish Biodiversity of North East India.

Table 1.3: Performance of Fish Species under Culture Conditions

Sl. No.	*Species*	*Growth (g/month)*	*Production (kg/600 m^2/6months)*	*Contributed production (%)*	*Rank*
1.	Silver carp	26.06	78.64	26.83	2
2.	Grass carp	21.42	76.54	26.11	3
3.	Common carp	39.52	137.95	47.06	1

Source: Radheyshyam, *et al.* (1988), Utilisation of Small Backyard Ponds for Fish Culture in Rural Areas.

found related to the quality and quantity of the grass and vegetable waste fed. Common carp including different phenotypes and feeding on unutilized feed, faecal matter of grass carp and benthic organisms contributed the bulk of the catch. The importance of supplementary feed in composite carp culture is well recognised. In a hilly district like West Kameng, the quantity and quality of supplementary feed played very important role. From the trial results and the data generated, dose of feed at the rate of 3 per cent body weight of fishes produced an average production of 293 kg/600 m^2/6 months. In a span of 6 months, silver carp (30%), grass carp (35%) and common carp (35%) attained the maximum individual weight of 235g, 300g and 500g respectively.

The fertilizers of organic nature like raw cow-dung, poultry litter in prescribed doses at weekly interval are important to produce natural food in ponds. Such fertilisation procedure play vital role in getting higher survival and growth of fish.

Based on the present market rate the estimated value of the carps produced was Rs. 9,570.00. Overall percentage composition of total expenditure on various items in carp production is depicted in Fig. 1.1. Maximum expenditure incurred in this venture was: (1) purchase of fish feeds (45.14%), followed by (2) purchase of quality seeds from neighbouring state Assam (37.62%), (3) renovation and maintenance cost (10.45%), (4) manpower (5.22%) and (5) purchase of necessary inputs (1.57%). The estimated total income was Rs. 35,160.00 at the rate of Rs. 120.00 per kg fish. The net profit/income on estimated expenditure of Rs. 33.00 per kg was Rs. 120.00 per kg, suggesting the economic profitability of the technology for participating rural tribe farmers.

The production figures indicate that culture of Chinese carps under the technique "Composite Carp Farming" is easy to operate, economically viable, eco-friendly as it is able to convert/recycle the cattle yard, agricultural, kitchen wastes into value added fish food. Therefore, this technology opens up the possibility of promoting exotic carp culture in hilly region of the district where existing production of indigenous fishery is very low.

REFERENCES

Ponniah, A.G., and Sarkar, U.K. (2000). *Fish Biodiversity of North East India*. NBFGR-NATP Publ.2

Radheyshyam, Satpathy, B.B., Singh, B.N., Sarkar, S.K., Verma, J.P., Kumar, K. and Dutta, B.R. (1988). Utilisation of small backyard ponds for fish culture in rural areas—a new perspective. *J. Zool. Res.* 1 (2): 129-139.

Sarma, D., Baruah, D. and Mahanta, P.C. (2010). Performance of three pronged Chinese carp farming in mid Himalayas of West Kameng district, Arunachal Pradesh. *J. Inland Fish. Soc. India,* 42(2): 48-51.

Tyagi, B.C., S. Sunder and M. Mohan, 2005. *Coldwater Fisheries Research and Development in North East Region of India*, NRCCWF (ICAR), Bhimtal.

2

Fish Husbandry in Vast Expanse of Water

A Perspective Platform for Livelihood and Sustainability in Arunachal Pradesh

P. Nath, D.N. Das and *S.C. Dey*

Introduction

Rivers convey the excess water of the land areas that they drain to larger bodies of water or directly to the oceans. Collectively, they represent the world's water resources, as they carry virtually all the water, that is, available for human management and use. Interestingly, on a global basis, the total water resource of the earth is to the tune of 0.14 per cent of which 0.01 per cent (Groiler, 1993) is the fresh water on which all the living forms depend. Besides, the four great civilisations of early human history developed in close dependence on river and the fertile, easily worked soils of their flood plains. On the whole, rivers and their valleys have continued to play important roles in the course of history.

In addition, the rivers providing direct sources of water for domestic, agriculture, and industrial uses. They produce energy directly through hydropower generation and also provide the cooling water for many fossil and nuclear fuelled power plants. The rivers also serve as transportation routes, as carriers and natural "treatment plants" for human wastes and as habitats for fish and wildlife.

In totality, it appears the shrinkage of fresh liquid water is certain in the days ahead of us for obvious reasons; therefore, the utmost effort has to be conserved water for multipurpose activities. And in the process, Aquaculture could play an important role not only for livelihood but at the same time would ensure food security and sustainability in the vast expanse of waters.

Necessity for Creation of Vast Expanse of Water

In the early civilisations, the reservoir (vast expanse of water) was created to control flooding to protect the city, to provide water for irrigation and especially to conserve water for domestic purposes particularly for use during dry spell of water and nevertheless for generation of power in the nineteenth and twentieth centuries. Interestingly, it may be noted that the Romans built impounded tank throughout their empire (Groiler, 1993). The concept for creation of Indian reservoir for drinking water supply first took place at the erstwhile Madhya Pradesh by the then Princess Durgabati of Eastern Uttar Pradesh in the early sixteenth century. Thereafter, several man-made lakes have been created primarily for irrigation, power generation and other water resource development purposes throughout the country including NE Region. Apart from this, North Eastern Region has been blessed with other forms of Wetlands in the form of beels and *jheels* in the Valleys due to change of river courses and lakes in the high altitude region owing to earthquakes etc. (Nath, 2012). In this respect Arunachal Pradesh is in the fore-runner lists of all forms of wetlands in this Region.

Water Bodies—An Economic Hub

The vast expanse of water often regarded as a sleeping giant of Indian fisheries. The aforesaid resources still remained an area of neglect (Kar, 2012; Nath, 2012), thereby exhibits a poor performance in fish production. If the resources are properly exploited through proper management practices, the present production of 15-20kg/ha could be increased to 10-15 times (Sugunan, 2010; Dube, 2010).

Poor Performance and the Challenges Thereof

The various challenges confronting proper management and development of available vast water bodies could be categorized as follows:

(i) **Shortfall of fingerlings production:** The present water area in our Country in terms of Nursery and Rearing ponds, is rather inadequate to fulfil our requirement of fingerlings as a stocking material not only for the land based fishery activities but also for the open water bodies. Virtually, the supply-demand is still very wide, thereby the market price of table fish is soaring day by day.

(ii) **Introduction of incompatible exotic fish spp:** In many of the Reservoirs without proper hydro-biological studies, several types of exotic species have been introduced which has proved detrimental to the ecosystem (Lakra, 2008).

(iii) **Lack of co-ordination:** The fishers solely dependent on their livelihood are self-centred and do not comply with regulation in force (during visit at Maithon, Tilaya and Konar Reservoirs, DVC Project, Jharkhand, 2013; Ranganadi, Arunachal Pradesh, 2011). There is no proper inventory of available fish species, lack of stocking of proper fish species including the ratio of stocking. Although co-operatives and farmers' club exit, but there is no cohesiveness, poor post-harvesting infrastructure and marketing net work in most of the reservoirs of our country including NE Region.

(iv) **Improper facilities for Tourists:** Lot of revenue could be generated through the visiting Tourists. There is a lack of even the simple facilities like the jetties, huts for viewing the lake proper in most of these water bodies.

(v) **Shortage of Supervising Manpower:** For obtaining the desired result from any production oriented unit time-to-time monitoring and evaluation of the stocked material needs assessment. In terms of funding, there is no hindrance, but no analytical data of harvest of the produce is being recorded, thereby the actual production per hectare is lacking in most of the Reservoirs. This has been attributed in the lapses of proper Manpower placement.

(vi) **Lack of documentation of Women involved in allied activities:** Women indirectly involve themselves in various fishery activities, but their experience and success stories has not been properly documented. Glaring examples needs mention here are: Womenfolk of Apatani Plateau of Arunachal Pradesh involves in Integrated fish farming including marketing (Chowdhary & Nath, 2009); Selling fish in Meghalaya/Tripura/ Manipur market and in many places of Assam and tribal belts of West Bengal, Jharkhand etc. (Mahanta, 2011).

Perspective of Fishery Production Oriented Programmes

On looking through the Window of N.E. Region, one cannot overlook the geography of the Tail end of snow capped Himalayan mountain. The major part of this mountain is in the State of Arunachal Pradesh, contributing to the richness of vast network of open waters. In the process, various multipurpose river valley projects have been in the offing whereby expectation is for creation of vast expanse of confined waters. These confined waters could be exploited and harnessed beside hydropower generation and irrigation purpose, perhaps for production of easily digestible protein, viz. Fish.

The production oriented programmes could be through various forms of Aquaculture practices, Aqua-Tourism in these waters and agro-based and other allied activities in the feasible landed area. In addition, other vast Resources in the form of Beels, *Jheels*, Swamps, Lakes contributing to the basket of the natural resources as well as rich deposit of fish germplasms (reported 131 spp, Nath & Dey, 2000; 165 spp., Bagra *et al.*, 2009) in the Region and 4 nos. of new spp. (*Amblyceps apangi & A. arunachalensis*, Nath & Dey, 1989; *Bhabania arunachalensis*, Nath *et al.*, 2007; *Barilius arunachalensis*, Nath *et al.*, 2010) offering immense potential for pisciculture practices.

Aquaculture Practices

Presently, culture-based Fisheries in the open waters (Stocking and recapture) suitable for small sized water bodies; Stock Enhancement (for large sized water bodies), imposing mesh regulations and conserving habitats to allow natural recruitment and growth of target species in which annual stocking is not done after the target species gets established are being encouraged in context to topography and agro-climatic condition of our country in general.

As indicated in the foregoing that shortage of land based fingerlings hinders the proper stocking of this vast water bodies which is also capital intensive and involves environmental risk while transportation. Thereby calls for alternative, innovative and economic fish seed raising unit and the CIFRI (2009) has been successful *in situ* rearing of fry to fingerlings through Cage and Pen culture of Indian Major Carps and Exotic Carps as well as Ornamental fish spp. in the open waters before releasing into it (Maithon reservoir, Jharkhand), which is conducive to the ecosystem of middle and lower belts, whereas lakes and reservoir of the upper belts may be stocked with exotic *Trouts, Schizothorax* spp. etc. (Sela lake, Arunachal Pradesh); while the landed feasible areas offers unparallel opportunities for establishment of fish farms with fish breeding hatcheries (Mithon Dam, 2013, Jharkhand).

Integrated Fish Farming

The culture practices are: rice-*cum*-fish culture (Apatani Plateau, Arunachal Pradesh) poultry-*cum*-fish culture, pig-*cum*-fish culture, horticulture/floriculture-*cum*-fish culture, cattle-*cum*-fish culture, sericulture-*cum*-fish culture, duck-*cum*-fish culture etc. in an around the damming area including go-bar-gas plant forms the best option whereby saving the recurring cost of feed and fertilizers through such culture system (Nath, 2001).

Other Ventures

This could be in the form of Ornamental fish culture (colourful fishes for aquarium), Net and Boat industry, Ice-factory, Cold storage, hygienic market etc.

Value Added Fish Products

The surplus production could be utilized for long shelf-life and better off-site prices (Smoked fish, Fermented fish, Ranganadi, Arunachal Pradesh), Canned fish, Fish Papad, Fish Kurkure etc.), rice-mill, vegetable Oil Industry (for rice bran and oilcakes being the fish feed), Hygienic fish market etc. (Kerala, Karnataka, Andhra Pradesh).

Aqua-tourism

In the form of rafting, boating (Brahmaputra festival being at Pasighat, Arunachal Pradesh; Maithon, Jharkhand), botanical garden, aforestation, mini-zoo, children park including boat-house (Srinagar, Kashmir; Bhimtal, Uttarakhand; Ward's Lake, Shillong, Meghalaya; Modali Park, Kolkata, West Bengal), hotel and motels, sport fishery (angling with rod and line at Umiam lake, Barapani, Meghalaya) etc. could be coupled with for attraction of tourists. Besides, academics, nature-lovers etc. could get a good platform in enhancement of their knowledge. All these activities are supposed to be the benchmark for development and protection of the environment affected for implementation of river valley projects.

Likelihood of Unforeseen Odds

In many of the existing wetlands many noticeable changes have been noticed and being noted as follows in respect to the fisheries in particular, they are: (i) The large water bodies are unmanageable in true sense and perhaps not economical. "Growth of aquatic weeds, floating or submerged usually hinders in fish netting operation, navigation and poor production. (ii) Outbreak of fish disease both in cages and pens and in water bodies deeply choked with floating vegetation cover. (iii) Mechanized boats affects the ecosystem through fuel spill-way. (iv) Human interference in dumping of garbage and other anthropogenic activities. (v) Loss of fish habitat downstream in view of non-implementation of proper engineering skill and feasible technology. (vi) Sudden release of excess water from the man-made reservoir during monsoon months thereby causing untold flooding down stream. Although lot of stocked fish escapes yet may be profitable to some one from the fish harvest and ferrying earning handsome revenue during the flooding period. (vii) Stocking of exotic species in many of the water bodies have affected the local population to a great extent (Thailand magur, Silver carp, Big head, Grass carp, *Pagasius suchi, Nile* Tilapia, Rainbow trout, Brown trout, NBFGR). The stocking of exotic spp. could be encouraged in feasible areas, *viz.*, Rainbow and Brown trout has been stocked in barren snow fed streams and High altitude lakes of Tawang and West Kameng district and Mehao lake of Lower Dibang Valley of Arunachal Pradesh.

Quarantine and Prophylactic Measures

The preventive measures suggested and in practice at Maithon Dam, DVC for fish diseases are: (i) After transportation from Nursery for rearing, fish seeds (fry to fingerlings and to table fish) should preferably be given alum bath or permanganate solution bath (500 mg in 20 litre of distilled water; (ii) For any ulcer diseases—bath with Betadine/Iodine solution (1 ml in 10 litre of distilled water) followed by Tetramycin/Tetracyclin solution bath (1 capsule of 500 mg in 20 litre of distilled water) and liming the pond 250-500 kg/ha; (iii) For bacterial diseases: (a) Tail and fin rot application of copper sulphate in affected parts followed by potassium solution bath (500 mg in 20 litre of distilled water); (b) dropsy-treatment of pond with potassium permanganate at the rate of 2 gram/m^3 and tetracyclin orally along with fish feed at the rate of 50-70 mg/kg feed; (c) Eye disease—Chloromycetin solution bath (500 mg in 20 litre of distilled water); (d) Fungal diseases—Melachite green (bath 2-5 mg in 20 litre of distilled water) and with fish feed orally Cifran or Teramycin capsule 500 mg/kg feed; (e) If *p*H level is low (below *p*H-5) being acidic mucous secretion from the gills of fish, the pond should be treated with powdered Calcium Carbonate and not quick-lime at the rate of 250-500 kg/ha; (f) If the pond is in excessive alkaline condition (>10.8) which usually often occurs due to liberation of excessive amount of oxygen during photosynthetic activities of aquatic plants thereby formation of insoluble calcium carbonate from calcium bicarbonate followed by the formation of calcium oxide with the elimination of Carbon dioxide in the water bodies. This can be prevented by means of suitable calcification or through the removal of excessive plant growth; and (g) Gas bubble disease—when the nitrogen in water exceeds the lethal range (>125%) thereby fish found to swim at an angle of 45° with head pointing down; this could be controlled by stirring the pond water.

Inference

Concomitantly, Aquaculture activities, as stated, have been identified (Nath, 2003) as one of the several management and developmental platforms promoting economic growth; boosts health and hygiene (Nath, 2007; Nath *et al.,* 2012); ensures conservation measures, which could be most effectively done through Community Participation (Nath *et al.*, 2001) of land and water for long term livelihood *vis-à-vis* food security and sustainability (Nath and Dey, 2012).

REFERENCES

Choudhary, K.K., Nath, P., (2004). *Paddy-cum-fish in Apatani Plateau,* Arunachal Pradesh. CCWFR (ICAR), Bhimtal.

Dainik Jagaram, (2013). **Parikshan Ka Udghatan** (published by the Local daily on 20.9.2013, Dhanbad, Jharkhand) in connection with visit of Dr. P. Nath, Ex.DF as a Resource Person at the inaugural session for Training on Management of Reservoir Fisheries held at Tilaya Dam (DVC Project).

Das, A.K. *et al.*, (2009). *Cage Culture in Indian Reservoir*, CIFRI, Barrackpur, pp. 1-22.

Dube, K. (2010). **Cage & Pen Culture Options for Rearing Fingerlings in Reservoirs**, A paper presented in Reservoir Fisheries Management Training, NFDB at Bangalore.

Groiler (1993). River Discharge and Watersheds: In *Encyclopedia of Knowledge*, Groiler Incorporated, Danbury, p. 101.

Groiler (1993). History of Dam. In *Encyclopedia of Knowledge*, Groiler Incorporaed, Danbury, pp. 412-413.

Lakra, W.S., (2008). Pamplet on *Introduced Fresh Water Fishes in India,* NBFGR, Lucknow.

Nath, P. and Dey, S.C., (2000). *Fish and Fisheries of NE India.* Narendra Publication Ltd., New Delhi, pp. 1-285.

Nath, P., (2003). *Pisciculure: An Entrepreneur Development Tool:* Proceedings of workshop on Multidisciplinary training on sustainable environmental technique for NGOs of N.E. Region, G.B. Pant Institute of Himalayan Environment, N.E.R., Itanagar, pp. 64-65.

Nath, P., (2007). Fish for Health and Environment and Importance of Aquaculture in Arunachal Pradesh. In souvenir on the occasion of Golden Jubilee Celebration of Arunachal Pradesh coperative Movement (1957-2007) A.P. State Co-operative Union, pp. 34-37.

Nath, P., and Dey, S.C. (1989). Two new species of Genus Amblyceps (Blyth) from Arunachal Pradesh, *Journal of Assam Science Society*, 32(**1**): (**8**) 1.6.

Nath, P., and Dey, S.C., (2012). Fish Health Management, **A Tool for Fishery Industry** in 1st National Symposium: "**Fish Parasites**" Department of Biotechnology, GOI, held at RGU, Itanagar, Arunachal Pradesh, p. 19.

Nath, P., and Dey, S.C., (2012). Wetland—A Sustainable Fishery Resources for Conservation and Management perspective to Assam. In National Symposium: "**WETLAND**" CSIR, DBT, NFDB, ICAR (GOI) held at Assam University, Silchar, p. 56.

Nath, P., Dam, D. & Kumar, Anil, (2010). A New Fish Species of the Genus ***Barilius*** (Cyprinidae) from river Siang, D'Ering Memorial Wildlife Sanctuary, Arunachal Pradesh, India. *Records of the Zoological Survey of India*, 110 (Part-3), pp. 19-33.

Nath, P., Dam, D., Bhutia, P., (2007). A New Fish Species of the Genus ***Bhavania*** (Homalopteridae) from river Noadhing Drainage, Arunachal Pradesh India. Zoological Survey of India: 107 (Part-3): pp. 71-78.

Nath, P., Gopi, G.V., (2008). *Fish culture challenges and opportunities for self-employment in Arunachal Pradesh.* In Souvenir in commemoration of state level "Farmers Development Workshop-*cum*-Kishan Mela" published by Directorate of Agriculture Ministry of Agriculture, G.O.I., pp. 98-99.

Nath, P., Riba, T., Das, D.N., (2001). Community participation in the conservation of fish germ plasm in Arunachal Pradesh: A Focus; Resarun, XXVII, pp. 82-87.

Prabhat Khabar. (2013). **Team Ne kiya fish farm Ka Nirikshan** (Published by the Local daily on 14.6.2013, from Dhanbad, Jharkhand) in connection with the visit of Dr. P. Nath, Ex. DF to the Maithon Dam, DVC, Jharkhand and Fish Farm for undertaking Fish Breeding CIFRI, Barrackpur and Fishery Division, Maithon Dam.

Sugunan, V.V., (2010). Opportunities, Challenges and the Way Forward: In *Reservoir Fisheries Management (Training Manual)* Regional Centre, CIFRI, Bangalore, pp. 1-7.

The Telegraph. (2013). Human Role in Warming: at the Intergovernmental Panel discussion on Climate Change held at Stockholm National Daily on 28.9.2013) in the caption: NATION, p. 12.

3

NERIST in Development of Social Welfare and Economic Growth of the North Eastern Region Through CATRD

Debabrata Maji

Introduction

The Board of Management of NERIST in its 62nd meeting held on August 11, 2007 has resolved to establish the Centre for Appropriate Technology and Rural Development (CATRD) at NERIST. It is a multi-functional and multi-disciplinary Centre to assist the needs of NE Region. Centre for Appropriate Technology and Rural Development started its activities since August 2007 at NERIST, Nirjuli, Arunachal Pradesh. It is an independent Centre of NERIST.

Aim and Objectives

- To cater the technical needs of the people living in Arunachal Pradesh and neighbouring states of the North Eastern Region.
- To support in Technical and Vocational Educational activities of the people of the NE Region.
- To assist the development of social welfare and economic growth of the people in NE Region.
- To establish a consortium of scientific and technical talents to undertake activities that will help to promote and provide Technical Manpower base to cater to Non-Formal Sector for Technical and Vocational Education and Training (TVET) for Rural Stakeholders.
- To encourage Appropriate Technology adaptation and transfer through conducting pilots studies on specific projects.

- To develop documentary films on the lives of the people of the region by use and application of science and technology in socio-economic growth and development.
- To preserve rural and indigenous technologies of the NE Region and assist in technical documentation and dissemination of knowledge.
- To conduct Certificate, Diploma, Degree, Post Graduate Diploma/ Degree and Research Degrees in Appropriate Technology and Rural Development for regular or sponsored candidates for State/ Central Government, UN sponsored organisations, SAARC Countries through Multilateral and bilateral agreements under UNDP, UNEP, UNESCO, WHO, UNIDO, NEC, ADB etc.
- To organize and support Research, Colloquium, Seminar, Workshops, Conference on various Scientific and Technological advancements leading to the social and economic growth and progress of the region.
- To use the concept of Remote Sensing (RS) to Sector Professionals and academic community for forecasting Disaster and ensure remedial measures.
- To solicit, receive and accept grant from Central and State Governments and other recognised agencies and also materials in the shape of equipments, technical knowledge, documents etc. and also from recognised international funding agencies.
- To initiate for generating financial resources from Central and State Governmental Agencies, NGOs (Indian and Foreign) etc.

Operational Activities of CATRD

- Providing non-formal vocational training to generate self-employment and establish micro-enterprise;
- Providing Technical support services to user group for propagation of appropriate and affordable technologies;
- Conducting technologies need analysis towards location specific HR development;
- Providing delivery system for appropriate technology information dissemination through establishing a glaring house on low cost affordable technology within the campus;
- To ascertain the felt needs of the community through techno-economic social survey, job potential survey etc.;
- To become focal points for technology transfer;
- To train youth, women, and other disadvantaged groups in employable skills;

- To provide technical and other support services for improving local capabilities; and
- To create awareness regarding development programmes for creating problem solving environment.

It is on this back ground that we solicit collaboration and cooperation from various nodal agencies to implement these activities through non-formal mode.

Social Development Activities

Low Cost Housing Technologies for Arunachal Pradesh

Colloquium on "Low Cost Construction—Prospects and Perspective Application through Social Sector" held at NERIST on February 21, 2007 emphasized low cost affordable technologies for housing sector in North East in general and Arunachal Pradesh in particular. It has been decided that pre-fabricated technologies and bamboo technologies may be adopted for low cost and affordable housing in Arunachal Pradesh with the locally available materials in order to create employment opportunities for the local youth. The Colloquium also suggested preparing an action plan of collaborative activities for implementation of pilot project to study the effectiveness of such technologies and to come out with standard specification for alternative materials. This work may be taken up by the CATRD and RD Nodal Officers in the various parts of Arunachal Pradesh.

KVIC Collaborative Project

In an Interaction Session chaired by KVIC Chairperson Ms. Kumud Joshi held at State Guest House, Naharlagun on May 23, 2007 on "NERIST-KVIC linkages in Non-formal Sector" proposed to set up a National Level Committee in collaboration with NERIST to provide a platform to make the successful implementation of the KVIC schemes in Arunachal Pradesh. The chairperson also stressed the need of non-formal vocational training of KVIC scheme with an active support by NERIST. Secretary, Regional Director, Dr. Banerjee and Regional Manager (SBI) T.K. Banerjee assured to provide all necessary help to NERIST in its collaborative efforts. It is also felt necessary that Non-formal Vocational Education is the need of the hour for upliftment of local artisans, casual workers, rural masses which cater more than 94 per cent of the jobs in unorganised sector.

Conservation based Development in Arunachal Pradesh

Exuberating the feeling on the natural beauty of Himalayan State as Arunachal Pradesh, the development-conservation conflict is globally common, but development should come with a strong will to defect the forces opposing development in the name of conservation. This has been narrated by Kolkata based American Centre Director Douglas G. Kelly, Director, Office of Public Affairs, Consulate General of the United States of America, Kolkata, during press meet held at Itanagar on June 15, 2007. Need is stressed to study the climate change comprehensive investigation for preparing data bank on global Warming which may be accessible to the public through collection of figures and images. It is pointed out that the Economic and Social problem which are faced by the individuals after any disasters like Earthquake, Tsunami, Tornado, Cyclone and other modes of disasters in the wake of Global warming, which lead to long term rehabilitation, Societal problem for castes, Problem of migration and Psychological problems among students community. Both Mr. Kelly, and Ms. Koruna Singh, Programme Manager, emphasized on having institutional tie-ups and academic exchange programmes between NERIST and other prominent institutes of the United States of America which was declared by them in the Workshop on "Global Warming *vis-à-vis* Climate Change: the Effects of Climate Change in the Eco-system' held at NERIST on June 15, 2007 to commemorate the World Environment Day.

Entrepreneurship holds Key to Expedite Socio-Economic Development

Addressing the gathering during the "Awareness-*cum*-Orientation Programme" held at NERIST on July 1, 2007, Mr. M.G. Radhakrishnan, the member of All India Handloom Board and North Frontier Railway Users Consultative Committee, stated that Entrepreneurship holds key to expedite socio-economic development of Arunachal Pradesh. Referring a classic example of what entrepreneurship can achieve he mentioned the case of like Israel, a small nation one-third in size as compared with Arunachal Pradesh, which has well developed enterprise without any natural resources. Floriculture, ginger and local handicrafts have high prospects in the state to encourage the local youth to take the entrepreneurship opportunities. The Women groups of Dirang hired international designers to upgrade their indigenous design of handloom products for competing in the international market is one such example for emulation by other entrepreneurs of this state. Exhorting the people for paying back their loans for smooth transaction of their business enterprises, Mr. T.K. Banerjee, Regional Manager (SBI) highlighted the need to remove the fear phobia revolving around banking institutions, stating that a customer is always held in high esteem by the Bank. APSS Chairman Rekhi Tana Tara called upon the trainees to make a holistic approach while venturing into any business enterprise and should lay more stress on indigenous products for competing with outside products.

Rural Manpower Development and Appropriate Technology Transfer

Three-day Sensitisation Programme on "Role of Technical Institutions in District Development Activities" held at NERIST during August 29-31, 2007 for field level professionals. In his Key-Note Address Dr. Banerjee stressed the Key role of Middle Management and implementation personnel dealing with Rural Technology Transfer process, awareness campaign and specifically communicating affordable technologies with the user group. He recommended the participating Officers that Sensitisation at every level is essential to extract maximum benefit on the investment made by Government. Prof. Kalyan Kumar, Director, NERIST, expressed the need for Technology options available. He added that the Centre for Appropriate Technology and Rural Development is working in this direction and stressed the importance of creating a sense of involvement by the implementing personnel in the Technologies and their acceptance by the people. Director, State Institute of Rural Development (SIRD), Shri Tope Bam who attended the programme as Guest of Honour described in detail the activities of SIRD in District Development works. He elaborated the need of more Collaborative programme with NERIST.

Summing up of the Panel discussion, the Director NERIST Prof. Kalyan Kumar raised some pertinent issues connected with rural manpower development and appropriate Technology transfer:

- Creation of a Consortium with Department of RD, NIC, PHED, SIRD, KVIC and other resource Institutions and centre for Appropriate Technology and Rural Development of NERIST.
- Initiation of a demand driven approach with input of Science and Technology.
- Creation of Extension activities with NIC in particular in the sector of IT for Rural areas to prepare database of various resources in the area.

- Create computer Service Centre (CSC) in the NERIST campus, assisting schools and other nodal departments in setting up of Community Information Centre for the use of Community members.

It was also mentioned that the Secretary (RD) Dr. B.S. Banerjee and Chief Coordinator Prof. P.K. Bhattacharya may coordinate the proposed concept of Consortium initially for the State of Arunachal Pradesh and later for other regions of NE States.

Arising out of the discussion the following recommendations were made for further action at appropriate level:

- It is felt that there is a technical need for finding the gaps in expertise among rural sector professionals in tackling field level situations towards professional management at grassroots level.
- There is scope for further enhancement of Communication skill of the sector professionals in dealing with community needs.
- It is observed that many of the gaps can be filled up through a professional study on demand generation-parametres and towards an approach of convergence towards proper utilisation of both materials and human resources in the rural sector.
- Centre for Appropriate Technology and Rural Development at NERIST can play the role of nodal agency for the proposed Consortium of organisations like NIC, KVIC, NIRD, SIRD, PHED, National Research laboratory and other allied organisations.
- It was further felt a duel system of Technical and Technological Education on taking care of the rural sector demands and satisfying the needs of local communities may be initiated in the Country under Centre for Appropriate Technology and Rural Development (CATRD) could play in lead role in this effort. It was further felt there is need for a comprehensive local level studies of Technology options and propagation at various levels.
- It was strongly suggested that the special role and appreciation of Women members of the community be addressed to in a respectable manner in the field of gender balance and drudgery reduction.
- It was unanimously suggested that NERIST through CATRD would initiate Vocational Education and Training at various levels on the lines of UNIVOC, Centre of UNESCO with particular

reference to production of Training and resource documents for user group in general.

- It was further stressed to identify the role of CATRD under NERIST to initiate HRD programme towards appropriate technology transfer at various levels on the line of Community Collages of West.

Water Quality Testing

Fifteen days Training Programme on "Water Quality Testing" was organised during October 2007 sponsored by Public Health Engineering Department, Government of Arunachal Pradesh. Thirty two trainees from various places of Arunachal Pradesh participated in the Training Programme.

Entrepreneurship Development Programme

Three days "Entrepreneurship Development Programme" for REGP beneficiaries was jointly organised at Multidisciplinary Training Centre, Doimukh during November 29 to December 1, 2007.

Role of Khadi Movement to Eradicate Rural Poverty and Unemployment

Addressing the workshop on "REGP Bankers" Meeting and Technology Selection for Vocational Programme' held at NERIST on January 23, 2008, Mr. Khoda Ruja, Chief Executive Officer (APKVIB) and Director (Textile & Handicrafts) explained that the new Industrial Policy of Arunachal Pradesh need to take fresh looks at the potentialities of rural areas for mass production of consumer goods so that the objectives of rural industrialisation are realised. The KVIC/KVIB has got an important role to play to eradicate rural poverty and unemployment through the *Khadi* movement. In order to make the rural credit related Government schemes like REGP more vibrant and people friendly, suitable policy has got to be adopted. Dr. Banerjee, Secretary (RD) attending the Valedictory Session as Chief Guest described in detail the provision of SGSY and other schemes for SHG. NABARD representative Mr. Talukdar gave assurances to the SHG members for providing all kinds of assistance for the setting up of tiny units.

For Effective implementation of SHG activities the action plan and recommendation were finalised in the REGP Bankers' Meeting and Technology Selection for Vocational Programme:

- The formation of SHG and providing support to deprived sections of Society.
- To include CATRD representative in Bankers' Coordination Committee as special invitees and subsequently as regular member.
- To make banking services more SHG-friendly particularly lower income group.
- To conduct Sensitisation and Orientation programmes sponsored by SBI to the SBI's banking facilitators.
- It has been agreed that APKVIB and KVIC (State Office) will include CATRD representatives.
- Sponsored R & D activities on technology options should be undertaken by CATRD with support from KVIC, KVIB, NABARD, DST and other nodal agencies.
- Short-term training for SHG at CATRD and appropriate technology information service infrastructure would be provided by NABARD.
- NERIST would be provided appropriate facilities and infrastructure support for SHG activities.

Students' Role Pivotal in Rural Development

An Essay Competition on "Entrepreneurship" as a part of People's Education Programme was jointly organised by CATRD and MDTC, Doimukh on January 30, 2008 in Kendriya Vidyalaya NERIST. The students were sensitised for the urgent need to incorporate the Entrepreneurship in school education and the role of the student community to fulfil the vision and the dream of Gandhiji on Entrepreneurship development in the rural areas and make the India a developed nation by 2020.

Strategies for Entrepreneurship Development should be part of School Curriculum

A Debate Competition with the theme of "Strategies for Entrepreneurship Development should be part of School Curriculum" through People's Education Programme on January 31, 2008 at New Seminar Hall,

NERIST. It was envisaged that there is a good scope to start a modular 4 year skill development programme in near future for the age groups 14 to 18 years in energy (Hydropower), Oil and Natural Gas (Bio-Diesel), Medicinal Herbs (Ayurvedic), Forestry and Bio-diversity, Agro based and Food Processing, Handicrafts and Transportation. Non-formal training and educational methods are to be adapted to the expected enrolment of 20-25 per cent in higher education from the present 7 per cent of age group 16-23 years, three to four fold increase in our colleges/universities is essential. Developing multi-skill expertise for the non-formal sector activities is yet another mechanism for developing successful Entrepreneurship. Considering the dearth of affordable community based technologies particularly in the vast hinterland of rural India and the North-East, it is essential that adequate information based along with a proper delivery system is available to the user group.

Strategies for Rural Industrialisation

Sensitisation programme on "Strategies for Rural Industrialisation" through People's Programme was organised at NERIST on January 31, 2008. More than 55 participants from Class-X to XII of KV NERIST participated in the programme. The need of introducing the Concept of Entrepreneurship in school curriculum was stressed.

Success Story of SHG at NERIST

The Success Story of SHG at NERIST has just begun with a new vision and would go a long way for the upliftment of deprived section of the society in Arunachal Pradesh.

Women-SHG

Fourteen-member Women-SHG (Welfare Organisation of Mahila Empowerment of NERIST) has been constituted after providing them Skill Development Vocational Training on "Candle and Agarbati Making' and started their venture within NERIST Campus. The Women-SHG has also participated in the State Level KHADI EXHIBITION held at Itanagar organised by Arunachal Pradesh *Khadi* and Village Industries Board (February 20-29, 2007) and *Khadi* and Village Industries Commission, State Office (March 1-7, 2007) respectively and got positive response and patronising their products. They have prepared an action plan to sustain their activities by introducing various types of Candle and Agarbati which are generally used in homes on different occasions.

AMAN-SHG

Twelve-member AMAN-SHG (Arunachal Mechanics Association of NERIST) have been constituted after providing them Skill Development Vocational Training on "Automobile Repairing and Maintenance and Rural Mechanic Course" and started their venture.

Collaborative Mode

IIFT & NEDFi

A Meeting was organised at NERIST on February 12, 2008 where Mr. Roderick Zapanta and Mr. Alan Repolles both are Designers from Republic of Philippines, and Prof. Madan Lal, Indian Institute of Fashion Technology, New Delhi, in connection with Development of Incubation Centre at NERIST. In the meeting, it was decided that NEDFi will help for the Development of Incubation Centre at NERIST under CATRD and Skill Development Programme will be conducted under CATRD from the forthcoming financial year. Possible help will be extended by both Indian Institute of Fashion Technology and NEDFi for marketing of product as produced by the SHG at NERIST.

D.J. Research & Consultancy Pvt. Ltd.

For infrastructure development in the existing Multidisciplinary Training Centres throughout the country, a meeting was organised at NERIST on February 7, 2008. Dr. Damodar Tripathy, IES (Retd.), International Development Economist and Managing Director of D.J. Research & Consultancy Pvt. Ltd., Ex-Fellow EDI, World Bank; Ex-Chief Division Manager, African Development Bank; Ex-Joint Adviser, Planning Commission, India (IES), focused his work and experience in the developing world of Asia and Africa prompt him to say that the way the NERIST as well as CATRD intend to disseminate knowledge and make North East a powerhouse of development and poverty reduction is laudable.

Project Profile

- A Pilot Project Proposal for "R & D Intervention for Technology options for Setting up Micro-Enterprises and initiating Pilot Project through Setting up Design and Infrastructure for Product Development and Service Centre" was submitted to Khadi and Village Industries Commission, Itanagar on August 21, 2007.
- Project proposal for "Setting up of Food Testing Laboratory" was submitted to Ministry of Food Processing Industries, New Delhi on August 22, 2007 and First meeting of Techno Scrutiny Committee (TSC) held on August 28, 2007 under the Chairmanship of Shri Goutam Sanyal, Joint Secretary, MFPI has recommended the proposal.
- A Proposal for Competency based "Technical Vocational Education & Training (TVET)" through Non-Formal mode in North Eastern Region was submitted to North East Council, Shillong on July 5, 2007.
- A Mini in House Project proposal on "Community Development and Outreach Programme" was submitted to Director, NERIST on August 2007.
- A Draft Approach Paper for the "Development of Arunachal Pradesh" was submitted to *Khadi* and Village Industries Commission, Guwahati during Convergence Resource Group Meeting held at Guwahati on June 5, 2007.

Dissemination of Information

- Rural Development Department, Government of Arunachal Pradesh and *Khadi* and Village Industries Commission sponsored in-house 'Booklet' on "Role of Technical Institutions in District Development Activities" has been prepared by CATRD.
- PHED Sponsored 'Training Manual' on "Water Quality Testing" has been prepared by CATRD.
- KVIC sponsored in house 'Training Manual' on "Entrepreneurship Development Programme" has been prepared by CATRD.
- KVIC sponsored in house 'Technopreneur Volume-I' has been prepared by CATRD.
- APKVIB sponsored in house 'Technopreneur Volume-II' has been prepared by CATRD.

- KVIC sponsored in house 'Technopreneur Volume-III' has been prepared by CATRD.

Growth Activities

Ph.D. Programme started in January 2008. One Scholar was selected, but could not join. The Resource Group Members under the CATRD are frequently invited by the various organisations to deliver invited talk/ lectures on various programmes in Arunachal Pradesh. During the year 2007-08, they have delivered more than 11 lectures, 28 papers presented/ published in the National/International Conferences and three numbers of papers are also published in different Books published by the renowned publishers in India. Resource Group Members have received recognition 14 times during the year 2007-08 in different functions.

Future Development

- To provide a Community-Institute interface so that Science and Technology inputs can be transferred to the grassroots level through skills training, technology transfer and organisation of support services;
- Ensuring for the rural society a fair share of benefits from the investments in technical education system and thus bringing socio-economic upliftment and improvement of quality of life of rural mass; and
- To sensitise students and faculty of polytechnics/College/ University towards existing problems of the community needing Science & Technology inputs.

REFERENCES

The Arunachal Front, Thursday, March 1, 2007, Vol. XV, No. 18, pp. 1 & 6.
The Arunachal Times, Sunday, May 27, 2007, Vol. 18, No. 342, p. 1.
The Arunachal Front, Thursday, May 31, 2007, Vol. XV, No. 31, p. 8.
The Arunachal Times, Saturday, June 16, 2007, Vol. 19, No. 11, p. 1.
The Arunachal Front, Thursday, June 21, 2007, Vol. XV, No. 34, p. 6.
The Dawnlit Post, Monday, July 2, 2007, Vol. X, No. 72, pp. 1-2.
The Arunachal Times, July 3, 2007, Vol. 19, No. 28, p. 6.
The Echo of Arunachal, Tuesday, July 3, 2007, Vol. XX, No. 128, pp. 1 2.
The Arunachal Front, Thursday, July 5, 2007, Vol. XV, No. 35, p. 5.

Annual Report of CATRD, 2007-08.
The Arunachal Times, Sunday, December 2, 2007, Vol.19, No. 175, p. 6.
The Dawnlit Post, Thursday, January 24, 2008, Vol. X, No. 271, pp. 1-2.
The Arunachal Front, Thursday, January 24, 2008, Vol. 1, No. 149, pp. 1 & 3.
Echo of Arunachal, Saturday, January 26, 2008, Vol. XX, p. 1.
The Dawnlit Post, Saturday, January 26, 2008, Vol. X, No. 273, p. 1.
The Arunachal Front, Saturday, January 26, 2008, Vol. 1, No. 151, p. 3.
The Dawnlit Post, Saturday, February 2, 2008, Vol. X, No. 279, p. 1.
The Dawnlit Post, Sunday, February 3, 2008, Vol. X, No. 280, p. 1.
The Dawnlit Post, Monday, February 4, 2008, Vol. X, No. 281, p. 1.

4

Poverty and We

A Brief Preview

Swapnali Baruah

Introduction

"Three members of a family, including one ten months old child, committed suicide in Assam's Guwahati city as they jumped into the Brahmaputra river on 23rd September, 2013" (www.newsKerala.com), "Couple jumps into river along with infant child" (*The Assam Tribune*, September 24, 2013) etc. and such were the news headlines of almost all news papers in Assam on 24th September, 2013. Question arises why it happened? The infant has been suffering from heart problem since birth and they belonged to a very poor class or we can call Below Poverty Line (BPL). They were unable to carry on the costly expenditure of their single daughter. And ultimately they decided to commit suicide. They were partly misguided to have free treatment by the Government of Assam regarding their kid. A family finished because of unconsciousness or poor guidance and above all because of Poverty. So, poverty brought climax to a family recently in Assam.

The above stated incident is not happening only in Assam, it is an usual news throughout India and World. "About 21,000 people die every day of hunger or hunger-related causes, according to the United Nations. This is one person every four seconds, as you can see on this display. Sadly, it is children who die most often..." (www.poverty.com). Actually, the main problem behind this picture is also "Poverty", i.e. one of the burning issues in the present day World is making the Globe more warming than Global Warming. Poverty is the root cause of all economic problems. In fact, all economic problems move around it. No part of the Globe is free from this problem. Question arises what is Poverty? Absence of money? Absence of rich people? People may (or not) agree with such definitions. But poverty is what poverty does. The trouble with being poor is what it takes up all your time (W. de Kooning). It is a condition characterized by severs deprivation of basic human needs (UN). It is a situation where a section of the society is denied of even the basic necessities of life, without their own fault (Vedanti). Poverty is the absence of all human rights (M. Yunns). The frustrations, hostility and anger generated by abject poverty cannot sustain peace in any society. For building stable peace we must find ways to provide opportunities for people to live decent lives. Poverty is parent of revolution and crime (Aristotle).

Poverty at the International Level: A Brief Review

Poverty is a global problem. There is hardly any country in the World free from it. The third World countries mainly suffer from it. 1.3 billion People (approx.) in developing countries live on \$1.25 a day or less. Between 1990 and 2008, the rate of people suffering poverty has decreased from 48 per cent to 26 per cent and now has started to show an increasing trend due to food price inflation at the international level. As per information, more than 80 per cent of the World population lives in such countries where income differentials are widening. According to the report of UNICEF, everyday 22,000 children die due to poverty and they die quietly in some poor places of the Earth. India is one of those countries where this feature can be observed easily. The country with more than 1 billion population is marching fast in the race of development, but still has low per capita income at \$1,527 in 2011, as per Economic Survey Report. India's wider poverty level is worse than that of her neighbouring country Pakistan. 41.6 per cent of Indian's 1.1 billion people earned less than 78 pence per day in comparison to 22.6 per cent of Pakistan's 173 million population using Multi-Dimensional Poverty Index. The report also says that 53.7 per cent of Indians suffering from broader kind of poverty, compared with 49 per cent in Pakistan. Although India has emerged as a Global player with the World's 4th largest economy but still fails to remove poverty at a large scale. Reasons for missing out this target of halving poverty by 2015 are uneven economic growth and population growth. According to the Report of UNDP, 33 per cent of population lives in India below the revised national poverty line. By the year 2013, this rate has become almost 30 per cent (2010 estimate). In the country with 46 per cent population living on less than a dollar a day

(UNDP). It is to be mentioned here that as per the definition of World Bank, the International Poverty line is $ 1-2 per day in 1993 Purchasing Power Parity (PPP).

Poverty in North East India

North East India is one of the backward regions of India from socio-economic development point of view. Throughout India, this Region is adding fuel to the fire of poverty. To put it in other words, N-E India has been suffering from poverty at high level. Poverty in Assam is not of recent origin. Dandekar and Rath in their study estimated the numbers of people living under BPL (at Rs. 48 as poverty line) at 5.53 lakh (40.14%) and 107.12 lakh (77.38%) in urban and rural areas respectively. For the period 1970-71, the 7th Finance Commission estimated proportion of people living under BPL in the state at 33.0 per cent, while in 1983, as per National Sample Survey estimate, the rate of rural and urban poverty in the state became 45 per cent and 33 per cent against 55 per cent and 30 per cent of all India average. In 1993, the estimated poverty level in Assam was 40.86 per cent (Planning Commission's Expert Group Report). And now in 2009-10, it has become 37.9 per cent as a whole.

It is observed from Tables 4.1 and 4.2 that following Tendulkar Methodology the percentage of population living below poverty line (BPL) by 2004-05, Tripura ranks 1st at about 40 per cent against 37.2 per cent of India at average. Even though the rate of Economic Development is high in Assam among all N-E states but during the considered period percentage of persons living BPL was about 34 per cent with about 98 lakh persons in absolute term. These digits have changed into 37.9 per cent and 116.4 lakh numbers in the year 2009-10, whereas in case of India as a whole it has declined from 4,072.2 lakh numbers to 3,546.8 lakh numbers in the year 2004-05 to 2009-10. At present (i.e. 2009-10) Manipur has 47.1 per cent of people living under BPL, Meghalaya 17.1 per cent, Mizoram 21.1 per cent, Tripura 17.4 per cent, Nagaland 20.9 per cent and Arunachal Pradesh 25.9 per cent. Hence, the level of poverty in Assam is increasing during the considered period. The state is suffering from rural-urban divisions. In rural Assam, four out of ten live under BPL and in urban Assam, it is less than one in ten.

Discussions and Results

The causes of poverty are many. Unequal distribution of income, high

Table 4.1: Poverty Ratios of NE States and All India—Number and Percentage of population under BPL by States 2004-05 (Tendulkar Methodology)

States	Rural		Urban		Total	
	%age of persons	No. of persons (Lakhs)	%age of persons	No. of persons (Lakhs)	%age of persons	No. of persons (Lakhs)
Arunachal Pradesh	33.6	3.2	23.5	0.6	31.4	3.8
Assam	36.4	89.4	21.8	8.3	34.4	97.7
Manipur	39.3	6.7	34.5	2.3	37.9	9
Meghalaya	14	2.9	24.7	1.2	16.1	4.1
Mizoram	23	1.1	7.9	0.4	15.4	1.5
Nagaland	10	1.5	4.3	0.2	8.8	1.7
Sikkim	31.8	1.5	25.9	0.2	30.9	1.7
Tripura	44.5	11.9	22.5	1.5	40	13.4
India	**42**	**3258.1**	**25.5**	**814.1**	**37.2**	**4072.2**

Note: Population as on March 1st, 2005 has been used for estimating number of persons under BPL (Revised on the basis of 2011 population census).

Source: www.mdoner.gov.in

Table 4.2 : Poverty Ratios of NE States and All India—Number and Percentage of population under BPL by States 2009-10 (Tendulkar Methodology)

States	Rural		Urban		Total	
	%age of persons	No. of persons (Lakhs)	%age of persons	No. of persons (Lakhs)	%age of persons	No. of persons (Lakhs)
Arunachal Pradesh	26.2	2.7	24.9	0.8	25.9	3.5
Assam	39.9	105.3	26.1	11.2	37.9	116.4
Manipur	47.4	8.8	46.4	3.7	47.1	12.5
Meghalaya	15.3	3.5	24.1	1.4	17.1	4.9
Mizoram	31.1	1.6	11.5	0.6	21.1	2.3
Nagaland	19.3	2.8	25.0	1.4	20.9	4.1
Sikkim	15.5	0.7	5.0	0.1	13.1	0.8
Tripura	19.8	5.4	10.0	0.9	17.4	6.3
India	**33.8**	**2782.1**	**20.9**	**764.7**	**29.8**	**3546.8**

Note: Population as on March 1st, 2010 has been used for estimating number of persons under BPL (Interpolated between 2001 and 2011 population census)

Source: www.mdoner.gov.in

population growth, illiteracy, caste system, improper training, slow job growth, failure of PDS etc. are some of them. As a whole, the process of economic development is responsible mainly for poverty in Assam. The N-E India inequality of per capita income (PCI) at a high level is noticed. From Table 4.2, it is observed that urban PCI is high than rural PCI throughout N-E India. But the picture is quite opposite in case of India at average (Table 4.3).

Table 4.3: State Specific Poverty Lines for 2009-10

States	*Monthly per capita (in Rs.)*	
	Rural	*Urban*
Arunachal Pradesh	773.7	925.2
Assam	691.7	871
Manipur	871	955
Meghalaya	686.9	989.8
Mizoram	850	939.3
Nagaland	1016.8	1147.6
Sikkim	728.9	1035.2
Tripura	663.4	782.7
India	**972.8**	**859.6**

Source: www.mdoner.gov.in

As mentioned above, reasons of poverty in Assam are many. One of them is population growth. Population in the state rises naturally as well as because of migration from neighbouring countries (mainly from Bangladesh). The UNDP has observed that poverty head count ratio for Muslims as the highest in Assam and it is one of the basic causes of poverty in the state. Hence, poverty exists in Assam and it causes malnutrition, illiteracy, diseases, long term health problems, unhygienic living conditions, lack of proper housing, high infant mortality rate, injustice to women, absence of social security schemes etc. Poverty causes high injustice to women and girls. From extreme poverty they suffer the most and statistics show it is 70 per cent of the one billion people living on less than $ 1 per day. The women constituting a big share of World population works two-third of World's working hours, produce half of the World's food and in return they earn only 10 per cent of the World's income and now less than 1 per cent of the Global property. This is the Global picture of women where they mostly suffer from chronic hunger of malnutrition. It is said educating a woman is equal to educate a family, empowering women is equal to build a better World for them.

Assam, a state where "Women's day" is celebrated with the rest of India on 3rd March every year, is far legging behind in empowering women. This statement is equally valid for India. In many parts of Assam, girls are not send to school with the mentality that working in households, gardens or factories is much more better than to waste time in schools. Even in the present date, women are deprived of their paternal property. They can enjoy only their dower. Bills are passed and laws are enacted but it will take time for Assam ladies to enjoy proper empowerment.

In addition to all these, poverty causes unemployment, i.e. another burning issue of the current date. In the state the level of unemployment has increased from 1.8 per cent (1980) to 6.4 per cent (2011). To get rid of poverty, many had committed suicide. In 2009, 141 people committed suicide, what have become 159 in 2010 and 268 in the following year 2011. At all India level the figures stood at 2987 (2009), 3047 (2010) and 2282 (2011). Comparison of Assam with the rest of India in this regard is not required. Question is why do the people are committing suicide? Answer is just one word: Unemployment. It is observed that poverty in the state is high in rural areas than in urban areas. Why? Rural Assam is mainly dependent on agriculture. It is the mainstay of rural people but it has not grown at the expected level.

Solutions

The reasons of every poblem themselves are the solutions. Time has come to change the mentality, to send girls to schools, to make them literate, modernise agriculture, and control the growth of population (both natural and migration) and above all women empowerment.

With 16.93 per cent decadal growth rate (2001-11), population of Assam has increased from 26,655,528 (2001) to 31,169,272 (2011). This drastic growth of population in the state is not the result of natural birth rate. The state has been experiencing migration also. Migration in today's World is shaped by a number of factors related to economic, political, religious, life risk and various ethnic and socio-cultural issues (Roy *et al.*, 2011). At the time of partition of India, a substantial Bangali Muslim immigrant population chose to stay back in Assam as Indian citizens. Thus, immigration from Bangladesh started to Assam (Dutta). This fact becomes clear from the assessed influx of Bangladeshis between 1971 and 1991. Between these periods the growth of Muslim population in Assam was 77.42 per cent against 41.89 per cent of Hindu population growth. In the decade 1991-2001 the growth for Muslim population remained abnormally high at 29.3 per cent as compared to Hindu growth at 14.9 per cent. Bangladeshi migration is remarkably high in the Dhubri district of Assam, where out of 74.29 per cent Muslim population 70.07 per cent speak Assamese, with the decadal growth of around 23 per cent and 941 persons per square km. as population density (2001 census report). As per the final electoral roll of Election Commission of India, Muslim population in Assam has risen from 24.68 per cent (1951) to 28.42 per cent (1991). The number of Muslim voters has become the highest in Barpeta district in Assam at 4.97 per cent growth. It is not necessary to say about the result of high rate if migration from the neighbouring country. The community violence in July 2012 in Kokrajhar district of Assam covered the headlines of news at national and international level. Government is taking steps to control this migration but it is just for name. Leaving the "Vote Bank" issue aside, steps must be taken effectively, otherwise within few decades indigenous Assamese will become refugees in Assam and the state language of Assam will be Bangla and above all Government of Assam will become Government of Bangladesh.

Assam economy is agro-based and this sector has not been well developed as per expectation. Improvement of cropping intensity, application of appropriate technological intervention, intra-crop shifting etc. can increase crop intensity from its present level of about 146 per cent to at least 200 per cent. Horticultural practice is another good option for a state like Assam, as its climate is conducive to grow a variety of crops at a large scale. Baruah (2012) suggests for intra-horticultural shift, keeping in view the feasibility of climate. To her, double or multiple cropping is much more beneficial than mono cropping to the farmers. This will not only ensure financial security, but also it will provide employment opportunity and eradicate poverty to a great extent.

Statistics shows female literacy in Assam has increased from 56.03 per cent to 67.27 per cent during 2001-11. With such a good statistical proof it is expected that Assam's females are in better position than the rest of the North East India. But it needs their empowerment. This is a process of enabling or authorizing an woman to think, behave, take action and control work in an autonomous way (Battliwala, 1994). This expands the assets and capabilities of woman to influence control and hold accountable institutions that affect their lives (*World Bank Resource Book*). In the words of Sahidullah, women's empowerment would be achieved only when the attitudes, ways of thinking, feeling and willing—as also ways of behaving men, women and society towards women become congenial and positive, so as to respect her as a person with an identity of her own, to be treated, as an equally worthy human being rather taking her as an commodity and primarily as a sex object to be abused, exploited, discriminated and ill-treated. Doing so, women can go for family planning themselves and thereby can control the growth of population, i.e. reduction of poverty to a great extent.

Provision of economic security for eradication of poverty and empowerment of women is one of the urgent needs of time. In our country, collaborative model among Banks, NGOs, MFIs and women's organisations is advancing fast. Such a model serves as a "Best Practice" than micro-finance for women empowerment in the country. At the same time it needs reduction of gender discrimination at a large scale. No need to say what is SHG. It is also a good step or model through which women can become financially dependent.

Health of women must also be highlighted while going for their empowerment in the fight of poverty. Because of an ill mother, whole family had to suffer. In the last few decades, Assam's health scenario has improved a lot, but the goal is too far to make Assam a "Healthy Assam".

Governments both at the Centre and State level are doing their level best. Many plans and programmes remain in papers, never reach the needy people. Question arises why? Answer is because maximum people are poor and illiterate and hence unable to enjoy the fruits of these Schemes. The 23rd September, 2013 suicide incident in Brahmaputra River (stated above) bears its proof. For them poverty is a curse, freedom from it brings power. And freedom from poverty is like a pot full of curd that hangs up by a string, one can see it, but one cannot get it (Quoted from various discussion groups). The basic solution to this burning problem is public consciousness and their alert participation.

Conclusion

To conclude, the President of World Bank Jim Yong Kim has correctly warned that ending the worst of Global poverty within a generation would prove a tougher challenge than tackling Aids. Control of poverty can handle many socio-economic problems adhered to it.

REFERENCES

Baruah, S., Prospects of Intra-horticultural shift for Economic Growth of Farmers: A Case study of Tinsukia District of Assam, unpublished Ph.D. thesis.

Bhattacharya, R., *Women in Assam:* What have been achieved till date?
Biswas, T., *Women Empowerment Through Micro Finance: A Boon for Development.*
Dutta, N., *The Myth of the Bangladesh and Violence in Assam.*
Goodpal, *Poverty in India: Am I Poor? Where is the Poverty Line?*
Narayan, D., Sen, B. and Hull, K., *Moving Out of Poverty in India: An overview.*
Roy, N., Debnath, A. (2011). *Impact of Migration on Economic Development*: A study of some selected States.
Sahidullah, F. T., *Status of Women in Assam.*

Anonymous

- *The Assam Tribune*, June 17, 2009; September 24, 2013.
- *The Hindu*, July 15, 2010.
- *The Indian Express*, April 7, 2013.
- *The Telegraph*, March 20, 2012.
- *The Telegraph*, April 12, 2013.
- *The Times of India*, January 25, 2013.

Internet

- m.guardian.co.uk
- m.medianexpress.com
- www.assamchronicle.com
- www.assamtribune.com
- www.care.org
- www.censusindia.gov.in
- www.defencefromindia.com
- www.goodpal.hubpages.com
- www.globalissues.org
- www.ibtl.in
- www.pedr.com
- www.isical.ac.in
- www.indiatoday.in
- www.infoplease.com
- www.indexmundi.com
- www.kafila.org
- www.mapsofindia.com
- www.mdover.gov.in
- www.newsKerala.com
- www.photins.com

- www.pib.nic.in
- www.planningcommission.nic.in
- www.poverty.com
- www.tradechakra.com
- www.thp.org
- www.un.org
- www.vedanti.com

5

PRI in Sustaining Livelihood in Arunachal Pradesh

Bijay Raji

Introduction

Decade of economic growth has produced new economic inequalities and disparities. The poor have given a right to ask what is in it for me. That human activity has already crossed several planetary limits. We may need global growth, along with radical redistribution so that countries or region thus for deprived can gain without further threatening the earth. Thus, the focus on increased livelihood security to be addressed on the issues of economic growth. Arunachal Pradesh is predominantly rural in character where nearly 90 per cent of its population dwells in the villages after elapse of 41 years of its formation as Union Territory and 26 years of its statehood.

Rural areas are of by and large described as a den of ignorance and localism. There is a vicious circle of poverty, which is torn lead to low rate or development. The situation worsens by the level of living standard as it has a cumulative effect on people's attitude and their institutions. Arunachal Pradesh is tribal state and each tribe of Arunachal Pradesh having strong traditional ethos. Their traditional social structure is very rigid. Therefore, for the overall progress of the Arunachal Pradesh, the first and foremost task is the development of the rural sector. The herculean task is to provide an infrastructure to rural area which can facilitate the process of systematic and regulated development. The process of rural development in general seeks to transform traditional rural culture into modern one. In this context rural development projects and programmes accelerate the process of change in individuals and in rural community as a whole.

Rural development imbibes brings about simultaneous development in physical, social, economic, technological, political and institutional aspect by involving the people directly in the process. It also implies that development is one dimensional is directly proportional to the development in other aspects, requiring an integrated effort for an embracing development process. These developments enhance the livelihood of the rural people. Road development seeks to improve the quality of rural life of all the people in all the sphere of human needs.

For proper flow of rural development, it urgently needs agency or linkage. So, that the Central scheme and State sponsored scheme can percolate at the grassroot level. There is no denying the fact that neither at the Centre nor in the State in the respective ministries dealing with all the aspects of rural development structurally integrated. They may collaborate in idyllic situation in unison, but they are not as integrated enough in formulation or implementation of the progress. The developmental compartmentalisation has not yet waned. However, generally Centre frames broad schemes and budgetary allocations and leaves at the disposal of State Government to implement them with local flexibility within the broad frame work of the scheme.

In 1957, it was felt that people's participation was not coming forth to make community development programme a success story. People's participation on institutional basis through elected representative was ardently advocated. For this, as remedy a new institutional device was thought out by Balwant Rai Mehta Committee—Democratic Decentralisation. This institutional arrangement for rural areas officially came to be known as Panchayati Raj.

Decentralisation of administration is essential since the rural development is to be implemented at the grassroots level where the villages form the basic social and economic units. It is necessary that the administrative structure dealing with development at the rural areas need to have one supervisory agency preferably are elected body such as Panchayat under which Project could be executed.

Since its inception, Panchayati Raj is playing vital role in sustaining livelihood in rural area. If functions as some sort of government in rural area. All development and public welfare scheme which are being sponsored by Central and State Governments are being utilized and supervised by the Panchayat. For betterment and improvement of functioning of Panchayat, from time to time various committees were constituted by Government of India. The 73rd Constitutional Amendment Act of 1992 armed with power structure to Panchayati Raj in India.

For the upliftment of rural areas, Government of India formed a separate Ministry of Rural Reconstruction in August 1979, which was formerly a Department of Ministry of Agriculture. In Arunachal Pradesh also, there was a Department of Agriculture and Community Development

In 1979, a separate Department of Rural Development was created and community development was brought to form the part of this Rural Development Department. Thus, all community development programmes are piloted through the Rural Development Department.

Rural Development Programmes, continued to be implemented under Deputy Commissioner, thought their *ex-officio* BDO till 1983. In pursuance to the national policy under Societies Registration Act Government of Arunachal Pradesh created 12 District Rural Development Agency (DRDA) the then 12 District of Arunachal Pradesh. Since 1983 DRDA acts as an autonomous body. Each DRDA functions under chairmanship of Deputy Commissioner, all projects and programmes of rural development are now executed through it.

Every year under IRDP, ASMF, JRY, TRYSEM, PMEGP etc. funds are released district-wise by the Central Government on 50:50 basis, except JRY where it is on 80:20 basis. In IRDP and ASMF the ceiling limit of government subsidy which was applied, but in the rest of India subsidy will be one-third only.

Rural poverty and rural unemployment are interlocked with each other to the extent of in separation. To eliminate rural poverty is one of the biggest challenges before the Government of India in general and Panchayat Raj in particular in rural India. To overcome this challenges "food for work" programme was replaced by the National Rural Employment Programme commencing from October 1980. Subsequently, Rural Landless Employment Guarantee Programme (RLEGP) was also made operational in order to provide minimum 100 days employment to at least one member of every rural landless labourer from each household in a year.

Jawahar Rojgar Yojana is the ever biggest employment giving programme chalked out by the Government of India. The fund allotted under this scheme, would be an additional fund to the existing NREP, RLEGP etc. it would subsequently absorb both NREP and RLEP in order to make more effective opportunity.

The objective of JRY was to generate gainful employment in rural area to create productive community assets for direct continuing benefits to Poverty groups for improving rural economic and social infrastructure to prepare the overall quality of rural life.

The new working strategy of the Jawahar Rojgar Yojana was unlike the earlier, the Central assistance for their programme is to be directly released to the DRDA/District. It give employment opportunities to one member of each family living below the poverty line who seeks unskilled employment under JRY. Thirty per cent of the employment opportunities are reserved for women and priority has been accorded to the SC/ST and other weaker sections of society.

In addition to other Yojana, the Mahatma Gandhi National Rural Employment Guarantee Act (MGNREGA) aims at enhancing the livelihood security of people in rural area by giving 100 days of wage-employment in financial year to rural households who volunteer to unskilled rural worker. Capacity building and planning are critical to successful implementation of scheme under MGNREGA, the flagship programme of the Centre is providing 100 days guaranteed employment. MGNREGA enhance sustainable development and professional institutional networks. The Panchayati Raj Act is a agent to implement MGNREGA in the rural area.

In Arunachal Pradesh, provision of paying wages in food grain form has not been kept and wages are to be paid in cash only. The wage would be paid as per prevailing rates approved by the government. In Arunachal Pradesh, release of fund to the Anchal Samitis will be decided on the basis of the number of Gram Panchayats under each Anchal Samiti. Each Gram Panchayat will be allocated fund in proportion to the population under it.

Apart from Central sponsored scheme, the Government of Arunachal Pradesh under the dynamic leadership of Shri Nabam Tuki launched Chief Minister's Paryatan Vikas Yujana and Chief Minister's Agri-mechanisation programme for livelihood for the rural people of Arunachal Pradesh. Under Chief Minister's Paryatan Vikas Yojana the unemployed youth are provided vehicles on 80:20 subsidies. On the one hand it is enhancing the livelihood of thousands of unemployed youth of state.

The Chief Minister's Agri-Mechanisation Programme promotes the Agriculture of the state. In this programme the farmers are given subsidies on 80:20 basis on agricultural tools and impements. The Chief Minister's Agri-Mechanisation Programme attracts the youth of state towards the Agricultural sector.

The Chief Minister's Paryatan Vikas Yojana and Chief Minister's Agri-Mechanisation Programme's beneficiaries' are selected by the Panchayats. After selection of beneficiaries panchayat forwarded beneficiaries' names to respective offices. The respective offices released the money to the dealer or company in the name of beneficiaries.

The responsibility of planning and selection of schemes and their implementation has been given to the Anchal Samitis. The Gram Panchayat will decide the schemes to be considered by their respective Anchal

Samitis and to be included in Anchal Plans finally. The release of funds by Director, Rural Development, shall be informed.

All the Anchal Samitis' Plans of particular district would be consolidated into district plan after the approval of governing body of District Rural Development Agency for which the constitution of DRDA has been expanded with representatives from Panchayati Raj bodies.

In Arunachal Pradesh, instead of spending money too thin over all the Gram Panchayats, it would be desirable to take up Projects during the year in selected Gram Panchayats with the money available with each Anchal Samiti. This arrangement will be subject to the condition that all Gram Panchayats under a particular Anchal Samiti should reach at a consensus as regard the Gram Pachayats/area where projects are to be implemented. The projects in any case, should be selected on the basis of consensus. Anchal Samitis will be responsible for planning and execution of Yojana.

The Executive Officers of Anchal Samitis will get works executed either through the agency or any working department depending on the types of schemes and workload involved. At the district level, besides the technical supervision, the entire work relating to co-ordination, review, monitor and supervision of the programme will be the responsibility of the DRDA and Zilla Parishads, the apex body of Panchayat.

Panchayat Raj is soul of rural India in general and Arunachal Pradesh in particular. The life and condition of rural people is purely dependent on the Panchayat. All the schemes and project relating to rural people in India flow through Panchayat. Panchayat Raj is power to people, Panchayat plays role of big brother in sustaining the livelihood in Arunachal Pradesh.

Villages have been sources of enormous innovation. So, rural revitalisation is a significant employment generator. The search for possibilities of relative self-reliance through decentralized, democratic economics, which dramatically cut unsustainable transportation, empower people to be in control of their own lives need more attentions by the policy-makers. So, livelihood issue will empower people to be on control of their own lives, democratise market and provide a sustainable basis for wider socio-economic relations across communities and may reverse distress migration of villages into cities. So, the need is for more radical transformation and governance. The Forest Right Act and the Panchayat (Extension to Schedule Areas) Act need to be implemented in letter and spirit in the tribal area in general and particular in Arunachal Pradesh, villages should be given land as an unconditional livelihood claim.

REFERENCES

Arunachal Times (Daily News Paper), Itanagar, 15th April, 2013.

Arunachal Times (Daily News Paper), Itanagar, 29th May, 2013.

Arunachal Review, Vol. V, No. 5, May 2013.

Arunachal Review, Vol. V, No. 6 June 2013.

Dubey, Sanjay (1991): *Dynamics of Tribal Local Polity and Panchayat Raj in Arunachal Pradesh*, New Delhi: Premier Publishing House.

Pandey, Dwanweth (1997): *Local Government in Arunachal Pradesh*, Delhi.

6

Strategies for Sustainable Socio-Economic Development in Arunachal Pradesh

Toku Chokio

Introduction

It is well recognised fact that availabilities of capital is a vital link in the development process in an economy and upliftment of poor masses in regards to their proper education, poverty alleviation and resource of regular income in the real socio-economic development.

Several Rural Development and Poverty Alleviation Programmes have been implemented by Government of India and the State Governments. While the objective of these programmes may be commendable, they are based on a belief that spending of money is in itself a necessary and sufficient condition for poverty alleviation. It has been the experience of many researchers that such programmes have not yielded the desired result. In Arunachal Pradesh where tribal population is dominated, these programmes have also not faired well.

So far the development consists of a series of poverty alleviation programmes, designed to widen the income earning opportunities for the poor to enhance their socio-economic status. When discussion on structural changes were done in the fifties and sixties, it basically related land reforms, credit reforms, introduction of Panchayati Raj and other such measures which not only improved the income earning power of the poor and the underprivileged, but also raised their bargaining power. A series of special programmes were launched in the seventies to strengthen the income-earning power of the small and the marginal farmers, Scheduled Castes and Tribes and those for the backward regions. The special programmes for wage, employment like MGNREGA were designed to empower the poor and the weaker section of the society including the tribals. These programmes not only failed to achieve the desired results as a whole, but also failed to attract the tribal's towards these programmes. The tribal's are very much skeptic about these poverty alleviation programmes. This does not mean that they are not growth oriented, but the programmes have not been prepared taking into consideration the regional and socio-economic structure of the tribal of this region.

In understanding the problems of economic development of the region the landscape where they reside, the people's typologies and their development and nature of poverty of the region needs to be analysed.

Situation Analysis of Arunachal Pradesh

It is the land of breath takingly beautiful sunrises (the "Land of dawn-Lit mountains",) lies between 26°28' to 29°30' N latitudes and 91°30' to 97°30' E longitudes with a total areas of 83,743 sq.km. It is bounded by Bhutan to the West (160 km), China to the North and North East (1,030 km), and Myanmar to the east (440 km). It shares inter-state boundary with Nagaland in the east and south-east and Assam in the south between skyrocketing mountains, sparkling rivers, lakes, and ample of snow. It is the Arunachal Pradesh; the vast expanse of rolling plains, hills, and beautiful water bodies at the far eastern edge of India. India shows diversity in every aspect, including its population distribution. Arunachal Pradesh is the Indian State with the least population density, with just over 13 lakh of people living in the vast area of over 80,000 square kilometres. The population density of Arunachal Pradesh is even less than 20 people per square kilometre of area, according to Arunachal Pradesh Census of 2011. Population growth rate is more than 25 per cent here, but has shown decrement since the last census.

Literacy in this state, however, is far more disappointing. With only over 60 per cent of literate citizens, it is one of the two states in India having lowest literacy. On the positive side, the literacy has increased since the last survey by more than 10 per cent. Additionally, the increase in female literacy is greater than that in males. Though large in size, the state of Arunachal Pradesh has far less area urbanised; making most of the population lives in rural areas. Whatever small urban areas exist, the gender ratio found in those is dissatisfactory, whereas the sex-ratio in villages shows above 900 females per 1000 males.

As vibrant is the land, so are the people living in it. Arunachal population speaks above 50 dialects in total owing to the cultural diversity. Yet, the official language is English. The state capital is Itanagar. Some other major cities like Bomdila, Bhismaknagar, and Bhalukpong are worth visiting. Numerous tribes reside in the state each following their own cultures and ceremonies. Owing to wide tourism opportunities due to the Buddhist monasteries and cultural fests, the state has been gradually progressing.

The capital city which is also the largest city in the state of Arunachal Pradesh is Itanagar. The languages spoken in the Arunachal Pradesh state includes English. In total Arunachal Pradesh (AR) state comprises 16 districts. The ISOCODE assigned by International Organisation for Standardisation for Arunachal Pradesh State is AR.

Arunachal Pradesh Population Growth Rate

The total population growth in this decade was 26.03 per cent while in previous decade it was 26.21 per cent. The population of Arunachal Pradesh forms 0.11 per cent of India in 2011. In 2001, the figure was also 0.11 per cent.

Arunachal Pradesh Literacy Rate, 2011

Literacy rate in Arunachal Pradesh has seen upward trend and is 65.38 per cent as per 2011 population census. Of that, male literacy stands at 72.55 per cent while female literacy is at 53.52 per cent. In 2001, literacy rate in Arunachal Pradesh stood at 54.34 per cent of which male and female were 65.43 per cent and 40.23 per cent literate respectively. In actual numbers, total literates in Arunachal Pradesh stands at 7,66,005 of which males were 4,39,868 and females were 3,26,137.

Population Density in Arunachal Pradesh Density, 2011

Total area of Arunachal Pradesh is 83,743 sq. km. As per population census 2011, population density of Arunachal Pradesh is 17 per sq. km. which is lower than national average 382 per sq. km. In 2001, density of Arunachal Pradesh was 13 per sq. km., while nation average in 2001 was 324 per sq. km.

Arunachal Pradesh Sex-Ratio

Sex-Ratio in Arunachal Pradesh is 938, i.e. 938 females for each 1000 males, which is below national average of 940 as per Census 2011. In 2001, the sex-ratio was 901 in Arunachal Pradesh.

Description	*2011*	*2001*
Approximate Population	13.84 Lakhs	10.98 Lakh
Actual Population	13,83,727	10,97,968
Male	7,13,912	5,79,941
Female	6,69,815	5,18,027
Population Growth	26.03%	26.21%
Percantage of Total Population	0.11%	0.11%
Sex-Ratio	938	901
Child Sex-Ratio	972	798
Density/km^2	17	13
Density/m^2	43	34
Area km^2	83,743	83,743
Area m^2	32,333	32,333
Total Child Population (0-6 Age)	2,12,188	2,05,871
Male Population (0-6 Age)	1,07,624	1,04,833
Female Population (0-6 Age)	1,04,564	1,01,038
Literacy	65.38%	54.34%
Male Literacy	72.55%	65.43%
Female Literacy	53.52%	40.23%
Total Literate	7,66,005	4,84,785
Male Literate	4,39,868	3,03,281
Female Literate	3,26,137	1,81,504

Source: Census of India, 2001, 2011.

Arunachal Pradesh Urban Population 2011

Out of total population of Arunachal Pradesh, 22.94 per cent people live in urban regions. The total figure of population living in urban areas is 3,17,369 of which 1,67,901 are males and while remaining 1,49,468 are females. The urban population in the last 10 years has increased by 22.94 per cent. Sex-Ratio in urban regions of Arunachal Pradesh was 890 females per 1000 males. For child (0-6) sex-ratio the figure for urban region stood at 957 girls per 1000 boys. Total children (0-6 age) living in urban areas of Arunachal Pradesh were 39,899. Of total population in urban region, 12.57 per cent were children (0-6). Average Literacy rate in Arunachal Pradesh for Urban regions was 82.93 per cent in which males were 88.45 per cent literate while female literacy stood at 67.14 per cent. Total literates in urban region of Arunachal Pradesh were 2,30,103.

Arunachal Pradesh Rural Population, 2011

Of the total population of Arunachal Pradesh state, around 77.06 per cent live in the villages of rural areas. In actual numbers, males and females were 5,46,011 and 5,20,347 respectively. Total population of rural areas of Arunachal Pradesh state was 10,66,358. The population growth rate recorded for this decade (2001-2011) was 77.06 per cent. In rural regions of Arunachal Pradesh state, female sex-ratio per 1000 males was 953 while same for the child (0-6 age) was 975 girls per 1000 boys. In Arunachal Pradesh, 1,72,289 children (0-6) live in rural areas. Child population forms 16.16 per cent of total rural population. In rural areas of Arunachal Pradesh, literacy rate for males and female stood at 67.44 per cent and 49.14 per cent. Average literacy rate in Arunachal Pradesh for rural areas was 59.94 per cent. Total literates in rural areas were 5,35,902.

Description	*Rural*	*Urban*
Population (%)	77.06%	22.94%
Total Population	10,66,358	3,17,369
Male Population	5,46,011	1,67,901
Female Population	5,20,347	1,49,468
Population Growth	22.56%	39.27%
Sex-Ratio	953	890
Child Sex-Ratio (0-6)	975	957
Child Population (0-6)	1,72,289	39,899
Child Percentage (0-6)	16.16%	12.57%
Literates	5,35,902	2,30,103
Average Literacy	59.94%	82.93%
Male Literacy	67.44%	88.45%
Female Literacy	49.14%	67.14%

Source: Census of India, 2011.

Arunachal Pradesh Census 2011 Conclusion

The official census 2011 of Arunachal Pradesh has been conducted by Directorate of Census Operations in Arunachal Pradesh. Enumeration of key persons including Chief Minister of Arunachal Pradesh was also done by officials conducting population census.

Figures of population census 2011 Arunachal Pradesh have been represented in following chart:

There is no city having population above 1 lakh in the State.

Largest District (km²)

1. Dibang Valley	9129
2. West Siang	8325
3. West Kameng	7422
4. Upper Subansiri	7032
5. Upper Siang	6590

Percentage of Child

1 East Kameng	18.59
2 Kurung Kumey	18.45
3 Tirap	17.90
4 Changlang	17.45
5. Lohit	16.40

Rural Urban Arunachal Pradesh

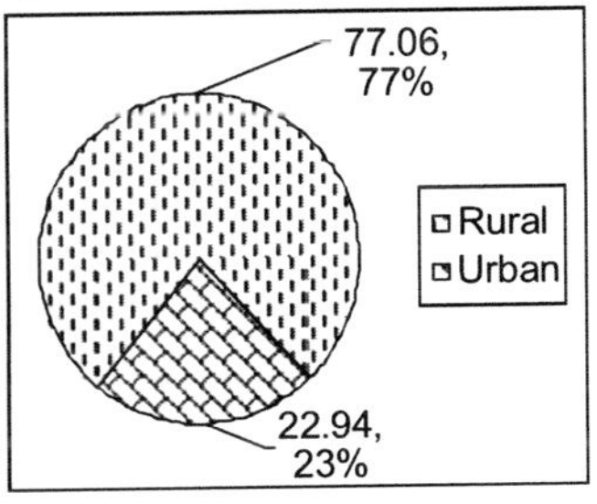

High Population Density

1. Papumpare	51
2. Tirap	47
3. Changlang	32
4. Lohit	28
5. East Siang	28

Top Population Growth (in %)

1. Kurung Kumey	116.56%
2. Upper Subansiri	50.78%
3 Lower Subansiri	49.00%
4. Papumpare	44.73%
5. East Kameng	37.62%

High Literacy (in %)

1. Papumpare	79.95%
2. Lower Subansiri	74.35%

3. East Siang	72.54
4. Lower Dibang Valley	69.13
5. Lohit	68.18

High Sex-Ratio

1. Kurung Kumey	1032
2. East Kameng	1029
3. Upper Subansiri	998
4. Lower Subansiri	984
5. East Siang	980

Political History of Arunachal Pradesh

Arunachal Pradesh economy has to be understood in the historical perspective. The tribal are considered to original settlers of Arunachal Pradesh. In early days they did not live permanently in any fixed part but generally migrated from one place to another in search of food and better accommodation, but after some time the tribal give up their migratory habit and took recourse to permanent settlement. The tribal of the region being mostly shifting cultivators and had only community ownership of land, Individual ownership of land was found to be prevalent in case of land under permanent cultivation. They are associated with land and forest for their livelihood. The characters of tribals are such that they are not being able to cope with the alternative means of livelihood easily.

Different movements were initiated in the region, whenever tribal right on land was disturbed. The beginning can be traced back to called "The Inner Line Regulation of 1873," for first time, separated some tracts inhabited by tribal people from the districts of Assam and British Authority. The areas were kept outside the purview of regular laws of the country and administered in different ways by passing regulations and framing procedures from time to time. When permanent settlement began in this area; then feudal structure was superimposed on the earlier tribal structure. The progressive erosion of the tribal ways of life, the break-up of their land system, land with ownership as clans, generation community land in the rural areas and by follow-up the British agenda for the protection of the Tribal people, the Government has imposed the rules and regulations that outsider people cannot be settled permanent on the land and cannot buy the land by outsiders and cannot sell to the outsiders by local tribal. But today dominance of outsiders as a part of Land Encroachment in the border area of Assam and Nagaland states are on the National border issues and moreover, International border with China and Bhutan, which is one of the burning issues. Collaboration with Government of India and Arunachal Pradesh has provoked the tribal into another series of revolts for preservation and protection of Tribal Identity. The present Arunachal movement is basically a tribal movement in protest against the totality of outsider intrusion, encroachment and dominance at all levels. During the last 70 years, significant demographic changes have taken place in Arunachal Pradesh through in-migration of Refugee-tribal called Chakmas-Hajoungs and non-migration of tribal, thus making the tribal a majority as complexity and land division in their occupied home land. The tribal of this region are more aggressive and opposed to the non-tribal from outsider states, who cannot dominate the region because of their British-political regulations. There is evidence of any confrontation between the Tribal and non-tribal (only the tribal sons of the soil) and the tribal of this state.

The State of Arunachal Pradesh which has rich mineral deposits of coal, limestone dolomite, graphite, quartzite, oil, yellow ochre, marbles, brine oil etc. and forest cover has then facing lot of problems. It has high rate of poverty ratio, low literacy, low level of agro-based industrialisation, low per capital-income, poor infrastructure and low credit deposits ratio and less development of eco-tourism.

So, this state needs proper and fair attention towards the poverty alleviation and upliftment of poor masses in all respect because as per the availability of mineral and wealth in the state, there exist great potential for the sustainable socio-economic growth with the development on agro-based and forest-based industries. The author has emphasis on the need of proper attention of poverty alleviation and credit delivery of fund to the poor masses for their upliftment in the real sense.

Arunachal Region did not receive due care in the past which it deserved and lagged behind in socio-economic development. The state requires a suitable mode for sustainable socio-economic development due to: because of continuous exploitation of this region by British imperialism and the colonial rule of the Assam Government, this region is still lagging behind of other states.

Different Development Programmers' in Arunachal Pradesh

The Government of India and the State Government has initiated special schemes for the development of tribal areas to supplement the benefits arising from general programmes of development in different field such as agriculture, co-operation, communication, health, housing etc. Arunachal Pradesh Government has also adopted tribal sub-plan to ensure higher degree of benefits to the tribal. This area has special provisions two Nagaland border districts as regarding, Tirap and Changlang Affairs Department and also special provisions to the remote area tribal people by programmes called Border Area Development Programmes (BADP).

The rural development in Arunachal Pradesh is either area specific which include Tribal Sub-Plan, Small Farmer Development Agency (SFDS), Draught Prone Area Programme (DPAP), Tribal Development Agency and recently Poverty Alleviation Programmes like. This area has also received special financial assistance under these programmes by different organisations. NGOs are also given grant-in-aid. But the impact of these programmes has been quite limited.

Various programme for the poverty alleviation and upliftment of poor masses which has been launched centrally sponsored and state sponsored but there is some weakness and shortcoming in the process of implementation of poverty alleviation scheme and credit delivery, so, it is necessary to identify these shortcomings which are related to these programmes.

So, that appropriate measures for the improving effective and impact of implementation of different scheme could be considered and secured.

Before identification of weak links, it is necessary to know about the different schemes for the poverty alleviation and upliftment of the rural poor masses, which has been sponsored by the Central and State Governments.

Centrally Sponsored Poverty Alleviation Programmes

I. Swarnajayanti Gram Swarojgar Yojana (SGSY): This scheme has been launched on 1st April, 1999 by the Government of India for the upliftment of rural poor, replaces the existing five following schemes:

1. Integrated Rural Development Programme (IRDP).
2. Training for Rural Youth for Self-Employment (TRYSE).
3. Development of Women and Child in Rural Area (DWCRA).
4. Supply of Improved Toolkits to Rural Artisan (SITRA).
5. Million Wells Scheme (MWS).

The objective of the scheme of SGSY is to organise the poorer into Self-help Group (SHG) and to provide training, technology, infrastructure and funs for community viable project and jobs.

II. Swarnajayanti Shahari Rojgar Yojana (SJSRY): The Scheme came into being with effect from 1st December, 1997 and replaced the three existing schemes:

1. Nehru Rojgar Yojana (NRY).
2. Urban Basic Services for the Poor (UBSP).
3. Prime Minister Integrated Urban Poverty Eradication Programme (PMIUPEP).

The main objective of SJSRY is to cover below poverty line family living in urban and semi-urban towns and special attention is to be given to women, ST and disabled persons.

In addition to that the following schemes are also in operation for the poverty alleviation and employment generation, such as:

(a) Prime Minister's Rojgar Yojana (PMRY),
(b) Margin Money Scheme of KVIC,
(c) Subsidy Linked Housing Scheme, and
(d) Nirmal Bharat Yojana (Sponsored by Central Government).

The Banks are implementing most of the schemes. So, the role of Banks particularly Lead Banks of each district is more significant for the proper implementation of various schemes in regard to socio-economic development. Because, all such schemes are dependant upon the adequate credit support to different segments of the economy for improving production, productivity and income generation in the economy by the Banks under Annual Credit Plans.

Some of the State Organisations, such as:

1. Scheduled Caste Co-operative Development Corporation; and
2. State Tribal Co-operative Development Corporation is also implementing credit linked schemes for ST in the Arunachal Pradesh. Even then, the mobilisation of credit for the needy people under different schemes is not satisfactory and found it much below the target.

Shortcoming and Weak-Links–(Issues)

The weak links related to implementation of poverty alleviation programmes in the state of Arunachal Pradesh are :

1. Lack of involvement of beneficiaries in the implementation process.
2. Implementing Nodal Agencies are more interested in achieving the target overlooking quality of implementation.
3. Selection of beneficiaries are not according to the norms and guidelines for the assistance.
4. Identification of key activities and development of project profiles on commercial lines is lacking in most of the districts in the State.
5. The existing training and skill development facilities are not adequate to meet the requirements.
6. Non-availability of quality assets like good quality milk animals, seeds, implements etc. adversely affect implementation.
7. Lack of direct vital link to the market centre to the majority of DWCRA ground.
8. Lack of creation of quality assets.
9. Lack of viable schemes suitable for beneficiaries.
10. Very poor recovery under the different schemes.
11. Panchayat election could not be held and this institution has not been able to perform its role and responsibilities in effective manner.
12. Proper assessment of credit and non-credit inputs for providing support to beneficiaries of key activities and preparation of project profiles to be made by only Bank Branches and it has not been taken care of on commercial and profession levels.
13. SGSY and SJSRY lay emphasis on group lending, but progress in formation and development of group is very slow resulting in low level performance.
14. Organising people in-group is a specialised job which require grassroots knowledge and information of the village. It requires times and patience on the part of the agencies/persons undertaking the job of organising people, so, there is lack of good and fair effective NGOs/VAs for this purpose.
15. Urban level bodies which are the Nodal Agencies for implementation are not able to play their role effectively in implementation of the schemes under SJSRY.

Weak-Links Related to Credit Delivery

1. Non-implementation of Land reform measures.
2. Irrigated area is very limited in the State.

3. Major area in under mono-crop and traditional culture, from its result in very low demand for production credit.
4. Lack of cold storage facilities it discourages farmers for growing potato, onion, vegetable etc. they do not get adequate remuneration price for the products.
5. Poor quality and erratic supply of power.
6. Co-operatives are not able to perform their role regarding providing production credit due to resource problems.
7. Most of the District Central Co-operative Banks have become financially weak and are unable to meet the credit demand of the solution.
8. Delay in disposal of cases filed under public debt recovery Act.
9. There is no instruction for bank to link recovery with fresh credit deployment.
10. Operating staffs are not particular not only for augmenting credit but also for improving recovery performance.

However, the fact remains that level of credit dispensation has not been commensurate with scope for utilisation of abundant and rich resource available in Arunachal Pradesh.

Prospect and Potential in Arunachal Pradesh State

1. Diverse agro-climatic conditions.
2. Suitability of soil for raising variety of crops vegetable and fruits plants.
3. Adequate availability of underground water.
4. Large wastes land area.
5. Availability of raw materials for agro-based industry and other.
6. Availability of abandon labour.
7. Prestigious institutions like Agriculture University, Engineering Colleges, Management Institutes etc. that can provide skilled personnel.
8. Availability of talented intellectual assets in the State.
9. Extensive network of Bank Branches.
10. Responsibility taken by NABARD, SIDBI, Lead Banks, NGOs, Ramkrishna Mission, Vivekananda, Mother Teresa Charitable, Oju Mission, Don Bosco, Holy Cross etc. for the upliftment of poor masses (BPL).

In view of the above facts, the following schemes and activities are more suitable for weaker section of the societies, such as:

(i) Sericulture and lac production, (ii) Mini Dairy Unit (Clusters), (iii) Poultry farming (Cluster), (iv) Minor Irrigation, (v) Sprinkler and drip Irrigation system, (vi) Bee-keeping, (vii) Vegetable cultivation, (viii) Piggery, (ix) Rural Artisans, x) Plantation and horticulture, (xi) Seed production, (xii) Fisheries, (xiii) Agro-base industries etc., and (xiv) Eco-tourism development.

On the basis of potential and classified available activities, flow of credit can be enhanced in Jharkhand state for the socio-economic development. It is the duty of the State Government, Development, Agencies, Banks, Financial Institution, NGOs VAs to take care and co-coordinated effort in initiating weaker sections for sustainable development.

Conclusion

With a view to overcome the above weaknesses and shortcoming and identified potential in Arunachal Pradesh state for the sustainable rural poverty reduction and socio-economic development, it is necessary to determined the objective for improving the financial services of commercial banks to the rural poor is the target group those who are living in below level, such as tribal, small/marginal farmers, landless, artisans, women headed households etc. and to promote saving mobilisation as the basic for lending to the people through formation development and operation of Self-Help Groups (SHGs). It will be much better for sustainable socio-economic development.

In this direction, fair and positive strategies should be linked with these rural poor, such as:

- Model should be sustainable rural poverty reduction from and socio-economic development.
- Developing people's participation in rural development making people 'own' the model of projects with collective decision-making.
- Access to saving and micro-finance-developing, saving habits and credit culture through Banks Self-help Groups.
- Improving financial services of Banks–developing appropriate rural financial mechanism.
- Process and mechanism to ensure people participation, people's institution, link—Village Development Assembly, Village Development Council etc.

It is found that if the conventional system fails to yield results, there is need to rethink about socio-economic institutions that should link resources, people and the government. People must cooperate and follow the rules set down by the community only if the use of the resources to be managed satisfies some of their very significant felt needs.

The Arunachal Pradesh statehood was not only for the sake of having a state but also for fulfilling aspirations of the people of the area in spite of the fact that this area has rich mineral wealth and natural resources. It requires due attention for the sustainable socio-economic development with honesty and in transparency.

REFERENCES

Arunachal Pradesh, "*Human Development Report*," (2005). Rajiv Gandhi University, Ronohills, Doimukh.

Baily, F.G (1960). *Tribe, Cast and Nation*, Oxford University Press, London.

Bakshi, S.R. and Kiran Bala, (2000). *Social and Economic Development of Scheduled Tribes*, Deep and Deep Publication Pvt. Ltd., New Delhi.

Bhattacharjee, R.P. (2002). *Economic Development of Arunachal Pradesh*, Himalaya Publication, New Delhi, Itanagar.

Das, Gurudas (1995). *The Tribes of Arunachal Pradesh in Transition*, Vikas Publishing House Pvt. Ltd., New Delhi, pp. 116-148.

Department of Rural Development of Arunachal Pradesh, (2010-2012), "with its every months workshop, seminars, conference etc., papers, policy, draft etc., from Government of Arunachal Pradesh and Central Government".

Eshi, Koge (1998). "Changing Agrarian Economy of Galos", A Study of Two Villages under West Siang District of Arunachal Pradesh.

Gopalkrishnan, R. (1991), *The North East India: Land, Economy and People*. Vikas Publishing Pvt. Ltd., New Delhi, pp. 65-73.

Government of Arunachal Pradesh, (2010, 2011, 2012, 2013), *Economic Review of Arunachal Pradesh*, Directorate of Economics and Statistics, Itanagar.

Government of India (2001), "Marginalisation of Tribals"; *Economic and Political Weekly*, Vol. 31, No. 47, pp. 4087-4091.

Jha, S.D. (1985), *The Wealth of Arunachal Pradesh*, Mittal Publications, Delhi, pp. 113-115.

Jodha, N.S. (1990), "Study of Rural Common Property Resources", Contribution and Crisis, *EPW*, Vol. XXV, No. 26.

Mandal, R.K., "The Human Resources Development of Arunachal Pradesh in respect of Education" a paper presented in National Seminar, organised by D.N. Government College, Itanagar, February, 2005, pp. 7-8.

Roy, N.C. and Kuri, P.K., *Land Reforms in Arunachal Pradesh*, Classical Publications, New Delhi

7

Rubber Cultivation as Sustainable Livelihood in Arunachal Pradesh

Amum Tamuk

Introduction

Many plant species produce natural rubber. Considerations of quality and economics, however, limit the source of natural rubber to one species, namely *Hevea brasiliensis*. It is a native of the Amazon basin and introduced from there to countries in the tropical belts of Asia and Africa during late nineteenth century. It can be termed as the most far reaching and successful of introduction in plant history resulting in plantations over 9.3 million hectares, 95 per cent of it across the globe in Asia.

Hevea brasiliensis, also known as the Para rubber tree after the Brazilian port of Para, is a quick growing, fairly sturdy, perennial tree of a height of 25 to 30 metres. It has a straight trunk and thick, somewhat soft, light brownish grey bark. The young plant shows characteristic growth pattern of alternating period of rapid elongation and consolidated development. The leaves are trifoliate with long stalks. The tree is deciduous in habit and winters from December to February in India. Refoliation is quick and copious flowering follows. Flowers are small but appearing in large clusters. Fruits are three lobed, each holding three seeds, quite like castor seed in appearance but much larger in size. The seeds are oil bearing.

Rubber (*Hevea brasiliensis*) is one of the important cash crops cultivated in India especially Kerala, Tripura, Odisha, Andhra Pradesh, Tamil Nadu etc. The rubber plantation can be categorized into two types, i.e. those with immature plants and other with mature trees. The rubber tree may live for a hundred years or even more. But, its economic life period in plantations, on general considerations is, only around 32 years—

7 years of immature phase and 25 years of productive phase. When the yields start decreasing beyond a certain level due to aging, the trees are usually cut and the area is replanted. Commercial cultivation of rubber in India was started in 1902.

In most of the rubber cultivated region, the cultivation meet the demands of rapid economic development. It has replaced more and more natural forest and fallow fields. There are two different viewpoints on rubber cultivation. One is that rubber cultivation improves local economics and social situations, while the other is that more rubber cultivation does not mean more sustainable rubber productions and that monoculture rubber plantation encounter many problems, example, pest, disease and erosion, pollution from chemical fertilizers and diversity loss. The chapter is an attempt to highlight contribution of rubber cultivation to the improvement of local economic situation along with intercropping in rubber cultivation.

Rubber Cultivation in Arunachal Pradesh

In a step to gainfully employ the unemployed youth in the State, the State Government of Arunachal Pradesh, under the Chief Minister's Mission Mode Project on plantation crops, through the Directorate of Trade and Commerce which is the nodal department, has planned to accommodate them in rubber plantation scheme by giving technical, material and financial assistance in the form of subsidy during the Twelfth Five Year Plan 2012-17 or during the next five years. Nine districts, i.e. East Siang, West Siang, Papumpare, East Kameng, Lohit, Lower Dibang Valley, Changlang, Tirap and Longding in the State are identified for rubber cultivation. Already rubber is cultivated around 2000 ha in the State by around 1800 growers. Around 23,000 ha are still available for rubber cultivation in the state; outside the areas classified as forest. Rubber is a viable and profitable cash crop for Arunachal Pradesh which could yield Rs. 2.7 lakh per hectare. Besides substituting the destructive and low yielding slash and burn cultivation, rubber plantations, if encouraged in right perspective would substantially increase the forest covers which stands at 82 per cent at present.

Climatic Requirements of the Rubber Tree

The rubber tree is native to the evergreen tropical rainforests usually occurring within the 5° latitude of the equator. The climate of this region is characterized by heavy rainfall and no distinct dry season. According to Rao and Vijayakumar (1992), the optimal climatic conditions for the genus *Hevea* are:

(i) Rubber can be grown in areas with elevation up to 450 metres from MSL (Mean Sea Level), avoiding low lying areas prone to water logging;
(ii) A rainfall of 2000 mm or more, evenly distributed throughout the year with no severe dry season and with 125-150 annual rainy days;
(iii) A maximum temperature of about 29-34°C, minimum of about 20°C and a monthly mean of 25-28°C;
(iv) High atmospheric humidity of about 80 per cent with moderate wind; and
(v) Bright sunshine for about 2000 hours in a year, at the rate of six hours a day in all months.

The growth and latex yield of a tree are affected in different ways by soil moisture. Moisture stress has more dramatic effects on the latex yield than on tree growth, as turgor pressure in latex vessels inside the trunk of the tree is required to facilitate the latex flow.

Soil Requirements of the Rubber Tree

Rubber can grow on many soils, the best options being well drained clayey and deep clay but it can withstand physical conditions ranging from stiff clay with poor drainage to well drained sandy loam. Soil water retention capacity, depth and soil moisture are important factors determining the suitability of a growing site. Ground covering plants can help in improving the soil physical properties. An optimal soil *p*H value for rubber is at 5-6. The performance of the tree can be restricted where there is rocky surface, heavy drainage or soil *p*H values above 6.5 or below 4 (Krishnakumar and Potty, 1992).

Rubber requires a modest level of soil nutrients when compared to coffee, tea, coconut and oil palm. Some fertilizer is, however, advantageous and can be needed to replace nutrients lost.

Block Cultivation

Traditionally most of the tribal population of Arunachal Pradesh practice shifting cultivation following the slash and burn method, known locally as *jhum* cultivation. It is even now practiced extensively in certain parts and is causing serious soil erosion and other ecological problems. In some region like East Siang District (includes villages like Depi, Nari, Detak, Debing, Rayang), rubber cultivation has already attracted large scale participation of tribals in proving to be an effective means of weaning away the *jhumias* to settled cultivation. Considering such situations, the Rubber Board of India in collaboration with some State Governments of North East like Tribal Welfare Department of Government of Tripura, has implemented a series of block planting programmes in which large blocks of tribal areas are planted up with rubber using the services of the beneficiaries and wage earners. The plantation on attaining maturity are handed over to the beneficiaries and they are held to set up a community processing centres to process the produce and market the rubber form the individual holdings. An integrated approach has been adopted by the rubber boards in this economics settlement programme under regular motivational efforts. The scheme envisages conversion of resources and facilitate a meaningful economic and social development at the same time ensuring eco-restoration. The rubber board has successfully evolved a model tribal development plan based on rubber under a World Bank assisted rubber project implementation in Tripura during 1994-2000. Block plantation project is also implemented in Odisha, Andhra Pradesh, Kerala, Karnataka. Where compact blocks of tribal land are available the tribal families in each hamlet are being held to raise rubber plantation on their individual land holdings. The recommended rubber plants are RRIM 600 (Malaysian Clone), RRIM 105 (Indian Clone), and GT 1 (Indonesian Clone). Along with rubber, energy plantation are also being raised in as much of fringe land as feasible for ensuring availability of fuel wood to the tribal families. Besides these, in most cases, they act as wind brakes and also enhance biodiversity. These patterns of block cultivation are proving to be highly successful and popular which can also be implemented in Arunachal Pradesh.

Other Additional Benefits from Rubber Cultivation

Intercropping

The Rubber Board of India has begun trial cultivation of rubber with tea in Bengal to change the perception that rubber is harmful to environment and other crops cannot be grown in rubber gardens. If the mission is successful then inter-cropping would be extended to other parts of the country. But, what exactly is intercropping?

Intercropping is the practice of growing two or more crops in proximity. The most common goal of intercropping is to produce a greater yield on a given piece of land by making use of resources that would otherwise not be utilised by a single crop. Taking into account the factors of soil, climate, crops, and varieties, careful planning is required. Intercropping of compatible plants also encourages biodiversity, by providing a habitat for a variety of insects and soil organisms that would not be present in a single-crop environment.

Rubber is an economic tree species that needs large investment and there is no return for at least eight years. In India we have a common idea that intercropping could not be done in rubber gardens. But experiments in South China show that in order to make full use of the land a large scale intercropping is done in rubber gardens.

It is a common practice that in monoculture rubber plantation to provide considerable space for the mature rubber trees, the spacing between two rows of rubber trees is generally set at 6 m, which is not only a waste of soil nutrients and solar energy, but also causes competition for light and soil nutrients between the rubber trees and ground vegetations. One can make use of these spaces by establishing intercrop rubber plantations. Crops like corn, upland rice, soybeans and pineapple, banana and sweet potato can be planted between young rubber trees before the canopy of rubber trees closes. Years later, plantation of short-term crops can be stopped and the monoculture rubber plantation can be managed. Shrubs or perennial herbaceous plant can also be planted in rubber plantation. Plants such as Pepper, Sugarcane, Tea, Coffee and *Amomun villusum* and other plants with high economic value can be planted along with rubber plantation. Rubber and Tea trees are usually planted at the same time. But, either of them can be planted one or two years after the other. Tea can be collected three years after planting, and its yield increases gradually year after year, until its peak at six or seven years. Further the tea tree intercropped with rubber accelerates the growth and prolongs the life of rubber trees.

Studies have revealed that rubber plantations composed of multiple species and layers not only bring out better income generation, but also benefit water and soil conservation.

The recommended planting distance for the inter-cropping with rubber depends on the characteristic of inter-crop. Process for this would be to plant smaller crops in the distance of about one metre from rubber rows and two metre for larger crops. At post-harvesting period they are recommended to conserve moisture and to improve the soil's physical properties.

It can be considered that correct inter-cropping in rubber plantations is a sustainable farming system. Initiative should be taken towards enhancing the productivity of existing yielding trees through improved agro-management practices like inter-cropping, soil moisture conservation, scientific crop exploitation and also the pace of adoption of these measures should be accelerated.

Beekeeping in Rubber Plantation

The rubber tree is prolific producer of honey. The joining part of young leaflets (petiole) of rubber leaves produce honey dew. At normal condition, the honey produced in rubber plants not completely collected by honey bees. By doing honey bee farming near rubber plantation, we can ensure most of these honey is collected by our bees. Honey flow period is between the months of January and March. As the rubber plantation area is large in India, honey bee farming has great scope. Various Governmental Agencies like Rubber Board of India, National Horticulture Board, NABARD, Khadi Board etc. give training and assistance to promote bee-keeping. Honey bee farming is a great way to reduce unemployment in rural areas. These also increase the availability of pure natural honey. These farming can avoid wastage of women work hours in village areas. Incorporating honey bee farming in current farm is always a sustainable method of farming.

It is estimated that the annual production of honey from rubber plantations in India is about 2750 tonnes, which forms 40 per cent of the total honey production in the country. Assuming even a production potential of 10 kg per hive and 15 hives per hectare, the total production in India could be enhanced to around 45,000 tonnes under scientific management. Assuming that 30 hives can be managed by a bee-keeper, the rubber plantation industry can give part-time employment to 1,50, 000 people.

Although rubber plantation was identified as a source of honey since 1920s, organised commercial exploitation of honey from rubber plantations in India is a relatively recent development under the auspices of Khadi and Village Industries Commission (KVIC). The available estimates on the production of apiary honey provided by KVIC underline the importance of rubber plantations as a source of honey.

Lack of honey flow in rubber during the prolonged dearth period from April to December necessitates alternate bee flora for off-season management in rubber plantation based apiaries.

The forage plants identified by the RRII are:

(a) *Antigonon leptopus* polygonaceae,
(b) *Callistemon lanceolatus* myrtaceae,
(c) *Manihot glaziovii* euphorbiaceae, and
(d) *Pongamia glabra* leguminoceae.

Apart from honey, other principal hive products are pollen, propolis, beeswax, royal jelly and bee venom, which also have industrial uses. The major consuming industries for honey in the domestic market are the Ayurvedic and Allopathic Pharmaceutical firms, bakery, confectionery, diary and tobacco manufacturing.

In order to provide an alternate source of income for the growers, the Rubber Board is encouraging bee-keeping among the rubber growers. A scheme for extending financial assistance for bee keeping was introduced by the Rubber Board in 1996-97. Under the scheme, the small growers owning a total rubber area between 0.5 and 2.50 acres and the tappers of small-holdings are eligible for bee keeping subsidy. The financial assistance granted per unit—consisting of 40 hives per S.H. Group will get Rs. 20,000. To become eligible for subsidy the hives and equipments should be purchased from agencies, approved by the Rubber Board.

To encourage bee-keeping in rubber plantations the Training and Technical Consultancy Department of Rubber Board conducts training programme in bee-keeping.

Rubber Plantation Insurance Scheme

The rubber plantations are exposed to perils like fire, lightning, forest fire, bush fire, flood, storm, tempest, inundation, landslide, rock slide, earthquake, draught etc. The peculiarity of rubber plantations is that if a few trees in a holding is damaged or perished, that particular patch of land cannot be used till the time the entire trees are cut and the area replanted. There are insurance schemes for rubber plantations. The scheme covers risks like damage caused by Fire, Lightning, Riot, Strike and Malicious Damage, Bush Fire, Forest Fire, Flood, Storm, Tempest, Inundation, Land Slide, Rock Slide, Earthquake and Drought provided the Block/Taluka concerned is declared as drought affected by the competent authority of the State Government. The policy is also extended to cover the loss or damage caused by road/rail vehicles and wild animals.

Conclusion

Rubber Board, under the Government of India, Ministry of Commerce & Industry, is the national agency to promote rubber cultivation in the country. The Board is giving all technical support and some financial assistance to the growers. Financial assistance provided by the Board meets only around 25 per cent of the cost of planting. Now, the cost of planting has increased due the hike in labour wages, price of plantation input materials etc. and the growers are finding it difficult to raise the required funds for scientifically maintenance of their rubber plantations. Therefore, the State Government proposes to support rubber plantation and related activities in 4000 ha in Arunachal Pradesh during the Twelfth Five Year Plan Period or the next five year.

From the discussion a conclusion can be drawn that rubber cultivation not only can improve the local economic situation, but also partially replaces traditional slash and burn agriculture, making possible economic sustainability.

REFERENCES

"Hon'ble Chief Ministers Mission Mode Project on Plantation Crops and Sharing a Cup of Tea Mission", Director (Trade & Commerce), Government of Arunachal Pradesh.

"*Intercropping in rubber plantation leads to economic benefit*", National Agricultural Portal "*Krishibhoomi.*"

"*Modalities, Guidelines and Implementation Scheme of Rubber Plantation in Arunachal Pradesh*" published by Director (Trade & Commerce), Government of Arunachal Pradesh.

Rubber Board of India website.

"Rubber Cultivation and Sustainable Development in Xishuangbanna, China", *International Journal of Sustainable Development & World Ecology.*

"*Rubber Cultivation as a Suitable Livelihood in Arunachal Pradesh*", published by Director (Trade & Commerce), Government of Arunachal Pradesh.

"Rubber inter-cropping to stop the falling yield growth", *Indian Express Newspaper* (Bombay Edition).

"*Rubber Plantation Insurance*", Agriculture Insurance Company of India Limited (AIC).

"*Tea and Rubber Board on Card*", *The Arunachal Times.*

8

Educational Attainment for Changing Livelihood in Arunachal Pradesh

Tumter Lollen

Introduction

Educational attainment in any society is regarded as important indicators of social, cultural, economical and technological development, because education creates skilled manpower, which plays a significant role in the economic and social development.

In today's globalised world one can not remain aloof or indifferent from phenomenal changes, that is taking place in every sphere of human life. The advancement achieved in economic, social and technological field in any country has been possible by its human resources. The best example may be cited of European nations on one hand and African nations on the other hand, where natural resource rich countries of Africa registers very poor social and economic development, whereas the human resource rich countries of Europe has attained very high index of social and economic advancements. The level of all-round development is achieved through its human resources, generated through quality education. Therefore, it is no wonder that UNESCO in its declaration of human rights has included education as one of the basic rights of every human being. The Government of India during its early part of independence also realized the significance of education and therefore, it incorporated in its directive principles the obligation of every state to provide universal and free elementary education to the children below 14 years of age. Further, for the overall development of its citizen it noted that, "education is the single most important factor in achieving rapid economic and technological progress..."

Educational attainment and knowledge is essential for eradicating disparity between rich and poor, for attaining higher standards of living, for overcoming ignorance, for sustainable development of its economy. Today, literacy has increased all over the world but at the same time literacy rate differs from developed nation to developing nation, from male to female, from one community to other. It is in this context that the present chapter seeks to analyse the role and significance of education as major generator of human resource and changing the livelihood practices of people living in one of the remotest region of India, i.e. Arunachal Pradesh.

Conceptual Framework

The concept of literacy varies from country to country. The Population Commission of the United Nations considers a person literate if he or she has the ability to both read and write a simple message with understanding in any language. The same definition of literate has been accepted in India and therefore, the Census of India also recognises a person as a literate who has the ability to read and write with understanding in any language. However, to consider a person as literate or illiterate consideration of age has to be taken in account in order to know what percentage of population is literate or not. On the basis of which a person is classified as literate also vary from country to country. In India from 1961 to 1981 Census, all children below the age of 5 years were regarded as illiterate. However, from 1991 Census all children below the age of 7 years were considered as illiterate. In addition formula for computing literacy rate also varied in both the Census periods that are before 1981 Census and after 1991 Census.

$$\text{Literacy rate (up to 1981 Census)} = \frac{\text{Number of Literate Persons}}{\text{Total Population}} \times 100$$

$$\text{Literacy rate (1991 Census onward)} = \frac{\text{Number of Literate Persons aged more than 7 years}}{\text{Total Population aged more than 7 years}} \times 100$$

Study Area

The state of Arunachal Pradesh is situated in the North Eastern region of India extending between 26° 28′ N to 29° 30′ N latitude and 91° 30′ E to 97° 30′ E longitude. It is a thinly populated state of India with lowest density of population with 17 persons per square kilometre (2011 Provisional Census Report). It is surrounded by Bhutan in the west, Tibet (China) in the north, Myanmar in the east and Assam and Nagaland in the south. Arunachal Pradesh is inhabited by numerous tribal communities who are in majority. There are around 25 major tribes and numerous sub-tribes in Arunachal Pradesh belonging to Indo-Mongoloid racial stock. In terms of economic and social development it is one of the least developed states of the country. Its backwardness may be attributed to its peripheral location, age-old isolation, rugged topography and extreme climatic condition, lack of infrastructural development, limited land for agricultural production, lack of industrialisation and urbanisation, problem of connectivity, limited use of its natural resources and perhaps imposition of Inner Line Regulation Act of 1873. Looking at the educational scenario of Arunachal Pradesh, education was introduced effectively only after the independence of the country, while other hilly states of North East states had educational institutes introduced by the Christian Missionaries during British rule. The British Government neither interfered in the matters of the tribes nor encouraged the Missionaries to do missionary work and kept the area under excluded and partially excluded category. However, because of missionary activities in the foothills of Assam-Arunachal border some private schools (Primary level) were established in the first quarter of twentieth century. Therefore, during Indian independence out of 12 Primary level schools only four were functioning in the entire state. After independence, all the plans and programmes for the development of the then North East Frontier Tract was introduced with the objective to integrate them with the rest of the country and therefore, the system of school education was linked to the Secondary Education Board of Assam till 1972. Since then, Arunachal Pradesh has made tremendous progress in the field of education even if the literacy rate is below national average.

Objective

The present study will analyse the growth of education in Arunachal Pradesh from the census year of 1961 onward. The study will make an attempt to understand the reason for low attainment of literacy rate and low level of education. Besides, it also aims to examine the implication of education on changing livelihood in the state.

Data Source

The study is based on secondary data collected from various Census Reports, Department of Economics and Statistics, Government of Arunachal Pradesh, *Gazetteer of Arunachal Pradesh*. The literacy rate, growth rate of education and percentage of workers at various sectors has been worked out.

Educational Scenario in Arunachal Pradesh

After Independence Government of India made an attempt to develop the tribal people of the region by providing the benefits of modern education. It was not an easy task to introduce modern education in the region where literacy rate was around 1 per cent. Therefore, in order to popularize modern education system, various types of concessions were extended to the students in the form of hostels, stipends, free books and uniforms etc. And in order to involve the people in new formal educational system, the community participation and involvement were encouraged. The village communities were encouraged to take part in the construction of school building, hostels and gardening work etc. An education officer was appointed and teachers from Assam were trained to open new schools. The school education was affiliated to the Secondary Education Board of Assam (SEBA). It was only after 1972 that the system of school education was affiliated to the Central Board of Secondary Education (CBSE) under Government of India. The major aims and objective of school education in Arunachal Pradesh were: (1) To remove backwardness and imbalances of the area; (2) To raise the economic level of the state; (3) To promote integration; (4) To eradicate illiteracy; (5) To universalize elementary education; and (6) To acquaint with modern science, technology, medicine and engineering.

In order to promote educational system in the state various policies and programmes were adopted at different stages on the basis of the National Policy on Education. During the initial Plan period impetus was given only on school education and that too upto secondary level. There were no Higher Secondary or Degree level educational institutions in Arunachal Pradesh till 1961 Census Report as evident from Table 8.1.

The first Higher Secondary school was established in the year 1966-67 in Khonsa, Tirap District. Thereafter, some Secondary level schools were upgraded to Higher Secondary Schools and till 1971 there were 16 Secondary schools, 7 Higher secondary schools and 1 Degree College in whole of Arunachal Pradesh. The first college in Arunachal Pradesh was established at Pasighat (East Siang District) in 1964-65 for only Arts stream offering B.A. Degree. It was only in 1973 that science stream was introduced in Jawaharlal Nehru College, Pasighat.

Table 8.1: Number of Educational Institutes at Various Levels in Various Census Years

Census Year	*Educational Institutes at various level*					
	Primary School	*Middle School*	*Secondary School*	*Higher School*	*Degree College*	*University*
1961	129	14	5	–	–	–
1971	506	47	16	7	1	–
1981	953	119	29	14	2	–
1991	1350	241	63	45	4	1
2001	1669	347	120	71	7	1
2011	1941	920	191	118	25	2

Source: Directorate of School Education and Directorate of Higher and Technical Education, Itanagar, Arunachal Pradesh.

The Census Reports show that there were no university in Arunachal Pradesh, only two degree colleges one at Pasighat and another in Itanagar with 385 numbers of students. The number of Primary and Middle schools were 953 and 119 respectively. There were only 29 Secondary and 14 Higher Secondary schools till 1981. However, in the last three decades, i.e. from 1981 to 2011 there has been tremendous growth in the number of educational institutes at various levels. The latest Census Report shows an appreciable number of educational institutes in Arunachal Pradesh, like 1941 Primary Schools, 920 Middle Schools, 191 Secondary Schools, 118 Higher Secondary Schools, 25 numbers of Degree Colleges, and two Universities. The Census report of 2011 shows considerable growth of educational institutes in the state from 1669 Primary schools to 1941 Primary Schools with 14 per cent growth. A very high growth rate of 62.28 per cent was registered in the number of Middle level schools from 347 to 920. Similarly, high growth rate in Secondary and Higher Secondary level was also registered with 37.17 per cent and 39.83 per cent respectively. But the highest growth rate of 72 per cent was registered in case of Degree colleges from 2001 to 2011 period. Tremendous growth in the number of educational institutes in recent years shows that access rate to education has also increased in recent years. The high growth could be because of growing awareness among the native masses on the significance of education for the overall well being of society on one hand and government's realisation for facilitating education at all levels to the nook and corner of the state. In addition, the State Government is also making every effort to implement various schemes under Central Government and UGC for not only opening up of new schools, but also in improving the infrastructure of educational institutes. In addition there are Institutions offering Degree, Diploma Courses in Engineering, Law Colleges and allied courses. A Homoeopathy College has also been opened. The growth in educational institutes were not only because of State Governments Initiatives, but also because of various NGOs like, Ramakrishna Mission Schools, Sharda Mission Schools, Vivekananda Kendriya Vidyalaya, Don Bosco Mission Schools, Private parties. In addition, the Central Government sponsored Sarva Shiksha Abhiyan schools at primary level helped in increasing the literacy rate in the State.

The growth of education in the initial years from 1947 to 1981 was quite slow not only in terms of number of educational institutions, but also in the number of students at various levels shown in Table 8.2. The growth in the number of students at various educational levels has been quite high with 2,22,378 (25%) at Primary level; (30.75%) at Middle level; 36,507 (32.64%) at Secondary level; 22,483 (47%) at Higher Secondary level and 15,492 (67.12%) at College level. The growth rate in the number of students shows increasing rate with increasing level of education.

Table 8.2: Number of Students at Various Levels in Different Census Year

Census Year	*Number of Students*					
	Primary	*Middle*	*Secondary*	*Higher Secondary*	*Degree*	*University*
1961	3899	1309	999	–	–	–
1971	16467	3998	2365	1479	88	–
1981	43311	15426	9373	7025	385	–
1991	125071	26089	10771	4925	1523	64
2001	166689	56104	24588	11728	5093	500
2011	222378	81022	36507	22483	15492	1078

Source: Directorate of School Education and Directorate of Higher and Technical Education, Itanagar, Arunachal Pradesh

Because of increasing awareness on the importance of education by the rural folks there has been considerable increase in enrolment of students in recent past. A large number of students from middle class and affluent families are studying outside the state for acquiring better education and exposure which has not been reflected in the given census data. The present data only gives us information of students studying at various educational levels in Arunachal Pradesh.

The teacher-students ratio is reflective of classroom teaching and accessibility of teachers by students for gaining knowledge and guidance. The teacher-student ratio at different level of education as shown in Table 8.3 appears to be fulfilling the required norms of a class but in actual practice there is huge dearth of teachers in many schools. The given ratio of teacher-students shows number of teacher appointed by the government, private institutes and NGO run schools, but the absentees of teachers in school from the place of posting especially in the rural and interior places while there is surplus number of teachers posted in urban places. Therefore, there is repeated demand for teachers especially in secondary and higher secondary schools from various districts in various local newspapers. Even the teacher-students ratio as worked out for colleges in Census Reports is actually spurious because in bigger colleges like Dera Natung Government College the overall teacher-student ratio is 1:100. It is more in English department for first year with 1: 500, which is against the prescribed norm of UGC. And in some smaller colleges the teacher-students ratio is even less then states average of 1:32. Again the teacher-students ratio is lesser in Science stream as compared to Arts stream both in schools, colleges and university. The private, public and Central Government schools have again lesser teacher-students ratio as compared to government run schools. Therefore, it is not correct to draw conclusion of good teacher-students ratio in Arunachal Pradesh as it is not a true reflection of teachers imparting knowledge to students for their intellectual development. Moreover, the absence of many teachers in the place of posting has adversely affected the quality of education in schools. The growing incidence of indiscipline and use of unfair means during examinations can be partly held responsible to the absence of qualified teachers in schools who is supposed to impart not only text book knowledge but also impart moral and ethical values to students in the budding stage.

Table 8.3: Teacher-Student Ratio at different levels as per 2011 Census Report (Provisional)

Teacher-Student Ratio at different levels					
Primary	*Middle*	*Secondary*	*Higher Secondary*	*College*	*University*
1 : 22	1 : 24	1 : 20	1 : 27	1 : 32	1 : 27

Source: Directorate of Economics and Statistics, Itanagar, Arunachal Pradesh.

Literacy Rate in Arunachal Pradesh

During Independence of the country the literacy rate in Arunachal Pradesh was around only one per cent but then there has been considerable increase in the literacy rate after 1980s. According to 2011 Census Report (Provisional) the literacy rate of 66.93 per cent in the state has been registered which is below national average of 74.04 per cent (Table 8.4) and one of the least literate states and last being Bihar with 63.82 per cent. A cursory glance at the growth of literacy rate in Arunachal Pradesh as compared to all India level shows much higher progress as shown in the given Fig. 8.1. While the growth of literacy in India has been slow and steady, while the growth of literacy has been quite rapid in Arunachal Pradesh. Tremendous growth was registered from 1971 to 1991 Census period and the possible reason for its growth could be because of attainment of status of Union Territory in 1971 and statehood in 1987 and shifting of state capital from Shillong to Itanagar in 1979 which made the administrative work much easier. The National Policy of Education, 1986 and its programme of Action as viewed in 1992 which stressed on improvement and expansion of education at all level and thereafter, the launch of Sarva Shiksha Abhiyan (SSA) during 2001-02 in the state may also be contributed for the growth of education in the state. In fact, the scenario of elementary education in Arunachal Pradesh has changed to some extent after the inception of SSA which is a centrally sponsored scheme with it objective to universalize elementary education.

Table 8.4: Literacy Rate in various Census Years

	1961	*1971*	*1981*	*1991*	*2001*	*2011*
Arunachal Pradesh	7.23%	11.29%	25.54%	41.59%	54.74%	66.93%
India	28.30%	34.45%	43.53%	52.31%	66.38%	74.04%

Source: Population Census, 2011, Various Issues.

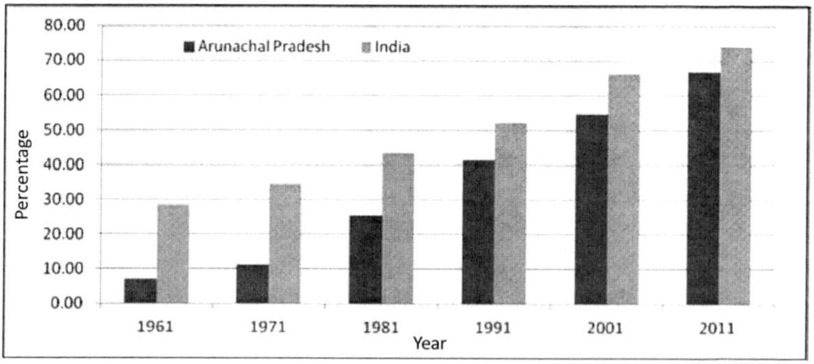

Fig. 8.1: Comparative Growth of Literacy in Arunachal Pradesh and in India
Source: Population census, 2011.

When we compare the status of literacy with the other eight North East Indian states, Arunachal Pradesh happened to be the least literate state as shown in Table 8.5 followed by Assam with 73.18 per cent and these two states have literacy below national average. Mizoram is not only the most literate state in the entire North East region with 91.58 per cent, but also third most literate state of India and the possible reason for high literacy rate is the influence of the Church on its 95 per cent Christian population. The other states with above 80 per cent literates are Tripura, Sikkim and Nagaland. The comparative low literacy rate in Arunachal Pradesh also implies that there is more number of Adult illiterates as because 40 per cent of total population belong to adult group and moreover, within juvenile age group children belonging up to age group of 7 years are also excluded from literate group. Therefore, it can be assumed that along with adult illiterates there are also non-school going children adding to the number of high illiterates in the state.

Table 8.5: Literacy Rate in North East States

States	Arunachal Pradesh	Assam	Manipur	Meghalaya	Mizoram	Nagaland	Sikkim	Tripura
Literacy Rate	66.95%	73.18%	79.85%	75.48%	91.58%	80.11%	82.20%	87.75%

Source: Population Census, 2011.

High growth in literacy over few decades does not necessarily mean that the level of education achieved is high as because out of 4200 habitations in the State only 1941 primary level schools are there. Moreover, the distribution of these educational institutions is also very uneven in different parts of Arunachal Pradesh as for example, there were only 15 Primary level Schools in the District of Dibang Valley as against 195 and 177 Primary schools in West Siang and Papum Pare Districts respectively. Such discrepancy in terms of distribution of educational institutions reflects the accessibility of education to children in the age group of elementary school level, which is against the very spirit of universalisation of elementary education.

Implication of Education on Changing Livelihood in Arunachal Pradesh

The potential for development of a state depends to a great extent on the human resource of that region. The quality of human resource will help in assessing the knowledge of the physical and natural resources of the region, it will also bring in awareness of the constraints and challenges in exploiting these resources, the skill they possess at varying levels of operations and management, their attitudes toward life and society, their work culture, their investment of time, money and energy, and their values and moral responsibility towards their personal as well as social life will undoubtedly bring in all round development in the state. The quality of human resource is determined by the spread, quality and content of education. With regard to quality of education in India it is important to note as given in the Approaches to the Eleventh Five Year Plan, which states that "*38 per cent of the children who have completed 4 years of schooling cannot read a small paragraph with short sentences meant to be read by second standard student and about 55 per cent of such children cannot divide a three digit number by a one digit number.*" It further adds that "*universalisation of education will not suffice in the knowledge economy*". These statement made by government is quite true with regard to Arunachal Pradesh. Many students in undergraduate level cannot write single correct sentences, while others are there who cannot read or tell the scales of centimetre and inches given in a 15 cm scale. Notwithstanding the phenomenal growth in educational level and literacy in Arunachal Pradesh, the State Government observes that "*there is still shortage of manpower for specialised jobs*". Does it mean that most of our educated manpower is unemployable in various white colour jobs? As per the government report the work participation rate have registered a declining trend in the last three decades, i.e. 52.59 per cent, 46.24 per cent and 43.61 per cent for 1981, 1991 and 2001 census period respectively. However, decadal rise in the number of workers in non-agriculture sector was higher. This trend is an indicator that the avenues of employment were created in non-agricultural sector, but these avenues were only in white colour jobs offered by government. It is a fact that in Arunachal Pradesh employment is generally understood to be employment in government undertakings. Since there is dearth of private undertaking and even if private jobs are there they are either underpaid or underemployed. Therefore, number of unemployed youth has increased by manifold during last few years. In addition, a very few educated youth seek employment outside the state as they either lack confidence or abhors long working hours in various MNCs or private companies. The possible reason for the increasing school and undergraduate unemployed youth could be spurious development in educational sector.

Even with high growth rate in educational sector the Census Report of 2001 records 62.3 per cent of its total workers engaged in farming activity. Government itself admits that "about 80 per cent of people living in rural areas where the main occupation is agriculture, the state will have to make substantial investment in agriculture and allied sector for creating employment opportunities". But our educated youth hardly engage themselves in primary sector although there is wide scope for self-employment in this sector. The educated youth look for employment opportunities in either government jobs or in contract (business) job in various governmental schemes and programmes.

Conclusion

The present study shows that a young state like Arunachal Pradesh has made tremendous progress in the area of educational sector, which had around 1 per cent literacy rate at the time of Independence of the country to 66.93 per cent during five and half decade of its existence as a state. The growth registered in the number of educational institutions at various level as well as increase in literacy rate is definitely noteworthy. Although, the growth attained in educational sector as compared to other North East Indian states is comparatively poor it may be attributed to its age long isolation and hostile physical condition. The study also shows that during this period the number of educational institutions at various level have increased manifold with the help of governments initiative as well as private sector and NGOs, which in turn helped in spread of education to different parts of the State. In order to attain universalisation of elementary education various incentives were provided to the students in the form of free books, stipend, hostel facilities, free uniform etc. many teachers were also appointed as a result the teacher-students ratio at various education level for entire state appears to be under the prescribed norms. The chapter also shows that number of educational institutions at undergraduate level has increased tremendously in the recent past, which helped the poor students to access to higher education within catchment area. Having made appreciable progress in educational sector the progress made so far appears to be spurious as the state is far from attaining the universalisation of elementary education, the problem of inadequate infrastructure is rampant at all level, the teacher-student ratio as given in the governmental reports is far from the required norms when analysed closely. The high literacy rate achieved over the past decades is yet to generate quality human resources and help in changing livelihood for increasing unemployed youth of the State.

REFERENCES

Aziz, Abdul (1996). *Regional Development: Problems and Policy Measures*, Concept Publishing Company, New Delhi.

Alam, K. (edited), (1985). *Planning in North East India*, Omsons Publications, Guwahati, Assam.

Agarwal, A.K. (1987). *Economic Problems and Planning in North East India*, Sterling Publishers Pvt. Ltd., New Delhi.

Begi, Joram (2007). Education in Arunachal Pradesh since 1947, *Constraints, Opportunities, Initiative and Needs*, Mittal Publications, New Delhi.

Bhattacharjee, R.P. (2000). *Economic Development of Arunachal Pradesh*, Himalayan Publishers, Itanagar, Arunachal Pradesh.

Chaube, P. (2005). *History of Indian Education*, Vinod Pustak Mandir, Agra, Uttar Pradesh.

Chaube, P. (2005). *Problems of Indian Education*, Vinod Pustak Mandir, Agra, Uttar Pradesh.

Choudhury, R.K.D. (2007). *Human Capital and Manpower Planning in North East*, Himalayan Publishers, Itanagar, Arunachal Pradesh.

Das, G. (1995). *Tribes of Arunachal Pradesh*, Omsons Publication, New Delhi.

Dey, S. and Rajput, K.S. (2003). "Population and Educational Profile of Meghalaya", *Hill Geographer*, Vol. XIX, Nos. 1 and 2, Shillong, Meghalaya.

Dutta, P.C. (1993). *Arunachal Pradesh: An Overview*, Directorate of Research, Government of Arunachal Pradesh, Itanagar, Arunachal Pradesh.

Government of Arunachal Pradesh: Statistical Abstract, 2011, Directorate of Economics and Statistics, Itanagar, Arunachal Pradesh.

Government of India, *Census Report*, Arunachal Pradesh, 1961,1971, 1981, 1991, 2001.

Jha, S.D. (1988), *Socio-Economic and Demographic Dimensions of Arunachal Pradesh*, Western Book Depot, Guwahati, Assam.

Lollen, Tumter (2001). "Impact of Developmental Planning on Tribal Communities: A Case Study of Arunachal Pradesh", Unpublished Ph.D. Thesis, JNU, New Delhi.

Mandal, R.K. (2005). *Arunachal Economy: Socio-Economic Transformation*, Champion Publishing, Itanagar, Arunachal Pradesh.

Mandal, R.K. (2009). *Socio-Economic Transformation of Arunachal Pradesh*, Omsons Publication, New Delhi.

Mitra, A. (2002). "Economic Development of Arunachal Pradesh: an introspection", *Resarun: Journal of the Directorate of Research*, Government of Arunachal Pradesh, Itanagar, Arunachal Pradesh.

Koley, R.N. (2002). "Evolution and Growth of Education in Arunachal Pradesh", *Arunachal Reviews*, Vol. V, No. 2 June-August.

Premi, M.K. (2006). *Population of India, in New Millennium*, Director, National Book Trust, India, New Delhi.

Raza, Moonis, *et al.* (1986). *Educational Planning: A Long Term Perspective*, Concept Publishing Company, New Delhi.

Rostov, W.W. (1971). *Politics and Stages of Growth*, Cambridge University Press, London.

Satyanaryan, M. (1990). "Tribal Development in India: A Trend Report", *Tribal Studies of India Series*, 5137, Inter-India Publication, New Delhi.

9

NGOs in Livelihood Strategies for Marginalised Differently Abled People

A Study on *Atmanirbhar—Ek* Challenge

Dipakshi Das, Ira Das and *Namita Das*

Introduction

Non-Governmental Organisations (NGOs)[1] across the world have existed for different purposes but with the common motive of providing help to the needy. In this regard it is worth emphasising the role of NGOs in the field of livelihood generation. In fact, NGOs are now a day's recognised as the third key sectors on the landscape of reforming livelihood status of different sections of people in the society.

Livelihood is a set of activities involving self-employment and/or wage employment by using one's endowments (human and material) to generate adequate resources (cash and non-cash) for meeting the requirements of self and the household usually carried out repeatedly and as such become a way of life. Thus, livelihood is the sum of ways and means by which individuals, households and communities make and sustain a living. But unfortunately there are very few scope and less opportunities for the differently abled people to earn a stable livelihood. There are an estimated 650 million disabled people with disabilities in the world (around 12% of the global population) and 80 per cent of these (i.e. 520 million) are concentrated in developing countries (UNDP, 2012). In India there are millions of people affected with different forms of disabilities such as blindness, hearing impairment, loco motor disability, mental retardation etc. According to Census 2011, there were approximately 26 million persons with disabilities in India. In Assam also it is estimated that the prevalence of disabilities is 1681 per lakh population.

All men and women with disabilities can and want to be productive members of the society and earn a livelihood of their own and thereby lead an independent and respectable life. But they encounter many difficulties in society and are often subject to stigma and discrimination. Further, they remain largely excluded from political and civil processes and voiceless on crucial issues that affect them and their societies (Wiesen, 2012). Thus, the primary reason to promote livelihood is the belief in the essential rights of all human beings to equal opportunity.

In India, provisions have been made with a view to promoting equality of opportunities and raising of livelihood options for the differently abled people. Equality for all is guaranteed under Articles 14, 16 and 21 of the Constitution of India. The Legislative framework for people with disabilities is provided by The Rehabilitation Council of India Act, 1992, The People with Disabilities Act, 1995 and The National Trust for Welfare of Persons with Autism, Cerebral Palsy, Mental Retardation and Multiple Disabilities Act, 1999. There are several livelihood or poverty reduction schemes, which have also existed and worked for livelihood generation of disabled persons along with other weaker sections of the society. Thus, it can be said that Government of India has been one of the largest agencies involved in such livelihood promotion efforts.

But the question arises is that whether these provisions have fully/ actually benefited the disabled people? The answer lies in the fact that the disabled people have not been able to fully avail of the benefits and are only partially benefited because the main problem is that the policies, legislation and schemes that are introduced by the government are not easy to access by the disabled persons. In India opportunities for persons with disabilities fell from 43 per cent in 1991 to 38 per cent in 2002 despite the galloping economic growth (World Bank, 2007). Information about schemes and benefits is not widely known and is difficult to avail because of bureaucratic lethargy and intransigence. In this context, NGOs can play the significant role in the livelihood generation of the differently abled people. NGOs can take the initiative to disseminate information among disabled persons so that they can take advantage of reservation in jobs, education and poverty reduction or livelihood schemes.

A recent study commissioned by the government put the number of such entities, accounted for till 2009 at 3.3 million (*The Indian Express*, 2010). In India there are not many NGOs working in the area of livelihood promotion for the disabled persons.

Atmanirbhar is a small, not for profit organisation working for economic rehabilitation of the differently abled people. It was established in 1996 in Guwahati and is the only organisation in Assam which is working for the livelihood promotion of the disabled people. *Atmanirbhar* shows that, given due consideration and facilities, the disabled can become productive and contributing members of the society. Thus, the organisation aims to enable disabled people with low socio-economic status to earn their livelihood, encourage artists and artisans with disabilities to show case their talent and create awareness on issues related to disability.

Therefore, in this chapter, a case study has been carried out on an NGO named *Atmanirbhar Ek* Challenge and the study tries to examine the objectives and strategies of *Atmanirbhar* in improving livelihood status of the marginalised differently abled people. The study has also focused on the achievements and strength of the organisation, the future plans of the organisations, their successes, weaknesses, and the obstacles that the organisation has come across in achieving its target.

Objectives of the Study

The objectives of the study are:

1. To examine the objectives and strategies of *Atmanirbhar* in improving livelihood status of the marginalised differently abled people.
2. To find out the achievements and strengths of *Atmanirbhar* in improvement of the livelihood level of the targeted communities.
3. To discuss the obstacles/problems and the weaknesses of *Atmanirbhar*.

Data Source and Methodology

The present study is based on primary data. The strategies and objectives of *Atmanirbhar* in improving livelihood status of the marginalised differently abled people is examined with the help of two questionnaires prepared for the beneficiaries and managements. Relevant questions are asked to the beneficiaries regarding the role played by *Atmanirbhar* for improvement of livelihood status. The achievements and strength of *Atmanirbhar* is examined with the help of the questionnaires. The obstacles/problems and weakness of *Atmanirbhar* are also derived with the help of the questionnaires. Simple arithmetical calculations are done to achieve the objectives in this study.

Results and Discussion

Examination of Objectives and Strategies of Atmanirbhar

The main objectives of *Atmanirbhar* are found as follows:

(a) To increase the number of beneficiaries from present 39 to 100 or more.
(b) To implement sustainable employment projects for the disabled.
(c) To improve quality of life of the marginalised living in welfare institutions.

In order to achieve the objectives *Atmanirbhar is* adopting different strategies. *Atmanirbhar* is very much concerned regarding the capabilities of its differently abled beneficiaries, so, its strategy is to implement those activities which the disabled people can easily perform considering their skills and abilities. The activities are:

(a) Packaging of tea and grocery items;
(b) Making and leasing out ornamental potted plants;
(c) Making paper shopping bags;
(d) Marketing of own tea and spices brand (on a small scale at present).

These are the activities with the help of which the differently abled people are earning their livelihood. *Atmanirbhar* is now concentrating on increasing business through job works, which has been a major activity, expand marketing of their products and services. Since *Atmanirbhar* is not associated and does not receive any financial and technical support from the government, so in the short run they are trying to take recourse for obtaining larger donation and sponsorships for stipend of their beneficiaries.

Examination of the Achievements and Strengths of Atmanirbhar in improving the Livelihood Status to the Marginalised Differently Abled Person

Achievements of Atmanirbhar

The achievements of the organisation can be studied under the following headings:

(i) Employment Generation

The organisation started with 5 disabled persons but at present there are 39 beneficiaries (both male and female) and 5 staff members on full time basis currently engaged in *Atmanirbhar*. It is found from the study that 80.55 per cent of the beneficiaries are literates and 19.44 per cent are illiterates. All targeted people are tried to employ in the organisation according to their education level and capabilities.

(ii) Improvement of Earning Status of the Beneficiaries.

When the survey was carried out only 36 out of 39 beneficiaries were present. Table 9.1 shows how *Atmanirbhar* has helped those disabled persons to earn an income of their own. It is clear from the table that 77.7 per cent (i.e. 28) of the beneficiaries had no earning source before joining *Atmanirbhar*. But at present 100 per cent (i.e. 36) of the beneficiaries are earning more than Rs. 2000 per month. Table 9.1 shows that those 22.2 per cent (i.e.) of the beneficiaries who were earning before joining *Atmanirbhar*, their income was less than Rs. 2000 per month but now they are earning more than Rs. 2500 per month. Thus, *Atmanirbhar* has helped in raising the income of the disabled persons.

Table 9.1: Improvement of Earning Status

Sl. No.	*Earning Status of Beneficiaries*	*Percentage of Beneficiaries*
1.	Beneficiaries not earning before joining *Atmanirbhar*	77.7
2.	Beneficiaries earning more than Rs. 2000 per month after joining *Atmanirbhar*	100
3.	Beneficiaries earning less than Rs. 2000 per month before joining *Atmanirbhar*	22.2
4.	Beneficiaries earning more than Rs. 2500 per month after joining *Atmanirbhar*	22.2

Source: Calculated from the questionnaire for the beneficiaries.

Table 9.1 can be represented suitably with the help of the Fig. 9.1.

(iii) Benefits Enjoyed by the Beneficiaries due to Improvement in Livelihood

With the improvement in livelihood of the beneficiaries of *Atmanirbhar* they have now been able enjoy benefits in certain related areas such as

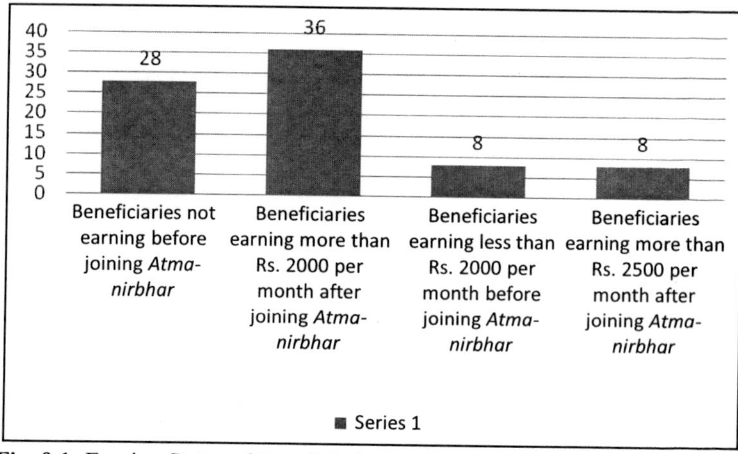

Fig. 9.1: Earning Status of Beneficiaries
Source: Field Study on the basis of No. of Beneficiaries

almost 100 per cent of the beneficiaries now feel socially secured and recognised. This has raised their level of confidence and self-respect. Moreover, they have now been able to utilise their income for further up gradation of their life such as they have access to better health and medical facilities, proper nutritious diet and spend for the purpose of education of their family members. Thus, almost 94.4 per cent of the beneficiaries' family are fairly benefited and 5.5 per cent of beneficiaries' family are fully benefited. This is shown in Table 9.2 below:

Table 9.2: Related Areas of Benefits

Serial No.	*Related areas of benefits enjoyed by the Beneficiaries of Atma Nirbhar*	*Beneficiaries in terms of %*
1.	Social security and recognition	100
2.	Raising of Confidence Level	100
3.	Beneficiaries' family fairly benefited	94.4
4.	Beneficiaries' family fully benefited	5.5
5.	Access to Health and Educational facilities	100

Source: Calculated from the questionnaire for the beneficiaries.

(iv) State of Living Condition of the Beneficiaries

Table 9.3 shows that 55.55 per cent of the disabled beneficiaries live in rented house and only 36.11 per cent live in their own house. Table 9.4 reveals the housing type and the source of drinking water of the beneficiaries. Nearly 36 per cent of the beneficiaries live in *Kuchcha* house like huts made of mud, 41.6 per cent lives in Assam type house and only 22.2 per cent live in R.C.C. buildings. Again only 2.77 per cent of the beneficiaries have access to running water, 13.88 per cent depends on supply water and 83.33 per cent relies on other sources such as well, stream, pond, hand-pump etc. Thus, Table 9.2 signifies that *Atmanirbhar* is working for livelihood promotion of those disabled persons who are literate as well as illiterate and those belonging to the middle class and the lower section of the society.

Table 9.3: Housing Condition of the Beneficiaries

Housing Condition of the Beneficiaries	*Beneficiaries in %*
Beneficiaries living in own house	36.11
Beneficiaries living in rented house	55.55
Beneficiaries living in quarters	8.33

Source: Calculated from the questionnaire for the beneficiaries.

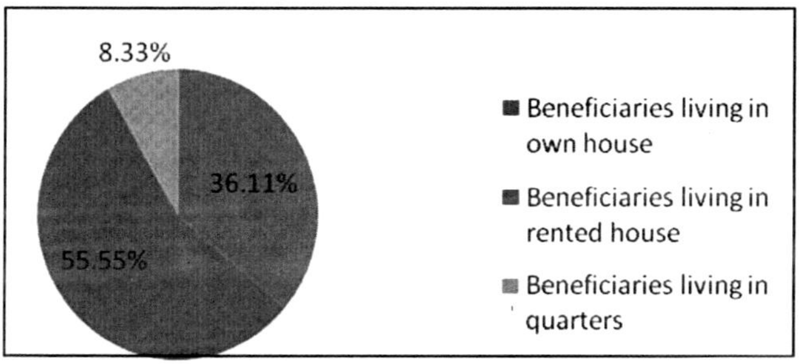

Fig. 9.2: Housing Condition of Beneficiaries
Source: Table 9.3.

Table 9.4: Status of Living Condition

Housing Type	*In %*	*Source of Drinking Water*	*In %*
R.C.C. Building	22.22	Running Water	2.77
Assam Type House	41.6	Supply Water	13.88
Kuchcha House	36.11	Other Source (e.g. Well, stream, hand-pump etc.)	83.33

Source: Calculated from the questionnaire for the beneficiaries.

The above results reveal that *Atmanirbhar* is mainly working for the marginalised poor section of differently abled person and due to poverty they cannot pursue education and thus remained illiterate. The scope of earning livelihood for the illiterate poor is very few and so *Atmanirbhar* has taken a bold attempt in this regard.

Strengths of Atmanirbhar

Atmanirbhar being the only organisation of its type in Assam attempting to provide the scope of employment opportunity to the differently able, with greater awareness about *Atmanirbhar* and consequent sensitisation of the required order, it can fulfil the need of the society to contribute to the objective of provision of a dignified life for the differently able. From the study the strengths of the organisation are found as—

(a) Committed team of managing committee members, supervisors and beneficiaries.
(b) Small but sensitised and committed team of business partners.
(c) Environment sensibility
(d) Focus on sustainability.

Recognitions of Atmanirbhar

Atmanirbhar has received the two most important national awards for promoting employment among the disabled: (1) The N.C.P.E.D.P.—Hellen Keller Award in 2000, from Congress Leader Mrs. Sonia Gandhi; (2) The National Award for the Welfare of Persons with Disabilities in 2004, from former President Dr. A.P.J. Abdul Kalam. Recently, it has also received The Chief Minister's Best Community Action Award for Development on the 15th August, 2012.

Future Plans

Atmanirbhar plans to take up new disabled-friendly income generating projects to offer employment opportunities to 50-100 more disabled people in a proposed "New Life Centre".

Again the organisation started a second project "Spreading Sunshine", in 1998, with the primary aim of improving the quality of life of marginalised people living in residential social welfare institutions, through assistance mobilised from the public. It provides educational aids, cloths, footwear to the residents.

Moreover, in order to provide access to better health and medical facilities to the beneficiaries as well as their family members *Atmanirbhar* have enrolled themselves under a well known scheme called Employees State Insurance (E.S.I.) which is in process but has not yet been implemented.

Problems and Weaknesses of *Atmanirbhar* in Achieving the Targets

Problems

The very objective of providing an avenue for leading a dignified life through employment for the disabled is itself fraught with difficulties. Obviously, persons with different abilities do not and cannot have the same productivity as the other persons do. The objective to provide employment through viable economic activities has not been fulfilled so far due to their low productivity and dearth of opportunities to establish a business which generates adequate revenues to sustain the beneficiaries without having to go in for donations. Other factors such as lack of finance, no support from the Government, would not stand in their way if they are able to establish a sufficient paying business for the upliftment of the beneficiaries.

Though *Atmanirbhar* has faced immense problems but it has managed to carry on so far because of receiving rents and regular donations from certain sources. Attempts are on the way to expand business by going on for hand-made paper articles, orchids etc.

Weaknesses

The weaknesses of the organisation are found as—

(a) The very nature of *Atmanirbhar* and its objectives, not wanting to rely on charity.
(b) Lack of awareness of *Atmanirbhar* in the market.

The main challenges to the organisation are scarce resources, paucity of reserves and general funds.

Conclusion

From the above discussion we can say that along with the Government, NGOs should also take the initiative in generating livelihood activities for the marginalised differently abled and the above analysis reveals that

Atmanirbhar has set a good example and has shown that how NGOs has helped in the livelihood generation of those marginalised disabled persons who are poor, illiterate and unskilled with few scope of employment in the private and Government sector. Though the organisation has faced with some difficulties in achieving its objectives, it has not lagged behind in realising the need and difficulties of disabled people and has tried to provide a helping hand to them by offering an opportunity to work with dignity and earn a livelihood. *Atmanirbhar* has done a commendable job by enabling the differently abled people specially those who are poor, illiterate, semi-literate and unskilled with few scope of employment in the government and private sector by engaging them in productive works suitable to their talents so that they could earn a living on their own.

NOTE

1. NGOs are primarily non-profit making organisations and are legally constituted corporations created by natural or legal people mostly operating independently from any form of government.

REFERENCES

Centre for Financial Inclusion (2010). "A New Financial Access Frontier: People with Disabilities", A concept paper from the Centre for Financial Inclusion at ACCION International June. Accessed from www.miusa.org/idd/resources/files/econinclusionresources/.../at.../file on 01-08-13.

The Indian Express (2010). First Official Estimate, July 7.

UNDP (2012). *Livelihood Opportunities for Persons with Disabilities*, Part 1, A Report prepared for United Nations Development Programmes, Published in India.

Wiesen, Caitlin (2012). Preface by Country Director, UNDP in *Livelihood Opportunities for Persons with Disabilities*. UNDP, India.

World Bank (2007). People with Disabilities in India: From Commitments to Outcomes, A Report, Human Development Unit, South Asia Region, The World Bank, May. Accessed from http://siteresources.worldbank.org/INDIAEXTN/Resources/295583117145632580/DISABILITYREPORTFINALNOV2007.pdf on 01-08-13.

SECTION-II

Tourism and Development

10

Problems and Prospects of Tourism

A Case Study of Kaziranga and Sibsagar in Assam

Mithilesh Kumar Sinha and *Mriganka Saikia*

Introduction

The habit of travelling is inherent and attached to human being from the very beginning. Early men travelled under the compulsion primarily to satisfy their basic necessities of life such as food, water, clothing, shelter and safety. In the latter ages, the emergence of various empires led to travel for political, business and religious purpose. With the evolution, growth and development of human civilisation, people started moving in large numbers to places away from their home with a desire for leisure and pleasure. This phenomenon today has evolved into one of the largest and fastest growing industries of the world as "Tourism sector".

The term 'tourism' is defined by different authors in different ways. Etymologically, the word "tour" is derived from the Latin word "tornare" and the Greek word "tornos" meaning "a lathe or circle", the movement around a central point or axis. This meaning is changed in modern English to represent 'One's turn.' The suffix—'ism' is defined as an action or process; typical behaviour or quality; whereas the suffix—'ist' denotes one that performs a given action. Thus, when the word 'tour' and the suffix—'ism' and—'ist' are combined, they suggest the action of movement around a circle. One can argue that a circle represents a starting point, which ultimately returns back to its beginning. Therefore, like a circle, a tour represents a journey, which is a round trip, i.e. the act of leaving and then returning to the original starting point. Therefore, one who takes such a journey can be called a tourist (Theobald, 1998). Finally, the most popular and widely accepted definition of tourism is given by the World Tourism Organisation (WTO) as "A tourist is a person who travels to a place other than his usual place of residence and stays at hotels or other accommodation establishment run on a commercial basis or in any rent free places for a duration of not less than 24 hours and not more than 6 months at a time, for any of the following purposes:

(i) Pleasure (holiday, leisure, sports etc.).
(ii) Pilgrimage, religious or social functions.
(iii) Study and health.
(iv) Meetings.
(v) Business. (Chattopadhyay, 1995)

However in India, the Tourist Department of Government of India, following the recommendation of the UN Conference of International Travel and Tourism, Rome adopted the definition of foreign tourist as "A person visiting India on a foreign passport for a period of not less than 24 hours for non-immigrant, non-employment tourist purposes" (Sharma, 2004).

Assam as Tourist Destination

Assam as a destination corresponds to a world of contrast and excitement with each place of the state having something amazing to offer. Some people call it a magic land while others call it green paradise. The state of Assam is one of the most beautiful and attractive region of India. There is hardly any other state as Assam has greater variety and colours in its natural scenery and in the cultural treasures of the people that inhabit it. The recorded history tells the Assam has been serving as the eastern gateway for passage and communication of people, commodities and ideas between Indian Subcontinent in the West and China and South-East Asia in the East (Acharyya, 1985). Assam did attract travellers and scholars both from the East and West. Valuable information regarding its trade routes, hills, mountains and people of the area would be found in the works of great scholar Ptolemy. It was further supplemented by the works of Huen Tsang, the great Chinese traveller, who came to Assam during the regime of Kumar Bhaskar Barman in the middle of the seventh century AD. Similarly, Ibn Batuta a Muslim traveller and writer visited this region in 1345 AD and narrated the physical landscape, commercial products and the ethnographic characteristics of its people. Subsequently, the knowledge about the region was further enriched by the writings of the European travellers and British military and civil officials in the eighteenth and nineteenth centuries.

Considering the importance of tourism in economic development, State like Assam has made planned effort to promote it in different parts of its region. The ungrudging blessings of nature have made tourism in Assam essentially nature-centric, despite the fact there are historical and religious places of tourist attraction. Thus, Assam has tremendous strength of tourist's attraction like scenic beauty, cultural variety, ethnic mixture and diverse flora and fauna. Such wealth of tourism resources endows Assam with comparative advantage over many other states. Yet for variety of reasons this advantage has not brought for Assam the prominent position that it deserves. It is, therefore, imperative to give a dynamic thrust to tourism promotion in the State.

Kaziranga National Park is a national park in the Golaghat and Nagaon districts of the state of Assam, India. A World Heritage Site, the park hosts two-thirds of the world's Great One-horned Rhinoceroses. Kaziranga boasts the highest density of tigers among protected areas in the world and was declared a Tiger Reserve in 2006. The park is home to large breeding populations of elephants, wild water buffalo, and swamp deer. Kaziranga is recognised as an *Important Bird Area* by Birdlife International for conservation of avifaunal species. Compared to other protected areas in India, Kaziranga has achieved notable success in wildlife conservation. Located on the edge of the Eastern Himalaya biodiversity hotspot, the park combines high species diversity and visibility.

Kaziranga is a vast expanse of tall elephant grass, marshland, and dense tropical moist broadleaf forests, crisscrossed by four major rivers, including the Brahmaputra, and the park includes numerous small bodies of water. Kaziranga has been the theme of several books, songs, and documentaries. The park celebrated its centennial in 2005 after its establishment in 1905 as a reserve forest. In 1985, Kaziranga was declared a World Heritage Site by UNESCO for its unique natural environment Kaziranga has witnessed several natural and human-made calamities in recent decades. Floods caused by overflowing of river Brahmaputra have led to significant losses of animal life. Encroachment by humans along the periphery also has led to a diminished forest cover and a loss of habitat.

Sivasagar is a town in Upper Assam, about 360 kilometre North East of Guwahati. It is the district headquarters of the Sivasagar district. It is well-known for its Ahom palaces and monuments. Sivasagar today is also an important centre for the tea and oil industries. This town's main feature is the water body from which it takes its name. This is a 257-acre tank, also known as the Borpukhuri, which is at a higher elevation than the rest of the town, with three temples on its banks. Of these temples, the most prominent is the Sivadol, standing tall at 104 feet (32 m), drawing large crowds on *Shiv Ratri*. The other temples are the Vishnudol and Devidol. The temples were built by Kuwori Ambika, wife of Swargadeo Siba Singha, in 1734. Joysagar, said to be the biggest man-made lake in the country, is spread over 318 acres of water on the edge of the town in an area called Rangpur, 5 kilometres away from the present town of Sivasagar. This lake was built by Swargadeo Rudra Singha in honour of his mother, Joymoti Gaurisagar.

The Ahom queen Bor Kuwori Phuleshwari Devi built this tank, which is spread over 150 acres. Rudrasagar, Swargadeo Lakshmi Singha built this tank, and dedicated it to his father Swargadeo Rudra Singha, in 1773. A Shiva Temple was also built on the bank of this beautifully constructed tank. It is 8 kilometres away from the town of Sivasagar.

It is in the above background that present chapter has been designed to highlight the problem and prospect of tourism taking two major spots of Assam.

Objectives

(a) To explore the potentiality from Assam which will maintain the prospect of economic development in terms of tourism industry in near future.
(b) To find out the barriers for developing tourism in Assam and provide some suggestions to overcome those.

Review of Litreature: A substantial volume of litreature both at the macro and micro level study were reviewed on the subject of tourism and its impacts on economic development of a state.

Bezbaruah (2001) says that the inflow of foreign visitors in India has registered a 6 per cent growth in fiscal year 2000-01. Foreign tourism fetched $3 billion to the Union exchequer making tourism the second highest net foreign exchange earned in the country.

Bhalla (2004), in his book "*Potential of Tourism—A Study of Himachal Pradesh*" studied how tourism had played a significant role in transforming mountain communities of the world by diversifying economy, generating employment opportunities and modernizing these societies. This book primarily deals with tourism in Kullu and Manali which is now a well accepted option for its economic development. It is simply because of its contribution towards income and employment generation in the area. Based on the empirical data the book is an attempt to assess the socio-cultural as well as the economic impact on the host environment.

Chattopadhyay (1995), in his book "*Economic Impact of Tourism Development: An Indian Experience*", provides a comprehensive overview of tourism development in the Third World. The first part of the book sets the analytical scaffolding of the study where he discusses the definition and type of tourism. The second part focuses on economic aspects of tourism development on the basis of available secondary data on the size of tourist flow, the expenditure per day etc. Part three deals with the process of tourism development through some case studies conducted under certain control situations. In the concluding part, an empirical model has been built on the international tourism demand for India.

Dutta (1980), in his study on tourism in North East region, analysed the problems faced by tourists in the region, like that inaccessibility to the forests, non-availability transport and accommodation and uncertain political condition of North East region. He also emphasized that this region is as yet under exploited, given the tourism potential of the region.

Gupta (1983), in his doctoral thesis, tried to analyse the income and employment effects tourism on the economy of Jammu & Kashmir. He is of the opinion that in developed countries the economic benefits from tourism ranged from 20 to 40 per cent.

Henderson (2011) in his research states that International visitors perceive a negative impression towards a destination with improper arrangement of infrastructure of a country. He also mentioned political instability, security and safety as an influential factor domestic and foreign tourist.

Waters (1986) estimated that tourism industry in the United States of America creates about 35,602 jobs, directly and indirectly, for each billion dollar spending by the tourists. He also reported that the tourism industry has better scope for developing countries where labour is cheap.

Justification of the Study

From the foregoing review of litreature it can be understood that though many studies have been conducted on different aspects of tourism in India and even in foreign countries, a study specifically for problems and prospects of tourism with SWOT analysis in Assam is missing in litreature. Hence, the study will make an attempt to examine present scenario and future prospect of tourism by highlighting the existing lacuna and drawbacks.

Methodology and Design

The study is based on both primary and secondary data covering a period of November 2012 to January 2013. Primary data is governed mostly by the questionnaires distributed amongst the concerned respondents. Secondary information was collected from Government publications/ records, State tourism statistics, periodicals, reports and related plan documents. Moreover, personal visit has been made to Kaziranga and Sibsagar in order to collect information/data. A sample of 45 international tourists and the similar number of domestic tourists were interviewed. And 50 local residents from each spot were also interviewed. Two types of questionnaires were administered—one for local people and the other for tourists. In the selection of the respondents, a stage stratified simple random sampling technique was adopted. The data have been mainly analysed by using Tabulation occupies a significant space in the process of analysis and interpretation.

Interview Responses of Tourists

Table 10.1: Tourists Attraction of Different Reasons of Visit

Item	*No. of respondents*	
Reasons for visit	*Domestic*	*International*
Unique cultural attractions	6(13.33)	8(17.77)
Unique wildlife attractions	14(31.11)	15(33.33)
Pilgrimage	11(24.44)	5(11.11)
Pleasant climate	5(11.11)	5(11.11)
Sightseeing	6(13.33)	11(24.44)
Fairs and festivals	1(2.22)	1(2.22)
Participation in events	2(4.44)	2(4.44)

Note: Figures in parentheses indicate percentage.
Source: Field study.

Table 10.1 reveals one thing clearly that about 31 per cent of our domestic tourists and 33 per cent of foreign tourists visited the place due to their wild life attraction and about 24.4 per cent of domestic and 24 per cent of foreigners came to these places for sightseeing. However, reasons for visit like pilgrimage, pleasant climate, and unique cultural attraction also encouraged to visit for many domestic as well as foreign tourists to these places of Assam.

Table 10.2: Purposes of Visit of the Tourists

Items	*No. of respondents*	
Purpose of the visit	*Domestic*	*International*
Holiday	25(55.56)	3(66.67)
Visit friends and relatives	6(13.33)	1(2.22)
Business	2(4.44)	5(11.11)
Attend conference	2(4.44)	2(4.44)
Study tour	7(15.56)	3(6.67)
Officials	3(6.67)	4(8.89)

Note: Figures in parentheses indicate percentage.
Source: Field study.

A study of the purposes of visit of the tourists is essential to identify their expectations of tourists spots. Our study reveals that majority of the domestic about 55 per cent and foreign tourists 66 per cent were visited the places for the purpose of holidaying. Hence tourism promotional activities in Assam should be oriented towards creating more facilities to generate fun and pleasure excursion. Around 15 per cent of the domestic and 7 per cent of the foreign tourists came for academic purposes, i.e. (to study wildlife, environmental status, native culture, visit to tea garden etc.).

Table 10.3: Types of Accommodation Tourists Stay

Items	*Number of respondents*	
Type of accommodation	*Domestic*	*International*
Three star hotel	5(11.11)	9(2.)
Government lodge	7(15.56)	5(11.11)
Private lodge	25(55.56)	3(66.67)
Guest house	2(4.44)	1(2.22)
Staying with friends and relatives	4(8.89)	nil
Others	2(4.44)	nil

Note: Figures in parentheses indicate percentage.
Source: Field study.

A significant 55 per cent of the domestic tourists and 66 per cent of the foreign tourists stayed in private lodge while only about 15 per cent and 11 per cent of domestic and foreign tourists respectively stayed in government lodge. It was mainly due to the lack of enough public sector lodges out there.

A summary of findings about trip duration and mode of travel is given in Tables 10.4 and 10.5 respectively. Seventy seven per cent of the

Table 10.4: Trip Duration of Tourist Travel

Items	*Number of respondents*	
Trip duration	*Domestic*	*International*
1 day	8(17.78)	2(4.44)
2–3 days	22(48.89)	4(8.89)
4–7 days	3(6.67)	2(4.44)
8–14 days	2(4.44)	Nil
15 and above	10(22.22)	37(82.22)

Note: Figures in parentheses indicate percentage.
Source: Field study.

international tourists were travelling under an inclusive tour package. As is usually the characteristic of all-inclusive tour package travel arrangements, most international tourists about 82 per cent stated that they were staying for a period of 15 and above days. On the other hand about half of the domestic tourists' stayed the places for 2-3 days and also 66 per cent of our domestic tourists arranged their travel independently.

Table 10.5: Trip Mode of Tourists Travel

Items	*Number of respondents*	
Mode of travel	*Domestic*	*International*
An inclusive tour package	15(33.33)	35(77.78)
Individual travel arrangements	30(66.67)	10(22.22)

Note: Figures in parentheses indicate percentage.
Source: Field study.

Table 10.6: Services in Packaged Tour of Tourist

Items	*No. of respondents*	
Services in packaged tour	*Domestic*	*International*
Return ticket	9(20.0)	20(40.45)
Accommodation	20(44.45)	20(40.45)
Car rental	10(22.22)	3(6.67)
Meals at restaurants	2(4.44)	Nil
Tickets for park entry, museum	1(2.22)	2(4.43)
Local tour (transportation)	3(6.67)	nil
Others	nil	nil

Note: Figures in parentheses indicate percentage.
Source: Field study.

Table 10.6 related to service in packaged tour revealed clearly that about 80 per cent foreign tourists came to visit these spots return tickets with accommodation facility while 60 per cent of the same domestic tourists had these two facilities in their tour package.

Responses of Local Residents

About sixty per cent of the local people affirmed that poverty is the most serious problem that they face. But only 22 per cent of them stated that tourism has, over the years, benefited the people of the region. When asked to state the forms of benefits that accrue to local people from tourism, 46 per cent listed business opportunities, followed by 42 per cent who listed the availability of employment opportunities (Table 10.6). In this regard, it is generally accepted that the development of tourism creates employment and business opportunities for both the local community and other tourism investors. Moreover, proponents of tourism viewed that, since the industry is labour-intensive, it has great potential in creating employment opportunities, particularly in a state like Assam where more than 85 per cent population are living in rural Assam. Hence,

Table 10.7: Showing the Reasons for Visit and benefit from Tourism

Items	*No. of respondents*	*In percentages (%)*
Reasons for visit		
(a) Climate	2	4.44
(b) Historical and wildlife attractions	14	31.11
(c) Tea tourism	2	4.44
(d) Cultural aspects	2	4.44
(e) Excellent tourist facilities	1	2.22
(f) Friendly people	8	17.78
(g) Holiday	16	35.56
Who benefit most from tourism		
(a) The Government	12	26.67
(b) Hoteliers	18	40.00
(c) Tour and travel firms	5	11.11
(d) Local residents	10	22.22
Benefits to the local residents		
(a) Employment creation	19	42.22
(b) Business opportunities	21	46.67
(c) Development of infrastructure	3	6.67
(d) Cross-cultural understanding	2	4.44

Source: Field study.

the tourism industry is perceived as a major source for much sought-after employment and other source of income. However, the majority of local residents who work in the tourism industry in Kaziranga and Sibsagar tend to occupy unskilled, servile and lowly paying positions including waiters, gardeners, porters, janitors and security guards. The local people have viewed that historical and wildlife attracts 31 per cent tourists whereas most of the tourists came to these places to make their holidays while the tea tourism could attract very insignificant number of tourist accounting of 4 per cent only. This is mainly because of lack of publicity about the tea tourism in Assam.

Positive and Negative Aspects of Destinations as Viewed by Tourists

In order to make the place of the destinations attractive and healthy, it is essential to know the views of the tourists. The tourism planners then can take the advantage of positive aspects and can try to eliminate the negative elements as perceived by tourists through their travel experience. To understand these aspects, tourists were asked to state their most liking and disliking experiences they faced during their visit to their destinations. Majority of the domestic tourists have positive experiences on natural beauty 26 per cent and wildlife 33 per cent whereas the tea tourism could attract very insignificant number of tourist accounting of 13 per cent only.

In case of foreign tourist, natural beauty and wildlife are most liking experience for 44 per cent and 26 per cent of tourists respectively. However, attractions like historical and tea gardens 11 per cent and 13 per cent of the state also contribute to positive experience for many foreign tourists respectively. However, the negative experiences of the foreign tourists are concerned, the poor quality of the road, poor service at stay places, unorganised Government tourism service etc. are the major aspects

Table 10.8: Foreign Tourist seen aspects of Natural Beauty, Wildlife etc.

Aspects	*No. of responses*	
	Domestic	*International*
Wildlife	15(33.33)	12(26.67)
Historical attractions	10(22.22)	5(11.11)
Nature beauty	12(26.67)	20(44.44)
Tea gardens	6(13.33)	6(13.33)
Hospitality of Local people	2(4.44)	2(4.44)

Note: Figures in parentheses indicate percentage.
Source: Field study.

of dissatisfaction, apart from inadequate public service, lack of better information about the tourists spots. It is analysed that both the positive and negative experience of the tourists in the tour period calls for a reorientation of development perspectives of tourism in the state. Strategies should be developed by the concerned agencies to exploit the positive aspects meaningfully for better tourism promotion. Similarly, except natural disturbances, other negative aspects can be removed to gear up our tourism promotion activities.

Negative Aspects of Destinations as Viewed by Tourists in Assam

Table 10.9: Negative Experiences of the Foreign Tourists Aspects of Destinations as View

Aspects	*No. of responses*	*Percentage*
Unorganized Govt. tourism service	15(33.33)	10(22.22)
Poor quality of road transport	7(15.56)	13(28.89)
Uncertain weather	1(2.22)	Nil
Poor railway service	10(22.22)	3(6.67)
Sense of insecurity	1(2.22)	1(2.22)
Poor service at stay places	7(15.56)	10(22.22)
Inadequate public service	3(6.67)	8(17.78)
No response	1(2.22)	Nil

Note: Figures in Parenthesis indicate percentage.
Source: Field Study.

SWOT Analysis of Tourism in Kaziranga and Sibsagar

To find out the competitive advantage of Kaziranga and Sibsagar as a popular tourist destination it is necessary to find the strength, weakness, opportunity and threat. It will be helpful for policy-makers to develop a planning map to establish these two spots particularly and Assam in general, as a popular tourist destination.

Strengths

1. Natural beauty
2. Pollution free environment
3. Cost effective transportation facility
4. Terrorism free state
5. Rich history and heritage
6. Hospitality of Local people
7. Folk Culture
8. Availability of Marvelous handicraft and handloom product

Weaknesses

1. Poor transportation system,
2. Lack of proper information,
3. Lack of adequate mode of communication,
4. Insufficient number of restaurant,
5. Lack of accommodation High price of resorts, hotel and motels,
6. Long time waiting for booking system, and
7. Many attractive location of Assam still remain unexplored.

Opportunities

1. Building awareness among tourist, policy-maker and local community,
2. Training programme to local community,
3. Huge campaign to create a positive attitude towards tourism,
4. To flourish handicraft and locally made organic food,
5. Establishing better transportation system,
6. Job creation,
7. Enriching standard of living, and
8. Eradication of Poverty.

Threats

1. Poor coordination among tourist, local community and policy-makers.
2. Fear of local communities for loss of land, traditional culture etc.
3. Misinterpretation about tourism in local communities.
4. Pollution.
5. Destruction of nature.
6. Fear of abduction.

Suggestions

1. Infrastructural system of the state should be improved.
2. The State Government should open four information centres at different cities and metros of the country to motivate both the domestic and foreign tourists to Assam.
3. There is an urgent need for tourism development strategies

centred mainly on expansion of local employment and self-employment, expansion of informal sector opportunities.

4. Development of partnership amongst public and private sectors, NGOs and local communities.
5. Improving social and cultural impacts and also ensuring proper involvement of local tribal community of the region.
6. Increasing local access to infrastructure and services provided for tourists.
7. Increasing participation of local people in decision-making process and capacity building to enable their participation.

Conclusion

This case study shows that current forms of tourism development in Assam have not reduced poverty or contributed to the socio-economic empowerment of local people. Local people are usually not involved in product development and product marketing, and derive minimal benefits from the tourism industry while bearing many of the costs. No clear tourism strategies and policies have been devised to enhance sustainable socio-economic development for local people.

The success of tourism should, therefore, not be measured in terms of increased numbers of international tourist arrivals and gross tourism revenues, but should be evaluated according to how the industry is integrated with the local and national economy, and how the industry contributes to the overall development of local people at grassroots level.

REFERENCES

Acharyya, N.N. (1985). *North East as Viewed by Foreigners*. New Delhi: Omsons Publications.

Baruah, Tirtha (2011). International Understanding Through Tourism and Tourism Scenario in Assam. In Jayanta Gogoi (Ed.), *Assam Tourism: Opportunities and Challenges* (p. 90). Guwahati: Jagaran Sahitya Prakashan.

Bezbaruah, M.P. (2001): *Speech at Conference on Tourism in Assam—Status and Prospects,* New Delhi, December.

Bhalla, Pankaj (2004). *Potential of Tourism—A Study of Himachal Pradesh*. New Delhi: Sonali Publications.

Chattopadhyay, Kunal (1995). *Economic Impact of Tourism Development—An Indian Experience.* New Delhi: Kanishka Publishers and Distributors.

Devi, Meena Kumari (2012). Ecotourism in Assam: A Promising Opportunity for development. *South Asian Journal of Tourism and Heritage*, Vol. 5(1), pp. 179-192.

Dutta, S. (1980). Eastern Region, Yet to make up to its potentials. *Eastern Economists, 33.*

Gupta, D.B. (1983). Income and Employment Effect of Tourism: A Case Study of Jammu & Kashmir State. Ph. D. Thesis, University of Jammu.

Henderson, J.C. (2011). Tourism and Politics Development, The Philippines. Tourismos: An International Multidisciplinary, *Journal of Tourism*, Vol. 6, No. 2, pp. 159-173.

Hussain, M.M. (2012). Role of Tourism in the Socio-Economic Development of Assam. *Dialogue*, Vol. 14(1).

Ministry of Tourism, Government of India (2003). Final Report on 20 years Perspective Tourism plan for the State of Assam. New Delhi: ES (I) Pvt. Ltd.

Sharma, Shashi Prabha (2004). *Tourism Education—Principles, Theories and Practices*. New Delhi: Kanishka Publishers and Distributors.

Website: www.wttc.org, www.assamtourism.org.

11

Tourism Development in Arunachal Pradesh

Opportunities and Challenges

Wangda Gyatso Gyana

Introduction

Tourism is a composite industry with multiple processes and activities arising from the relationship of tourists with service providers, local community, local government, and the environment. It is a multi-fragmented industry that encompasses many industries under its broad umbrella. The UNWTO, the apex global tourism body, in 1995 defined tourism as comprising "the activities of persons travelling to and staying in places outside their usual environment for not more than one consecutive year for leisure, business, and other purposes".[1] Tourism, in fact involves short-term movements of people to the destinations outside the place where they normally live and work, and their activities at those destinations.

Tourism industry is one of the largest and fastest growing industries in the world. It has a tremendous income and employment generating capacity contributing to the sustainable economic development with least environmental concerns. As per the World Travel and Tourism Council (WTTC) report of 2005, tourism generated $ 4.7 trillion constituting 11 per cent of the world's total Gross Domestic Product (GDP) and over 221 million jobs constituting 8 per cent of the total world employment. The report also projected that tourism would create 8.5 million new jobs every year until 2015.[2]

In India, tourism is one of the most profitable industries and substantially contributes to the foreign exchange. It is the third largest generator of foreign exchange earnings. In the WTTC 2004 forecast for 174 countries, India ranked second one notch above China where demand for travel and tourism is expected to grow fastest between 2005–2015. Almost 20 million people are at present engaged in the industry. According to the latest Tourism Satellite Accounting (TSA) research released by the WTTC and its strategic partner Accenture, India's tourism is expected to generate US $ 275.5 billion approximately by 2018.

A huge amount of opportunities in tourism sector are looming large over the North East India including the state of Arunachal Pradesh. Back to back national and international events such as South Asia Travel and Tourism Exchange (SATTE) Exhibition, 2008 at Pragati Maidan (India), World Tourism Mart, 2013 at London (United Kingdom), International Tourism Mart, 2013 (First Edition) at Guwahati (India), ASEAN Tourist Summit, 2013 in Laos, International Tourism Mart, 2013 (Second Edition) at Tawang (India), Adventure Festival, 2013 at Menchukha (India), Arunachal Angling Festival, 2013 at Pitapool, Yazali (India), Meen Festival, 2013 (a fish based Aqua-tourism festival) at Itanagar (India), Panyor River Festival, 2013 at Yazali (India) etc. organised in the recent past showcase the region's tremendous tourism potentials to the national and international markets. The Centre is taking a number of steps to promote tourism in the region by projecting it as an alluring destination under the tag of "Paradise Unexplored", a sub-theme under the "Incredible India" campaign of the Ministry of Tourism (MoT), Government of India (GoI). The MoT has been spending about 15 to 20 per cent of its budget for developing tourism in the region against the Central Government's policy to allocate 10 per cent of budget for each region and has spent Rs. 560 crore during the Eleventh Five Year Plan for developing quality tourism infrastructure in the region. The number of international tourists having visited the region shot up to 58,920 in 2011 from 50,950 in 2010.[3]

Objectives of the Study

The following are the objectives of the study:

1. to identify and study the tourism potential in Arunachal Pradesh;
2. to study Arunachal Pradesh Tourism as an opportunity for employment and income generation;
3. to identify and study the issues in developing tourism in Arunachal Pradesh; and
4. to suggest measures to develop Arunachal Pradesh Tourism.

Research Methodology

The proposed study is both empirical and descriptive in analysis. The scope of the study in terms of geographical area has been confined to the whole of state of Arunachal Pradesh covering all the 11 government approved travel circuits. The study is based mainly on secondary data which include standard published national and international books, publications of Ministry of Tourism (MoT), Government of India (GoI), the Department of Tourism (DoT), Government of Arunachal Pradesh (GoAP), leading national and international books, journals and magazines, newspapers, booklets and pamphlets. Besides, primary data collected through observation and interview methods were used in the study.

Review of Litreature

For the purpose of the study, the following books and materials were consulted to have a relevant and objective perspective in the study area:

Arpita Mathur (2010), in her book *Tourism, Marketing and Travel Agency Business,* has stressed upon to adopt a proactive attitude and to use a wide spectrum of marketing skills and strategies to maintain and develop tourism. She has discussed in detail the principles and practices of marketing that can be used in the context of Twenty First Century Global Travel and Tourism. She has also tried to discuss the concepts through various case studies.

K. Chauhan & B.K. Punia (2009), in their research endeavour *Success Factors of E-Commerce in Indian Tourism Industry,* have attempted to study the status of Indian tourism marketing through e-commerce. They stated that the security of transactions, skill shortage, and payment facilities are the dominant hindrances on the way of effective and successful e-tourism.

S.K. Swain & J.M. Mishra (2012), in their book *Tourism: Principles and Practices,* stated that the new millennium tech-savvy tourists are experience seekers and that they gather information about the cognitive, behavioural, and affective dimensions of a destination before embarking on travel itself. They are better educated, more conscious of value for money, more demanding, curious for new products and are more health and hygiene oriented. They adopted an integrated multi-disciplinary approach to explain the various dimensions of tourism business. Further, they have discussed the tourism principles and practices with the help of case studies.

H.N. Das and Seemanti Ramanath (2008), in their book *Tourism in the North East and Other Essays,* have remarked that in a region like North East India, where the scope of heavy industries is minuscule, and wherein, the rich natural resources and an army of unemployed educated youth are very much there, tourism industry is the best suited industry to be developed in the region. They opined that the region can become a tourism hub if the planners (the political leaders) take a disaggregated view of the market for development of tourism in the region and have the foresight to take the region on the path of development, implementing plans accordingly. They emphasized the need of a top-class infrastructure in the region.

Manjula Chaudhary (2010), in her book *Tourism Marketing,* holds that the creation of memorable experience is the essence of tourism marketing. She opines that the relationship building among tourists and marketers is the key to achieving success in tourism marketing. Further, she has elaborately discussed the environment of tourism marketing, market segmentation, targeting, positioning, competitive marketing strategies, dynamics of tourism marketing, tourism product distribution, pricing and promotion. She has also illustrated real life tourism marketing strategies through comprehensive case studies.

Sandeep Kulshreshtha (2005), in his study *Destination Branding,* exhaustively discussed the various issues related to destination branding and attempted to analyse the new initiative and achievements of "Incredible India" campaign of Ministry of Tourism, Government of India. He stated that destination branding is one of today's hottest topics among place marketers. He further stated that places are potentially the world's biggest tourism brands and must be emotionally appealing with high conversational and celebrity value. He opined that future battle for customers in destination market place will be fought not over price but over hearts and minds. Brand identity is needed for global recognition and to access and penetrate new markets.

M. Selvam (1989), in his book *Tourism Industry in India*, stated that India is a country with vast potentials and it is up to the planners and the government to develop the necessary infrastructure so that the tourism industry grows to greater heights to become a real big business contributing substantially to the development of the national economy. He opined that bold decisions are required to revitalize the industry with the long-term benefits in view.

Devashish Dasgupta (2011), in his book *Tourism Marketing*, has opined that in tourism the greatest role is played by the destination and that it is the final influence on the decision to visit a place. He further stated that the greatest challenge in tourism marketing is always from a destination perspective. He exhaustively discussed various aspects of tourism marketing based on a well researched structure of marketing. Tourism market environment scanning, tourist consumer behaviour, customer value, marketing issues in tourism, differentiation and positioning in tourism, tourist market segmentation, targeting, tourism life cycle etc. have been studied in detail by him.

G. Ganesan and K. Chandra Shekar Rao (2005), in their study *Visit India as a Tourism Brand*, have stated that India is one of the fast growing tourist destinations in the world and that it has realized its tourism potential and its importance to the national economy. They opined that the country has a lot of untapped potential to be tapped as early as possible so as to increase foreign exchange earnings. They have analysed the present trend and growth prospects of Indian tourism.

Kamal Yadav (2005), in his research endeavour *Mass Customisation: Concept and Application*, has stated that the concept of mass customisation has evoked widespread interest among the marketers in both manufacturing as well as service sectors so as to maintain or gain a competitive advantage. He further opined that mass customisation strategy is adopted in a big way in hospitality services, and that the tour and travel agencies create mass customisation by offering standard modules that can be combined in unique ways.

Tapan Kumar Panda (2006), in his book *Tourism Marketing*, has exhaustively studied tourism marketing in Indian as well as international contexts. He discussed in detail the aspects such as external deterrents and barriers to tourism marketing in South Asia, destination marketing, alternative methods for developing new tourist products, application of E-Commerce in tourism and hospitality industry etc.

P.K. Yadav, Sanjay Misra, Swatantra Kumar and Harminder Kaur (2005), in their study *Brand India Its Implications on Tourism,* have opined that brand is the most powerful single determinant in the long-term success of any business and that if the nations in the tourism sector do the exercise of branding well, they can attract more customers. They further stated that India has got huge potential as a mother brand in tourism. They analysed in detail the various impediments which hamper the fullest realisation of Indian tourism potential.

Kamal Nayan Kapil (2011), in his study *Incredible India: Building a Country as a Tourism Brand,* has stated that nation branding is an important and vital concept in today's era of global village and that countries compete to attract the attention, respect and trust of tourists, investors, donors, business delegates, media and the governments of other nations. He opined that there must be a consistent single unified strategy to promote India as a brand.

Alastair M. Morrison (2013), in his book *Marketing and Managing Tourism Destinations*, has studied in detail how destination is planned, implemented and evaluated. Further, he has studied the management organisations, their conductance of business, major opportunities, challenges, and issues faced by them to compete for the global leisure and business travel markets.

Tourism Prospects in Arunachal Pradesh

Arunachal Pradesh known as "the Land of Rising Sun", is the easternmost state of India with an area of 83,743 sq. km. sharing international borders with China in the north, Myanmar in the east, Bhutan in the west, and national borders with Assam and Nagaland in the south. The state is a tribal state inhabited by 26 major tribes and over 100 sub-tribes. The state has a great potential for tourism development and hence, has been named as the "Hidden Paradise". It has been chosen as the 4th Best Region amongst the top ten tourist destinations in the world for the year 2012 by the BBC's globally circulated magazine and one of the leading travelogues, viz. the Lonely Planet; the top three destinations being Coastal Wales, La Ruta Maya and Northern Kenya. Also, the voting and the subsequent awarding of the state as the Favourite Upcoming Tourist Destination, only recently in the month of January 2013 through a survey conducted by the Outlook Traveller, one of the country's leading travel magazines, indicates that the state can be a perfect tourist hot spot not only in the national tourism map but also in the world tourism map.[4] It is here only one can still experience the nature in its true colours. Its enchanting virgin beauty has made it a perfect, a unique and a fascinating tourist destination. Far away from the busy and maddening crowd, it offers the ultimate solace and delight for the visitors where they can relax, refresh and rejuvenate right in the lap of mother nature. The state offers diverse tourist attractions and products making it a perfect holiday destination waiting to be explored.

The state is naturally and abundantly blessed with all the necessary resources that are needed to develop travel and tourism industry. In fact, the state is a treasure house of unique, rich, refreshing, enchanting and diverse experiences that a tourist seeks in a life time—the variegated climate, the turbulent fresh water rivers, tough terrains, the serried hills, mountains and peaks, rich and green valleys, the rich sub-tropical to alpine forest cover and the vast canopy of rain-forest with its dynamic blend of amazing plethora of flora and fauna, the numerous ancient monuments, the tribes and their picturesque villages, rich culture, traditions and customs, their diversified forms of art and handicrafts etc. and above all, their warm hospitality. There is a tremendous scope for development of a varied categories of tourism in the state viz., adventure tourism, rural tourism, history tourism, religious and spiritual tourism, cultural tourism, heritage tourism, wild life tourism, eco-tourism, festival tourism, golf tourism, tea tourism, health tourism etc.

Tourism is as much a part of socio-economic development process as any other related activity. It can play a vital role in bringing about sustainable economic development of the industrially backward state that too with least environmental concerns! Given the vast scope, industrialisation of the state can be brought about in the tourism sector in the lines of other successful tourist destinations viz. Sikkim, Meghalaya, Jammu & Kashmir, Kerala, Goa etc. In fact, it can be a major wealth creating industrial activity. Successful tourism would bring about enormous economic benefits. It is the only sector which could generate massive self-employment avenues while enriching the state exchequer. Being labour-intensive industry, it would increase employment opportunities, thus solving the ever growing unemployment menace in the state. Numerous jobs—direct and indirect jobs, would be created in a variety of tourism related ancillary activities—resorts, hotels, restaurants, tours and travels agencies, guides, handloom and handicrafts etc. State tourism, if efficiently managed would also contribute to increased income and revenue generation, and development of tourism related infrastructures.

Given the huge tourism potential, a strong tourism-allied economic activities linkage is very much possible and viable which could offer a strong economic base for the local resource-based industrialisation process in the state. Tourism has the potential to stimulate the allied economic activities through the strong forward and backward linkages, and cross sectional synergies with agriculture, horticulture, poultry, dairy, fishery, handloom and handicraft, transportation and communication, construction, accommodation and hospitality etc. It induces a chain of economic transactions requiring continuous supply of goods and services from the allied sectors. As the result, income and employment opportunities would be generated, which could effectively solve the ever-growing unemployment and poverty problems in the state. The economic benefits that flow in to the economy through the growth of tourism in terms of increased state revenues, business receipts, employment wages and salary incomes, increase in tax receipts can contribute towards the accelerated all-round socio-economic development and growth of the state. Sensing the vast tourism potential, the State Government created the separate and independent Department of Tourism (DoT) in 1995, i.e. just 18 years back. Since then, the government has been making concerted efforts to develop and promote tourism industry in the state through various plans, policies, programmes, schemes etc. The chart below depicts the employment and income generation opportunity that can be offered by tourism in the state.

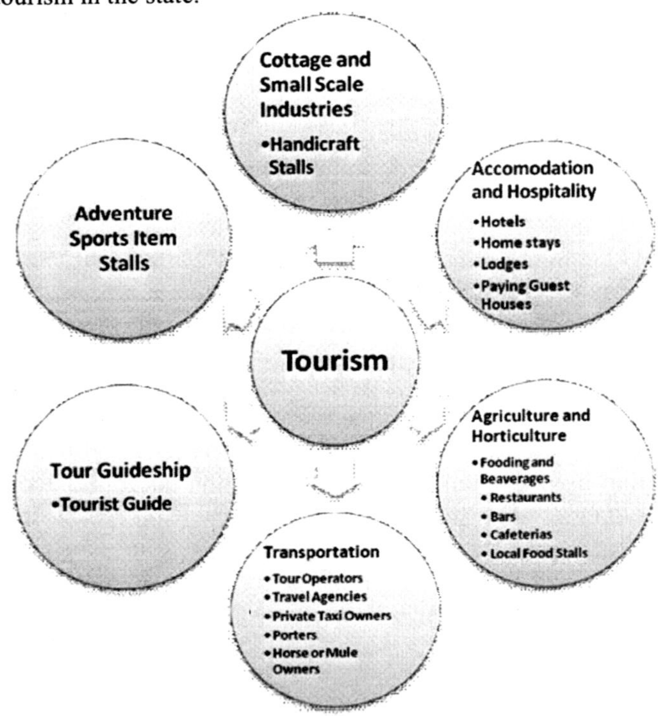

Categories of Tourism in Arunachal Pradesh

There is a tremendous scope for development of a varied categories of tourism in the state. Table 11.1 below, shows the categories of tourism that can be gainfully taken up in the state.

Table 11.1: Promising Tourism Categories in Arunachal Pradesh

Sl. No.	*Tourism Category*	*Tourism Product*
1.	*Adventure Tourism*	Arunachal Pradesh is endowed with thick evergreen forests covering more than 80 per cent of the total area and has five major rivers—Kameng, Subansiri, Lohit, Siang, and Tirap along with their tributaries winding their ways through the sylvan mountains and hills. The geographical landscape is very rich and diverse consisting of snow-capped and high-up mountains, peaks, enchanting valleys, gushing fresh rivers, dense forests, plateaus and plains. The state, especially the upper reaches offer the perfect landscape in the natural settings ideal for trekking, hiking, angling, rock climbing, para-gliding, rafting, base camping, mountain biking, trap shooting, bungee jumping, mountaineering, skiing, backpacking, river expeditions, etc. Menchukha (West Siang district), Tawang (Tawang district), Pasighat (East Siang district), Bhalukpong (West Kameng district), etc. can become hotspots for adventure tourism in the state.
2.	Rural Tourism	Arunachal Pradesh is a rural state. Majority of the population live in villages. As the state is home to 26 major and the sub-tribes, it has a huge potential to develop rural tourism. Each tribe has its own unique and rich way of life. Their religions, festivals, attires, cuisines and beverages, art and crafts, beliefs and ritual practices, healing system and folk-medicines, folk-lores, folk-music, folk-songs, folk-dances, folk-games and sports, material culture etc. being nurtured through ages are one of the most uniquely diverse and colourful in the world. The rural areas can facilitate this sector of tourism as the villagers are hospitable and eager to welcome visitors. The tourists can visit the rural areas in the state and have invaluable experience the tribal ways of life and attractions in fresh environment which is not available in urban settings.
3.	History and Heritage Tourism	Arunachal Pradesh finds mention in the literature of *Kalika Purana* and *Mahabharata*. It is home to many monuments and archaeological sites of

(*Contd.*)

Sl. No.	Tourism Category	Tourism Product
		historical importance. The heritage list includes Parashuram Kund (Lohit), 17th Century Tawang Monastery (Asia's oldest and second largest Buddhist Monastery), the Indo-China War (1962), Memorial (Tawang district), Gorsam Chorten (Tawang district), Urgelling Gompa, the birth place of the 6th Dalai Lama (Tawang district), Samden Yangcha Monastery (Menchukha, West Siang district), Malinithan (West Siang district), Itafort (Papum Pare district), Bhismaknagar (Lower Dibang Valley district), Komsing (East Siang district), Kekar Monying, the Black Rock (East Siang district), the Still Well road built by the allied forces (Changlang district), the Second World War cemetery (Changlang district) etc.
4.	Religious and Spiritual Tourism	Arunachal Pradesh can be a religious and spiritual treat especially for the Buddhist and Hindu pilgrims. Tawang Monastery (Tawang district), Urgelling Gompa, the birth place of the 6th Dalai Lama (Tawang district), Gorsam Chorten (Tawang district), Malinithan (West Siang district), Samden Yangcha Monastery (Menchukha, West Siang district) Parashuram Kund (Lohit), Shivaling (Kardo Hills, Lower Subansiri district) etc. are few of the important pilgrimage destinations.
5.	Cultural Tourism	Arunachal Pradesh is inhabited by at least 26 major and a number of sub-tribes each with its rich customs and traditions. Their festivals, attires, cuisines and beverages, art and crafts, religions, beliefs, ritual practices, folklores, healing system and folk-medicines, folk-music, folk-songs, folk-dances, folk-games and sports, material culture etc. ways of life being nurtured through ages are one of the most uniquely diverse and colourful in the world. This cultural potential of the state can offer a "never before seen" experience in this part of tribal world. Nyishi, Memba, Monpa, Adi, Galo, Apatani, Tagin, Tangsa are few of the tribes to name.
6.	Wildlife Tourism	Arunachal Pradesh is a treasure of rich wildlife. The extensive geographical diversity and corresponding climatic conditions varying from the tropical to the temperate and the alpine have blessed the state

(*Contd.*)

Sl. No.	*Tourism Category*	*Tourism Product*
		with a rich variety of wild life, flora and fauna which, has been acclaimed as one of the richest bio-diversities and heritage spots in the world. The wide variety of altitudinal and climatic conditions have resulted in different forest types providing natural shelter and food etc., to varieties of wildlife many of which are found only the state. Arunachal Pradesh is the only state that can claim to have four major varieties of big cats—tiger, leopard, clouded leopard and snow leopard. Then there are lesser feline species like the golden cat and marbled cat. Seven species of primates, i.e. hoolock gibbon, slow loris, Assamese macaque, rhesus macaque, pigtailed macaque, stumptailed macaque and capped *langur* are also found in the state. All the three goat antelopes *viz*., serow, goral and takin are found. Infact, Arunachal Pradesh is the only state in India, where takin is found. Highly endangerd species like hispid hare have been reported to be found in the low latitudinal grassy lands. The list of wild animals also include tigers, elephants, gaurs, musk deers, bharals, Himalayan black bears, red panda etc. The majestic Yaks and Mithuns need special mention. More than 500 bird species have been recorded, many of which are highly endangered and found only in this state such as white winged duck, sclater monal, temminck's tragopan, etc. The state is very rich in peasants with about 10 species record. The state is equally rich in reptiles, amphibians and pisces. Numerous invertebrate species of butterflies, moths, beetles etc. are also found. On the other hand, the flora of the state is equally diverse and rich. Dr D Fring Wildlife Sanctuary (East Siang district), Namdapha Wildlife Sanctuary (Changlang district), Mouling National Park (Upper Siang district), Pakke Tiger Reserve (East Kameng), Pakhui Wildlife Sanctuary (East Kameng), Dihang-Debang Biosphere Reserve (Upper Siang and Dibang Valley districts), Mehao Wildlife Sanctuary (Lower Dibang Valley district) etc. are important wildlife spots to visit.

(*Contd.*)

Sl. No.	Tourism Category	Tourism Product
7.	Festival Tourism	Arunachal Pradesh can also be known as the "Land of Festivals". Almost all the tribes have festivals which they have been celebrating since time immemorial. Infact, these are the mirror of tribal culture. Festivals are celebrated throughout the year in the state by one or the other tribe. This treasure of festivals could be based upon to develop festival tourism in the state. Lossar (Memba, Khamba, Monpa etc. Buddhist tribes of Mahayana sect), Sangken (Khampti tribe), Nyokum (Nyishi tribe), Solung (Adi tribe), Dree (Apatani tribe), Mopin (Galo tribe), Reh (Idu Mishmi tribe), Ojiyale (Wancho tribe), Si-Donyi (Tagin tribe), Moh-Mol (Tangsa tribe), etc. are few of the tribal festivals. Furthermore, tourism festivals, marts, fairs etc. based on the rich and diverse natural scenic beauty and tribal cultures can be organised in the state. The Arunachal Adventure Festival, 2013 at Mechukha (West Siang district), the Tawang Festival, 2013 at Tawang (Tawang district), India's second edition of International Tourism Mart, 2013 at Tawang (Tawang district), Meen Festival, 2013 at Itanagar (Papum Pare district) etc. are the important tourism festivals successfully celebrated in the recent past.
8.	Golf Tourism	Arunachal Pradesh has been blessed with the requisite landscape with perfect climatic conditions and abundant natural features, which can be developed into appealing golf courses of international standards. Golf can be developed as the niche tourism product for attracting golfers. Golf courses could be developed at Menchukha (West Siang district), Tawang (Tawang district), Ziro (Lower Subansiri district) etc.
9.	Tea Tourism	Arunachal Pradesh has a good scope for developing tea tourism. More number of tea gardens with undulating beauty in serene environment can be developed in the state. Tea tourism can be encouraged in the districts like East Siang, Papum Pare, Changlang, Tirap, Lohit, Lower Dibang Valley etc.

(*Contd.*)

Sl. No.	*Tourism Category*	*Tourism Product*
10.	Helicopter Tourism	The incredible and mesmerizing natural beauty of Arunachal Pradesh comprising of beautiful landscapes viz. snowcapped and knife sharp mountains, rugged terrains, plains, valleys, waterfalls, ridges, gorges, dense forests, foothills, rivers, lakes, etc. provides a strong base for developing helicopter tourism. Depending on weather conditions, scenic helicopter sight seeing tours can be organised throughout the year.
11.	Orchid Tourism	Arunachal Pradesh is considered to be the "Orchid Paradise" of the country. There are about 20,000 orchid species distributed all over the world. India accounts for about 1,150 orchid species in the world and out of which 601 species, i.e. about 52 per cent of the total known orchid species are found in the state itself. Nearly 175 species have been considered rare and endangered. Orchids such as Dendrobium hookerianum, Cleisostoma williamsonii, Arundina gramminifolia etc. orchids are found in the state which can be used for multiple purposes especially for ornamental and medicinal purposes. The orchid treasure of the state can be a life time treat for the tourists with special crave for orchids such as scholars, botanists etc. One of the Asia's largest orchidarium is at Tippi (West Kameng district). The state has an orchid sanctuary at Sessa (West Kameng district).
12.	Eco-tourism	Arunachal Pradesh has a huge potential to be developed into a perfect tourist destination. The tourism resources in terms of natural scenic beauty, tribal art and culture, wildlife etc. are abundant and the state tourism must be developed carefully on the principle of sustainable development. As the state is in its initial stage of tourism development, the opportunity must taken to sustainably and responsibly develop the sector so that environment-physical, socio-cultural and economic, is protected from any negative impact so that the future generation may experience the state as the destination, relatively untouched by human intervention free from degradation and pollution.

Government Approved Travel Circuits in Arunachal Pradesh

At present, to increase the inflow of tourists and to boost tourism, 11 travel circuits have been identified and approved by the State Government. Each circuit is complete within itself choosing from varied fields of interest *viz.*, nature, adventure, culture and tradition, heritage, religion, art and craft, etc. Table 11.2 below, depicts the government approved travel circuits in the State.

Table 11.2: Government Approved Travel Circuits in Arunachal Pradesh

Sl. No.	*Travel Circuit*
1.	Tezpur—Bhalukpung – Bomdila – Tawang Circuit
2.	Itanagar – Ziro – Daporijo – Aalo – Pasighat Circuit
3.	Aalo – Mechukha Circuit
4.	Margherita—Miao – Namdapha Circuit
5.	Dibrugarh – Roing – Mayudia—Anini Circuit
6.	Tinsukia – Tezu – Hayuliang Circuit
7.	Pasighat – Jenging – Yingkiong – Tuting Circuit
8.	Tezpur – Seijosa – Bhalukpong Circuit
9.	Ziro – Palin – Nyapin – Sangram – Koloriang Circuit
10.	Doimukh – Sagalee – Pakke Kesang – Seppa Circuit
11.	Daporijo—Taliha – Siyum – Nacho Circuit

Source: Arunachal Pradesh Tourist Guide Map, Directorate of Tourism, GoAP, Itanagar, Arunachal Pradesh.

Challenges in Developing Tourism in Arunachal Pradesh

In the process of successful development of tourism, Arunachal Pradesh has to solve the following standing issues:

1. Infrastructural and Support Services Bottleneck

There is an inadequate tourism infrastructural and support services facilities which are in fact, prerequisites for the successful tourism development in the state. All-weather road connectivity to the tourist destinations is the need of the hour. The ambitious Trans-Arunachal Highway project which is presently underway is an effort towards this. The air communication to and in the state for the tourists is negligible. The helicopter service has been discontinued for the last few years which has taken a huge toll on the tourist arrivals into the state. Also the state needs to streamline and strengthen its telecommunication and internet service system. Further, there is a dearth of well-furnished government and private lodging facility. Most of the government lodges are ill-maintained and understaffed. Special medical facility for the tourists is absent in the state. There is no proper health centre concerning to the tourists in all the tourist destinations. No matter how potentially the state is in tourism, but unless the basic infrastructure and support services bottleneck is fixed, it can never capitalize upon and tourism cannot be developed. Frequent load-shedding and irregular electric power supply in various tourist destinations too has added to the problem.

2. Inadequate Government Initiatives

An exclusive and practical State Tourism Policy supplemented with procedural guidelines based on the local situations to promote tourism is still awaited. At present, the state tourism development is based on the tourism policy formulated by the Central Government, which has been found improper and lacking clear perspective *vis-à-vis* the unique local circumstances. There is dearth of initiatives on the part of the government, both Central and State. The government is yet to have sound planning and follow-up programmes. Besides, the government incentives and schemes are inadequate to motivate genuine entrepreneurs. The State Government needs to do more under its flagship programme, "Mukhya Mantri Paryatan Vikas Yojana" launched during 2012-13 as a pilot project. Along with the scheme of providing subsidized tourist cabs, other allied services must be given due encouragement under the programme through various schemes.

3. Long and Tiresome Administrative Processes

It has always proved to be long and tiresome task in processing the Protected Area Permit (PAP) and the Inner Line Permit (ILP) for the foreign tourists and the domestic tourists respectively. The permit must be issued for a longer period too so that the tourists can stay comfortably for longer period. At present PAP is issued to the foreign tourists in a group of 2 or more persons for a period of only 30 days.

4. Inadequate Marketing

One of the obvious reasons for the poor show is the improper and inadequate marketing. Majority of the tourist destinations and other tourism products, which have otherwise high potential to attract a large number of tourists if marketed properly to the world, ultimately remain idle and unproductive with no consumers. In fact, there is the need to market Arunachal Pradesh as the global tourism brand so as to draw the attention of both domestic and international tourists. The brand identity is needed for global recognition and to access and penetrate into newer markets. Therefore, it is high time to frame a suitable marketing management model taking into consideration the attitude, mindset and problems of the first generation tour and travel operators, and other service providers in the state. A unique marketable option for the state is the need of the hour to promote it as one of the most leading 365-day tourism destinations of India. In fact, aggressive marketing must be undertaken by the marketers with an assertion to take state tourism to its desired level.

5. Inadequate Entrepreneurship

Tourism requires specialised, trained and skilled entrepreneurs in all the allied services whether it be in tour and travel agency, hospitality, hotels, resorts, restaurants, cafeterias, bars, tourist information centres, counters, tourist guideship etc. It calls for a world-class professionalism in the field. There is an acute shortage of genuine tourism entrepreneurs in the state. A negligible private party participation in the sector is observed.

Conclusion and Suggestions

Tourism is such an economic activity which requires least investment, provides massive employment opportunity, earns huge profit and contributes substantially to the country's Gross Domestic Product (GDP) that too with minimal environmental degradation. Arunachal Pradesh has just recently embarked on the process of developing tourism sector. In fact, tourism can prove to be a major game changer in the sustainable socio-economic development process in Arunachal Pradesh. The mystic beauty of the state has always fascinated travellers. The tourism resources blessed by mother nature needs to be capitalized upon and marketed through concerted efforts by keeping the concept of sustainable development in mind on the part of both the government and the public. If this is achieved, then the day is not far when Arunachal Pradesh will be the most sought-after tourist destination in the country and the world. In fact, the state would become one of the most leading 365-days tourism destinations of India. Many tourism experts unhesitatingly remark "What oil is to Arab countries, tourism is to the State. It could be the largest earning source for the State."

Therefore, it is high time to develop and manage this sector of the economy sensibly and intelligently so that Arunachal Pradesh can ensure sustainable development *vis-à-vis* economic supremacy. In this regard the following suggestions are putforth:

1. Environmental and Socio-cultural Conservation and Sustainable Development

In the process of developing state tourism, the natural environment must be protected by sensibly using, avoiding over exploitation of the resources, and minimizing environmental pollution. Besides, it must be also taken care of that the rich and unique tribal socio-cultural fabric remains intact and is not influenced by any foreign culture. As Arunachal Pradesh is a late starter in the tourism development arena, it has a relative advantage in the sense that it can still learn from the mistakes of other regions who have actually indiscriminately exploited environmental resources and lost the very socio-cultural fabric in the run for bringing drastic economic development. In fact, it is an opportunity in disguise to sustainably develop the tourism sector of the State.

2. Adequate Tourism Infrastructural and Support Services Facilities

The tourism infrastructural and support services facilities are prerequisites for the successful tourism development in the State. All-weather road connectivity to the tourist destinations is the need of the hour. The air communication to and in the State for the tourists must be developed. The helicopter service must be restarted. Green field airports must be developed in the State. Also the State needs to streamline and strengthen its telecommunication and internet service system. Further, there must be adequate and well-furnished government and private lodging facility. The government lodges must be maintained and staffed adequately. Special medical facility for the tourists must be available. In this regard proper health centres concerning to the tourists in all the tourist destinations must be set up. There must be adequate and regular power supply in all the destinations. Arunachal Pradesh must not be interested in bulk tourists until enough accommodation facility and other logistics are ready. As the government alone cannot develop all the tourism infrastructure and the allied services facility, private party participation in the process is very much essential. The Public-Private-Partnership (PPP) and the Design-Build-Own-Operate (DBOO) models for investment in tourism sector, including resorts, star hotels, budget hotels, guest houses etc. with the government to provide land on long term lease basis on a revenue sharing basis can prove fruitful in this regard.

3. Adequate Government Initiatives

The State Government must work-out an exclusive and practical State Tourism Policy supplemented with procedural guidelines based on the local situations to promote tourism. The Government, both Central and State must take more and more initiatives in the State Tourism Sector. The Government must have sound planning and follow-up programmes. It must provide adequate incentives and schemes to motivate genuine entrepreneurs. The State Government must deliver more under its flagship programme, "Mukhya Mantri Paryatan Vikas Yojana." Along with the scheme of providing subsidized tourist cabs, other allied services must be given due encouragement under the programme through various schemes.

4. Adequate and Efficient Marketing

One needs to adopt a proactive attitude and use a wide spectrum of marketing skills and strategies to promote, develop and sustain the State tourism industry. Tourism marketers need to have an insight into the why, what, when, where, how etc., of tourist behaviour to deliver the desired satisfaction in the most efficient manner. A tourism marketing strategy for the State must be devised with an integrated approach keeping all the eight Ps of tourism marketing mix in mind—Product, Price, Place, Promotion, People, Physical evidence, Programming and Partnership. Promotional spree must be adequately undertaken through organising tourism festivals, tourism marts, fairs etc. showcasing the State tourism potential, and the unique, rich and varied tribal way of life. The mass media can play a proactive role of tourism ambassadors. A celebrity of both national and international stature may be appointed as the tourism brand ambassador for the State. In fact, there is the need to market Arunachal Pradesh as the global tourism brand so as to draw the attention of both domestic and international tourists. The brand identity is needed for global recognition and to access and penetrate into newer markets. Resorting to e-marketing can prove very efficient and fruitful. Arunachal Tourism Information Counters must be set up in both the national and international airports. Constitution of a Marketing Board drawing public representatives from the departments of Tourism, Information Technology, Art & Culture, Trade & Commerce etc. and private representatives from hotels, tour operators, travel agents etc. is also suggested. Over all, aggressive niche marketing is suggested.

5. Simpler, Efficient and Tourist-friendly Administrative Processes

The whole administrative processes regarding the granting of the Protected Area Permit (PAP) and the Inner Line Permit (ILP) to the foreign tourists and the domestic tourists respectively must be made simpler, efficient and tourist friendly. The permit must be issued for a longer period too so that the tourists can stay comfortably for a longer period. In this regard, the internet services can prove very handy and useful by saving time, money and energy of the tourists. The whole processes can be completed on-line.

6. Genuine Tourism Entrepreneurship

As tourism requires specialised services and a world-class professionalism of the personnels whether it be in tour and travel agency, hospitality, hotels, resorts, restaurants, bars, tourist information centres, counters, tourist guideship etc., effort must be made to nurture genuine tourism entrepreneurs by the government and the private individuals through various programmes, schemes etc.

7. Home Stay Facility

To meet the problem of inadequate accommodation, the locals can operate and offer home stay facility to the tourists. The home stays must be constructed and operated on traditional lines by keeping the rich traditional designs and culture in mind. This could attract a good number of tourists as they are always fascinated by the rich tribal tradition and culture. They would rather prefer cozy and eco-friendly accommodation in home stays to the accommodation in concrete hotels and lodges. The venture can be a good revenue generating machine for the home stay entrepreneurs.

8. Local Cuisines, Beverages and Handicrafts

Most of the hotels, restaurants and lodges in the tourist destinations provide main-land Indian and other foreign cuisines such as Chinese, Continental etc. Tribal cuisines and beverages being simple, fresh, organic and healthy, and in particular unique in taste, can prove a good option in the menu list. Tribal food stalls and bars could be set up at the tourist destinations. This could prove a profitable business venture. Also, stalls dealing in the traditional handicraft products must be set up at the tourist destinations which the tourists can take back home as souvenir. In fact, tourists are very interested in tribal cuisines, beverages and handicraft products and other aspects of tribal way of life.

NOTES

1. Swain, Sampad Kumar and Mishra, Jitendra Mohan, 2012, *Tourism: Principles and Practices,* Oxford University Press, New Delhi, p. 4.
2. *Ibid.*, p. 28.
3. *The Arunachal Times*, 19th January, 2013, p. 1.
4. *Ibid.*

REFERENCES

Bhatia, A.K. (2008). *Tourism in India*, Sterling Publishers Pvt. Ltd., New Delhi.

Chaudhary, Manjula (2010). *Tourism Marketing,* Oxford University Press, New Delhi, India.

Chauhan, K. and Punia, B.K. (2009). Success Factors of E-Commerce in Indian Tourism Industry, *The Indian Journal of Commerce*, Vol. 62, No. 4, pp. 91- 97.

Das, H.N. and Ramanath, Seemanti (2008). *Tourism in the North East and Other Essays,* M/s. Today's Communications, Guwahati, Assam (India).

Ganesan, G. and Rao, K. Chandra Shekar (2005). Visit India as a Tourism Brand, *The Indian Journal of Commerce*, Vol. 58, No. 3, pp. 41-46.

Gratzer, M., Werthner, H. and Waniwarter, W. (2004). Electronic Business in Tourism, *International Journal of Electronic Business*, 2 (5): 450-459.

M. Morrison, Alastair (2013). *Marketing and Managing Tourism Destinations*, Routledge, Taylor & Francis Group, USA.

Pender, Lesley and Sharpley, Richard (2005). *The Management of Tourism*, Sage Publications, New Delhi.

Seth, P.N. (2006). *Successful Tourism Management: Fundamental of Tourism,* Sterling Publishers Pvt. Ltd., New Delhi.

SECTION-III

Women Empowerment for Sustainable Society

12

Dipshikha Beneficiaries' Participation in Women Empowerment Activities

M.S. Ali and *M.M. Islam*

Introduction

The word 'Dipshikha' was derived from two Bengali words—'Dip' and 'Shikha'. 'Dip' means light or lamp and 'shikha' means flame or spark of light. So, the meaning of Dipshikha stands as sparkling flame of lamp, which never puts out and continues illuminating people and places. The conceptual meaning of 'Dipshikha' is more interesting and more attractive. The sparkling flame of light is the symbol of socio-cultural and economic development of people through "helping people help themselves" (Bhuiyan and Ali, 2009). Dipshikha helps people in such a way that they can proceed forward from ignorant to wisdom and knowledge, from illiteracy to literacy, from conservatism to modernity, and from narrowness to broadness. Thus, Dipshikha has commitment of mass education, leadership development, democracy, economic emancipation, social empowerment, women empowerment, and so forth. Actually, Dipshikha is working for the development of rural poor especially for the rural women.

Women empowerment in Bangladesh means giving women of the country the power to rule and govern their own lives, away from traditional and social constraints. The women empowerment movement in Bangladesh focuses on giving women the power and authority they need to be men's equals. Women must have intellectual resources that can be acquired through good education and material resources that can be accumulated with the help of a solid job. Women in Bangladesh work in rural areas and do most of the manufacturing labour as well as most of the harvesting.

This traditional practice needs to stop. The violence against women must also stop. Women need to gain a lot more power over their decision-making process. They should not be seen as fertility machines that have only the goal of reproducing. Various economic and social development indicators show that in the last 25 years, Bangladesh, a poor, Muslim-majority country in the classic patriarchal belt, has made substantial progress in increasing women's access to education and healthcare (including increasing life-expectancy), and in improving women's participation in the labour force (Hossain, *et al.*, 2011). The population of Bangladesh is about 161 million and the male ratio is about 50:50 [0.95 male/female (BBS, 2012)]. As the half of the population is female in Bangladesh, it is very important to empower women for the total development of Bangladesh. Dipshikha as an NGO is working for empowering women in Bangladesh. Dipshikha claimed that its beneficiaries often participate in women empowering activities. Therefore, it is necessary to rate the participation of Dipshikha beneficiaries in women empowering activities. On these considerations, the researchers of the present study felt necessity to conduct this piece of research on the following objectives:

Objectives

- To determine the extent of Dipshikha beneficiaries' participation in women empowerment activities before and after involvement with Dipshikha.
- To determine the rate of changes of Dipshikha beneficiaries' participation in women empowerment activities after involving with Dipshikha.
- To compare item-wise changes of participation in women empowerment activities.

Methodology

Study Area: In Bangladesh, Dipshikha is working in five upazillas under Dinajpur districts, namely Birol, Kaharol, Bochaganj, Birganj and Ghoraghat and two upazillas of Sirajganj district namely Tarash and Raiganj. All these seven upazillas were selected as the study area.

Population: There are two types of approaches of Dipshikha for the development of their target beneficiaries, namely Group Based Approach (GBA) and Family Development Approach (FDA). Dipshikha reported that it works with GBA in four areas with 4487 group members and with FDA in three areas with 7896 families. These group members and family heads constituted the population of the study.

Sample and Sampling Procedure: Data were collected from the sample of the population rather than the whole population. A total of 373 members containing 135 group members from GBA and 238 family heads from FDA were selected as the sample of the study by stratified random sampling method with the help of sample size calculator suggested by Creative Research System (1982).

Data Collection: Data were collected with the help of pre-tested interview schedule by the Data Collectors during the period from 1 to 31 May, 2013.

Measurement of Participation in Women Empowerment Activities: Dipshikha has been working for the development of the rural poor especially for the rural women of Bangladesh since 1984. Eleven-item scale was considered to measure the participation of the Dipshikha beneficiaries in women empowerment. These items were collected from the scale developed by Bhuiyan and Ali (2009). Bhuiyan and Ali (2009) reported that they collected the items after thorough consultation with the Dipshikha personnel, review of related litreatures and based on pretest information. Respondents were asked to response against each of these items with four alternative responses as 'regularly', 'occasionally', 'seldom' and 'not at all' and weights were assigned to these alternative responses as 3, 2, 1 and 0 respectively. Thus, Participation of the respondents in women empowerment activities could range from 0 to 33, where '0' indicated no participation and '33' indicated highest participation in women empowerment activities. Participation in women empowerment activities before and after involvement with Dipshikha was determined separately based on the responses of the respondents. Changes of participation in women empowerment activities before and after involvement with Dipshikha was also determined and item-wise rank order of changes was again made for comparing the change items. Full procedures of these issues are discussed in the results and discussion section.

Results and Discussion

Participation of the Dipshikha Beneficiaries in Women Empowerment Activities

Salient features like observed range, sum, mean and standard deviation of participation of the Dipshikha beneficiaries in women empowerment activities before and after involvement in Dipshikha are presented in Table 12.1.

Table 12.1: Salient Features of Participation of the Dipshikha Beneficiaries in Women Empowerment Activities Before and After Involvement with Dipshikha

Approaches	*Number of respondent interviewed*	*Period*	*Observed range*	*Sum*	*Mean*	*SD*
Group based approach (GBA)	135	Before involvement	0 – 28	995	7.37	5.76
		After involvement	1 – 33	3825	18.33	6.85
Family development approach (FDA)	238	Before involvement	0 – 32	2116	8.89	5.29
		After involvement	0 – 33	4336	18.22	6.81
Overall	**373**	Before involvement	0 – 32	**3111**	**8.34**	**5.62**
		After involvement	0 – 33	**8161**	**21.88**	**6.84**

Source: Field Survey.

Findings revealed that mean of Dipshikha beneficiaries' participation in women empowerment activities after involvement in Dipshikha was higher than before involvement with Dipshikha in all the cases like GBA, FDA and overall.

Respondents were classified into four categories according to their participation in women empowerment activities on the basis of the following way:

Categories	*Basis of Categorisation (Score)*
No participation	0
Low participation	1–11
Medium participation	12–22
High participation	23–33

The detail number and percentage distribution of the respondents according to their participation in women empowerment activities are presented in Table 12.2.

Findings revealed that majority proportion (76.7%) of the respondents had no or low participation in women empowerment activities before involvement with Dipshikha. But overwhelming majority (86.9%) of the beneficiaries had medium to high participation in women empowerment activities after involvement with Dipshikha. The overall achievement of

Table 12.2: Distribution of the Dipshikha Beneficiaries According to Their Participation in Women Empowerment Activities

Approaches	*Categories according to participation in women empowerment activities*	*Before involvement with Dipshikha, respondents*		*After involvement with Dipshikha, respondents*	
		Number	%	Number	%
Group based approach (GBA)	No participation	7	5.2	0	0.0
	Low participation	101	74.8	20	14.8
	Medium participation	24	17.8	79	58.5
	High participation	3	2.2	36	26.7
	Total	**135**	**100**	**135**	**100**
Family Development approach (FDA)	No participation	13	5.5	0	0.0
	Low participation	165	69.3	29	12.2
	Medium participation	57	23.9	157	66.0
	High participation	3	1.3	52	21.8
	Total	**238**	**100**	**238**	**100**
Overall	No participation	20	5.4	0	0.0
	Low participation	266	71.3	49	13.1
	Medium participation	81	21.7	236	63.3
	High participation	6	1.6	88	23.6
	Total	**373**	**100**	**373**	**100**

Source: Field Survey.

Dipshikha can be asserted from the reducing tendency of no participation and low participation in women empowerment activities.

Changes in Participation in Women Empowerment Activities after Involving with Dipshikha

Attempt had been made to determine the changes of participation in women empowerment activities after involvement Dipshikha with the help of the following formula:

$$Cpw = Apw - Bpw$$

Where, Cpw = Changes of participation in women empowerment activities (score)

Apw = Participation in women empowerment activities after involving with Dipshikha (score)

Bpw = Participation in women empowerment activities before involving with Dipshikha (score)

The possible and observed range of score of changes of participation in women empowerment activities of the respondents was 0 to 33, where '0' indicated no change and '33' indicated highest changes in participation in women empowerment activities. The respondents were again classified into four categories according to their changes of participation in women empowerment activities on the basis of the following way:

Categories	*Basis of categorisation (score)*
No change	0
Slightly increase of participation	1–11
Moderately increase of participation	12–22
Highly increase of participation	23–33

Source: Field Survey.

Data revealed that overwhelming majority (91.2%) of the respondent beneficiaries increased their participation in women empowerment activities ranged from slightly to moderate level compared to 2.4 per cent respondents increased at high level and rest 6.4 per cent of the respondents did not change their participation in women empowerment activities. Moderate and high increase of participation in women empowerment in GBA and FDA was found to be 51.1 per cent and 31.5 per cent respondents respectively. It means that increase of participation in women empowerment in GBA was higher than FDA. Therefore, it may be concluded that the family alone can not increase women empowerment but the group. These findings were slightly higher than the findings of Bhuiyan and Ali (2009). It again means that Dipshikha increased its women empowerment activities more than previous days. The salient features of changes of participation in women empowerment activities of the respondents due to involvement in Dipshikha are presented in Table 12.3 with the number and per cent distribution of the respondents.

Item-wise Change of Participation in Women Empowerment Activities

Further attempt had been made to determine the item-wise change of participation in women empowerment activities. In this regard, change of participation in women empowerment activities index (CPWAI) had been determined for each item with the following formula:

Table 12.3: Salient Features of Changes of Participation in Women Empowerment Activities of the Respondents Due to Involvement in Dipshikha with the Number and Per cent Distribution of the Respondents

Approaches	*Categories according to changes in participation in women empowerment activities*	*Respondents'*		*Mean*	*SD*
		Number	%		
Group based approach (GBA)	No change	4	3.0	11.39	6.02
	Slightly increase of participation	62	45.9		
	Moderately increase of participation	64	47.4		
	Highly increase of participation	5	3.7		
	Total	**135**	**100**		
Family development approach (FDA)	No change	20	8.4	9.15	6.46
	Slightly increase of participation	143	60.1		
	Moderately increase of participation	71	29.8		
	Highly increase of participation	4	1.7		
	Total	**238**	**100**		
Overall	No change	24	6.4	10.13	6.24
	Slightly increase of participation	205	55.0		
	Moderately increase of participation	135	36.2		
	Highly increase of participation	9	2.4		
	Total	**373**	**100**		

$$CPWAI = C_h \times 3 + C_m \times 2 + C_s \times 1 + C_s \times 0$$

Where, CPWAI= Change of participation in women empowerment activities index.

C_h = Per cent of beneficiaries had highly increased their participation in women empowerment activities.

C_m = Per cent of beneficiaries had moderately increased their participation in women empowerment activities.

C_s = Per cent of beneficiaries had slightly increased their participation in women empowerment activities.

C_n = Per cent of beneficiaries had no change of participation in women empowerment activities.

Thus, CPWAI of the items could range from 0–300, where '0' indicated no change and '300' indicated highest increase. For better comparison, rank order had been made depending on the descending order of the CPWAI of the items.

Findings revealed that highest increase of participation in women empowerment was occurred in "ensuring equal importance for boys and girls in education" followed by "ensuring equal importance for male and female in decision-making", "ensure female freedom in income generating activities" and "participation female in buying and selling activities". Bhuiyan and Ali (2009) also found more or less similar results. Rank order of changes of other items of participation in women empowerment is presented in Table 12.4.

Table 12.4: Change of Participation in Women Empowerment Activities Index with Rank Order

Change items	*Per cent of beneficiaries*					*CPWAI*	*Rank order*
	Highly increase	*Moderately increase*	*Slightly increase*	*No change*	*Total*		
(1)	(2)	(3)	(4)	(5)	(6)	(7)	(8)
1. Ensuring equal importance for boys and girls in education	33	54	12	1	100	219	1
2. Ensuring equal importance for male and female in decision making	11	83	6	0	100	205	2
3. Ensure female freedom in income generating activities	7	79	14	0	100	193	3
4. Participation female in buying and selling activities	9	74	17	0	100	192	4
5. Ensuring equal importance for male and female in wealth distribution	4	65	30	1	100	172	5
6. Ensuring female freedom for vote casting	3	58	39	0	100	164	6
7. Ensuring free movement for female	2	53	45	0	100	157	7

(Contd.)

(1)	(2)	(3)	(4)	(5)	(6)	(7)	(8)
8. Movement for logical rights	1	48	48	3	100	147	8
9. Movement against child Marriage	1	33	64	2	100	133	9
10. Movement against Dowary	1	26	65	8	100	120	10
11. Ensuring political activities for female	1	2	85	12	100	92	11

Source: Field Survey.

Conclusion

Proverb goes that "the happiness of a family lies with the virtues of women". But without empowering women how a practical society can desire happy and prosperous life? In deed, family is a joint venture of women and men. So, women and men should equally be empowered in running a family. But, in Bangladesh, traditionally women's backward position in all spheres of life is socially structured and culturally conditioned. It is very difficult to bringing about changes regarding women empowerment in the Bangladesh contest. However, Dipshikha had taken policy initiatives aiming at empowering women in its jurisdictions. The research team observed that Dipshikha achieved a lot for increasing participation in women empowering activities and hoped that in near future women could be able to assume and exercise all the delegated powers.

REFERENCES

BBS. (2012). *Statistical Year Book of Bangladesh*. Bangladesh Bureau of Statistics. Planning Division, Ministry of Planning, Government of the People's Republic of Bangladesh.

Bhuiyan, M.H. and M.S. Ali. (2009). *Spark of Light in Poverty Alleviation and Rural Development for a Quarter Century.*

CRS. (1982) Sample Size Calculator. Creative Research System.

Hossain, N., S. Nazneen, and M. Sultan. (2011). *National Discourses on Women's Empowerment in Bangladesh: Continuities and Change.* URI: http://hdl.handle.net/10361/1532

13

Socio-Economic and Culture of the Backward Muslim Women in Basirhat Block-II of North 24 Parganas, in West Bengal, 2011-12

Kaniska Sarkar

Introduction

After seven decades of Independence majority of Muslim women are one of the most disadvantaged, least literate, economically impoverished and politically marginalised sections of Indian society. It has also restricted the Muslim women from making significant economic contributions, either towards their own independence or towards the economic expenditure of the family. Patriarchy system is very much popular in Muslim religion such as it is commonly found that early marriage is also very common among the Muslims. It creates problems in acquiring education for women. After marriage, Muslim women are not allowed to move out without escort; as a result, they cannot continue their education and other economic spheres after marriage. Divorce was commonly practiced; Muslim husbands quite frequently avail this opportunity. As a result, Muslim women are becoming poor in the field of economy, education and social interaction as well as self-respect. Begumpur Bibipur Gram Panchayat is an example to identify the poor condition of the Muslim women especially thus Muslim women who are belonging BPL. These backward Muslim women, their socio-economic and cultural analysis is the main study of this chapter.

Need of the Study

The study area is selected based on a particular social problem faced by a group, which is socio-economically and culturally degradation backward Muslim women. This problem is identified by the different categories of socio-economic and cultural scenario of the society. In the past no such type of job was done particularly on the said topic in the rural area. The Gram Panchayat, namely Begumpur Bibipur is suffering for lack of literacy, income, occupation, awareness of good livelihood. To discuss the problems of the backward Muslim women all the social contents will be analysed and compared to each other. On the other hand the way of remedy and steps to reduce the problem will also be discussed.

Objectives

To study of the present status of the backward Muslim women of the study area, the literacy rate, age group, marriage age group, income group, level of social status, level of torture on them will be discussed.

(i) To enquire the possible reason for the backwardness of the mentioned Muslim women in the field of social, economy and culture, we will also show the present scenario of the problem.

(ii) To study the nature of torture and negligence on the backward Muslim women, proper projection will be highlighted on the study field.

(iii) To suggest the possible steps to overcome the problems of the backward Muslim women, proper remedies will also be discussed.

Major Issues and Aspects on the Subject

Lack of education, scarcity of schooling and traditional technique of teaching are the main reasons of illiteracy among the poor people as well as the backward Muslim women. Superstitions among the Muslim religion and especially among the Muslim women are the more or less main reason for social, economic and cultural degradation. Traditional wrong treatment among the Muslim women and habit to denial to go to registered doctor is the main reason for their health degradation and wrong process of fertility. These wrong treatments also break up the scientific policy of family planning which is very much essential for building up a strong social group. So, it is urgent to discuss about the present status of literacy rate, income group, child birth rate of the victimized backward Muslim women and also urgent to discuss as remedy about their healthy and normal livelihood in the study area to abolish the act of different types of torture.

Methodology

The data was derived from a door-to-door survey was conducted to evaluate the socio-economic background and level of knowledge about the status of backward Muslim women of the study area. Data was also collected from two types of sources: (i) Primary data—Field work was conducted through questionnaire survey of villagers and interview office staffs like hospitals, clinics, Police Stations, Protection Office, Family welfare society etc.; and (ii) Secondary data got from Litreature (reports) from different offices. The survey covered 88 (Eighty eight) families which was selected by random process and related to this subject. The house hold schedules were completed with information on age, sex, marital status, place of birth etc. When a member of the household was absent his/her data was obtained from some elder member (s) of the household. The fertility schedule was completed with information from married females and the widows on their reproductive performance including wastages. Genealogies were collected by cross-checking on fertility data. The data on reproductive wastage has not been utilized in view of the possibility that they might be considered under-reported because of recall lapse. Social, economical and cultural degradation of backward Muslim women are hampered at study area due to different burning issues like population explosion, weak economic condition/poverty, increasing of number of illiterate persons, superstitions, increasing of political disturbances, Illegal migration from Bangladesh etc.

Study Area

The study area is Basirhat Block-II which is one of the Blocks of the North 24 Parganas District. The area of North 24 Pargana District is 4,094.00 sq. km. and location 23°15′2″ North to 22°11′6″ North latitude and 89°5′ East to 88°20′ East longitude. Bangladesh covers its eastern and partly northern boundary and the tributaries of Ichhamati River also regionalise from Bangladesh on the same boundary. District of South 24 Pargana covers on its south runs coastal area of Sundarban. Nadia district stands in the partly northern boundary. On the western boundary there are Kolkata, Howrah and Hoogly districts.

The study area is Basirhat Block-II whose area is 132.54 sq. km. The maps in Fig. 13.1 will show the Geographical location and boundary of the study area.

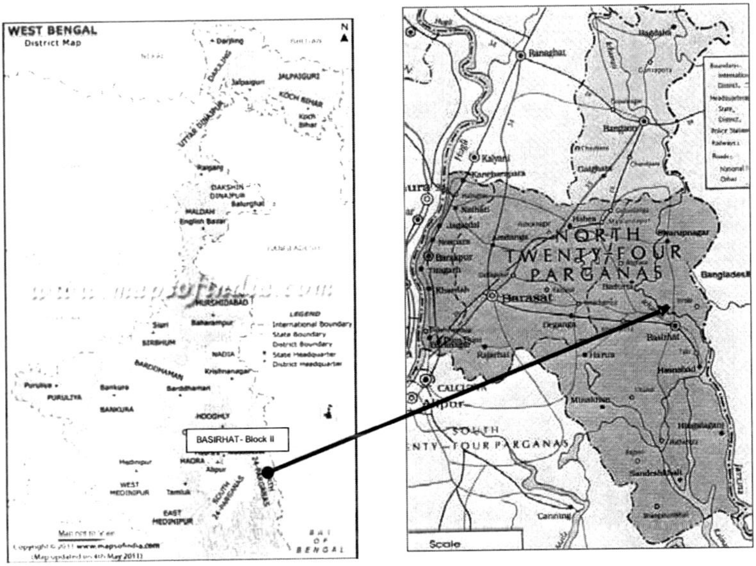

Fig. 13.1: Geography Location of the Study Area
Note: Map not to scale.
Source: www.mapofindia.com

Basirhat Block-II Profile: Basirhat Block-II has a high concentration of Muslim population. The percentage of Minority Community in the District is 24.67 per cent (Muslim share is 24.22% as per Census 2001) whereas the percentage of Muslim population in the Basirhat Block-II is 70.36 per cent. The total population of the Block is 1,89,850 and out of this Muslim population is 1,33,582. This Block was formed with nine Gram Panchayats.

The details of the GP and related villages are as following—

Name of Gram Panchayat	*Name of Village*
Ghoraras Gram Panchayat (G.P.)	Korapara Beler Dhanyakuria Zafarpur Jaypur Gopmahal Gadarati
Kholapota G.P.	Swaruppur Mathurapur Maynali Raghunathpur

(Contd.)

Name of Gram Panchayat	*Name of Village*
Rajendrapur G.P.	Tyantra Neora Jhuruli Dakshin Devipur
Begumpur Bibipur G.P.	Begumpur Paschim Bibipur
Srinagar Matia G.P.	Srinagar Sangberia Matia
Dhanyakuria G.P.	Nehalpur Nadia
Rajendrapur G.P.	Tyantra Neora Jhuruli Dakshin Devipur
Champapukur G.P.	Uttar Devipur
Kachua G.P.	Kachua Goblia Kankra Mirzanagar

Source: Directory of District, Sub-division, Panchayat Samiti/Block and Gram Panchayats in West Bengal, March 2008.

As per 2001 Census, Basirhat Block-II has a total population of 1,94,006 out of which 99,295 were males and 94,711 were females. Density of population per sq. km. is 1523 and P.C. of Population to District Population is 2.17. Basirhat Block-II registered a population growth of 18.30 per cent during the 1991-2001 decade. Decadal growth for the district was 22.40 per cent. Decadal growth in West Bengal was 17.84 per cent.

Nature of the Problem in the Study Area: The backward Muslim women in the study area are suffering due to low social status, weak economic infrastructure and superstitious cultural background. The following statistical based diagrams of different types of features of livelihood of human being will interpret the present scenario of this specific group of population.

Age group of the backward Muslim women: Age group of the women is divided in five classes. The women who are under the age of 24 years to 29 years are tortured in maximum level. Then the second group is under the age of 30 years to 35 years. Other age groups are also suffering accordingly (*see* Fig. 13.2).

Age group of the women during their marriage: Maximum of the victimized women of this study are bound to get married in the age group from 16 years to 18 years. The women who got married at the age of

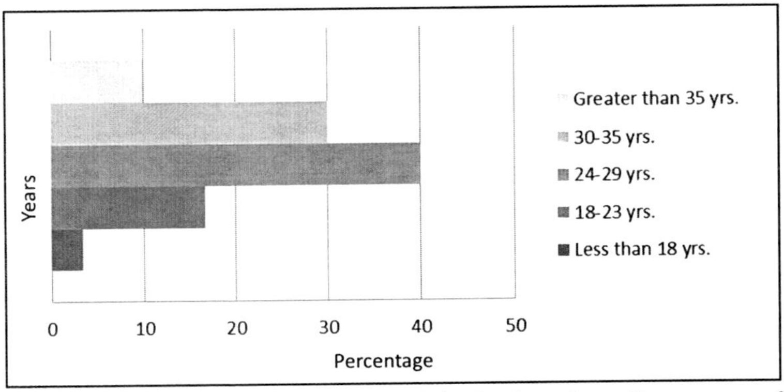

Fig. 13.2: Age Group in percentage of the backward muslim women of Begumpur Bibipur GP, Basirhat Block-II, North 24 Parganas, 2011-12.

Source: Household survey and NGO counselling centre.

below 16 years are also placed in second position in case of level of tortured by matrimonial. It is also found that, the underaged married women become victimized due to their vulnerability and immaturity (Fig. 13.3).

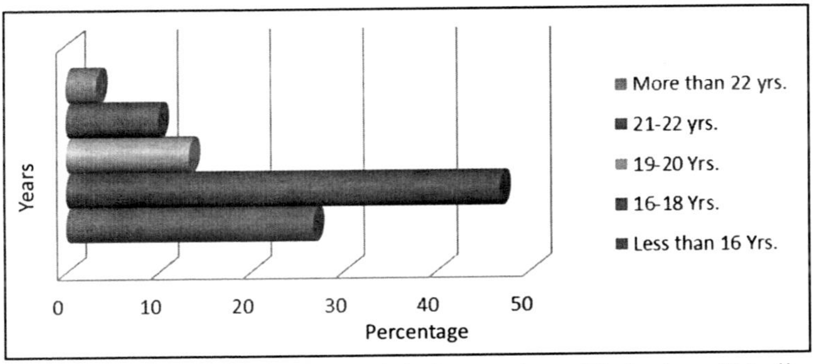

Fig. 13.3: Age Group (In percentage) during marriage of the backward Muslim women of Begumpur Bibipur GP, Basirhat Block-II, North 24 Parganas, 2011-12.

Source: Household survey and NGO counselling centre.

Education status of the women: Lack of education is the main reason among the women to tolerate the violation of fundamental rights and different kinds of torture. It is also found that forty per cent of the women are illiterate and only twenty six per cent women can write their name. And rest of them are not very much educated to establish or protect themselves (*see* Fig. 13.4).

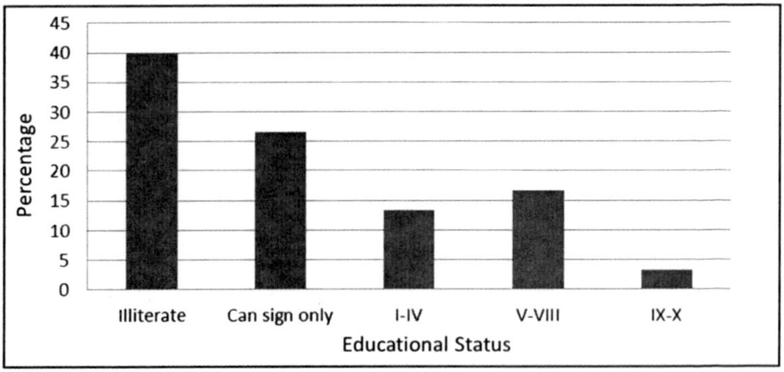

Fig. 13.4: Educational status (in percentage) of the backward Muslim women of Begumpur Bibipur GP, Basirhat Block-II, North 24 Parganas, 2011-12.

Source: Household survey and NGO counselling centre.

Occupational status of the women: Sixty seven per cent women are not able to earn and they are behaved like a domestic slave. Only thirty three per cent women can earn a few amount of money from the occupation of maid servant, handycraft-maker, labour of agricultural field, brick field labour or otherwise (*see* Fig. 13.5).

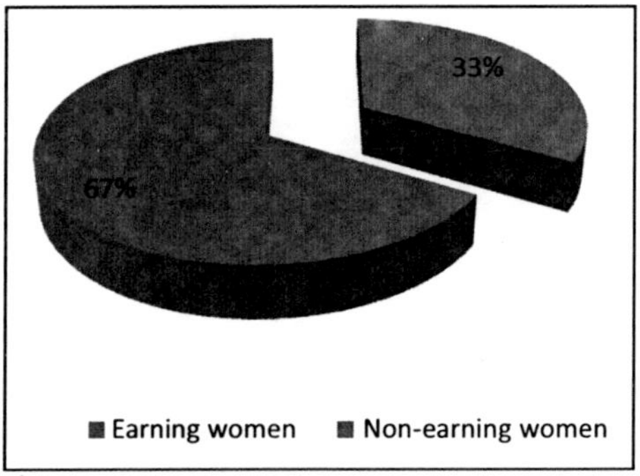

Fig. 13.5: Percentage on earning and non-earning backward Muslim women of Begumpur Bibipur GP, Basirhat Block-II, North 24 Parganas, 2011-12.

Source: Household survey and NGO counselling centre.

Different earning groups: Among the 66 per cent of earning women; three classes (i.e. from less than four hundred rupees to more than six hundred rupees per month) of earning amount can be found. This low income of the women is not capable to fulfil their own demands (*see* Fig. 13.6).

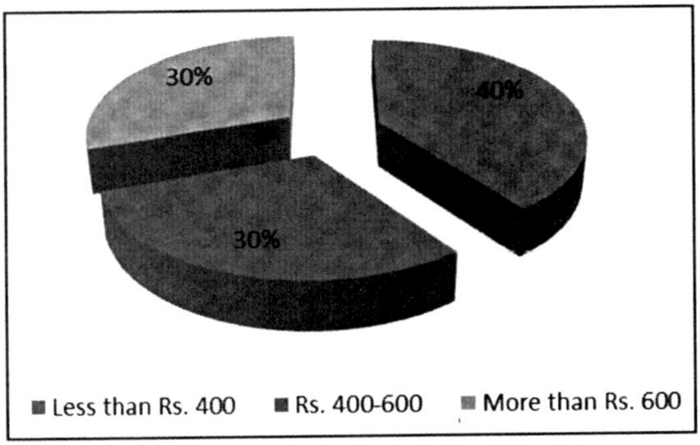

Fig. 13.6: Percentage on different source of income of the backward Muslim women of Begumpur Bibipur GP, Basirhat Block-II, North 24 Parganas, 2011-12.

Source: Household survey and NGO counselling centre.

Torture by matrimonial house: Sixty per cent women are tortured physically, mentally, economically and sexually by their matrimonial house. Beating, denial of food, untouchables, use of filthy words, dowry demand, insult, denial to meet or talk with others, negligence etc. are the main way to torture on the women. A few of women who can earn for their family or bring money or property from their paternal house get relief from the torture (*see* Fig. 13.7).

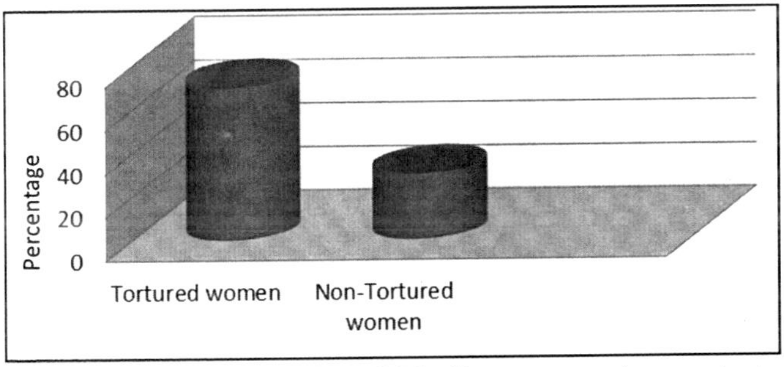

Fig. 13.7: Percentage of backward Muslim women who was tortured by matrimonial house in Begumpur Bibipur GP, Basirhat Block-II, North 24 Parganas, 2011-12.

Source: House hold survey and NGO counselling centre.

Source of physical treatment for the women: Most of the women (63%) are being mentally and physically tortured by refusing them from the proper physical treatment during their illness or pregnancy. On the other hand Government hospitals or private nursing homes are not very developed or affordable in the study area. Most of the women are bound to go to non-registered doctor or village *Dai* by their family heads during their delivery which is very dangerous for their life.

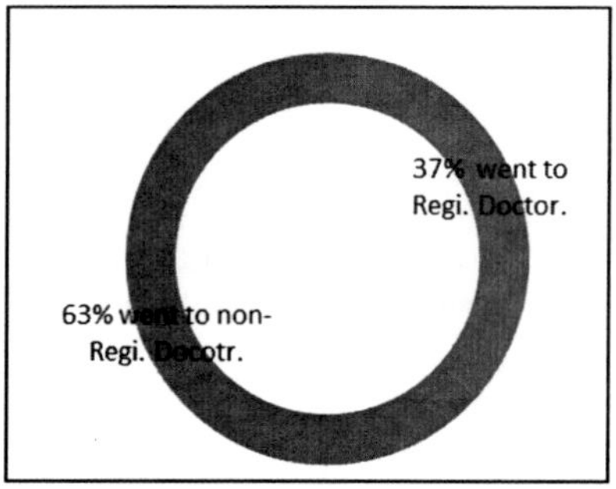

Fig. 13.8: Percentage of backward Muslim women who got treatment from different sources in Begumpur Bibipur GP, Basirhat Block-II, North 24 Parganas, 2011-12.

Source: Household survey and NGO counselling centre.

Different types of torture on the women: In case of different types of torture, maximum women are tortured due to denial of nutritious food, denial of meals, forced to marriage in minor age and especially physical torture (*see* Fig. 13.9).

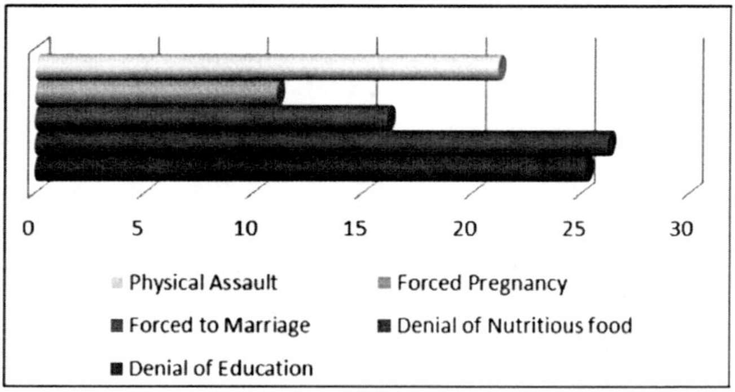

Fig. 13.9: Percentage on different types of torture on Muslim backward women of Begumpur Bibipur GP, Basirhat Block-II, North 24 Parganas, 2011-12.

Source: Household survey and NGO counselling centre.

Conclusion and Suggestion

Being 25.25 per cent of Bengal's total population Muslims form the principal minority group. The present study identifies some notable characteristic on the basis of which certain finding can be drawn. The review of socio-economic and cultural data on Muslims women in the study area shows that they are poor and by far educationally lagging behind. They are least educated and the further educational status is too low. They are economically and educationally very poor. Their literacy rate is very low, which will not be able to combat with any kind of violation as well as crime. Under present socio-economic situation and low level of education in Basirhat Block-II in particular the Muslim women pull them in frustrations, insecurity, anxiety, fear psychosis, helpless and hopeless. So in discussion for remedy to get freedom from this vast problems we can discuss the below mentioned topics for the better coming days of the Muslim women in the study area.

1. Education should be free and mandatory for all. Proper education and its implementation in practical field will develop the society. Female must be educated to boost up the backbone of the society.
2. Money is one of the main factors to develop the society. So source of income must be oriented especially for the weak and needy Muslim women.
3. The study area Basirhat Block-II, should be aware in all corners of socio-economic development.
4. Strong law implementation should be done to stop female exploitation through detachment from education and other problems; like lack of awareness of happy life, social domination by males, physical and mental torture in parental and matrimonial houses.
5. To stop all the offences, exploitation, mismanagement of Government aid for development; it is the responsibilities of Governmental agencies through the law and its implementation.
6. The Muslim women of the study area is mainly affected due to believe on religious unjustified explanations. So, it is necessary to make a common platform for all human being to express scientific explanation before the superstitious activities.
7. N.G.O. should take part to stop the social offences by helping the law implement agencies and the affected community through the government aid.

8. All kind of help from national or international level is very much needed in Basirhat Block-II of North 24 Parganas District, West Bengal to drive out the main problems of Muslim women.

REFERENCES

Bagchi, Jasodhara. (Ed.) (2000). *The Changing Status of Women in West Bengal, 1970-2000, The Challenge Ahead*, Sage Publications, New Delhi/Thousands Oaks/London.

Bakshi, S.R. and Kiran Bala. (Edited) (1999). *Women, Children and Weaker Sections: Social and Economic Development of Schedule Tribes.* Deep and Deep Publications, New Delhi.

Dak, T.M. (1988). *Women and Work in Indian Society*, Discovery Publishing House, New Delhi.

GOI, (2006). *Social, Economic and Educational Status of Muslim Community of India—A Report,* Prime Minister's High Level Committee, Cabinet Secretariat, Government of India, New Delhi (Chairperson Justice Rajinder Sacher).

Ishita Mukhopadhyay (eds.) (2002). *Violence Against Women, A Popular Intervention*. Vyas Prakashan, Kolkata.

Krishnaraj Maithreyi (eds.) (1998). *Gender, Population and Development.* Oxford University Press, New Delhi, India.

Nuna, S.C. (1989). *Regional Disparities in Educational Development—Policy and Planning Implication*, paper presented in the National Seminar on Regional Disparities in Educational Development, September 25-27, NIEPA, New Delhi.

"Population Explosion in West Bengal: A Survey", A Study by South Asia Research Society, Calcutta, Statistical Abstract, West Bengal, 1978-89 (Combined Issue), Bureau of Applied Economics and Statistics. http://www.voiceofdharma.org/books/tfst/appii1.html

Raza, M. and Agarwal, Y.P. (1986). Inequalities in the level of literacy in India, in Shafi and Raza, R. (eds.) *Spectram of Modern Geography*, Concept Publishing Company, New Delhi, pp.193-225.

Robert Keener (2007). *Functional Literacy in Rural India*, for more information or networking contact Bob.Keener@sinclair.edu

Sharma, A. (2002). *Women in Indian Religions*, New Delhi: Oxford University Press.

Siddiqui, F. A. and Nazmul Hussain: *Muslim Women Work Participation in West Bengal*, An Article Publication.

Siddiqui, M.K.A. (1984). *Educating a Backward Minority*, Abadi Publication, Calcutta.

Upreti, H.C. and Nandini Upreti (2000). *Women and Problems of Gender Discrimination.* India: Pointer Publishers.

14

Self-Help Groups on Socio-Economic Empowerment of the Rural Women

A Case Study of Cachar District, Assam

Subhrabaran Das and *A. Pushpalata Singh*

Introduction

The need to bring women into the mainstream of development has been a national concern since early fifties. Recent UN conferences have advocated that women's empowerment is central to development. The United Nations Conference on Environment and Development (UNCED) Agenda 21 mentions women's advancement and empowerment in decision-making, including women's participation in "national and international ecosystem management and control of environment degradation" as a key area for sustainable development (Wee and Heyzer, 1995). The Copenhagen Declaration of the World Summit on Social Development (WSSD),1995 recognised that empowering people, particularly women, to strengthen their own capacities is the main objective of development, and that empowerment requires the full participation of people in the formulation, implementation and evaluation of decisions determining the functioning and well-being of societies. This shows that the involvement of women in the development process is equally important as that of men and so their empowerment is a prime necessity. This is supported by the World Summit in 2005 where governments of all nations agreed that progress for women is progress for all. The Report of the UN Fourth World Conference on Women also called its platform for action "an agenda for women's empowerment" meaning that "the principle of shared power and responsibility should be established between women and men at home, in the workplace and in the wider national and international communities" (UN, 1995a).[1]

But, in spite of all these it is seen that the social, political, economic and cultural status of women is far less than that of men especially in the rural areas. Women are the true nation builders as they primarily build the future generation of a country. So, investment in women's capabilities for empowering them to expand their choices is not only important and valuable, but is also the surest way to contribute to the economic growth and development of the nation. Unless women are given opportunities for developing her vision, proper health care, respect and political and socio-economic status, her efforts may not achieve the ultimate objective of a strong, civilized and prosperous nation. So, empowerment of women has become one of the vital issues in the route of development of all developing countries in the world.

Majority of the women with lack of assets cannot contribute for improving their empowerment and well-being, so economic independence through self-employment and entrepreneurial development need to be paid more attention for their self-reliance. As Self-Help Groups (SHGs) are an effective tool to promote rural savings and gainful employment so it can transfer the real economic power in the hands of women and can considerably reduce their dependence on men. This can improve empowerment of women and build their self-confidence. Women's access to savings and credit gives them a greater economic role in decision-making through their decision about savings and credit. When women control decisions regarding credit and savings, they can optimize their own as well as their family welfare. It also strengthens women's position not only in their family, but also in the society as a whole. Economic solvency would enable them to increase expenditure on their overall well-being. There exists a large body of evidence which shows that increasing resources in the hands of female household members has a greater impact on family welfare (Thomas, 1990). However, the role of SHGs is yet to spread its wings all over India. Assam is generally considered as the economically backward State. The majority of the people belong to the rural areas and they depend on the village economy. In the era of globalisation and industrialisation, still now these rural areas are far from the main stream of the country's growth and development process. Especially, rural women are not included in the country's growth process. Government has focused on inclusive growth. Inclusive growth is the growth in totality by including all sections of the society. The Government has emphasized on the inclusive growth through the formation of Self-Help Group (SHG).

Self-Help Group (SHG) is a small voluntary association of poor people, preferably from the same socio-economic background. It can be all-women group, all-men group or even a mixed group. It is a group of about 10 to 20 people, usually women, from a similar class and region, who come together to form savings and credit organisation. They also come together for the purpose of solving their common problems through self-help and mutual help. The SHG promotes small savings among its members. The savings are kept with a bank. This common fund is in the name of the SHG.

In India, women Self-Help Groups (SHGs) were initiated by NABARD (National Bank of Agriculture and Rural Development), with the support of local NGOs. In March 1999, about 0.56 million families engaged in micro-enterprises were financed under the scheme through 33,000 SHGs (of which 84% were women SHGs). In all 202 banks, 64 per cent Regional Rural Bank (RRBs), 19 per cent Commercial Banks and 17 per cent Co-operative Banks are participated in the programme. A total of 550 NGOs were involved. The aggregate outstanding loan was Rs. 570 million. The average outstanding loan per SHG and per micro-entrepreneur worked out to Rs. 17,297 and Rs. 1,019 respectively. The average number of micro-entrepreneurs per SHG was 19. As of 2010, the total number of SHGs directly linked to banks stood at 69.53 lakh, with a savings amount of Rs. 6,199 crore and loan outstanding of Rs. 28,038 crore, according to the recently released "Status of Micro-finance in India" report by NABARD (Bhavani, 2011). The SHG approach helps the poor to build their self-confidence through community action. An interaction in group meetings and collective decision-making enables them in identification and prioritisation of their needs and resources. This process would ultimately lead to the strengthening and socio-economic empowerment of the rural poor as well as improve their collective bargaining power.

Review of Litreature

There are so many litreatures in this field, but some of them are discussed here.

Matheswaran (2008) made a case study of Tamil Nadu for studying how Self-Help Group (SHG) movement can promote women empowerment for attaining sustainable development. He has found that SHGs really help the women-folk to participate in organised activities apart from helping members to mobilise funds. This case study reveals that given the assistance and guidance, the SHGs are bound to help not only in empowering women, but also to tap and hither the unutilised power of women for sustainable development of the society as a whole. He concludes that education particularly distance education is an enabling factor for women empowerment and sustainable development of the society.

Raghavalu (2007) in his study attempted to analyse the role played by women entrepreneurs through Self-help Groups in Bellary district of Karnataka. About 20 women belonging to Swarnajayanti Gram Swarozgar Yojana (SGSY) Scheme were interviewed on random basis covering four trades, viz. Bamboo Products, Dairy, Handicrafts and Tailoring. It has been found from the study that the SGSY scheme in rural Bellary is effectively working as the employment and income of the women who were working in these groups have improved. Though the members are facing problems in their groups, some problems are tentative and should be solved in the short period. It is also evident from the field study that their efficiency and awareness of production process and developmental activities is insignificant. This is because of lack of training and awareness camps, which has not been conducted by the concerned agencies.

Biswas (2007) has attempted to put forward how micro-finance has received recognition as a strategy for economic empowerment of women and to examine the impact of micro-finance with respect to poverty alleviation and socio-economic empowerment of rural women. A conclusion that emerges from the study is that micro-finance can contribute to solve the problems of inadequate housing and urban services as an integral part of poverty alleviation programmes. The author has suggested for providing multipurpose loan or composite credit for income generation, housing improvement and consumption support so that it could match the multiple credit requirements of the low income borrower without imposing unbearably high cost of monitoring its end use upon the lenders.

Sahu and Das (2007) have examined the role and performance of SHGs in promoting women's empowerment in the Gajapati District of Odisha. To achieve this, the main objectives of the study were to analyse the economic gains derived by the members after joining the SHGs and to examine the social benefits derived by the members. The study has also analysed the operating system of SHGs for the mobilisation of saving, delivery of credit to the needy, management of group funds, repayment of loans, in building up leadership, and establishing linkage with banks. The study covers 498 SHGs with 800 members. The study reveals that habits of savings, economic independence, self-confidence, social cohesion, asset ownership, freedom from debt, additional employment, etc. are derived by the SHG members. SHGs play a vital role in incorporating women's aspirations, dynamism and involvement. Thus, the authors suggest that there is a need for the development of an innovative and diversified micro-finance sector, which will make a real contribution to women empowerment.

The present study attempts to assess the role of SHGs for improving the status of women in Cachar District of Assam. The study is based on the following objectives:

Objectives

- To investigate the activities of SHGs operated by women members.
- To examine whether SHGs can improve women's socio-economic empowerment or not.

Hypothesis

- SHGs operated by women are doing several activities for their economic improvement.
- There is a significant difference in socio-economic empowerment between the women belonging to SHG group and non-SHG group.

Methodology

For the study, the data have been collected from both primary sources and secondary sources. The primary data has been collected from the rural area of Cachar District by using three-stage stratified random sampling method. In the first stage, 3 blocks, viz. Sonai, Udharbond and Narshingpur have been selected from the 15 blocks in Cachar District based on large demographic size. In the second stage, 5 large villages have been selected according to demographic size from the each selected block. So, a total of 15 villages have been selected. In the last stage, 8 households have been randomly selected from each selected of the selected villages. So, finally a total of 120 households have been selected. Moreover, the primary data have been collected by taking interview from an adult married woman of each household through a scheduled questionnaire.

Secondary data have been collected from different government publications, books and journals, Census Reports of Assam, Human

Resource Development Reports and Statistical Handbook of Assam, Panchayat and Rural Development Department, different websites etc.

To measure decision-making power of women on six different aspects, coding and scaling has been used. As decision-making is a quality aspect we have taken a binary option to quantify this. If the women have no decision-making power then the value has been considered 0 otherwise it has been considered as 1. In some cases it is observed that they have taken some crucial decision jointly like children's education, children's marriage etc. For these crucial decisions, joint decision is commonly preferable than the single decision. So, it is important to check whether the women are playing participatory role in this decision-making process or not. For the total six aspects maximum value of the coding will be 6. To measure the degree of autonomy in the decision-making process, we have used three scaling; the value of the coding up to 2 out of 6 have been considered as low degree of autonomy, up to 4 as medium degree and above 4 as high degree of autonomy.

To investigate the problems faced by the women, different responses have come from the interviewed women. These problems have been divided into four different heads of categories and analysed accordingly.

Findings

Activities of Women SHGs

There are 592 SHGs in Sonai block, 500 in Udharbond block and 367 in Narsingpur block in Cachar District. In all these blocks, number of female operated SHGs is higher than male operated SHGs. There are few SHGs in all these blocks which is operated by both males and females. Total number of female members involved is 4589 in Sonai block, 4302 in Udharbond block and 3447 in Narsingpur block (Table 14.1).

Table 14.2 reveals that the activities of SHGs of different blocks operated by female members. It is commonly observed that in all these three blocks, women are involved in different types of activities such as maintaining live stocks and other activities. There are different types of livestock activities such as poultry farm, goatary, dairy etc. The other type of activities in which women are involved are weaving, tailoring, small business etc.

The status and strength of SHG is reflected by grading. Grading is done in SHGs after the period of six months. In the first grading the assistant project officer verifies the group activities in the past six months.

Table 14.1: Classification of Self-Help Group in Three Blocks of Cachar District

Blocks Category	*Sonai*	*Udharband*	*Narsingpur*
SHG operated by both male and female	47	16	29
SHG operated by male only	166	105	39
SHG operated by female only	379	379	299
Total number of female members	4589	4302	3447

Source: Panchayat and Rural Development Department, Government of Assam, 2009.

Table 14.2: Activities of the Self-Help Group of the Blocks

Blocks Variables	*Sonai*	*Udharbond*	*Narsingpur*
Main activities of the female operated SHG (No.)	Poultry (133) Goatary (72) Dairy (57) Weaving (39)	Poultry (80) Tailoring (72) Weaving (56) Business (53)	Poultry (55) Dairy (55) Weaving (54) Goatary (33)
Grade I	138	117	55
Grade II	26	36	48

Source: Panchayat and Rural Development Department, Government of Assam, 2009.

After the verification the SHG is subjected to get revolving fund from bank. The second phase grading is done after the period of one year. In this grading they verify the repaying capability of the groups. After the second grading the groups are eligible to get the amount of four times of their savings in bank.

Table 14.2 shows that number of SHGs of Grade-I are more than Grade-II. It is noticeable that most of the SHGs the repaying capability of the groups are poor. Among the three blocks, it is seen that number of SHGs getting Grade-I is highest in Sonai block and lowest in Narsingpur block while that of SHGs getting Grade-II is highest in Narsingpur block and lowest in Sonai block.

Socio-economic Status of Women

From Fig. 14.1, it is seen that 90.63 per cent of the SHG women are literate while only 26.09 per cent of non-SHG employed women are literate which is even less than the literate of non-SHG unemployed women (56.92%). It is important to note that majority of non-SHG employed women are employed in the tea garden as female labour who are mostly illiterate.

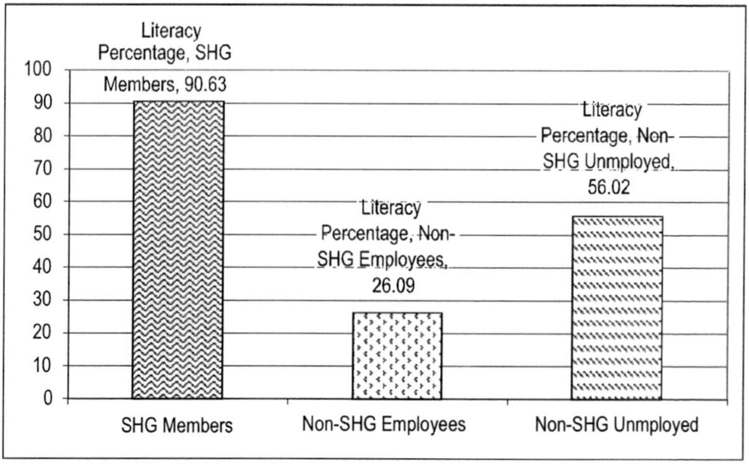

Fig. 141: Literacy percentage among different groups of women,
Source: Field study.

One of the most important indicators of women empowerment is decision-making power. There are six aspects, viz; purchase of daily household needs, visit to relatives, family planning, children's education, sons and daughter's marriage and major household decisions. By considering maximum 6 point scaling, it is observed from the survey that about 50 per cent of SHG women in Cachar district have high degree, 37 per cent of them have moderate degree and 12.50 per cent of them have low degree of autonomy for taking decision in their family. For non-SHG employed, only 26.09 per cent of the women have high degree of autonomy, 39.13 per cent have moderate degree and 34.78 per cent have high degree of autonomy. Regarding non-SHG unemployed, 31 per cent of them have high degree which is better than the non-SHG employed women (Table 14.3).

Table 14.4 reveals that the greater percentage of SHG women have freedom to participate in making-decisions like purchase of daily household needs, visit to relatives, family planning and son's and daughter's marriage. Regarding major household decisions, greater percentage of SHG women are enjoying freedom to participate in it than the non-SHG women.

Free mobility of women is another indicator of women empowerment. From the survey, it is found that the greater percentage of women are allowed to go within the residential area alone while very few of them are allowed to go outside the residential area alone. Comparing these three groups it is observed that non-SHG members are enjoying more freedom

Table 14.3: Degree of Autonomy for Taking the Decision in the Family

	Low (≤2)	Moderate (≤4)	High (≤6)
SHGs	12.50	37.50	50
Non-SHGs Employed	34.78	39.13	26.09
Non-SHGs Unemployed	40.91	27.27	31.82

Source: Primary Field Survey, November, 2010.

Table 14.4: Household Decision-Making Empowerment of Different Groups of Women

Different Groups of Women	Percentage of women who usually make specific decisions alone or jointly					
	Purchase of daily HH needs	Visit to relatives	Family Planning	Children's Education	Son's & Daughter's Marriage	Major HH decisions
SHGs	100	84.38	71.88	56.25	81.25	43.75
Non-SHG Employed	91.30	91.30	26.09	30.43	69.57	34.78
Non-SHG Unemployed	83.08	73.85	43.08	43.08	76.92	23.08

Source: Primary Field Survey, November, 2010.

of going within the residential area alone while SHG members are enjoying more freedom of going outside the residential area alone (Fig. 14.2).

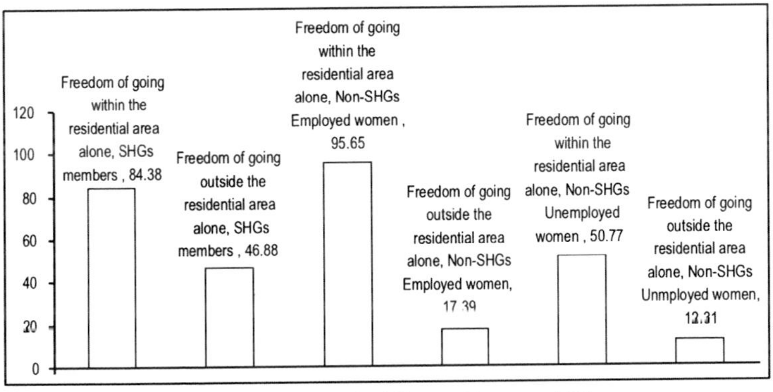

Fig. 14.2: Freedom of Movement of Different Groups of Women

Source: Field Survey.

Further, it is observed that about 65.63 per cent of SHG women have access to money for small purchases while only 9.38 per cent of them have access to money for large purchases and surprisingly, none of the non-SHG unemployed have any access to money for large purchases. Comparing these three groups, it is seen that SHG women are having greater access to money for both small and large purchases than the non-SHG women. It is also observed that 50 per cent of the women have bank account though only 18.25 per cent of them have ATM facilities and operate themselves. On the other side, only 17.39 per cent of the non-SHG employed women have bank account while 50 per cent of them have ATM facilities and operate themselves (Table 14.5). This reflects very poor economic and social empowerment of women especially for non-SHG employed and non-SHG unemployed.

Table 14.5: Access to Money of the Different Groups of Women

(in %)

Different Groups of Women	*Percentage of women having*				
	Access to Money for Small Purchases	*Access to Money for Large Purchases*	*Bank Account*	*ATM facilities those who have Bank Account*	*Own operation of ATM*
SHGs women	65.63	9.38	50	18.25	18.75
Non-SHG Employed	34.78	4.35	17.39	50	50
Non-SHG Unemployed	35.38	0	20	23.08	23.08

Source: Primary Field Survey, November 2010.

Problems Faced by Women

From the sample survey, it has been found that women in Cachar district are facing various types of problems but, these problems are categorised into four heads (Table 14.6) which is discussed below.

Employment of women is very much important for raising the status of women, but employment and cash earnings are more likely to empower women if women make decisions about their own earnings alone or jointly with their husband rather than their husband alone. Forty per cent of SHG women are not free from family obligations while 69.57 per cent of non-SHG employed women are not free from family obligation and 39.13 per cent are not having financial autonomy to spend or save from their own earnings.

Table 14.6: Problems Faced by Different Group of Women

(in %)

Different Types of Problems	*SHG members*	*Non-SHG Employed*	*Non-SHG Unemployed*
Employed but not free from family obligation	40	69.57	—
No financial autonomy to spend/ save from own earnings	0	39.13	—
Willing to study but not having educational freedom	50	45.45	60.53
Physically/Domestically humiliated by family members	25	52.17	46.15

Source: Primary Field Survey, November 2010.

The educational status of women in Cachar district is very low and one of the reasons may be that the women are willing to study but they are not having educational freedom. 60.53 per cent of non-SHG unemployed women who are willing to study are not getting educational freedom, followed by SHG members (50%) and non-SHG employed women (45.45%). It is observed that the percentage of women belonging to non-SHG unemployed group have more willingness to study compare to non-SHG employed who are mainly tea garden labourer.

Domestic violence is yet another important factor which affects the process of women empowerment. It has been observed from the survey that 52.17 per cent of the non-SHG employed women are either physically or domestically humiliated by their husbands or other family members while only 25 per cent of the SHG women are victimized by domestic violence.

Conclusion

In the Cachar district there are many SHGs operated by women. Women of the SHGs are generating their income through maintaining live stock and weaving, tailoring etc. Most of the women working under the SHG are literate compare to other group of women. Regarding decision making and other important activities SHG women are enjoying more empowerment compare to other group of women as they are self-sufficient in their earning status. So, it is concluded that SHG can improve economic empowerment and that leads finally the social empowerment of the women.

REFERENCES

Bhavani, R.V. (2011): "The bank-SHG model of microfinance in India", *Infochange News and Features*.

Biswas, Tiyas (2007): "Women Empowerment Through Micro Finance: A Boon for Development", downloaded from http://www.isical.ac.in/~wemp/index1.html.

Ghadoliya, M.K. (2004): "Empowering Women Through Selh-Help Groups: Role of Distance Education".

Kabeer Naila (2001): "Conflicts over credit: re-evaluating the empowerment potential of loans to women in rural Bangladesh", *World Development*, 29(1): 63-84.

Matheswaran, V.P. (2008): "Women Empowerment for Sustainable Development Through Self-Help Group Movement in Tamil Nadu", Presented at International Conference on "Issues in Public Policy and Sustainable Development", IGNOU, New Delhi, March 26-28.

Raghavalu, M.V. (2007): "Women Entrepreneurship Through Self-Help Groups in Rural Areas", *Journal of Social and Economic Policy*, Vol. 4, No. 2, pp. 211-216.

Rahman Aminur (1999): *"Women and Microcredit in Rural Bangladesh: Anthropological Study of the Rhetoric and Realities of Grameen Bank Lending"*, Westview Press, Boulder.

Reddy C.S (2005): "Self-Help Groups: A Keystone of Microfinance in India—Women Empowerment and Social Security".

Sahu, Ananta Basudev and Das, Sandhya Rani (2007): "Women Empowerment Through Self-Help Groups—A Case Study", Paper presented at a seminar on Gender Issues and Empowerment of Women, Indian Statistical Institute, February 1-2.

Swain, R.B. and F.Y. Wallentin (2007): "Does Microfinance Empower Women? Evidence from SHGs in India", downloaded from http://www.nek.uu.se

Thomas Duncan (1990): "Intra-household resource allocation: an inferential approach", *Journal of Human Resources*, 25(4): 635-664.

UN (1995a): *Report of the Fourth World Conference in Women*, Beijing, China.

Wee Vivienne and Heyzer Noeleen (1995): "Gender, Poverty and Sustainable Development", Engender, Singapore.

15

Woman Empowerment through Self-Help Group

A Case Study of Women SHG in Kapili Development Block of Morigaon District of Assam

Pankaj Saikia

Introduction

Empowerment of women is one of the vital issues of development, especially in developing countries, where they appear to form the largest of the poor, marginalised and vulnerable group. They usually have no choice regarding their course of life as well as no opportunities to improve their condition. Women's empowerment and their full participation on the basis of equality in all spheres of society, including participation in the decision-making process and access to power, are fundamental for the achievement of equality, development and peace (UN, 1995).

In all parts of globe, women have played an important role since the beginning of human life on earth. Though, men and women are equal, but women are not given equal status to men. This unequal gender role in socialisation process is operated in every society. Women comprise half of the population and if that half of the population is neglected, how nation's development can be achieved? All-round development and harmonious growth of a nation would be possible only when women are considered as equal partners in progress with men. An ideal society cannot be created without the voices of women.

Though, the increasing international awareness on gender issues, but in reality many countries have failed to eliminate the increasing gender gap. Even several countries do not capitalise the potentiality of women and misallocating their human resources and undermining their competitive potential in developmental quest. In most of the developing and under-developing countries, gender inequality is a major obstacle in meeting the target of Millennium Development Goals. In reality, achieving the goals will not be feasible without closing the gaps between women and men in terms of capacities, access to resources and opportunities.

Origin of the Research Problem

In the name of liberal democracy the Western developed countries tries to gain the economic interest of developing and under-developing countries. The process of globalisation de-legitimises the role of state on collective welfare system and strongly argues for free market economy. It recommends only minimum level of social protection. It has brought instability and insecurity among the people and under mines the capacity of the government to provide education, health care and social protection. It gives much priority to the commercialisation of entire economy and neglects the social aspects especially in the informal economy of rural areas.

Since 1970s, the idea and practice of self-help has developed world wide as a major social phenomenon. It has been widely acknowledged in the development literature that SHGs is one of the means to empower women by providing easy access to credits. Accessibility of women to credit will enable them into income generating activities by establishing micro-enterprises which will provide additional income to the household. The ability to generate own income will perhaps help them to have more power and choices related to household decision-making with regards to household's consumption, education and health, as well as participation in the political process.

Self-Help Group model has become one of the most widely adopted means for alleviating rural poverty. It is used as a channel for both individual and community development through people's self-effort and self-reliance.[1] The main intention is to empower individuals within organisation or group to create innovative solutions to the problems facing them. This process becomes an opportunity for individuals or communities to realise their problem-solving capacity and resources in order to be self-sufficient (Duffy & Wong, 2000). According to Drower (2005), groups challenge the sense of isolation, separation and loneliness.

Theoretical Framework

From history of social development, it has been seen that various theories emerged from time to time for better functioning of societies. In development discourse gender equality and empowerment of women is accepted universally as an important aspect. The "welfare approach" originated back 1950s to the 1970s during the era of decolonisation and political transitioning in most African and Asian countries. International development agencies applied Western approach towards newly independent nation's development. These brought about a negative impact and outcome towards developing nation's development.

Since 1970s, the concept of empowerment has been used by feminist literature and became popular in the developmental field from the 1980s.[2] The origin of empowerment as a form of theory was traced back to the Brazilian humanitarian and educator, Freire (1973), when he suggested a plan for liberating the oppressed people of the world through education (Hur Mann Hyung, 2006).[3] The neo-liberal policies and developmental agencies used to mobilise women through self-help groups as better economic and social change agents. Neo-liberalist stands on the freedom of individuals to make their own decisions and rejects the culture of dependency. It glorifies the self-control ethos of self-management, self-reliance and discipline (Harvey David, 2005).[4] It favoured the role of state is to create and preserve institutional framework to appropriate such practices. But this approach left out large section of people in the development process especially in developing and underdeveloped countries.

In this perspective, the libertarian concept developed by John Rawls is significant. His theory has great significance with the perspective of empowerment for establishing social justice. The concept of empowerment related with those who are powerless and need states intervention to give them power. Rawls developed the theory of justice, which is to be understood by means of fairness and demands that society should distribute goods according to merit and needs (Rawls John, 1971).[5] His theory is based on two principles, i.e. the principle of equality and principle of inequality. Principle of inequality is important for brining gender equality which is the prime aim of this study for strengthening grassroots democracy and to bring participation of deprived section in society.

Concept of Empowerment

Empowerment is a multidimensional process which enables an individual to realise his/her full identity and power in all spheres of life. The word 'empowerment' means giving power and power means having the capacity and the means to direct one's life towards desired goals. The term "power" is the root in empowerment. It has been one of the most contested concepts in social and political theory. Power can be understood in different ways: power over, power to, power with, power within (Oxaal & Baden, 1997).[6] Jo Rowlands (1996) identified four different forms of power while discussing empowerment.[7]

Power over: control or influence over others which is an instrumentation of domination.

Power to: considered as generative or productive power which creates new possibilities and actions without domination.

Power with: refers to collective action, recognising that more can be achieved by group than by individuals alone.

Power within: Its basis is self-acceptance and self-respect which extend respect and acceptance of others equally.

Michel Foucault (1976) refers power is knowledge and derived from below. It requires micro-political channels to disseminate throughout the social body (Banu Zenab, 2001: 17).[8] It relates to how individuals can recognize through analysing their experience, how power operates in their lives, and gain the confidence to act, influence and change. It focuses participation into decision-making and challenges oppression and inequality with a bottom-up process. It is aimed at decentralising authority and getting the participation of the deprived section in the decision-making process.

Power is unevenly distributed among stratified groups in society. Stratification is commonly based on differences in gender, age, income, race, ethnicity, religion, ability, class, and sexual orientation. Even, there is a high gender gap in literacy, voiceless, lack of information, awareness, skills, low wages and income earning capacity, gender discrimination excludes poor access to resources, power, and control over their own lives.

Amartya Sen's (1999) approach on "development as freedom" has been a starting point for many recent definitions of empowerment.[9,10] According to him the goal of development is to increase choices. Kabeer (1999) uses this approach in her definition of empowerment as the movement from an inability to an ability to make choices. According to Sen greater freedom will enhance the ability of people to help them and also to influence the world which is important for the process of development.

Narayan (2002, 2005), Alsop and Heinsohn (2005), Petesh, Smulovitz and Walton (2005), and Alsop, Bertelsen and Holland (2006) have come together with common conceptual frameworks for understanding empowerment. The World Bank publication on Empowerment and Poverty: A Sourcebook is to be viewed empowerment broadly as increasing poor people's freedom of choice and action to shape their own lives (Narayan, 2002).[11] It also implies more participatory, bottom-up approaches towards development objectives. Poor people's choices are extremely limited. They are lack of assets and their powerlessness excluded from participation in state institutions both formal and informal. So, poor people need assets and capabilities to increase their well-being and security, as well as their self-confidence.[12] Empowerment is the expansion of assets and capabilities of poor people to participate in, negotiate with, influence, control, and hold accountable the institution that affects their lives.

Ruth Alsop and others (2005) at the World Bank defined empowerment as the process of enhancing an individual's or group's capacity to make purposive choices and to transform those choices into desired actions and outcomes. Thus, empowerment is considered as an outcome of agency and opportunity structure. Agency is defined as the ability on the part of an individual or group to make meaningful choices. They consider agency to be strongly determined by people's individual assets (such as land, housing, livestock, savings) and capabilities of all types: human (such as good health and education), social (such as social belonging, a sense of identity, leadership relations) and psychological (self-esteem, self-confidence, the ability to imagine and aspire to a better future), and by people's collective assets and capabilities, such as voice, organisation, representation and identity. People's agency plays an important role in human development and capability approach (Sen A, 1999). The opportunity structure comprises the institutions that govern people's behaviour and which influence the success or failure of the choices that they make. The opportunity structure refers to the broader institutional, social, and political context of formal and informal rules and norms within which actors pursue their interests. In other words, the opportunity structure is what enables (or not) agents to become effective.

According to Narayan (2002), the opportunity structure encompasses both the institutional climate and the social and political structures. In turn, the institutional climate may include access to information, the degree of inclusion and participation in the economic life (e.g., poor people may not be able to participate in all markets, such as credit), the degree of accountability of the public sector and the capacity of local organisation.

The social and political structures refer to the degree of openness that poor people have to make use of opportunities and services.

From the theoretical analysis, empowerment can be conceptualised as a social process of recognising, promoting and enhancing people's abilities to meet their own needs, solve their own problems, and mobilise the necessary resources in order to control of their own lives.

Concept of SHG

Self-Help Group is voluntary apolitical associations of women or men, residing in a given area, formed democratically and come together for a common collective purpose. SHGs are small informal associations created for the purpose of enabling members to reap economic benefit out of mutual help, solidarity, and joint responsibility (Jaya S. Anand, 2002).[13] That members have come together to share a common experience and eventually create an opportunity to mobilise resources in the pursuit of needs and interests (Kurtz, 1981).[14] Katz and Bender (1976) defined self-help groups are voluntary, small group structures for mutual aid to the accomplishment of purpose. In India, it was piloted by NGOs, notably MYRADA (Mysore Resettlement and Development Agency), with a mission of "Building poor people's institution" in the mid-1980s, in order to provide financial services to poor people which become a movement for social empowerment for rural poor people in general and women in particular (Fernandez P. Aloysius, 2007).[15]

SHG is synonymously used as with the words of Abraham Lincoln's definition of democracy "for the people, by the people and of the people". It serves the principle "by the women, of the women and for the women". The basic principles on which self-help groups function are group approach, mutual trust, organisation of poor manageable small groups, group cohesiveness, spirit of thrift, demand based lending, collateral free, friendly loan, peer group pressure in repayment, skill training, capacity building and empowerment. SHG is such an organisation of poor people, particularly for women through which they can become self-reliant and self-sufficient to take active part in decision-making process in their day-to-day life. The self-help approach is a unique form of help that can lead to improving skill, self-esteem and personal growth and collective mobilisation for social change and service innovation and today this phenomenon becomes an integral part of the human services (Yeheskel Hasenfeld and Benjamin Gidron, 1993).[16]

Review of Literature

Zubair Meenai (2003), S. Galab and N. Chandrasekhara Rao (2003) Sahu and Tripathy (2005), Umashankar Deepti (2006), Suguna B. (2006), Reddy C.S. & Reddy, M.B.S., (2008), Jayasheela, Shriprasad H. and Dinesha P. T. (2009), Dhavamani P. (2010), Usha Pitta (2010), Vasanthakumari P. (2011), Dolly Sunny and Marina Pereira (2011), Sushil Kumar Mehta, Hari Govind Mishra & Amrinder Singh (2011), Manonmani, I.K. and Prabhakaran.V.P. (2011), Manga, B.V.L.A. (2011), Soroushmehr Homa (2012) etc. studies revealed that Self-help groups (SHGs) plays very important role in socio-economic and political empowerment of people. It also revealed that SHGs generates self-employment, increasing their confidence and improved the access of women to credit. This has helped women in reducing their dependence on moneylenders. Women have been able to achieve consciousness about the function of local self-government, politics, health awareness and child health care.

On the other hand, Kabeer, Naila (2005), and K. Lalitha and G. Prasad (2011) mentioned that the impact of SHG activity can access to financial services and does make important contributions to the economic productivity and social well-being of poor women and their households. They were not properly facilitated through conducting periodical meetings, training programmes and awareness camps for their improvement. Their active participation in economic activities was very much limited due to the lack of adequate approach by the NGOs for which they have poor decision-making capacity for their self-development. It does not "automatically" empower women. There is need for various supportive interventions for social transformation which should be related with commitment and capacity for the realisation of potentiality. Various studies suggested that in respect of poverty alleviation and women empowerment, the government should focus attention on developing the rural economy by activating agriculture and non-agriculture sectors and removing infra-structural inadequacies to widen the self-employment choices for the SHG members. Otherwise, the potential benefits cannot be realised on a sustainable basis.

Significance of the Study

Various studies reveal that SHG helps to reduce rural unemployment, poverty and strengthening rural services in the process of women empowerment. It gives them sufficient scope to develop capabilities, to take part in decision-making, planning, political participation and various rural development activities. The present study will stress on the rationality for devolution of power to the SHGs and to formulate policy keeping the view of social justice and social security. It also helps to reduce the administrative red-tappism and corruption and bring administrative transparency and accountability. The study also helps to reduce the rural-urban gap, population explosion, poverty, family conflict, violence against women etc. to achieve inclusive development. The study has been designed to focus on the contribution of rural women towards the strengthening of grassroots democracy and the extent of participation in governmental policy in rural area.

Profile of the Study Area

My study covers the Morigaon district, an area of 10,83,165 *Bighas* and Lessas (1450.02 sq.kms). The district is bounded by the mighty Brahmaputra on the north, Karbi-Anglong on the south, Morigaon district on the east and Kamrup district on the west. It is situated between 26.15 Degrees North and 26.5 degrees North latitude and between 92 degrees East longitude. The district is situated 78 km from Dispur, the State Capital. In the Morigaon district, where the bulk of the Tiwas are concentrated, they constitute 76.6 per cent of the total tribal population of the district. There are 7 development blocks in Morigaon District, i.e. Moirabari, Mayong, Lahorighat, Dolongghat, Bhurbandha, Kapili and Batadrava. Out of 653 villages in Morigaon District 67 villages in Moirabari, 45 in Dolonghat, 223 in Mayong, 178 in Lahorighat, 21 in Kapili, 117 in Bhurbandha and 4 villages in Batadrava Development Block. For the purpose of this study Kapili Block is selected as it is situated in the flood prone area of the river Brahmaputra. In every year the flood and erosion creates many problems in the life of people of this area.

SHG Status in Assam

The Self-Help Groups have become the focal point of development schemes under the unified poverty alleviation programme, "Swarnajayanti Gram Swarozgar Yojana" (SGSY) for Gram Panchayats and "Swarnajayanti Shahari Swa-Rozgar Yojana" (SJSRY), for Town Panchayats, Municipalities and corporations launched by the Government of India on 1st April, 1999. The scheme was initiated to promote self-employment among the rural poor. This scheme is based under joint liability through forming Self-Help Group. Since 1999, a large number of rural people particularly women have been mobilised into Self-Help Groups in Assam. The SGSY programme emphasised more on Group approach than individual approach. Under this programme, the self-help groups are developed through series of activities and then graded and arrangements are made for their bank loan with subsidy.

Status of Women SHGs in Kapili Block

The status of women SHGs in Kapili Development Block of Morigaon formed and registered under SGSY scheme since April 1, 1999 to March 31, 2012 as follows:

Table: Year-wise Details of Women SHGs

Sl. No.	*Year*	*No. of Women SHG Kapili*
1.	1999-2000	47
2.	2000-2001	72
3.	2001-2002	103
4.	2002-2003	86
5.	2003-2004	72
6.	2004-2005	120
7.	2005-2006	52
8.	2006-2007	61
9.	2007-2008	42
10.	2008-2009	66
11.	2009-2010	75
12.	2010-2011	101
13.	2011-2012	21
	Total	**918 nos.**

Source: Block Development Office, Kapili.

Objectives of the Study

The main objectives are:

(1) To study the socio economic background of the women members of SHGs.
(2) To study the factors to engage women for formation of SHG.
(3) To study the impact of SHG in socio-economic and political empowerment of women.
(4) To find out the problems of empowerment and make suggestions for effective working of SHG.

Hypotheses

1. The poor people are unaware about benefits of SHGs.
2. The potentiality and capabilities of SHGs has not been fully realised by rural women.
3. SHGs do not able to empower women members socially and economically.

Methodology

Both qualitative and quantitative methods will be used in the methodology of this research. The study is based on collection of data and information both from primary and secondary sources. The primary data will be collected through randomly selected sample survey (SHG members) with the help of well structured questionnaires. Secondary data will be obtained from various published and unpublished records, books, journals and information given by the Blocks and District offices. Further, qualitative method will be used through focused group discussions (FGD) for gathering information regarding the general functioning of the groups and feeling of empowerment of the respondents.

The simple random sampling technique is used for selection of respondents of the study. The SHGs are selected from the block which has been registered under SGSY scheme since April 1, 1999 to March 31, 2012. The total number of registered women SHGs in Kapili Block is 918. On the basis of continuity of their functioning, Block Development offices have provided the data of only 327 groups with proper address. Out of 327 SHGs, 10 per cent, that is 32 groups is selected and one member from each SHG is interviewed for the study.

Discussion and Findings of Study

Socio-Economic Background of the Respondents

Age of the Respondents

Age is interrelated of any activities. The young and middle age group people can actively participate in the socio-economic activities. Table 15.1 reveals that majority of the respondents (50%) are belonged to the age group of 35-44 yrs. and 15 per cent belong to the age group of 25-34 yrs, which indicates larger portion of respondents are belong to responsible

Table 15.1: Age group of the Respondents

Age Group	*Total*	
	No.	*%*
Below 15 yr.	Nil	—
15 yr-24 yr	8	25
25 yr-34 yr	5	15.625
35 yr-44 yr	6	50
45 yr- above	3	9.375
Total	**32**	**100**

Source: Field Survey.

and matured women group. Generally, at this age group people are dynamic, enthusiastic and hard working. It is equally important for proper functioning of SHGs through young spirit for creating healthy society.

Religion of the Respondents

Religion also has an influence on the attitudes of members towards their efforts. Analysis shows that Majority (44%) of the respondents belonged to Hindus followed by Muslims (36%) and the remaining 20 per cent other community (Schedule Tribes).

Table 15.2: Religion of the Respondents

Religion/Community		
	No.	*%*
Hindu	14	44
Muslim	12	36
Total	**26**	**80**

Source: Field Survey.

Educational Qualification of the Respondents

Education plays a crucial role in the social and economic development of women. Though, no specific educational qualification has been prescribed for those who wish to enroll themselves in SHG, but, possession of education could help to acquire necessary skills and knowledge for

Table 15.3: Education of the Respondents

Educational qualification	*Total*	
	No.	%
Illiterate	10	31.25
Literate	16	50
Below H.S.L.C.	5	15.625
H.S.	1	3.125
Degree	Nil	—
Other qualification	—	—

Source: Field Survey.

empowerment and economic upliftment. Even, high educational standard of the members have helped them to take up leadership positions and lead the SHGs in a responsible manner. Table 15.3 indicates that majorities (50%) of the respondents having educational qualification literate followed by 31 per cent of the respondents are illiterate and 3 per cent are H.S. and 15 per cent respondents are below H.S.L.C. The situation is due to the poor educational facilities in rural areas, less preference by the family for girls and intention to kept women inside the four walls of house. Therefore, there is need for giving more training to enhance the skills and abilities.

Marital Status of the Respondents

SHG members should preferably be married women and women who remain unmarried could also be included in the SHG. Table 15.4 shows that majorities (81%) of the respondents are married and 19 per cent women are widows. It indicated that majority of the members of the SHGs are responsible housewives. Even marriage has direct influence in women's life on the attitude, commitment and time available for work. Though, the membership is open to all but married women with the responsibility of a family showed more interest to join the SHGs.

Influence in Starting the Group

From Table 15.5 it has revealed that majority of the respondents (37%) starts the SHGs from the influence of family members. There is also 31 per cent of groups are formed from the influence of friends and relatives.

Table 15.4: Marital Status of the Respondents

Marital Status	*Total*	
	No.	*%*
Married	26	81.25
Unmarried	Nil	—
Never married	Nil	—
Widow	6	18.75
Separated	Nil	—
Others	32	100

Source: Field Survey.

Table 15.5: Influencing Agents in Starting SHGs

Influenced by	*Total*	
	No.	*%*
Bank	2	6.25
NGO	Nil	–
Self	8	25
Family members	12	37.5
Friends/Relatives	10	31.25
Total	**32**	**100**

Source: Field Survey.

There are no NGO influencing in the formation of groups. Only 6 per cent groups are formed by the influence of bank or governmental institutions. Though, NGOs and Governmental institutions are played an important influencing role in the formation of groups, but it is not reflected in this study area.

Economic Empowerment of Women

Economic empowerment is recognised as an important goal of the SHGs. Economic empowerment may be defined where the SHG members are able to fulfil their basic needs through reasonable opportunities for income generation and to own assets through their activity. On the other hand economic aspects are important in empowerment, as it significantly influence on social and political aspects of people. The economic empowerment of women is very important not only for reducing the disproportionate levels of poverty among women, but also as an important step towards raising household income and encouraging economic development in countries as a whole. To study the economic empowerment of the respondents, the study concentrated on the occupation, monthly income and activities performed by the respondents after joining the SHGs.

Activity Performed by SHGs

From Table 15.6 it is clear that 31 per cent of the members of SHGs have not performed any activity whereas 28 per cent respondent performed the activity of animal husbandry like goat, cow and piggery, 12 per cent respondents performed the activity of food processing and 18 per cent respondents related with the activity of bamboo products. Only 6 per cent respondents performed activities like pickle-making and production of goods from jute. It has clear from the study that all the respondents expect more training programmes and government support for effective functioning of SHGs and their empowerment.

Table 15.6: Activity Performed by SHGs

Activity performed by SHGs	*Total*	
	No.	%
No activity	10	31.25
Bamboo products	6	18.75
Pickle-making	2	6.25
Animal Husbandry	9	28.125
Food processing	4	12.5
Jute production	1	3.125

Source: Field Survey.

Household Income, Saving Habits and Expenditure

To access the economic condition of the respondent questionnaire was prepared to know the household income, saving habits and expenditure of respondents has increased or not. From the above Table 15.7 it has found that all the respondent's family income and saving habits has increased after joining the groups. The reason is that the SHG members have been economically benefited by joining the group because of saving habits and taking up income generating activities. It has also reveals that 62 per cent of the respondents reported that there is increasing in the expenditure level in family which indicates the change of standard of

Table 15.7: Household Income, Saving Habits and Expenditure

Statements		*Total*	
		No.	%
Household income	Increased	32	100
	Remained same	Nil	—
	Decrease	—	—
Saving habits	Increased	32	100
	Remained same	Nil	—
	Decrease	—	—
Family expenditure	Increased	20	62.5
	Remained same	12	37.5
	Decrease	Nil	—

Source: Field Survey.

living in rural area. It also reveals that 38 per cent respondent's family expenditure remained same because they are mainly preferred on savings.

Monthly Income of the Respondent Family

Income is a major determinant to study the respondent's living standard and their empowerment. The table below shows that majority 31 per cent of the respondents had monthly income of between Rs.1500-2000. It is due to their participation in income generating activities. This implies after becoming the member of SHGs monthly income of their family is increased because of saving habits and engaging in income generating activities.

Table 15.8: Monthly Income of the Family

Monthly income of the family	*Total*	
	No.	*%*
< 500	Nil	—
500 – 1000	4	12.5
1001 – 1500	9	28.125
1501 – 2000	10	31.25
2001 – 3000	6	18.75
3001 – 4000	3	9.375
More than 4000	**Nil**	—

Source: Field Survey.

Bank Account/Post-Office Account

From the below table it has revealed that majorities (90%) of the respondents did not have any bank or post-office account before the joining of group. It has also revealed that after the joining the group there is improvement in bank or post-office account. Fifty three per cent respondents having bank account whereas 45 per cent said that they have no bank account. It is because the account of the group is opened only in the name of president and secretary. The study indicates that despite the large rural banking network majority of rural population have no access to bank because of problems like distance, communication system etc. Actually in practice, banks are established only in urban area.

Table 15.9: Bank Account/Post-Office Account

Having Bank account or Post-Office account.		*Total*	
		No.	*%*
Before	Yes	3	9.375
	No	29	90.625
	Total	**32**	**100**
After	Yes	17	53.125
	No	15	46.875
	Total	**32**	**100**

Source: Field Survey.

The study reveals that SHGs enhanced the credit of respondents but they are not getting recognition of their contribution by their families as 44 per cent respondents said that their contribution is not recognised by their family. Even eighty per cent respondents are not able to spent money according to their own discretion. Seventy four per cent respondents are not financially independent and they are depended on others and 68 per cent respondents are not free to go local markets for marketing commodity. From the study it has revealed some improvements in the ability in domestic financial decision-making process whereas 66 per cent respondent viewed that the increase the ability in domestic financial decision-making process and 56 per cent respondent viewed that they are participate in decision-making about family budget (Table 15.10).

Social and Personal Empowerment of Women

The positive outcome of the respondents revealed that SHGs helps to

Table 15.10: Economic Empowerment of Respondents

Statements	*Total*	*Yes*	*No*
Enhancement of credit	%	—	—
Recognition of women's economic contribution	No	18	14
	%	56	44
Spend money according to own discretion	No	6	26
	%	20	80
Free from financial dependency on others	No	9	23
	%	26	74
Bargaining power is increased	No	10	22
	%	32	68
Free to go local market for marketing any commodity	No	10	22
	%	32	68
Increase the ability in domestic financial decision-making process	No	11	21
	%	34	66
Participate in decision-making about the family budget	No	16	16
	%	50	50

Source: Field Survey.

increase the self-confidence. Majority of the respondents (80%) viewed that SHGs helps to increases the communication capacity and 66 per cent respondents claimed that enhancement of capacity in involving decision-making and taking process. The 66 per cent respondents are feel that they are free to move abroad. The study also revealed that 44 per cent respondents are aware and getting ability to access health care system. With regard to family planning 34 per cent respondents know about family planning which is totally unknown before the joining of SHG and this has possible through discussion within the group members. It also reveals that the impact of SHGs increase the feelings of self-esteem/ self-reliance among respondent (68%) and (78%) respondents said that after enrolled in the SHGs decreases the family conflict/domestic violence. There is also increasing in household decision-making process whereas 66 per cent respondent said that they are participates in household decision-making process (Table 15.11).

Political Empowerment

Besides, social and economic empowerment, political aspects also looked by the present study. The indicators like awareness on government scheme, legal process, participation in political activity, membership in local bodies, knowledge of political system, the right to vote, participation in decision-making process have been taken for political empowerment.

Table 15.11: Social empowerment of women

Statements	*Total*	*Yes*	*No*
Increase in self-confidence	No	21	11
	%	66	34
Aware and getting ability to access health care system	No	14	18
	%	44	56
Increase in social status	No	16	16
	%	50	50
Family planning	No	11	21
	%	34	66
Participation in household decision-making process	No	21	11
	%	66	34
Taking decision independently	No	24	8
	%	74	26
Feelings of self-esteem/self-reliance	No	22	10
	%	68	32
Decreases the family conflict/domestic violence	No	24	8
	%	74	26
Increase the communication capacity	No	26	6
	%	80	20
Enhancement of capacity involving in decision-making/taking	No	21	11
	%	66	34
Free to move abroad	No	21	26
	%	66	80

Source: Field Survey.

Table 15.12: Political Empowerment

Statements	*Total*	*Yes*	*No*
Awareness on government schemes	32	23	9
Taking independent decision on vote	32	24	8
Involving public/governmental activities	32	21	11
Participation in political process	32	11	21
Participating in the activities of Panchayati Raj institution	32	6	26
Participation in gaon sabha	32	9	23
Increases awareness in legal and political matters	32	8	24
Participation in decision-making process	32	12	20

Source: Field Survey.

The study reveals that majority (72%) of respondents are aware about Governmental programmes and policies. The positive outcome of the respondents after the joining of SHGs they are aware about legal and political matters. It helps to increase the voting behaviour whereas 75 per cent respondents take an independent decision about their right to vote at the time of election. The study reveals that majority of the respondents not participate in the Panchayati Raj activities, gaon sabha and political decision-making process and stressed on the importance of involving SHG members in the activities of panchayats for strengthening the process of grassroots democracy. They are very optimistic for engaging in the panchayats activities as they are kept legging behind by the male members. They give their opinion about the necessities of government steps for involvement of SHG for proper implementation of government policy in grassroots level, which will help to reduce corruption and proper implementation of government policies.

Problems and Challenges: From the study following challenges can be mentioned in the empowerment of women:

(1) Manipulation of Below Poverty Line List with the help of officials sidelines the real beneficiaries and people Above Poverty Line (APL) gets benefit.
(2) Indifferent attitude of some government officials de-motivate the proper functioning of groups.
(3) Lack of proper management of groups for empowering women.
(4) Some groups are form only with the expectation of subsidy and once they get the benefits of subsidy, members are not interested for utilising the credit properly. Because of prevailing rumour in society that if the groups once get the loan; they will not avail the loan facility in future.
(5) Absence of NGOs to motivate the rural people for the formation of groups and their empowerment.
(6) SHG concept is not fully covered actual members especially those are Below Poverty Line in the villages.
(7) Irregularity in savings and group meeting.

Positive outcome of women SHGs: In the study it has found the following positive outcome of women SHGs in the study area:

(1) Women have started taking joint decisions with their husbands. Previously there was no involvement of women at all.
(2) Awareness about child health has increased among the members of the groups.
(3) Awareness about various government programmes.
(4) Changed attitude and increased confidence for better living.
(5) Greater participation in family decision-making.
(6) Improved family income.

(7) Better access to education of their children.
(8) Access financial support to strengthen their husband's occupation.
(9) Awareness about family health, nutrition etc.
(10) Awareness about legal marriage age, child marriage and other social issues.
(11) Change in behaviour, attitude and communication skills.

Suggestions for Better Functioning of SHGs and Empowerment of Women

(1) Provide subsidy loan for women SHGs for innovative projects.
(2) Provide self-employment loan for individual SHG members.
(3) Providing marketing facilities to the SHG products and it should be arranged by the Government.
(4) Formed SHG federation village-wise, panchayats-wise and block-wise for devolution some power for taking step in social problems and better execution government policies.
(5) Provide self-employment training to the rural people by government.
(6) Conducive atmosphere should be established among government, NGOs and SHGs.
(7) Ensure participation of women SHG member under the auspicious of government in social issues and community works.
(8) Ensure the groups only formed by Below Poverty Line and provide loan under close supervision of Governmental agency.

NOTES

1. Sabhlok, G. Smita. Development and Women: The role of trust in Self-Help Groups, *Indian Journal of Gender Studies*, Sage Publications, Los Angeles, London, New Delhi, Singapore, Washington DC, 18 (2), 2011. pp. 241-242.
2. Desai, Manisha, Hope in Hard Times: Women's Empowerment and Human Development, United Nations Development Programme, *Human Development Reports*, Research Paper 2010/14, July 2010, p. 4.
3. Hur Mann Hyung, Empowerment in terms of Theoretical Perspectives: Exploring a Typology of the Process and Components across Disciplines, *Journal of Community Psychology, Wiley Inter Science* (www.interscience.wiley.com).Vol. 34, No. 5, 2006. pp. 523–540,
4. Harvey, David (2005). *A Brief History of Neo Liberalism*, Oxford University Press.

5. Rawls John, A. (1971). *Theory of Justice*, Revised Edition, Harvard University Press, Cambridge.
6. Oxaal, Z. and Baden, S., 1997. Gender and Empowerment: Definitions, Approaches and Implications for Policy Report no. 40, Briefing prepared for the Swedish International Development Cooperation Agency (SIDCA), Institute of Development Studies, UK, 1997.
7. Rowlands Jo. (1996). "Empowerment examined" Introduced by Mary, B. Anderson, *Development and Social Diversity*, Oxfam (UK and Ireland), pp. 86-91.
8. Banu Zenab, 2001, *Tribal Women Empowerment and Gender Issues*, Kanishka Publishers, Distributors, New Delhi, p. 17.
9. Sen, A.K. (1999). *Development as Freedom*, Knopf Press, New York.
10. *Ibid.*
11. Narayan, D. (2002). *Empowerment and Poverty Reduction: A Sourcebook*, PREM, World Bank, Washington.
12. Narayan, D., Patel, R., Schafft, K., Rademacher, A., Koch-Schulte, S., 2000. *Voices of the Poor, Can Anyone Hear Us?* Oxford University Press, World Bank.
13. Anand S. Jaya, "Self-Help Groups in Empowering Women: Case Study of Selected SHGs and NHGs", Kerala Research Programme on Local Level Development, Centre for Development Studies, Discussion Paper No. 38, 2002.
14. Katz, H. Alfred (1981). "Self-help and Mutual Aid: An Emerging Social Movement?", *Annual Review of Sociology*, Vol. 7.
15. Fernandez P. Aloysius, *History and Spread of the Self-help Affinity Group Movement in India*, The Asia and the Pacific Division, IFAD, 2007.
16. Hasenfeld Yeheskel and Gidron Benjamin, "Self-Help Groups and Human Service Organisations: An Interorganisational Perspective", The University of Chicago Press, *The Social Service Review*, Vol. 67, No. 2 (June, 1993), pp. 217-236.

REFERENCES

Alsop Ruth and Heinsohn Nina, Measuring Empowerment in Practice: Structuring Analysis and Framing Indicators, World Bank Policy Research Working Paper 3510, February 2005.

Alsop, R., Bertelsen, M. and Holland, J. (2006) *Empowerment in Practice: From Analysis to Implementation*, Washington, DC: World Bank.

Banu, Zenab (2001). *Tribal Women Empowerment and Gender Issues*, Kanishka Publishers & Distributors, New Delhi.

Batliwala, Srilatha (2011). Feminist Leadership for Social Transformation Clearing the Conceptual Cloud, CREA.

Bhandari, Ramesh (2010). *Entrepreneurship and Women Empowerment*, Alfa Publications, New Delhi.

Devi, Lakshmi (1998). *Women Employment and Societal Improvement*, Anmol Publications, New Delhi.

Fernandez, P. Aloysius (2007). *History and Spread of the Self-Help Affinity Group Movement in India*, The Asia and the Pacific Division, IFAD.

Jayasheela, H. Shriprasad and P.T. Dinesha (2009). *Microfinance in India a Tool for Women Empowerment*, Serials Publications, New Delhi.

Kabeer Naila, *Gender Equality and Women's Empowerment: A Critical Analysis of the Third Millennium Development Goal, Gender and Development*, Vol. 13, No. 1, Taylor & Francis Ltd. on behalf of Oxfam GB, Millennium Development Goals (March, 2005), pp. 13-24.

Kabeer Naila (2001). *Gender Mainstreaming in Poverty Eradication and the Millennium Development Goals: A Handbook for Policy-Makers and Other Stakeholders*, International Development Research Centre.

Kabeer, Naila, Is Microfinance a 'magic bullet' for women's empowerment? Analysis of findings from South Asia, *Economic and Political Weekly*, Vol. 40, No. 44/45, October 29–November 4, 2005.

Kabeer, Naila. The Conditions and Consequences of Choice: Reflections on the Measurement of Women's Empowerment, United Nations Research Institute for Social Development, Discussion Paper No. 108, August 1999.

Manga, B.V.L.A. (2011). *Empowering Rural Women through Self-Help Group*, Akanksha Publishing House, New Delhi.

Mayoux, Linda. Women's Empowerment through Sustainable Micro-finance: Rethinking best Practice, Discussion draft, September 2005.

Meenai Zubair (2003). *Rural Women: An Approach to Empowering Women through Credit-Based Self-Help Groups*, Aakar Books. New Delhi.

Narayan, D. (2002). *Empowerment and Poverty Reduction: A Sourcebook, Poverty Reduction and Economic Management (PREM)*, World Bank, Washington.

Suguna B. (2006). *Empowerment of Rural Women through Self-Help Groups*, Discovery Publishing House, New Delhi.

Usha Pitta (2010). *Empowerment of Women and Self-Help Groups*, Sonali Publications, New Delhi.

Vasanthakumari, P. (2011). *Study on Performance of Self-Help Groups in India*, Madhav Books, Gurgaon, Haryana.

16

Leadership Pattern in LAMPS in Karbi Anglong District of Assam

Beena Rongpipi and *Uttambir Basumatary*

Introduction

A co-operative society is a democratic and voluntary organisation of the people formed with the object achieving some economic goals. If the group of people by whom the society is formed are to achieved their objective, some of them will have to take initiative, prepare plan and scheme, make proposal, take responsibilities, inspire the group to work and motivate them for active participation. These are the persons thus entrusted to guide the activities of the co-operation become co-operation leaders. In the words D.G. Karve, "Leadership consists in a capacity to shoulder responsibility and carry it out. Even the mere membership of a co-operative body involves a deliberate action, which has attendant responsibility organising co-operative societies of different sort and running them successfully involves leadership of the higher order", G.S. Kamat defines "Leadership" as "interpersonal influence, exercised in situation and diverted through the communication process towards attainment of specified goals." Leadership is a trait which reflects through behaviourial pattern in human beings. Therefore, leadership is a process of influencing the activities of individual or group for goal achievement in a given situation. As such leadership is an important factor for making an organisation successfully since an organisation is basically deliberate creation of human beings for certain specified objectives and the activities of its members need to be directed in a certain way. The co-operative movement is a movement of the people, by the people and for the people. It is, therefore, the co-operative has important role to play in the socio-economic development of a society. Hence, the responsibility of co-operative leadership has increased manifold with the diversification of activities of co-operative. The enlightened and dedicated leadership has an important role to play in the success of the movement. Similarly, a co-operative organisation is a democratic unit. Policy-making in co-operative is a function of leaders chosen or elected with the consent of at least majority of members of the co-operative. It may, therefore, be considered that leadership in co-operative is an element that makes democracy dynamic. Thus, the role guide the society in a manner which enables it to grow from strength to strength for the solution of economic problem on a voluntary, universal, democratic and non-profit-making basic, giving the members not only economic satisfaction but also a feeling of spiritual happiness. In co-operatives, a leader is to play the role of friend, philosopher, and guide to the members to set up the organisation, to undertake the business and conduct it through proper decision-making process. Further, the co-operative leader must have clear-understanding of the real nature of co-operation, its principles and philosophy. Equally important is the knowledge about business process, strategy formulation and implementation as well as management of co-operative organisation.

There are three types of co-operative leaders, *viz.* (i) management leaders, (ii) official leaders, and (iii) membership or non-official leaders. The management leaders are the professional men for day-to-day management of the affairs of the co-operatives. Official leaders include the extension workers and the Government official who are engaged in the administration of Co-operative Societies Acts and in the organisation, administration and supervision of co-operatives. The membership or non-official leaders include initiators and promoters of co-operatives and Directors elected by the members. In the proper function and success of co-operatives, the contribution of membership or non-official leaders is of great significance. In the first place, such leaders are instrument for articulating the aspirations and views of general body members. Secondly, it is the co-operative leaders who are mainly responsible for preventing co-operative from degeneration into purely bureaucratic organisation controlled by their employees. The co-operative movement in the developing countries were initiated and fostered by governments, i.e. by the colonial rulers to ameliorate the conditions of the rural people. Such leadership from Government in the early stage was inevitable in view of the widespread poverty and low education levels of the people. Further during the colonial regime, the scope for the emergence of democratic leadership was less. There was a special reason for this. The need to maintain an alien regime necessary led to discouragement of any large upsurge of spontaneous among governed societies as this lead eventually to agitation for change in the colonial regime. So, the government officers supplied, in the main, leadership in the co-operative organisations. Moreover, illiteracy among the people, formalism of government administration, the dominance of foreign officials and of foreign language made the emergence of genuine co-operative leadership at the basic level very difficult. However, with the independence, socio-economic spheres underwent a radical change. So, did the pattern of co-operative leadership. With the adoption of democratic constitution adult suffrage, the co-operatives had come to be seen by many as training places for development socio-political leadership from the grassroots. Business of the radical changes mentioned above, the constraints for the development of the co-operative movement has been removed by and large and hence there is reason today as to why section of non-officials should keep away from co-operative activity. Leadership has become a democratic function which. According to circumstance may be exercised by person with no special gift or training for it. In a democracy, leadership is not expected to be imposed from above or from outside. In co-operation it had to spring from among the members themselves. In the initial periods after post-independence, the pattern of co-operative in rural areas in India was not very encouraging. A study of the structure of co-operative leadership in rural areas in India has documented the following conclusion:

(i) Majority of the presidents of co-operatives are big landlords.
(ii) All presidents belong to the dominant castes.
(iii) Election of presidents were unanimous and ritualistic.
(iv) Most of the office-bearers had political affiliations.

However, under changing circumstance and realisation for convicted leadership, it has facilitated the emergence of democratic leadership in the co-operative by reducing the role of traditional factors like sex, age, cast, religion, ownership of land, income and occupation in the society on the one hand and giving rise to other competitive factors like education, political involvement participation in the community organisation for determining co-operative leadership on the other. A study of the socio-economic background educational attainment, political background and participation in communication of leaders is expected to reveal the changing pattern of co-operative leadership in rural area. The social background which in their turn determine the success of co-operative movement. In this chapter, an attempt has been made to find out the social background of Leadership of the Large Seized Multipurpose Co-operative Societies (LAMPS) in Assam.

In Assam, in accordance with the provisions of the existing bye laws of the LAMPS, the management structure consists of General Assembly, Managing Committee and paid employees. The General Assembly is formed consisting of one member of each family of the area of operation of a LAMPS. The members of the managing committee are elected by the General Assembly and they exercise their powers and manage the society on behalf of the members of the General Assembly. The paid employees execute the policies taken by the Committee. As per the byelaw, the Managing Committee of the LAMPS consist of eight elected members including the Chairman and the Vice-chairman, one appointed Secretary and four nominated members. In all, the number of members comes to thirteen. Although, according to same, leaders include all the thirteen members, but for the purpose of study, only the eight elected representatives of the Managing Committee of the LAMPS are included in the category of leaders. The term of office of the above leaders is three years and nominated members term depends on their respective nominating authorities. In the hill district of Karbi Anglong of Assam apart from other types of co-operative societies LAMPS with the object of supplying credit needs and agricultural inputs of the rural hill people and marketing their surplus produces and undertake distribution of essential and other consumer commodities in the hill areas. The co-operative has important role to play in the socio-economic development of a society of the rural people of the district.

Objectives of the Study

1. To examine the socio-economic characteristics of the leaders of the LAMPS.
2. To find out the type of leadership that is emerging in the LAMPS.

Methodology

Nature: The Study Involves Both Descriptive and Analytical in Nature

Data used: The study is based on both primary and secondary data. There are 52 LAMPS societies covering 3008 villages in the hill districts of Assam apart from other types of co-operative societies. For the study data has been collected 32 leaders of 4 LAMPS belonging to the three

Sub-Divisions of the Karbi Anglong district. Two from Diphu Sub-division, i.e. Dokmoka LAMPS and Lumbajong LAMPS, one from Bokajani, i.e. Bokajan LAMPS and one from Hamren Sub-division, i.e. Baithalangso LAMPS have been selected.

Data collection: The selected LAMPS were personally interviewed. For this study, five interview schedules were prepared and employed to general members, office-bearers and managing committee members of the selected LAMPS. The secondary data were collected from various periodicals, journals, books and websites.

Findings of the Study

Below is the examination of social background of all elected 32 leaders of 4 LAMPS belonging to the 3 sub-divisions of the Karbi Anglong district. All those leaders were personally interviewed during 2006-07 co-operative years.

Sex Composition

Leadership has been the monopoly of the males in tradition bound rural India. It is only after the adoption of democratic Constitution based upon adult suffrage that leadership avenues have been opened for both male and female in the rural areas. Though no special provision is made for the election of women member to the Managing Committee/Committees of the LAMPS by the Assam Co-operative Societies Act, 1949 (as amended up to date) or by the Model Byelaws for LAMPS, yet the door is open for both the sexes. However, the findings of the study show that all the thirty-two (32) leaders of the four (4) LAMPS studied in three sub-divisions of Karbi Anglong district are males.

Thus, it appears that even after five decades of democratic rules which provides equal opportunities for leadership to both sexes, the females have not succeeded in utilising this opportunity owing to a number of social handicaps.

Age Composition

Here age has been classified into five categories, i.e. 18 to 20, 21 to 30, 31 to 40, 41 to 50 and 51 and above. Though, it has previlage of the elders traditionally to occupy important positions in the village; this position is not prevalent among the tribal communities of hill district because of two reasons. Firstly, majority of elders are illiterate and hence, they are hesitant to hold position in any formal organisations. They prefer to hold positions in ritual works and in an informal environment. As a result, positions in a formal organisation are mostly occupied by a comparatively younger generation who are also happened to be first generation education learner as is obivious from Table 16.1, which gives the distribution of leaders by age.

Table 16.1: Distribution of Leaders by Age

Age Group	*Sub-Divisions*			*District Total*
	Diphu	*Bokajan*	*Hamren*	
18 – 20	—	—	—	—
21 – 30	3	—	—	3
31 – 40	7	1	2	10
41 – 50	6	6	5	17
51 & above	—	1	1	2

Sources: Field Survey.

It is revealed that maximum number (17) of leaders is found in the age group of 41–50 which is followed by upper age group of 31–40 (10). Another significant findings made that leaders of age group of 41 and above are majority non-tribals whereas leaders below the age of 40 are tribals. Another reason for not too many leaders belonging to the highest age group of 51 and above is lower average like expectancy in rural area, specially among the hills tribes, than that of urban people. It is also observed that 3 per cent leaders of age group 21–30 is an indication that younger generation is taking interest in sharing leadership of LAMPS.

Religion and Caste Composition

Religion has been classified into four categories, viz. Hinduism, Islam, Christianity and 'others', which include Buddhism etc. It has been found that out of 32 leaders studied as many as 25 are Hindus, 5 Christians and 2 leaders belong to Islam religion. There is no leader belong to Buddhism religion. This is more or less reflection of demographic composition (religion-wise) of the villager/area under the surveyed LAMPS.

Caste is seen playing a vital role in determining the leadership pattern in village India. Leadership in traditional village institutions like Panchayats, local authorities, co-operatives in generally found in the hands of upper caste. But due to introduction of statutory institutions and provisions for reservation of seats for women, Scheduled Castes, Scheduled Tribes; the composition of leadership has changed in rural institutions. Moreover, among the tribal communities, support to their respective clan and clan dominance is found prevalent rather than upper caste dominance. Further, the Model Byelaws of LAMPS has clear guidelines regarding reservation of sears. As the LAMPS is intended for tribal areas, the majority of leaders belong to tribal communities.

Analysis of response on identity of caste of LAMPS leaders, it is found that out of 32 leaders 29 belong to tribal communities. Of the 29 tribal leaders, 28 from Karbi tribes followed by 1 Dimasa Kacharies and 3 are general. The majority from Karbi tribes (48) are obvious as the Karbi population is a major hill tribe in the state of Assam and is mostly located in Karbi Anglong district, which is largest tribal population composition of the district in general and 4 LAMPS surveyed in particular.

Marital Status

Table 16.2 gives the marital status of the LAMPS leaders.

Table 16.2: Distribution of the LAMPS Leaders by Marital Status

Marital Stutus	*Sub-Divisions*			*District Total*
	Diphu	*Bokajan*	*Hamren*	
Married	14	8	8	30
Unmarried	2	—	—	2
Divorced	—	—	—	—
Widower	—	—	—	—

Sources: Field Survey.

Table 16.2 reveals that an overwhelming number of leaders, 30 out of 32, are married. Early marriage among rural people is a common practice, especially amount the tribal population. Even 5 out of 13 in the age group of 21–30 are found married. Two leaders found unmarried; of which belong to the age group of 21-30. No widower is found among the leaders and no divorced leader was found. Thus, it appears that people generally prefer to married people as their leaders.

Family Profile (Type, Size, Status)

Type of family is another important variable which can be classified into 'nuclear' and 'joint' families and the later by definition, is larger in size than the former. It is found from analysis of responses, that majority of LAMPS leaders, 15 out of 32, belong to nuclear family. It is also observed that families residing within town area or near the periphery of town area are used to adopt nuclear family type than that families residing in remote village areas. This may be attributed to the fact the leaders/members of nuclear families are engaged in non-agricultural activities, which require less manpower and exposure to modern amenities. Leaders from remote villages prefer joint family type as they are mostly engaged in agricultural activities, which require more persons to work in the farm. However, the tendency to nuclear family system from joint family is observed due to growth of population and fragmentation of agricultural land holding.

The size of the family is also play a role on the emergence of leadership. The larger the size of family is expected to spare an adult member to take the responsibilities of a leader in the areas of social and economic development of the community. Table 16.3 provides the family profile of leaders.

Analysis of Table 16.3 reveals that majority of leaders, 16 out of 32, come from families having 1–5 members. Sixteen leaders from family having 6–10 members and no leaders from having family members 10 and above. Therefore, it appears that family having small size families and that of family having moderately large number of members are same.

Table 16.3: Distribution of Leaders by Type, Size and Status of Family

Profile (family)	*Sub-Divisions*			*District Total*
	Diphu	*Bokajan*	*Hamren*	
Type of Family :				
Nuclear	7	2	6	15
Joint	9	6	2	16
Size of Family :				
1 – 5 Nos.	8	6	2	16
6 – 10 Nos.	8	2	6	16
10 & above Nos.	–	–	–	–
Status in Family :				
Head	10	7	7	24
Non-Head	6	1	1	8

Sources: Field Survey.

Small size families cannot expect to spare an adult member to take the responsibilities of a leader while very large family members also act as disincentive for leadership as these families reside in remote villages and engaged in family farming activities.

Regarding the status of leaders in the family, leaders have been classified as Head or Non-Head of the families concerned. Table 16.3 also reveals that 24 out of 32 leaders are heads of their respective families. Since the head manages the affairs of the families and take all decisions regarding the families, they stand better chance of becoming leaders. Non-Heads have to abide by the decisions of the heads and hence their chances of becoming leaders grow less. However, 8 leaders emerged, though Non-Heads in their families, because of non-participation of Heads on such matters.

Income

It is seen that people with considerable wealth and high income level were generally respected by the villagers in rural India. Even, because of their better economic conditions they could get hold leadership positions in various social and economic organisations at rural areas. It is, therefore, pertinent to examine the role of income level on the emergence of LAMPS leaders has played Table 16.4 presents the distribution of leaders by income groups.

Table 16.4: Distribution of Leaders by Income Group

(Per annum)

Income Group Rs. P.A.	*Sub-Divisions*			*District Total*
	Diphu	*Bokajan*	*Hamren*	
0 – 10,000	—	1	—	1
10,001 – 20,000	—	3	—	3
20,001 – 30,000	4	3	—	7
30,001 – 40,000	4	1	—	5
40,001 – 50,000	—	—	—	—
50,001 & above	8	—	8	16

Sources: Field Survey.

An analysis of the above Table 16.4 shows that majority of leaders, 16 out of 32, belong to the income group of Rs. 50,001 and above followed by 7 in the income of Rs. 20001–30000 and 5 leaders in the group of Rs. 30001–40000. It is also evident from the table a total 4 leaders belong to category of below poverty line (BPL has been identified considering

DRDA rating having an annual income of Rs.1900 or less). Of course, a majority of LAMPS leaders hails from the better economic condition. However, one fact has observed that people even belonging to below poverty line could get represented to the LAMPS managing committee countering the traditional belief that better economic wealth plays an important role in the election of leaders. This trend likely to attribute for domocratisation of rural level institutions like LAMPS.

Occupation

Occupation is also an important factor in determining the LAMPS leadership because people of those occupations can afford to be leaders who get leisure time and also ordinarily stay in the rural areas. Table 16.5 presents the distribution of leaders by their occupations. This also presents the landholding pattern of those leaders whose occupations are agricultural activities.

Table 16.5: Distribution of Leaders by their Occupation and Landholding

Items	*Sub-Divisions*			*District Total*
	Diphu	*Bokajan*	*Hamren*	
(A) Occupation :				
(i) Cultivators	6	1	3	10
(ii) Labours	–	–	–	–
(iii) Livestock Fishery etc.	–	–	–	–
(iv) Cottage Industry	–	–	–	–
(v) Construction	10	2	3	15
(vi) Trade & Commerce	–	3	–	3
(vii) Other Service	–	2	2	4
(viii) Non-workers	–	–	–	–
(B) Landholding : (Owned in *Bighas*)				
(i) Landless	–	–	–	–
(ii) Marginal Farmers	–	1	–	1
(iii) Small Farmers	–	2	–	2
(iv) Semi-medium Farmers	–	1	8	9
(v) Medium Farmers	16	1	–	17
(vi) Large Farmer	–	3	–	3

Sources: Field Survey.

It is evident from Table 16.5 that majority number of leaders 15 belong to occupation group of construction. Ten belong to 'trade and commerce', 4 to 'other services' etc. However, occupation stated by leaders were prime occupations. Apart from prime occupations, they also had engagement in other activities, but casually and spent very little time therein. By and large this is reflective of the occupational distribution of the general population. The cultivation pattern is characterised by monocropping, which leaves sufficient time to them for doing other works. This explains why the majority of leaders from the occupation group of cultivation could shoulder the responsibilities of leaders. As to landholding pattern, for the purpose of study, leaders are classified into 6 categories according to the size of their landholding, *viz.* (i) landless—having no cultivable land; (ii) marginal farmers—having below 1 hectare; (iii) small farmers—with landholding between 1 and 2 hectares; (iv) semi-medium farmers—with landholding between 2 and 4 hectares; (v) medium farmers—with landholding between 4 and 10 hectares; and (vi) large farmers—with landholding 10 hectares and above. In the district of Karbi Anglong, a different land tenure system is prevalent where the village head is the custodian of the village land under the overall control of the District Autonomous Council. A household is free to select a suitable plot out of village land for its annual jhumming with the consent of village head but devoid of any ownership right on that plot except for the period of cultivation. Flat lands suitable for wet-cultivation or other permanent cultivation are given in settlement to individual villagers on an annual/periodic lease at a prescribed rate. The leaseholder is also devoid of any right of inheritance and transfer without the prior approval of the Karbi Anglong Autonomous Council 10 under the study, landholding for permanent cultivation given in settlement are considered. Lands under shifting cultivation are not covered as such lands are given for one cultivation period. Table 16.5 shows the maximum leaders numbering 17 belonging to medium farmers group, followed by 9 leaders of semi-medium farmers groups, 3 leaders belonging to large farmers, and 2 leaders belonging to small farmers group and 1 belonging to marginal farmers. As a whole, taking marginal and small farmers, they constitute 3 of leaders, while semi-medium, medium and large farmers constitute 29 leaders. Thus, it appears that holding of lands does play a significant role in determining leadership of LAMPS. Although, the number of leaders does not increase with an increase in the size of operational holding, the maximum numbers of leaders do possess some land. The reason for poor representation from marginal and small farmers categories may be that there are very few farmers on these two sizes holdings among the hill tribes where jhumming cultivation on community basis still in practice and land in settlement is newly developed phenomenon among the tribe.

Educational Status

Table 16.6 shows the Educational Status of LAMPS Leaders.

Table 16.6: Distribution of LAMPS Leaders by Educational Status

Educational Status	*Sub-Divisions*			*District Total*
	Diphu	*Bokajan*	*Hamren*	
Illiterate	—	—	—	—
Up to Primary level	5	—	—	5
Up to School level (Under Matric)	10	1	6	17
Up to College level (Under Graduate)	1	5	2	8
Above graduate level	—	2	—	2

Sources: Field Survey.

Table 16.6 reveals that all the LAMPS leasers are literate. A maximum number of the leaders 17 out of 32 are found to have education up to school level, i.e. below matric. Eight of leaders are found to have education up to college level (under Graduate), 5 of leaders are found to have education up to primary level and 2 of leaders college above Graduate level. Thus, the education seems to be an important criterion in determining LAMPS leadership. As the LAMPS leaders are to follow a number of official procedures for managing the affairs of society, communication with departmental officials and general members as well as popularisation of co-operative movement, the education of leaders is only to be expected. At the same time a high level of educational attainment cannot be expected from them, as for the general tendency to move out for employment in urban areas.

Political Background

Table 16.7 shows the political background of LAMPS leaders.

It is seen from Table 16.7 that 29 out of 32 leaders had contested LAMPS elections in the past, and 3 leaders had contested KAAC elections in past. Assembly elections earlier. It is also clear that 32 leaders have been found to have political background. Thus, it seems that political background of person has a role in the determination of LAMPS leaders.

Participation in Community Organisation

Participation in community organisation is gaining importance in recent

Table 16.7: Distribution of LAMPS Leaders by Political Background

Election contested earlier	*Sub-Divisions*			*District Total*
	Diphu	*Bokajan*	*Hamren*	
LAMPS election	15	7	7	29
Karbi Anglong Autonomous Council (KAAC) election	1	1	1	3
Assembly Election	—	—	—	—
Parliamentary Election	—	—	—	—
Never Contested	—	—	—	—

Sources: Field Survey.

year as determining factors of rural leadership. A villager cannot be a leader in the true sense of the term unless he takes interest in public activities and tries to channelise his influence through some organisation. An attempt has been made to find out the level of participation of LAMPS leaders in organisations connected with various development activities such as education, culture, religion, youth welfare, sports etc.

Table 16.8 presents leaders participation in various community organisations.

Table 16.8: Distribution of Leaders by Participation in Community organisation

Community Organisation(s)	*Sub-Divisions*			*District Total*
	Diphu	*Bokajan*	*Hamren*	
(a) Educational Organisation	4	2	—	6
(b) Cultural Organisation	10	3	1	14
(c) Religious Organisation	12	2	1	15
(d) Trade Union Organisation	7	1	—	8
(e) Youth Club	10	8	—	18
(f) Sports Club	10	8	2	20
(g) Non-participant	1	—	4	5

Sources: Field Survey.

An analysis of Table 16.8 shows that as many as 20 leaders have been associated in some form of sports club organisation. Some of them are found to be associated in number of such organisations. However, 5 leaders have shown their non-participation in any community organisation. Majority of leaders are found to be associated with Cultural and Religious organisation. Generally, the tribal community are found of celebration and their festivals in a colourful and in a District manner preserving their own tradition and customs wherein participation of every member of the community is spontaneous. Moreover, several religious/ritual functions are also performed by the tribals involving all members of the community. Hence, participation of leaders in such community organisation is to be expected. Thus, it appears that persons associated with community organisation have greater chances of emerging as LAMPS leaders.

Thus, the foregoing analysis shows that the attainment of independence and subsequent adoption of democratic constitution with adult suffrage have brought some changes in the leadership composition of co-operatives. In this connection, the hypothesis that accretive character of LAMPS leadership is gradually disappearing seems to be supported by the findings. The finding shows that the role of traditional factors like age, caste, religion, landholding, income and occupation is on decline. It is found that the younger generation are taking part in the co-operative movement. Therefore, no definite role can be assigned to age factors for determination of LAMPS leadership. However, as to sex factor, male members are still dominating in LAMPS leadership, where no any female leaders are found though few female shareholders are enlisted in the LAMPS. Regarding religion composition, there are as many as 25 leaders are Hindus and that is only to be expected being reflective of demographic profile of the area of operation of the respective LAMPS. In the same manner, in determining the LAMPS are meant for Scheduled Tribes and the Model Byelaws have set clear guidelines or representation of caste and non-caste people in the LAMPS leadership. So far as nature of family is concerned, nuclear family system is gaining importance on the emergence of LAMPS leadership and at the same time, joint-family system is on decline. It is also seen that 16 leaders have come from family having member more than 6 and mostly family head are spared to take responsibilities of leadership. Thus, there is a shift from traditional joint family system to nuclear family and family having a moderate number of members are joining leadership. It is also found that newly emerged LAMPS leadership are cultivators belonging to marginal, small and semi-medium farming families having land less than 4 hectares and an annual income less than Rs. 30,000 along with a sizeable numbers of leaders from below poverty line category. On the other hand, competitive factors like education, political background and participation of leaders in community organisation have influenced in determination of LAMPS leadership. In case of education, all the 32 leaders are found educated though a majority (22) of them have below matric level education. Again a majority number of leaders (32) are found to have political background and an overwhelming majority (81) are found to have participated in various community organisations. Thus, the role of traditional factors like age, caste, income, landholding, occupation, nature of family is on the decline and being replaced by competitive factors like education, political background and participation in community organisation in determining the emergence of LAMPS leadership. The study also shows that the tribal society is no longer a static one; it has reflected the socio-political changes brought about after the attainment of independence.

Conclusion

LAMPS leaders play a crucial role in efficient management of tribal co-operatives, their social background, participation in community. The politicisation of leaders of the LAMPS has been measured with reference to the leaders' political awareness and participation, and political linkage with high-up leaders. On the other hand, because of state patronage some degree of political influence in co-operative is inevitable, thereby facilitating a group of leaders using the society for their self-interest. Therefore, in order to ascertain whether vested interest had developed in the LAMPS studied and role of LAMPS in economic development of tribal community there is need of co-operative education for success of co-operative democracy. In the study the leaders were found to have used the machinery and other equipments of the society for personal benefit. The success of co-operative movement in tribal areas is very much dependent on these societies. Because of this reason, it is essential to make an in depth study of this type of societies.

NOTES AND REFERENCES

1. D.G. Karve, "Pattern of Co-operative Leadership" in *Co-operative Leadership in South-East Asia*, p. 62.
2. G.S. Kamat, *New Dimensions Co-operative Management*, p. 63.
3. D.R. Gadgil, "Socio-Economic Factors Underlying Pattern of Leadership" in *Co-operative Leadership in South-East Asia*, p. 69.
4. B.S. Baviskar, "Co-operative and Politics", *Economic and Political Weekly*, March 32, 1968, p. 490.
5. C.R. Samader, *Co-operative Movement in Assam*, p. 289.
6. *Byelaws 28: Model Byelaws for LAMPS of Assam*, p. 6.
7. P.E. Weeraman, "The President, Secretaries, Treasures and Committee Members are Leaders", in *Co-operative Leadership in South-East Asia*, p. 32.

8. The term of Managing Committee is extended up to 3 years w.e.f. 1998-99 vide order from the Registrar of Co-operative Societies, No. GPSS.28/87/83 Dtd 29th June, 1998.
9. Byelaw 27(1) of Model Byelaws of LAMPS, ASCU.

   Provided that Eight members shall be elected by the General Assembly from among individual members holding 'A' class shares subject to the following conditions:

   (a) If the tribal population in the area of operation exceeds 70 per cent of the population, only tribal residing in the area of operation would be eligible to be elected to the Board of Management.

   (b) If the tribal population in the area of operation falls below 70 per cent of the population the representation of the total tribals in the Managing Committee shall not be less than two-thirds of the total strengths of the committee.
10. S. Sikidar, *Economic Development of Tribal India*, p. 14.

17

Self-Help Groups in Development and Empowerment

With Special Reference to Assam

Sanjay Kanti Das

Introduction

Economic and social marginalisation of poor by formal credit agencies including co-operatives led to the emergence of self-help groups (henceforth SHGs). SHGs are an outcome of the neo-liberal paradigm of development, where the poor take charge of their lives and fashion new improved future through self-reliant and socially sustainable efforts (Chitagubbi & Naik, 2011[1]). SHG is a voluntary association of the poor with a common goal of social and economic empowerment (Ganesh Murthy *et al.*, 2002[2]). Further, SHGs are forum for the collective voice of the poor against common oppression and exploitation to understand individual and common problems and improving their skills and capacities to manage resources (Dwarakanath, 2002[3]). Women SHGs represent a form of intervention that is a radical departure from most current programmes. They are an effective strategy for poverty alleviation, women development and social empowerment. The women SHGs have enhanced the status of women as participant decision-makers and beneficiaries on the democratic, economic, social and cultural spheres of life and sensitised the women members to take active part in socio-economic progress of rural India. SHGs in social change imply not only the change of outer form of a community or a society, but also in the social institutions as well as ideas of the people living in that society.

SHGs have been instrumental in empowerment by enabling women to work together in collective agency. A good number of researchers including MFIs claimed that this movement helped in empowering women

(Das, 2012[4]; Cheston & Kuhn, 2004[5]; Sahu and Tripathy, 2005[6]). Micro-finance and SHGs are effective in reducing poverty, empowering women, creating awareness and ensure sustainability of environment, which finally results in sustainable development of the nation. In India, the SHGs constitute a widely accepted development strategy for poverty reduction as they are perceived as powerful vehicles for the promotion of micro-credit and micro-finance especially for women (Chen *et al.*, 2007[7]). In recent years SHGs are emerging as alternative credit source to the poor. SHGs are playing a major role in removing poverty in the rural India today. The group-based model of self-help is widely practiced for rural development, poverty alleviation and empowerment of women (Singh *et al.*, 2009[8]). Self-help as a strategy for social development places emphasis on self reliance, human agency and action. It aims to mobilise people, to give them voice and build people's organisations that will overcome barriers to participation and empowerment. Central to the idea of self-help is the formation of groups, concept of a community and the development of egalitarian relationships that will promote people's well being (Chattopadhya & Bhagel, 2009[9]). SHGs serve as a medium of delivering micro-credit to the members. It is reported that SHGs are now emerging as the predominant model for poverty eradication, women empowerment and development agencies (Panda, 2005[10]). The application of the strategy through UN's Millennium Development Goal (MDGs) has made provision of financial support to the poor or low income people by realising the fact that instead of targeting individual development, it would be more useful to apply this idea in case of group development and interesting the result found in most cases is very positive.

Review of Literature

In this section, an effort is made to review studies that have undertaken so far in respect to the various qualities, sustainability and socio-economic issues related to SHGs in India. Most of the studies focus on SHGs performance and its role in upliftment of the vulnerable sections of society (Agarwal, 2007[11]; Gopisetti, 2007[12]; Gaonkar, 2008[13]; Sarkar, 2008[14]; Nagarajan, 2009[15]). Some studies were conducted on poverty reduction and empowerment (Prakash, 2009[16]). Some researchers have also worked on group based credit programmes (Sarangi, 2008[17]). There were many studies where the researcher has evaluated the performance of Commercial Banks, Co-operative Banks & Regional Rural Banks in micro-finance mainly SBLP (Abdul, 2005[18]; Das, 2012a[19]; Das, 2012b[20], Das, 2013[21]).

Some studies were found to focus on the relationship between micro-finance, SHGS and micro-enterprises (Kanaskar, 2008[22]; Natarajan, 2007[23]).

Studies like Pattanaik (2003[24]) emphasised the role of SHGs for socio-economic development of women in particular and society as a whole. Narasiah (2004[25]) opined that micro-credit plays crucial role in empowering women. Manimekalai (2004[26]) also remarked that SHGs have the enough potential for establishing capacity building and self-efficiency among women.

Sinha (2005[27]) in his work observed that micro-finance contributed significantly to saving and borrowing of the poorer section of the country. Suguna (2006[28]) also remarked that the emergence of SHGs as silent revolution in the spread of rural credit for rural development. Lolheihzovi (2007[29]) considered SHGs as best engine for growth of human resource. In addition, some remarkable studies have been done by Ali-Akpajiak & Pyke (2000[30]), Krishna (2003[31]), Panda (2005), Jerinabi (2006[32]) and Chen *et al.* (2007) regarding role of SHGs in development of poor people.

Singh (2006[33]) conducted a study on People's Education and Development Organisation's (PEDO) SHGs programme and makes an attempt to evaluate social and economic impact on households of SHGs members. They observed that members involved in SHGs programme have increased involvement in decision-making, awareness about various programmes and organisations. Mukerjee (2006[34]) reported that SHGs have positive impact on economic, political, household decision-making and awareness level of the members with respect to social and health issues. Gurumoorthy (2002[35]) reported that SHG have the power to create a social economic revolution in the rural areas of the country and can act as an important tool for socio-economic empowerment of the poor, particularly women (Roy, 2011[36]). It is also reported that the members of SHGs are prepared to undertake entrepreneurial activities at a smaller level with minimum capital requirements (Kamaraj, 2005[37]) and can promote self-employment opportunities to the rural women (Manimekalai and Rajeswari, 2000[38]). Pati and Benjamin (2011[39]) reported that micro-finance through SHGs has had a positive impact on income, expenditure and savings of the women clients in Meghalaya. The same observation is also revealed by Aruna & Jyothirmayi (2011[40]) in case of Hyderabad and also reported considerable improvement in self worthiness and decision-making level of women members because of participation. Meetei (2011[41]) reported that micro-finance through SHGs promoting during the last 10 years in Manipur increases average monthly income, earning capacity and in turn, saving capacity and effective productivity of SHG members and have ensured better economic life of rural women in Manipur. Centre for Micro-Finance & Livelihood (2009[42]) in a survey in Arunachal Pradesh reported that though the micro-finance through SHGs have a positive impact, but due to low population density, lack of information and training etc. the progress of the movement is not up to the mark.

Sharma (2007[43]) observed that the SHG movement has not successfully implemented in some North Eastern States of India because of the region's peculiar geographical location and other infrastructural problems. The study also observed that the banking constraints as a factor that hinders the quality of SHG in North East India. APMAS (2009[44]) reported that the SHG programme has resulted in social and economic benefits to a significant percentage of the sample groups. Despite of all round support from the Government of Assam, NABARD, NGOs, RRBs and active participation of primary members, the condition of SHGs in the State is far from satisfaction. The study also reveals that the proliferation of SHG has posed a serious challenge to sustain this movement by maintaining quality of SHGs and hence, the quality assessment of SHGs is now being considered as a key concern. The study also articulated some serious challenges like uneven growth of SHGs in different parts and uneven quality of SHGs across the country and issues related to their sustainability.

Sa-Dhan, 2003[45] made a comparative study of assessment tools developed by various organisation *viz.* NABARD, BASIX, MYRADA, CARE, APAMAS etc. and have identified eight broad thematic areas with various indicators and their relative benchmarks. The study also felt that unless a tool could provide an instant and clear analysis of the state of affairs of SHG, it would not popular in practice. Reddy (2005[46]) observes that the state of SHGs identifies key areas of weakness which undermine the sustainability of SHG movement. APMAS (2006[47]) on the SBLP in India, addressed a wide range of issues including cases of dropouts from SHGs, internal politics, issues of social harmony and social justice, community actions, book-keepings, equity, defaults and recoveries etc., and sustainability of SHGs. Roy (2007[48]) undertaken quality assessment of SHGs in West Bengal and this was done by using twenty indicators like group meeting, members' participation, group discipline, savings, micro-credit, financial management, economic and social initiatives and linkages with institutions. Kumar (2010[49]) while comparing the differences in quality of SHGs between SHGs under the umbrella of federations and other SHGs which are not part of federation observed that federation type SHGs are functioning well. Sahu (2010[50]) assessed the quality of SHG in Northwest India based on the 13 indicators observed that 27 per cent of the groups are found to be strong and stable. Das (2012[51]) observed that only 6 per cent SHGs are found good while 20 per cent to 30 per cent sample SHGs are levelled as grade 'Average', and hence constant support from SHPI is necessary to make them improved.

It is observed that there are abundant literature on micro-finance, SHG approach, but have dearth of research on quality assessment studies in the country in general and Assam in particular. But the assessment tools that are devised by different agencies for different purposes and different set of users. Several rating systems for micro-finance interventions and SHGs have been developed in the past. But most of these were restricted to understanding the creditworthiness of SHGs and employed indicators on performance on basic group functions and credit absorption capabilities. Social, empowerment and behavioural aspects of SHG functioning rarely found a place in the rating system. Further, these rating tools speak different languages in assessing the quality of SHGs. The present study differs from earlier studies as it covers qualitative aspects and perception of members on impact of SHGs functioning in three districts of Assam. Here, in this study an effort is also made to assess the normal quality practices and performance of the SHGs in Assam towards empowerment and development of masses. Further, this chapter tries to explore perceptions of SHG members on impact of SHG on different aspects like social, psychological and economic and to analyse the strengths, weaknesses, opportunities and threats (SWOT) of the SHG members in micro-finance management.

Objectives

The specific objectives of the study includes—

1. To assess the quality practices of SHGs and to identify performance of SHGs in Assam.
2. To study the perception of SHG members on impact of SHG on different aspects.
3. To study strengths, weaknesses, opportunities and threats of the sample respondents in micro-finance management.
4. To outline conclusions and recommendations based on the findings of the study.

Research Design and Methodology

The research design and methodology devised in this study is being presented which has been designed keeping in mind the focused objectives and with the aim of acquiring accurate and authentic data. The study was restricted to only three districts of Assam out of twenty seven districts under both judgement and convenience sampling methods, viz. Nagaon, Dima Hasao and Karbi Anglong. Three development blocks from each district were selected under first level of random sampling. Again, from each development block five revenue villages were selected under second level of random sampling mostly those revenue villages, which are featured with high proliferation of SHGs. Again from five revenue villages five SHGs representing one member from each are selected on third level of random sampling. Data has been collected from primary sources. Only SHGs under SGSY which are enlisted with Directorate of SHGs, Assam under SGSY, for the year 2008-09 and completed one year of existence, are covered in the study and primary data are collected during the first half of 2011. Initially, 75 (75 SHGs from each district covering both male and women) SHGs are randomly selected from selected revenue villages out of which researchers could collect 150 (50 SHGs from each district) useful filled questionnaires from the selected districts, due to

Study Area in Assam

1. Nagaon District
Development Blocks:
Odali, Raha and Binakandi
2. Karbi Anglong
Development Blocks:
Lumbajong, Langsomepi and Bokajan
3. Dima Hasao
Development Blocks:
Jatinga Valley, Diyung Valley and New Sangbar
***Total Sample: 150**
***Analytical Research**
***Primary source and Secondary Source**
***Data collected during Jan. to April, 2011.**

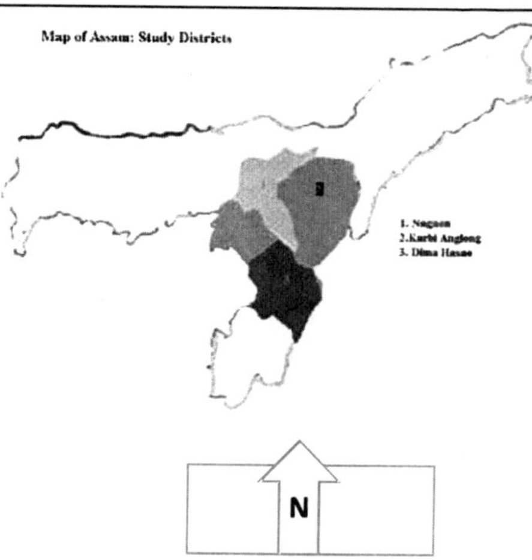

Profile of Study Districts of Assam: Nagaon, Karbi Anglong and Dima Hasao

time shortage, apathy of group members, defunct SHGs and distance constraints.

A set of questionnaires are being prepared for assessing the quality, performance and impact of the SHGs of the study area. These questionnaires are framed suitably by studying the existing literature on quality and impact assessment of SHGs.

SECTION I

Analysis and Interpretation on Quality Practices

Socio-Economic Profile of the Respondents

The respondents of the study mainly belong to the age group of 30–40 yrs. as 60.5 per cent of the respondents belong to that group. The respondents in the study cover all sections of society wherein representation of Hindu (64%), Muslims (35%) and Christian (1%) are ensured. Moreover, out of 150 respondents 55 belong to general caste, 49 belong to SC community, 24 belong to ST and 22 belong to OBC and MOBC. Further, 67 per cent of the respondents have completed Vth–Xth standard category of education level. Moreover, majority of the respondents are married and they live in nuclear family. The duration of membership of the respondents varies from 3 years to 8 years. However, 47 per cent of the respondents are members for a period of 4 years, 33.5 per cent for a period of 5 yrs and respondents belonging to 2 yrs and 3 yrs category are insignificant.

Reasons for Forming the SHGs

The reasons for forming the Self-Help Group in the study area are presented in Fig. 17.1.

It is found from Fig. 17.1 that 51 (34%) groups are formed to obtain the financial support from the government, the NGOs and the financial institutions. Twenty five (17%) groups are formed to improve their economic status. Another 11 (7%) groups are formed to improve social status while 23 (15%) groups are formed to promote saving habit among the members. Yet another 16 (11%) groups are formed to initiate group activities, only 11 (7%) groups are formed to take up community development activities and 13 groups (9%) are formed by the influence of friends and relatives.

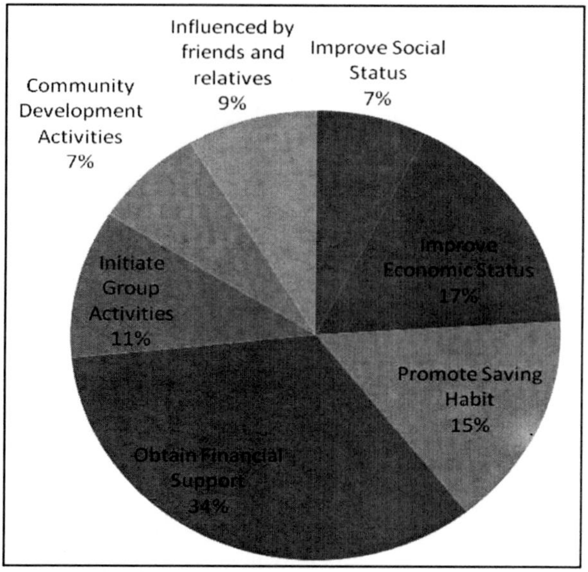

Fig. 17.1: Reasons for forming SHGs.
Source: Primary data

Homogeneity of the Group

SHGs become cohesive in the long run only if they are homogenous. Social mobilisation is an important step in the formation of SHGs. It requires a high degree of motivation, morale and management skill. The individuals possess a distinguishing character and conduct of their own. They establish their individuality in their personal and social life. The heterogeneity behaviour of the members makes the management of the SHGs difficult and hence members with homogeneous character are to be identified.

Homogeneity of members enables the SHG to select economic activities, which are common to many members. For the efficient functioning of the SHGs homogeneity of the members is essential. The members in each group can take collective decision because they are like-minded.

Among the 150 sample groups selected for the study, a majority of the members in each group are below poverty level. The homogeneity of members has been measured in terms of the percentage of the below poverty level to the total members. This is measured by the following formula:

$$\frac{\text{Number of below poverty level in the Group}}{\text{Total Number of Members of Group}} \times 100$$

Fig. 17.2 shows the distribution of the sample SHGs based on the percentage of the below poverty level to the total members.

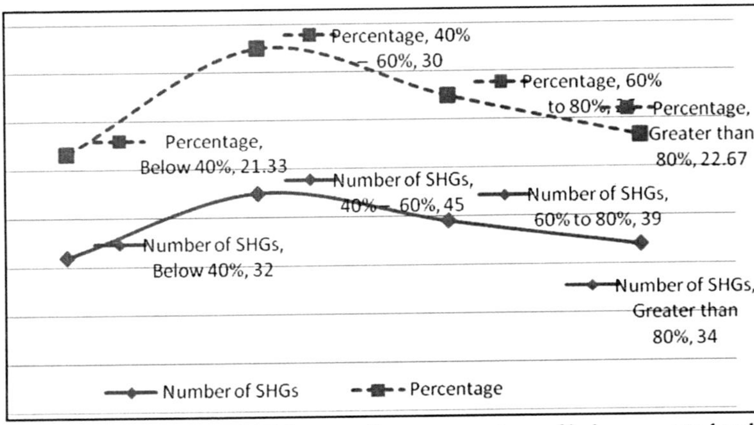

Fig. 17.2: Distribution of SHGs according to percentage of below poverty level
Source: Primary data.

It could be seen from Fig. 17.2 that 32 (21.33%) of the sample SHGs had reported that the percentage of homogeneity was up to 40 per cent while 45 SHGs had reported that the percentage of homogeneity was in between 40 per cent and 60 per cent. In case of 39 sample SHGs, they had reported that the percentage of homogeneity was in between 60 per cent to 80 per cent. Further, 34 sample SHGs had reported that the percentage of homogeneity was above 80 per cent.

Frequency of Meetings

The main activity of the SHGs is conducting group meetings in a common place at fixed intervals. Group meeting is very essential for all groups. They have to discuss their savings, common problems, performances and so on in the meeting. In addition to this, the occasion is used to discuss their economic and social problems and other issues that need to be sorted out through intervention of the group or its members. Hence, the frequency of conducting meetings is considered an important factor for judging the performance of the SHGs.

The allotment of the sample SHGs on the basis of the regularity in conduct of meetings is given in Table 17.1.

Table 17.1 indicates that 47 (31.33%) SHGs do not have any specific interval regarding the holding of group meetings. 38 (25.33%) conducted their meetings once in a week, whereas 48 (32%) groups conducted their meetings once in a fortnight. Further, the table reveals that 25 (16.67%) SHGs conducted their meetings on monthly basis.

Table 17.1: Distribution of SHGs based on Frequency of Meetings

Sl. No.	Frequency of Meeting	Number of SHGs	Percentage
1.	No specific interval	47	31.33
2.	Once in a Week	38	25.33
3.	Fortnightly	48	32.00
4.	Monthly	25	16.67
	Total	**150**	**100.00**

Source: Primary data.

Regularity in Attendance

The SHG members are required to attend the meeting of the SHGs and other meeting organised by the NGOs and the government to know more about the SHGs and government schemes. Hence, the more the attendance of the members the more will be the utilisation of the SHGs and corresponding Government schemes. In the study the level of attendance is identified as one of the indicators for measuring performance.

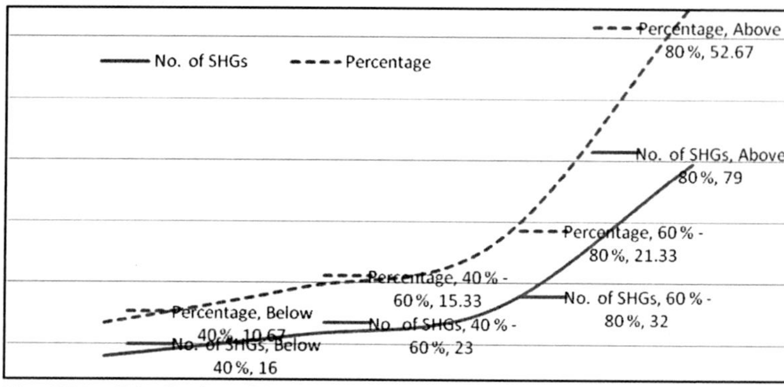

Fig. 17.3: Distribution of Group according to Regularity of Attendance in Meetings
Source: Primary data.

From Fig. 17.3, it could be seen that 79 groups (52.67%) recorded more than 80 per cent of members' attendance in the group meetings, which indicated active involvement of the members. Further, Fig. 17.3 depicts that 23 SHGs (15.33%) have 40 per cent to 60 per cent attendance in the group meetings, while 32 (21.33%) of the SHGs have 60 per cent to 80 per cent attendance in the group meetings and only 16 (10.67%) of the SHGs has less than 40 per cent attendance in the group meetings.

Participation of NGOs/MFIs in Meetings

The NGOs/MFIs attended a few meetings of the SHGs at the inception period in order to impart the required skill to the SHGs in conducting the proceedings. They gradually reduce their participation to make the SHGs independent in conducting the meetings. The participation of the NGOs/MFIs in meetings will facilitate the monitoring of each and every activity of the group so that the performance of the group improves. The participation of the NGOs in meetings has been measured in terms of the percentage of the number of meetings attended by the NGOs to the total number of meetings conducted by a group in a year. Fig. 17.4 shows the participation of the NGOs/MFIs in the meetings of the SHGs.

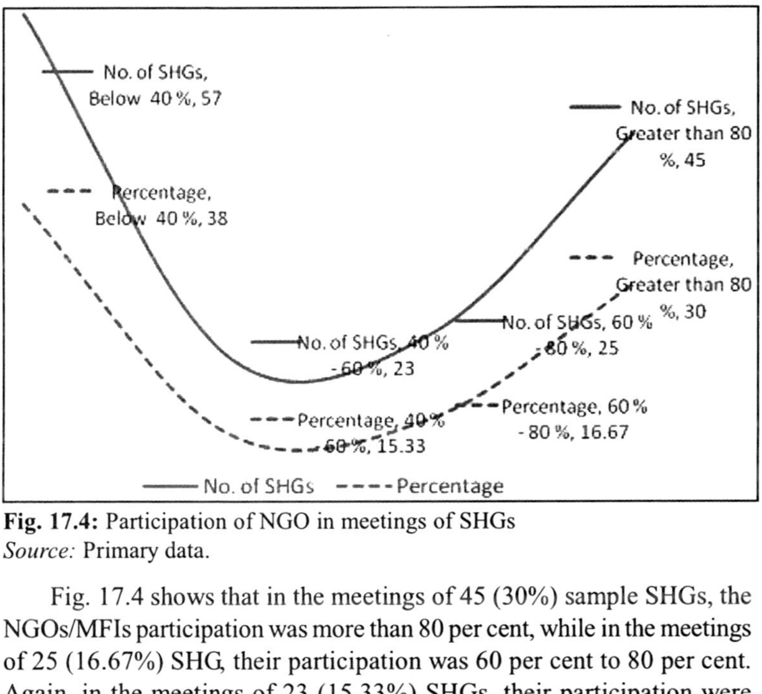

Fig. 17.4: Participation of NGO in meetings of SHGs
Source: Primary data.

Fig. 17.4 shows that in the meetings of 45 (30%) sample SHGs, the NGOs/MFIs participation was more than 80 per cent, while in the meetings of 25 (16.67%) SHG, their participation was 60 per cent to 80 per cent. Again, in the meetings of 23 (15.33%) SHGs, their participation were 40 per cent to 60 per cent. However, in the meetings of 57 (38%) groups, the participation of NGOs/MFIs in the meeting was less than 40 per cent.

Repayment Performance

The savings of the SHGs can be rotated smoothly when there is a prompt and regular repayment and that will also motivate the lending agencies like bank to lend more number of SHGs. From the point of view of the SHGs, the performance of repayment can be considered an important criterion while studying the overall performance. Hence, the performance of repayment has been taken as an indicator for judging the performance of the groups.

The distribution of the sample SHGs according to the level of repayment performance is shown in Fig. 17.5.

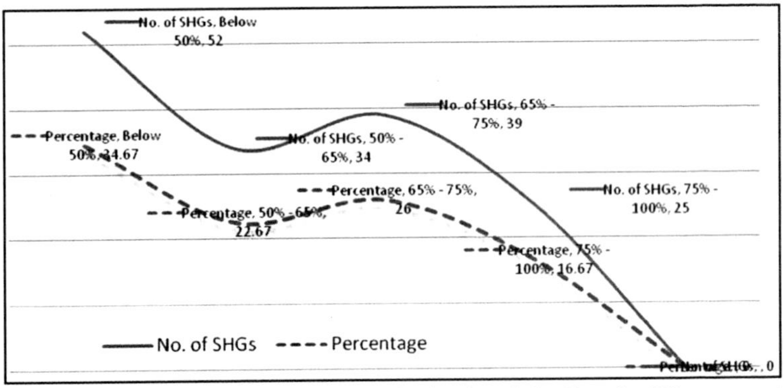

Fig. 17.5: Distribution of SHGs on the basis of the Level of Repayment Performance

Source: Primary data.

As it could be seen from Fig. 17.5, the performance of repayment is not at all good in all groups. Fifty two SHGs (34.67% of respondent groups) have recorded below 50 per cent of repayment performance. Among the sample SHGs, only 34 (22.67%) groups have recorded 50 per cent to 65 per cent, while 39 (26%) SHGs have recorded 65 per cent to 75 per cent of repayment. Further, 25 (16.67%) groups have recorded 75 per cent to 100 per cent of repayments.

Decision on Financial Transactions

Collective decision is the tool for effective functioning of the SHGs. If majority of the members in a group are involved in decision-making, definitely there will be more commitment on the part of the members. Usually, if the leader of the group does not force the members to accept a decision taken by him, the performance of the group will be good. Table 17.2 shows the distribution of the sample SHGs according to the decision on the financial transactions.

As it could be seen from Table 17.2 that in 16 (10.67%) sample groups, the decisions relating to financial transactions are taken by the NGOs, while in 45 (30%) SHGs the decisions are taken by the group leader and ratified. Again, in 63 (42%) sample groups, the decisions

Table 17.2: Distribution of SHGs based on the decision of financial transactions

Sl. No.	*Decision*	*No. of SHGs*	*Percentage*
1.	Taken by NGOs/MFIs	16	10.67
2.	Taken by Group Leader and Ratified	45	30.00
3.	Taken by Few Members	63	42.00
4.	Taken by Majority members	26	17.33
	Total	**150**	**100.00**

Source: Primary data.

relating to financial transactions are taken by few members. The remaining 26 (17.33%) SHGs have recorded that majority of the members take decisions. It is evident that NGOs play a minimum role in taking decisions on the financial transactions. Finally, it is observed that most of the financial decisions are taken by a few members who are the policy-makers of the groups.

Utilisation of Common Fund

Common fund includes the savings, the penalty imposed on members, the grants from government, subsidy from the banks and the like. This common fund of the SHGs forms their lendable resource. The utilisation of the common fund is measured in terms of percentage of the fund availed by the members as loan from the total common fund. If the group keeps the common fund idle, it indicates the lower performance of the SHG and hence, it has been taken as one of the indicators to judge the performance of the SHGs.

Fig. 17.6 shows the distribution of the sample SHGs according to the utilisation of the common fund.

From Fig. 17.6 it could be seen that 83 sample SHGs have recorded more than 75 per cent utilisation of common fund while 14 SHGs have recorded between 60 and 75 per cent utilisation of common fund. Thrity two SHGs have recorded between 40% and 60% utilisation of common funds. However, 21 groups reported that the utilisation of common fund is less than 40%.

Training of Members

The members are given training in tailoring, book-binding, poultry, dairy

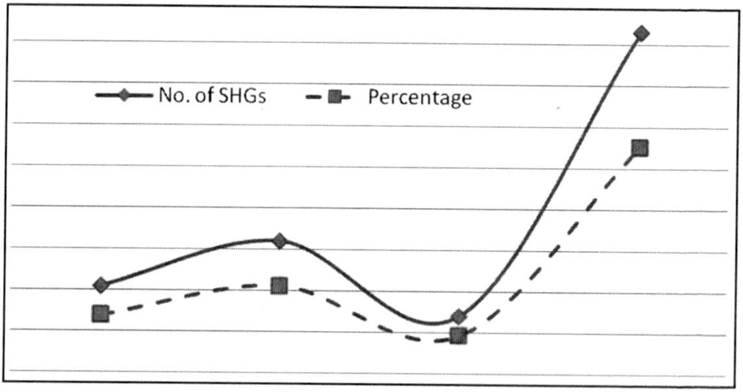

Fig. 17.6: Distribution of SHGs based on the Utilisation of Common Fund
Source: Primary data.

farming and management related aspects like leadership and book-keeping. The prime importance is given to training as the project is fundamentally a human resource development project. Training in certain topics is imparted by experts of the IIE and DIC officials. Occasionally local academicians, experienced entrepreneur and group leader also imparted knowledge to the group members. In addition to regular training, refresher training is also provided to the leaders by the specialised institute meant for that purpose on selection basis. In a group, if more persons are trained, the effectiveness of the group increases.

Table 17.3 shows the percentage of the sample SHGs members who attended the training programmes.

Table 17.3: Training of Members

Sl. No.	*No. of Members (in percentage)*	*No. of SHGs*	*Percentage*
1.	Below 25%	57	38
2.	25–50%	31	20.67
3.	50–65%	23	15.33
5.	65–75%	18	12
4.	Above 75%	21	14
	Total	**150**	**100**

Source: Primary data.

It is evident from Table 17.3 that 57 SHGs (38%) had imparted training to less than 25 per cent of their members while 31 SHGs (20.67%) provided training to 25 to 50 per cent of their members. It is to be noted that in the case of 18 SHGs, training was given only 65 per cent to 75 of their members. Only 14 per cent selected SHGs, training was imparted above 75 per cent which was the sad part of SHG performance in the study area.

Awareness of Rules and Regulations

For the smooth functioning of the SHGs, the rules and regulations must be known by all its members. If the members are not familiar with the rules and regulations, it is difficult to manage the affairs of the SHGs. From this viewpoint of the SHGs management, the level of awareness of rules and regulations of the SHGs by their members is a decisive factor while evaluating the performance of the group.

Table 17.4 depicts the distribution of the sample SHGs on the level of members in respect of rules and regulations.

Table 17.4: Awareness of Rules and Regulations

Sl. No.	*Awareness Level*	*No. of SHGs*	*Percentage*
1.	Less than 25%	11	7.33
2.	25%–50%	21	14
3.	50%–65%	24	16
4.	65%–75%	42	28
5.	Above 75%	52	34.67
	Total	**150**	**100**

Source: Primary data.

From Table 17.4, it was observed that 52 SHGs reported that the awareness of rules and regulation was more than 75 per cent and another 42 per cent SHGs reported that their awareness level was in between 65 and 75 per cent. Twenty one SHGs reported that the awareness level was in between 25 to 50 per cent while 24 reported 50 to 65 per cent. Only 11 SHGs (7.33%) reported that the awareness level was less than 25 per cent.

Maintenance of Books of Accounts

The proper maintenance of books of accounts (cash book, ledger books and final accounts either in single or double entry system) is very essential for the smooth functioning of the SHGs. The proper and update keeping of accounts will enable the SHGs to get grants, loans from banks and any other financial institutions. The group leader is responsible to maintain the accounts with the help of other members. In order to assess the performance of the SHGs, it is inevitable to consider the level of maintenance of books of accounts by the SHGs. Table 17.5 shows the distribution of sample SHGs according to the level of maintenance of books of accounts.

Table 17.5: Books of Accounts Maintained by the Sample SHGs

Sl. No.	*Level of Maintenance*	*No. of SHGs*	*Percentage*
1.	Below 40%	20	13.33
2.	40–60%	27	18
3.	60–75%	44	29.33
4.	Above 75%	59	39.33
	Total	**150**	**100**

Source: Primary data.

From Table 17.5, it could be inferred that in case of 59 SHGs (39.33%) the level of maintenance of books and accounts was more than 80 per cent while in 44 SHGs (29.33%) it was between 60 and 75 per cent. Further, 27 SHGs (18%) the level of maintenance of books and accounts lies in between 40 to 60 per cent. In the remaining 20 SHGs the level of books of accounts maintained was below 40 per cent.

Problems Faced by the SHGs

SHG members are facing a number of problems from the initial stage of group promotion to the stage of income generating units and thereafter too. The problems faced by the SHG are depicted in the following Fig. 17.7.

It is found from Fig. 17.7 that the major problem faced by the SHGs is delay in sanctioning the loan (22.67%) followed by poor response of authorities (22%), lack of administrative experience (16.67%), lack of cooperation among the members (11.33%), in adequate loan amount (10.67%), difficulty to approach the authorities (8.67%), and the problem of limited number of installment for repayment of Loan (8%).

Business Activities of SHG Members

The SHGs in the study area are mostly engaged in different types of business activities which are shown in Fig. 17.8.

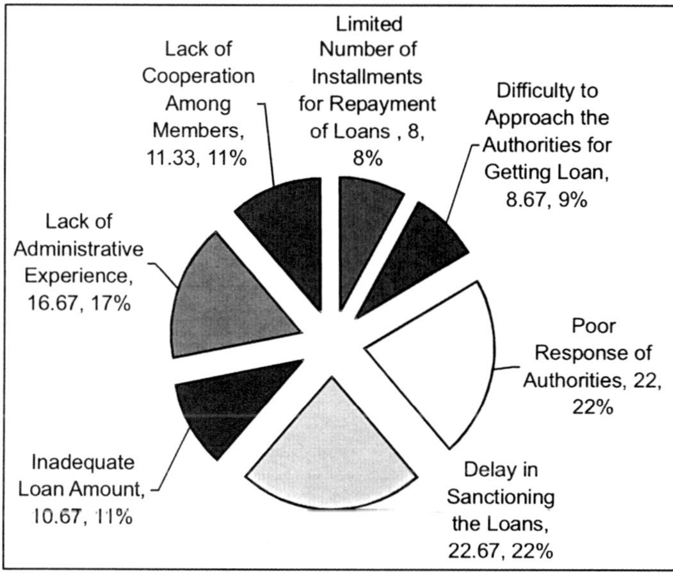

Fig. 17.7: Problems of SHG members.
Source: Primary data.

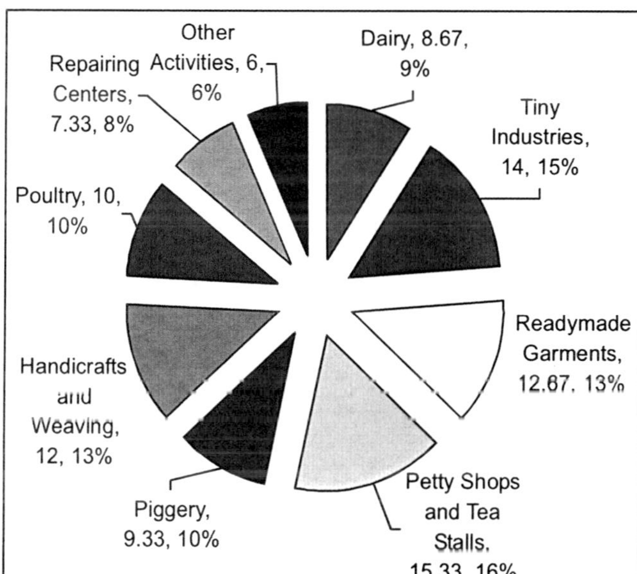

Fig. 17.8: Business activities undertaken by SHG members.
Source: Primary data.

Figure 17.8 shows distribution of category-wise respondents by type of economic activity. It is clear from Table 17.3 that comparatively larger number of members is found in petty shops (15.33%) followed by economic activities (14%) and then readymade garments (12.67%). Dairy and piggery farms also the other thrust area of business activities of SHGs in the study area.

Normal Practices of SHGs in Selected Districts

The variations in practices at SHG level have been spurring innovations in terms of products, systems and methodologies and encouraging new standards in SHG promotion and practices; nevertheless it has brought lot of incongruity in the established practices. However, from the present study in selected Development Blocks in Nagaon districts, it is observed that each and every SHGs are performing some common practices which are depicted in Table 17.6.

General Observations

1. The actual number of SHGs that are really present on the ground is not available. It is observed from the study that a good number of SHGs in selected districts mostly in Hill districts are defunct in nature and they are just in records only.
2. It is further observed from the study that though most of the SHGs in selected districts have some guidelines regarding holding of fortnightly group meeting, but there is no regularity in holding such meetings. However, the SHGs in Nagaon district mostly hold regular meetings either on monthly or fortnightly basis.
3. Regarding participation of members in decision-making process, it is observed that in most of the SHGs in selected districts where a few members of the SHGs are actively engaged in decision-making process.
4. Though in most of the SHGs in selected districts are guided by well established rules and regulations for organising and managing the same, but these are in many cases not known to majority of members.
5. "One time saving in a month" is the maxim in most of the SHGs in selected districts, but majority of the SHG members does not follow that. Regarding savings and its frequency, minimum amount and mode of collection etc. are often discussed in the

Table 17.6: Analysis of Some Existing Practices

Sl. No.	*Quality Assessment Parameters*	*Normal Practices*
1.	Group Meetings	SHGs take it as a rigour to meet frequently.
2.	Subsidy dependence	SHGs deriving more subsidies and more and more are moving on towards subsidy regime.
3.	New financial services	SHGs are comfortable only with credit and savings and consider other services as not falling within the mandate for which they are and need not directly deal with such are established.
4.	Affiliation to federation	SHGs remain, as stand-alone piece without any affiliation to SHG-upstream like clusters/federations and more often feel their role will be limited in a federal set up.
5.	Inter-group lending	SHGs do not lend to other groups as a matter of policy though more of idle funds are locked up within SHG, as the scope of lending within the group is limited beyond certain extent.
6.	Rotation of leadership	Rotation of leadership is not seriously taken, with the result clients with poor leadership qualities come to manage the SHGs very often on turn basis.
7.	Multiple membership within the family	Sometimes, promoters find it easy to include members from the same family for easy management of groups.
8.	Common economic activity	Common economic activity is preferred in some cases like SGSY groups due to project compulsions.
9.	Encouraging visitors	SHGs believe that visitors may borrow their own concepts and keep certain things within as tricks of trade and do not encourage visitors.

Source: Author.

member's meetings. It is further observed that most of the savings collections are done on at the desire of the member.

6. It is also observed that most of the SHGs in the selected districts are promoted to economic units. However, it is aptly observed that the rate of conversion to 'Grade I' are very high while the said conversion from Grades I to II is very low in all the selected districts. Further, it is observed that only a few SHGs in Dima Hasao districts has converted their units into economic units, but a large percentage of SHGs in Nagaon and Karbi Anglong districts has converted into viable economic units. Dairy farming, piggery, weaving, goatary and poultry and other traditional

economic units are the major economic units that are promoted by SHGs in Nagaon and Karbi Anglong districts. However, dairy farming appears to be the most lucrative project of the SHGs in Nagaon while weaving, piggery and poultry are considered the first choice in Karbi Anglong district.

SECTION II

Perceptions of the SHG Members on Impact

An almost infinite array of variables can be identified to assess impacts on different units. To be of use these must be able to be defined with precision and must be measurable. Conventionally, economic indicators have dominated micro-finance impact assessments with assessors particularly keen to measure changes in income despite the enormous problems. Other popular variables have been levels and patterns of expenditure, consumption and assets. A strong case can be made that assets are a particularly useful indicator of impact because their level does not fluctuate as greatly as other economic indicators and is not simply based on an annual estimate (Barnes, 1996[52]). The social indicators that became popular in the early 1980s (e.g. educational status, access to health services, nutritional levels, anthropometric measures etc.) have recently been extended into the socio-political arena in an attempt to assess whether micro-finance can promote empowerment (Mayoux, 1997[53]; Goetz and Sen Gupta, 1996[54]; Schuler and Hashemi, 1994[55]; Hashemi *et al.*, 1995[56]). This has led to the measurement of individual control over resources, involvement in household and community decision-making, levels of participation in community activities and social networks and electoral participation. The bulk of this work has focused on changes in gender relations, but there are sometimes partially formulated assessments of class relations within it (Fuglesang and Chandler, 1993[57]).

For assessing the comparative analysis on the impact of SBLP in Assam in comparison to All India level, the reports of NCAER, 2008 is duly analysed. The NCAER (2008[58]) survey was carriedout for the country as a whole covering a total of 4791 households from 961 SHGs spread over six sample States from five different regions, *viz.*, Andhra Pradesh and Karnataka (South), Maharashtra (West), Odisha (East), Uttar Pradesh (Central) and Assam (North East). The study observed the difference in the impact of SBLP in India and Assam as depicted in Tables 17.7 to 17.11 which are self-explanatory.

Table 17.7: Impact of SBLP on Level and Growth of Annual Net Household Income

State/Model	Annual Income Per Household	
	Base Level (Rupees)	CAGR (%)
Assam	28004	6.4
All India	34786	6.1

Source: NCAER (2008).

Table 17.8: Impact of SBLP on Level and Growth of Annual Expenditure Per Household

State	Consumption Expenditure on Food		Consumption Expenditure on Non-food		Expenditure on Education		Expenditure on Health	
	Base Level (Rs.)	CGAR (%)	Base Level (Rs.)	CGAR (%)	Base Level (Rs.)	CGAR (%)	Base Level (Rs.)	CGAR (%)
Assam	3468	5.1	1023	4.7	119	Neg.	112	5.9
All India	3040	5.1	1529	5.4	180	5.6	193	5.5

Source: NCAER (2008).

Table 17.9: Impact of SBLP on Poverty

State	Percentage of households below poverty line			CAGR (%)
	Base Level	2006	Net Reduction	
Assam	66.1	41.4	24.7	9.24
All India	58.3	33.0	25.3	10.00

Source: NCAER (2008).

Table 17.10: HHs Reporting Improved Social Empowerment of Women after Joining SHGs

State	Percentage of SHG Households
Assam	86.5
All India	92.0

Source: NCAER (2008).

The vital function of the SHG is to provide access to credit in the context of poverty reduction and empowerment of women. With the aim to meet the MDGs and micro-finance programmer's role in supporting it,

Table 17.11: HHs Reporting Improved Social Empowerment of Women after Joining SHGS

State	*Percentage of SHG Households*
Assam	86.5
All India	92.0

Source: NCAER (2008).

there has been an increasing expectation on their impact on women empowerment. However, the perception and expectations of the members of the SHGs vary from person to person. This section examines the perceptions of the sample members, who are engaged in different income generating activities, in terms of economic impact, social impact and psychological impact.

A. Perceptions of the SHG Members on Economic Impact

An individual's development purely depends on the positive economic impact. The SHGs are helping to improve the economic conditions of its members. The improvements can be reflected from increase in income, savings, value of assets, amount of borrowing and amount of expenditure and provision of employment opportunities etc. The perception of the sample members on the economic impact has been examined by taking into account the opinion of members on the economic variables like the capacity to spend more, increase in the value of assets, rise in income, improvement in savings habit and provision of employment opportunities.

Capacity to Spend More

Sample respondents are asked to express their perception on the statement that membership in SHGs increases capacity to spend more. Table 17.12 depicts the distribution of respondents by their perception on membership in SHGs increases to spend more. It is observed from table that 71.33 per cent of the sample respondents have strongly agreed to the statement that membership in SHG increases capacity to spend more, while 2 per cent of the respondents have disagreed to this statement.

Increases in the Value of Assets

Sample respondents are also asked to express their opinion whether

Table 17.12: Perception of SHG Member's on Increase in Capacities to Spend More

Category	*Membership in SHG increases capacity to spend more*					*Total*
	Strongly Agree	*Agree*	*Neither Agree Nor Disagree*	*Disagree*	*Strongly Disagree*	
Members' of SHG	107(71.33)	34(22.67)	6(4.00)	3(2.00)	0(0)	150

Source: Primary data.

membership in SHGs increases the value of assets. Distribution of the respondents by perception of the respondents on the statement that membership in SHG increases the value of assets is provided in Table 17.13, it is portrayed from table that 18.67 per cent of the respondents have strongly agreed to this statement, while 58 per cent of the respondents have agreed. On the otherhand, 13.33 per cent of the respondents have disagreed and only 4 per cent of the respondents are strongly disagreed. As a whole, merely 76 per cent of the respondents agreed with this statement.

Table 17.13: Perception of SHG Member's on Increase in the Value of Assets

Category	*Membership in SHG increases the value of assets*					*Total*
	Strongly Agree	*Agree*	*Neither Agree Nor Disagree*	*Disagree*	*Strongly Disagree*	
Members' of SHG	28(18.67)	87(58.00)	9(6.00)	20(13.33)	6(4.00)	150

Source: Primary data.

Changes in the Income

To examine the perception of the SHG members on the changes in income after joining SHG, it is observed that 95.33 per cent of sample respondents agreed that there income is changed in the positive direction. Table 17.14 presents distribution of the respondents by their perception on increase in income after joining SHGs. It is seen from table that 69.33 per cent of the sample respondents have strongly agreed that their incomes are increased after joining SHGs. On the other hand, only 4.67 per cent of the respondents could not make any comment about increase in income after joining SHGs.

Table 17.14: Perception of SHG Member's on Increase in Income

Category	*Membership in SHG increases the income*					*Total*
	Strongly Agree	*Agree*	*Neither Agree Nor Disagree*	*Disagree*	*Strongly Disagree*	
Members of SHG	104(69.33)	39(26.00)	7(4.67)	0(0)	0(0)	150

Source: Primary data.

Changes in the Savings Level

From Table 17.15, it is observed that 96 per cent of the sample respondents have a positive comment towards changes in income after becoming a member in SHG. It is further deduced from the table that no sample respondents have any disagreement this statement. Thus, the study reveals that membership in SHGs increases the savings.

Table 17.15: Perception of SHG Member's on Increase in Savings

Category	*Membership in SHG increases the savings*					*Total*
	Strongly Agree	*Agree*	*Neither Agree Nor Disagree*	*Disagree*	*Strongly Disagree*	
Members of SHG	108(72.00)	36(24.00)	6(4.00)	0(0)	0(0)	150

Source: Primary data.

Employment Opportunities

Sample respondents are asked to express their opinion as to membership in SHGs provides employment opportunities. It is observed from Table 17.16 that as many as 68 per cent of the sample respondents have strongly agreed with the statement that membership in SHGs provide employment opportunities, while the proportion of sample respondents, who have agreed with this statement is 26 per cent. Only 9 (6%) of the respondents neither agree nor disagree with this statement. However, there is no one who denied the statement that involving with SHG does not promote employment opportunities.

B. Perceptions of the SHG Members on Social Impact

The SHGs create social awareness among its members. To access the

Table 17.16: Perception of SHG Member's on Increase in Employment Opportunities

Category	Membership in SHG provides employment opportunities					Total
	Strongly agree	Agree	Neither Agree Nor Disagree	Disagree	Strongly disagree	
Members' of SHG	102 (68.00)	39 (26.00)	09 (6.00)	0 (0)	0 (0)	150

Source: Primary data.

perceptions of SHG members on impact of SHG towards social aspects, the following statements were asked. The perceptions of the sample respondents on the social impact are examined with the help of statements like membership in SHGs increase power of decision-making, creates better awareness about health and induces social responsibility.

Decision-making Power

To access the perception of SHG members on the social impact of SHG, the sample respondents were asked about the impact of SHG on increase in decision-making power in their family. Table 17.17 depicts distribution of the respondents by their perceptions as to whether membership in SHGs increases decision-making power in their family. Of the sample surveyed, 56 per cent of the sample respondents had strongly agreed that membership in SHGs increase decision-making power in the family, whereas 18 per cent of the respondents agreed to this statement. On the other hand, sample respondents constituting 19.33 per cent of the sample opined that they have no objection to this question, while merely 5.33 per cent of the respondents have disagreed and 1.33 per cent of the respondents are strongly disagreed to this statement. In fact, it is observed that decision-making power of the sample women in their family is increased after joining SHGs.

Awareness about Health

Table 17.18 shows distribution of the respondents by their opinion on whether membership in SHGs creates better awareness about health. It is found from table that more than half of the sample respondents (58%) have strongly agreed to this statement, while 24 per cent of the respondents have agreed to this statement, whilst 4 per cent of the respondents do not make any comment. Only 12.67 per cent of the respondents have disagreed

Table 17.17: Perception of Member's on Increase in Power of Decision-Making in Family

Category	Membership in SHG increases power of decision-making					Total
	Strongly Agree	Agree	Neither Agree Nor Disagree	Disagree	Strongly Disagree	
Members of SHG	84(56.00)	27(18.00)	29(19.33)	8(5.33)	2(1.33)	150

Source: Primary data.

as to membership in SHGs creates better awareness about health, whereas only 1.33 per cent of the respondents are strongly disagreed to this statement. In conclusion, majority of the sample respondents aware about good health practices after joining SHGs.

Table 17.18: Perception of SHG Members on Creating Better Awareness about Health

Category	Membership in SHG creates better awareness about Health					Total
	Strongly Agree	Agree	Neither Agree Nor Disagree	Disagree	Strongly Disagree	
Members of SHG	87(58.00)	36(24.00)	6(4.00)	19(12.67)	2(1.33)	150

Source: Primary data.

Social Responsibility

Sample respondents are asked to express their opinion as to whether membership in SHGs induces social responsibility. Table 17.19 presents distribution of the respondents by their opinion on the perception that membership is SHGs induces social responsibility. It is evident from table that 58 per cent of the sample respondents have strongly agreed that membership in SHGs induces socialresponsibility, while 12 per cent of them have agreed. On the other hand, 9.33 per cent of the respondents expressed no objection, whereas 20.67 per cent of them have disagreed with this statement. It is concluded that by and large membership in SHGs induces social responsibility in the opinion of the majority of the respondents.

Table 17.19: Perception of SHG Member's on Inducement on Social Responsibility

Category	Membership in SHG induces social responsibility					Total
	Strongly Agree	Agree	Neither Agree Nor Disagree	Disagree	Strongly Disagree	
Members of SHG	87(58.00)	18(12.00)	14(9.33)	31(20.67)	0 (0)	150

Source: Primary data.

C. Perceptions of the SHG Members on Psychological Impact

This paragraph portrays the perceptions of the sample respondents on psychological impact. SHG provides scope for the improvement of mind and development of the body of an individual. The psychological impact constitutes improving confidence, awareness on self-reliance, societal status, improving literacy and communication skills and improving leadership skills. The perception of members on the psychological impact has been analysed with the help of following points, *viz.* SHG creates confidence to face problems, creates awareness about self-reliance, gives societal status, improves literacy and communication skills and improves leadership skills.

Confidence to Face Problems

Sample respondents are asked to express their opinion as to membership in SHGs creates confidence to face problems. Table 17.20 indicates distribution of the respondents by their opinion on whether membership in SHGs creates confidence to face problems. It is noted from the table that sample respondents constituting 68 per cent of the respondents have strongly agreed to this question, while 22 per cent of the respondents have agreed, whilst 7.33 per cent of the respondents said no objection on the whole. On the other hand, 2.67 per cent of the respondents have disagreed to this question. Thus, SHGs create confidence to the sample members to face problems. Majority of the sample respondents reported confidence to face problems after joining SHGs. However, some of the respondents of some income generating activities only reported no confidence to face problems.

Table 17.20: Perception of SHG Member's on Increase in Confidence to Face Problems

Category	*Membership in SHG creates confidence to face problems*					*Total*
	Strongly Agree	*Agree*	*Neither Agree Nor Disagree*	*Disagree*	*Strongly Disagree*	
Members of SHG	102(68.00)	33(22.00)	11(7.33)	4(2.67)	0(0)	150

Source: Primary data.

Awareness about Self-Reliance

Sample respondents are asked to express their opinion on the statement that membership in SHGs creates awareness about self-reliance. Table 17.21 presents distribution of the respondents by their opinion on the statement that membership in SHGs creates awareness about self-reliance. Of the sample surveyed, 64.67 per cent of the respondents strongly agreed to this statement, 12 per cent of them agreed, 6.67 per cent of them expressed no objection and the rest 16.67 per cent disagreed with this statement. Thus, by and large, most of the respondents felt that membership in SHGs create awareness about self-reliance.

Table 17.21: Perception of SHG Member's on Increase Awareness About Self-reliance

Category	*Membership in SHG creates awareness about self-reliance*					*Total*
	Strongly agree	*Agree*	*Neither Agree Nor Disagree*	*Disagree*	*Strongly Disagree*	
Members of SHG	97(64.67)	18(12.00)	10(6.67)	25(16.67)	0(0)	150

Source: Primary data.

Social Status

Sample respondents are asked to state their opinion on the statement that membership in SHGs gives social status. Table 17.22 shows distribution of the respondents by their opinion on the statement that membership in SHGs gives social status. The data show that 62.67 per cent of the respondents opined that they strongly agreed with this statement, while 25.33 per cent of the respondents agreed with this statement and 2.67 per cent of the respondents stated no objection. As against this, merely 9.33 per cent of the respondents disagreed with this statement. It is concluded that by and large majority of the respondents felt that membership in SHGs gives social status. Interestingly, majority of the respondents of all income generating activities also stated the same.

Table 17.22: Perception of SHG Members on Increase in Social Status

Category	*Membership in SHG gives social status*					*Total*
	Strongly Agree	*Agree*	*Neither Agree Nor Disagree*	*Disagree*	*Strongly Disagree*	
Members' of SHG	94(62.67)	38(25.33)	4(2.67)	14(9.33)	0(0)	150

Source: Primary data.

Literacy and Communication Skills

Sample respondents are asked to express their opinion on the statement that membership in SHGs improves literacy and communication skills. Table 17.23 shows distribution of the respondents by their opinion on the statement that membership in SHGs improves literacy and communication skills. Of the sample surveyed, 62.67 per cent of the respondents strongly agreed with this statement, 28 per cent of the respondents agreed, 1.33 per cent of the respondents stated no objection, 5.33 per cent of the respondents disagreed and the rest 2.67 per cent of the respondents strongly disagreed. It is concluded that on the whole majority of the respondents feel that membership in SHGs improves literacy and communication skills. The same is observed across the strata also.

Table 17.23: Perception of Member's on Improvements in Literacy and Communication Skill

Category	*Membership in SHG improves literacy and communication skill*					*Total*
	Strongly Agree	*Agree*	*Neither Agree Nor Disagree*	*Disagree*	*Strongly Disagree*	
Members of SHG	94(62.67)	42(28.00)	2(1.33)	8(5.33)	4(2.67)	150

Source: Primary data.

However, half of the fish vending business women reported that literacy and communication skills are not improved after joining SHGs.

Leadership Skills

Sample respondents are asked to express their opinion on the statement that membership in SHGs improves leadership skills. Table 17.24 depicts distribution of the respondents by their opinion on the statement that membership in SHGs improves leadership skills. It is evident from the table that 62.67 per cent of the respondents have strongly agreed with this statement, while 16 per cent of the respondents have agreed with this statement, whilst another 12 per cent of the respondents disagreed to this statement and a little percentage (2.67%) of the respondents strongly disagreed with this statement. Some of the respondents stated no objection to this statement (6.67%).

Table 17.24: Perception of SHG Members Improves Leadership Skills

Category	*Membership in SHG improves leadership skill*					*Total*
	Strongly Agree	*Agree*	*Neither Agree Nor Disagree*	*Disagree*	*Strongly Disagree*	
Members of SHG	94(62.67)	24(16.00)	10(6.67)	18(12.00)	4(2.67)	150

Source: Primary data.

From the above analysis, it is observed that 71.33 per cent of the sample respondent strongly agrees that their involvement in SHG increases their capacities to spend more while 72 per cent of the sample respondent agrees that there is an increase in their income after involving with SHG. Again, 69.33 per cent of the sample respondents strongly agree that their income increases after joining SHG. On the social impact sphere, 56 per cent strongly agree that involvement in SHG promotes decision-making power while 58 per cent of the sample respondents claimed that involvement in SHG induces social responsibility and created better awareness about health and environment. On psychological impact sphere, 68 per cent of the sample respondents believed that their involvement in SHG creates confidence to face problems while 64.67 per cent of the respondents strongly agree that involvement in SHG creates awareness about self-reliance. To sum-up, it can be said that majority of the respondents opined that membership in SHGs has positive socio-economic and psychological impact.

SECTION III

SWOT Analysis of the SHG Management

An attempt is made in the present chapter to examine the strengths, weaknesses, threats and opportunities of sample SHGs so as to analyse the prospects of SHGs in micro-finance management. This section presents the SWOT analysis of the sample respondents. SWOT analysis is a qualitative tool which by identifying the strengths, weakness, opportunities and threats to the SHGs makes an overall assessment of the performance of the groups. The primary data are collected from the sample respondents to measure SWOT on the basis of their perceptions and expressed in percentage.

Strengths

The study has identified various aspects of group functioning as their strengths. Strengths of the sample respondents are shown in Table 17.25. Proper rationale behind joining SHGs is found to be their strength since all the members under study joined SHGs with various reasons. Small group size is also found to be strength of the sample SHGs as management of the group is easy with small number of members.

Selection of group leader, who is acceptable to all members, is also the strength of the group as members have the option to select their leader at their cause. It is found from the field data that a member, who is literate, prudent and acceptable to all the members, was selected as the group leader. The study shows unity among the sample respondents, which results in fewer conflicts among the group members. It is evident from the study that conducting of meetings regularly, holding of meetings whenever and wherever necessary and providing chance to every member to raise voice in the meetings are also the strengths of the sample SHGs. Conducting of meetings in such manner enables the sustainability of the groups and gives a chance to discuss and overcome their problems. This provision is also their strength. Of the sample surveyed, 62 per cent of the sample respondents regularly attend to the group meetings. Of the sample surveyed, 93 per cent of the members under study know rules and regulations of SHGs. This is also the strength of sample SHGs. Further, it is also found from the study that sample respondents are updating

Table 17.25: Strengths of SHG Members

Sl. No.	*Strengths*	*% of Respondents*
1.	Justified rationale behind joining SHGs	100
2.	Flexibility in amount of savings	100
3.	Flexibility in internal group loan norms	100
4.	Flexibility in recovery of bank loan	100
5.	Proper utilisation of interest accrued	100
6.	Holding of meetings at the desire of members	98
7.	Having awareness about rules and regulations	93
8.	Regular savings	92
9.	Democratic selection of group leader	90
10.	Running of IGA	89
11.	Equal right of members in decision-making	88
12.	Unanimous decisions	87
13.	Regular updating of SHG passbook	83
14.	Regular updating of books of accounts	82
15.	Regular updating of member's passbooks	80
16.	Regular repayment of bank loan installment	79
17.	Unity among group members	72
18.	Regular attendance of the members to the group meetings	62
19.	Marketing on own	62
20.	Family support	14

Source: Computed from Primary data.

the books of accounts regularly. They also update the passbook of the group as well as the members regularly. This is also their strength in the functioning of their group. Again, group cohesiveness *per se* is observed in the present study. This shows the good organisational sustainability of the sample SHGs. This is also the one of the strengths of the sample SHGs as drop-out of members from the group (though existence is low) may lead to certain problems in the sustainability of the groups. Further, the sample respondents reported that they determine the amount of savings. They also have the right to determine the norms for internal group lending as well as disbursement of bank loan. Thus, they have the flexibility to this extent in managing their group. This flexibility in management is also one of their strength in managing the group. The payment of thrift amount regularly is found to be one of the strength of the sample SHGs.

As regards strengths of the sample respondents, it is found that proper rationale behind joining SHGs, selection of Group Leader, who is acceptable to all members, regular conducting of meetings, holding of meetings whenever necessary, unanimous decisions, providing chance to every member to raise their voice, flexibility in group management in terms of amount of savings, flexibility in group management in terms of, norms for internal group loan, flexibility in group management in terms of disbursement of bank loan etc., regular payment of thrift amount, proper utilisation of interest accrued on savings amount, having awareness about rules and regulations to all the members, regular updating of books of accounts, regular updating of member's passbooks, regular updating of SHG passbook, regular repayment of bank loan installment amount, regular repayment of internal group loan installment amount, regular attendance of the members to the group meetings and marketing on own are the major strengths of the sample respondents.

Weaknesses

There are certain attributes in which the sample SHGs assessed to be weak or deficient. Weaknesses are shown in Table 17.26. Lack of periodical appraisal of the performance of the group, rotation of the group leader, lack of capital adequacy and absence of quality assessment are found to be one of the major weaknesses of the sample members. It is found from the study that sample respondents are not intimating in advance about their absence to the group meetings. This is found to be weakness in the functioning of the group.

Table 17.26: Weakness of SHG Members

Sl. No.	*Weaknesses*	*% of Respondents*
1.	Non-intimation of leave of absence to the group meetings	100
2.	Absence of quality assessment	100
3.	Lack of periodical appraisal on the performance of the group	98
4.	Absence of group leader rotation	95
5.	Regularity in conducting of group meetings	94
6.	Update minutes	92
7.	Presence of drop-out of members in the group	91
8.	Low follow-up action by the promoter	86
9.	Selection of IGA without feasibility study	55
10.	Lack of capital adequacy	54
11.	Low recovery rate in the repayment of internal group loan	45
12.	Low recovery rate on Bank loan	43
13.	Poor attendance in group meeting	32
14.	Irregular practice of updating of books of accounts	15
15.	Irregularity in updating of SHG passbook	15
16.	Irregular updating of SHG passbook	12
17.	Lack of awareness about rules and regulations of SHG	10

Source: Computed from Primary data.

With regard to weaknesses of the sample, the study reveals that non-intimation of absence to the group meetings in case it is not possible to attend the meeting, lack of rotation of group leaders and lack of awareness about rules and regulations of SHG etc. are the prominent weaknesses of the sample respondents.

Opportunities

Most of the SHGs are conscious of opportunities available to consolidate strengths and overcome weaknesses. There are certain opportunities too. Table 17.27 presents the opportunities of the sample respondents. Topping the list is the increases the income and savings, opportunity to participate in social activities and providing employment opportunities.

Table 17.27: Opportunities of SHG Members

Sl. No.	*Opportunities*	*% of Respondents*
1.	Increases income	98
2.	Increases savings	98
3.	Capacity to spend more	98
4.	Create employment opportunities	97
5.	Creates confidence to face problems	97
6.	Participation in social activities and organise social events	96
7.	Increases decision-making power in the household	94
8.	Creates better awareness about health and environment	86
9.	Earning for livelihood	83
10.	Enhances social status	82
11.	Improves leadership skill	81
12.	Increase in value of assets	78
13.	Improves literacy and communication skill	76
14.	Creates awareness about self-reliance	76
15.	Induces social responsibility	72

Source: Computed from Primary data.

Other opportunities include capacity to spend more on food as well as non-food expenditure; creating confidence to face problems; increasing of decision-making power in the family; improving literacy and communication skill; giving social status; creates better awareness about health; increase in the value of assets; creating awareness about self-reliance; improving leadership skill and inducing social responsibility.

Threats

For any collective entity to survive, it is necessary for the members of the collective entity to have the capacity to identify threat factors and take steps to ensure that these threats do not affect sustainability. In the SWOT exercise, 10 threats have been identified. Threats of the sample respondents are shown in Table 17.28:

Table 17.28: Threats of SHG Members

Sl. No.	*Threats*	*% of Respondents*
1.	Lack of training	100
2.	Subsidy and target oriented promotion strategy	98
3.	Lack of quality and sustainability approach	87
4.	Absence of follow-up action by the promoter, donor etc.	82
5.	Lack of impact assessment	76
6.	Dependence on others for marketing	35
7.	Lack of family support	24
8.	Lack of support from Government machinery	24
9.	Group conflicts and training on conflict management	12
10.	Problem of raw materials	12

Source: Computed from Primary data.

It is evident from Table 17.22 that lack of training to the SHGs on conflict management is found to be major threat. Subsidy and target oriented promotion strategy of the promoter and donor is also reported to be one of the threats as perceived by 98 per cent of the sample respondents. At the next level, lack of quality and sustainability approach of the promoter and financier including donor is found to be threat as reported by 87 per cent of the sample respondents. Although, the government machinery provides support to the SHG under different structure, due to lack of heartfelt cooperation they are still depending on self. Hence, this needs to be addressed. Less prominent threats are group conflicts (12%), lack of family support (24%), and problem of raw-materials (12%)

To sum-up, it can be said that SWOT analysis of sample SHGs shows that strengths and opportunities are found to be higher in degree when compared to weakness and threats. This is the ample evidence of the fact that members in the SHG are confident of overcoming the minor weaknesses and threats utilising the major strengths and opportunities that they possess.

Recommendations

Considering the findings of the study and also if the quality of the SHGs is taken into care, the role of SHGs towards empowerment will undoubtedly improved. The following recommendations are forwarded in this connection.

- Literacy and numeric training is essential for the poor women to benefit from the micro-credit schemes. Further, training in legal literacy, rights and gender awareness are important complements to micro-credit for the empowerment of women. The members should be given necessary training and guidance for the successful operation of the group.
- The members of the SHG should be more active, enthusiastic and dynamic to mobilise their savings by group actions. In this process NGOs and other agencies should act as a facilitator and motivator.
- The office bearers managing the group should be given nominal financial benefits, which will enable them to be more involved in the activities of the Group.
- The bank should advance adequate credit to the SHG according to their needs. The procedure of the banks in sanctioning credit to SHG should be simple and quick.
- Uniformity should be maintained in formation and extension of financial assistance to them by banks in all blocks.
- Access to bank credit should be increased by taking various simple operational decisions and steps like standardising the set of documents to be furnished by an SHG for opening its bank account or for accessing credit.
- Multiple agencies in the State are implementing SHG programmes with different objectives and approaches; this garbles the message that reaches the ground. This goes against the holistic support and collaboration requirements of SHGs and SHG programmes.
- Marketing facilities for the sale of products of SHG may be created. Periodical exhibitions at block-level may be organised where the products of SHG can be displayed.
- Meetings and Seminars may be organised where the members will get a chance to exchange their views and be able to develop their group strength by interactions.

- Government and other institutions need to implement their development projects through SHG so that the members of the SHG get ample scope for getting empowered in both social and psychological sphere.
- Steps needs to be ensured that the promoter and donor must come forwarded to provide skill development and training to the members. Constant monitoring and collection of feedback from member SHGs is quite necessary.
- Federation and Joint Liability Groups of SHG functioning needs to promote.
- Active intervention by district administration, professional bodies and voluntary organisations is precondition for the successful conception of micro-enterprises in terms of skill training, designing products, providing new technology and access to market.
- There is a need for conciseness about the well established and well recognised quality assessment tools without biasness.

Conclusion

In Assam, the SHGs primarily concentrate on women and economically backward classes. The size of the groups ranges between 10 and 15. Most of the members are the poorest of the poor, mainly landless agricultural labourers. Uniform socio-economic status and living together in the same rural community are observed to be the homogeneous factors among groups. The main reason for forming the SHGs in the study area is to obtain the financial support from the Government, the NGOs and the Banks in order to improve the economic status of the members.

The major discipline observed by the SHGs in the State is regularity in meetings (at least once in a month), attendance in the meetings (at least 60%) and regular savings. It has also been observed that in the initial period members of the Banks/NGOs/MFIs etc. attended all the group meetings and year after year they gradually reduced their participation to create the autonomy of the group. There payment performance of loan is more than 65 per cent. It is found that the main problems faced by the SHGs are delay in sanctioning the loans by the Government authorities and the bank officials. Further, the SHGs are facing the problems of marketing, basic infrastructure, training and skill development avenues, lack of administrative experience in managing the affairs of the groups.

The quality of groups is quite low in the selected districts in comparison to other blocks or states. Strict random selection of sample could be one of the reasons. Further, it is observed that SHGs has a positive impact on women member and in many cases it is proved that SHG promotes empowerment in the study districts. It is observed from the perceptions of the respondents about the impact of SHG, majority of the respondent strongly agrees that their involvement in SHG increases their income, savings and their capacities to spend more. Further, in social impact sphere, majority of the respondent strongly agree that involvement in SHG promotes decision-making power and involvement in SHG further induces social responsibility and created better awareness about health and environment. Moreover, on psychological impact sphere, majority of the sample respondents believed that their involvement in SHG creates confidence to face problems and their involvement in SHG creates awareness about self-reliance.

Moreover, it can be said that SWOT analysis of sample SHGs shows that strengths and opportunities are found to be higher in degree when compared to weakness and threats. This is the ample evidence of the fact that members in the SHGs are confident of overcoming the minor weaknesses and threats utilising the major strengths and opportunities that they possess.

Finally, it is observed that due to fast growing of the SHG-Bank linkage programme in the country, the quality of SHG has come under stress. Some of the factors affecting the quality of SHGs are: (i) the target oriented approach of the government preparing group; (ii) inadequate incentive to NGO's for nurturing their groups; (iii) lack of proper monitoring; (iv) absence of quality enhancement mechanism etc. It is further observed that quality of SHGs should not be stressed upon more than their numbers (i.e., quantity). Hence, the situations demand quality assessment of SHGs and financial institutions, MFIs, NGOs, Promoters must be engaged to study the qualitative aspects in further funding and promotion of SHGs in the state. In fine, quality parameters would include not just financial and physical performance of the group, but also parameters to assess economic and livelihood goal achievement, social status improvement and entitlement access facilitation. In fact, rating of SHGs assumes importance as it is not only a pre-appraisal tool, but as well a self-monitoring yardstick for the SHGs themselves for self-evaluation, which is a continuous process. Quality assessment of SHGs has come to be accepted as an important tool to ensure standards in SHGs.

Policy Implications

In this twenty first century, we must take along an active people-centred and growth-oriented poverty alleviation strategy—a strategy, which seems to incorporate women's aspirations, dynamism and involvement. It is envisaged that self-help groups will play a vital role in such strategy. But there is a need for structural orientation of the groups to suit the requirements of new business.

Micro-credit movement has to be viewed from a long-term perspective under SHG framework, which underlines the need for a deliberate policy implication in favour of assurance in terms of technology back-up, product market and human resource development. Hence, there is a need for the development of an innovative and diversified micro-finance sector, which will make a real contribution to women empowerment and rural development.

NOTES

1. Chitagubbi, Geeta and Naik, D. Murahari (2011). *Women Self-Help Groups: A Developmental Approach*, Germany: VDM Publishing.
2. Ganesh Murthy and V.S. Radha (2002). A study on Thrift and Credit Utilisation pattern of Self-Help Group (SHG) in Lakshmi Vilas Bank Suriyampalyam Branch, Irode. *Indian Journal of Marketing*, 34 (1): 12-24.
3. Dwarakanath, H.D. (2002). Rural Credit and women Self-Help Groups. *Kurukshetra*. 51(1):10.
4. Das, S.K. (2012). Micro-Finance and Women Empowerment: Does Self-Help Group Empowers Women? *International Journal of Management and Business Studies*, 2(2): 71-79.
5. Cheston, Susy and Lisa Kuhn (2000). Empowering Women through Micro-finance. Unpublished Background Paper for the Micro-credit Summit 15, New York. Retrieved from http://.www.microcreditsummit.org.
6. Sahu and Tripathy (2005). *Self-Help Groups and Women Empowerment*. New Delhi: Anmol Publications Pvt. Ltd.
7. Chen, M., Jhabvala, R., Kanbur, R. and Richards, C. (2007). *Membership Based Organisations of the Poor: Concepts, Experience and Policy*. London and New York: Routledge.
8. Singh, J. Godwin Prem; Parthesarathy and Mudiappan, M. (2009). Micro-Credit as a Strategy for Women's Empowerment. In Singh, J. Godwin Prem, Anita Priya Raja, and Florence, Shalini (Eds.), *Millennium Development Goals: A Social Science Perspectives* (pp. 170-176). New Delhi. Allied Publishers.

9. Chattopadhya, H.P. and Bhagel, Indu (2009). *Theory of Public Administration* (vol. 1). New Delhi: Global Vision Publishing House. pp. 215-240.
10. Panda, R.K. (2005). *Emerging Issues on Rural Credit*, (1st Ed.). New Delhi: APH Publishing Corporation.
11. Agarwal, S. (2007). Self-Help Groups and Bank Linkages: Performance and socio-economic impact with respect to women empowerment in Agra District. Unpublished doctoral dissertation, Dayalbagh Educational Institute, Agra, India.
12. Gopisetti, R. (2007).Working of Self-Help Groups in Andhra Pradesh: A study of marketing and financial aspects.Unpublished doctoral dissertation, Osmania University, Hyderabad, India.
13. Gaonkar, M.S. (2008). Financing of Self-Help Groups by Commercial banks: A case study of Uttarakhand District. Unpublished doctoral dissertation, Karnataka University, Dharavad, India.
14. Sarkar, S. (2008). Self-Help Groups: A study of systems operations and constraints of a micro-finance programme with special reference to Jalpaiguri district. Unpublished doctoral dissertation, University of North Bengal, Raja Rammohanpur, Jalpaiguri, India.
15. Nagarajan, P. S. (2009). Marketing problems of self-help groups: A study with respect to Kanyakumari district, unpublished doctoral dissertation, Alagappa University, Kakaikudi, India.
16. Prakash, J. (2009). Micro-finance for poverty reduction and empowerment A Study of urban poor households in the Visakhapatnam city Andhra Pradesh.Unpublished doctoral dissertation, Andhra University, Visakhapatnam, India.
17. Sarangi, N. (2008). Micro-finance and the rural poor: A study of group based credit programmes in Madhya Pradesh in India. Unpublished doctoral dissertation, Centre for the study of Regional Development, Jawaharlal Nehru University, New Delhi.
18. Abdul, H. (2005). An Assessment of the performance of Regional Rural Banks in West Bengal with respect to Murshidabad Gramin Bank, Unpublished doctoral dissertation, University of North Bengal, Raja Ramshunpur, Darjeeling, India.
19. Das, S.K. (2012a). Performance of Regional Rural Bank's in Micro-Financing in North East India: A Case Study, *IJSSR-Indian Journal of Social Sciences Research*, Hyderabad Institute of Social Sciences, Hyderabad, 1(3): 6-18.
20. Das, S.K. (2012b). Performance of Formal Financial Institutions in Self-Help Bank Linkage Programme (SBLP) in North East India: An Assessment, *International Journal of Development Studies*, IV (1): 67-79.
21. Das, S.K. (2013). RRB's Performance towards Micro-Financing in North East India, *Assam Economic Journal*, XXVI: 65-86.
22. Kanaskar, M.P. (2008). Study of micro-enterprises and micro-financing

systems in rural non-firm sector with respect to Jawahar Tribal Block in Maharashtra. Unpublished doctoral dissertation. Bharati Vidyapeeth, Pune, India.

23. Natarajan, J. (2007). Micro-finance for promotion of micro-enterprises: Emerging challenges. Unpublished doctoral dissertation, Gandhigram Rural Institute, Gandhigram, Dindigul, India.
24. Patanaik, Sunanda (2003). *Empowerment through SHG: A Case Study of Gajapati District, Smaraika*. 2003. Retrieved from http://www.isical.ac.in/.../Paper
25. Narasiah, M.L. (2004). *Micro-credit and Women*, (1st Ed.). New Delhi: Discovery Publishing House.
26. Manimekalai, N., Rajeswari, G. (2000). Empowerment of Women through Self-help Groups. *Margin*, 32(4):74-77.
27. Sinha, F. (2005). Access, Use and Contribution of Microfinance in India, Findings from a National Study, *Economic and Political Weekly*, XL (17): 1714-1732.
28. Suguna, B. (2006). *Employment of Rural Women through Self-Help Groups* (1st Ed.). New Delhi: Discovery Publishing House.
29. Lalneihzovi (2007). *Women's Development in India* (1st Ed.). New Delhi: Mittal Publication.
30. Ali-Akpajiak, C.A. & Pyke, T. (2003). *Measuring Poverty in Nigeria* (1st ed.), UK Oxfam GB 33.
31. Krishna, M. (2003). *Poverty Alleviation and Rural Poor* (1st Ed.), New Delhi: Mittal Publication.
32. Jerinabi, U. (2006). *Micro-Credit Management by Women's Self-Help Groups* (1st Ed.). New Delhi: Discovery Publishing House.
33. Singh, Jai Pal (2006). *PEDO's SHG Programme Impact Assessment: A Draft Report, Centre for Micro-finance*. Retrieved from http://www.solutionexchange-un.net.in/mf.
34. Mukerjee, Tuhin (2006). Impact assessment study of SGSY programme on empowerment of women at Babpur village, Vidyasagar School of Social Work.
35. Gurumoorthy, T. R. (2002). SHGs-Economic Empowerment through Self-Reliance, *Social Welfare*, 49(7): 14-17.
36. Roy, S. (2011). Extending Micro-finance services through SHGs: An Assessment of Self-Help Groups particularly Assam. Paper presented at seminar BIRD in collaboration with IIBM on Micro-finance in North East, 2011, 28th-29th January, Guwahati: 26-39.
37. Kamaraj, J.M. Arul (2005). Self-Help Groups New Mantra for Empowerment, *Readers Shelf*, 2(2): 13-16.
38. Manimekalai, N. and Rajeswari, G. (2000). Empowerment of Women through Self-help Groups. *Margin*, 32(4): 74-77.
39. Pati, A.P. and Lyngdoh, Benjamin F. (2011). Microfinance and Socio-economic change. An Assessment of Meghalaya. Paper presented at

seminar BIRD in collaboration with IIBM on Microfinance in North East, 2011, 28th-29th January, Guwahati: 12-17.

40. Aruna and Joythirmayi (2011). The Role of Micro-Finance in Women Empowerment: A study on SHG-Bank linkage programme in Hyderabad, *Indian Journal of Commerce and Management Studies*, 11 (4): 77-85.
41. Meetei, K.I. (2011). The Impact of MF Accessibility through Group initiative to Rural Women in Manipur—A case study. Paper presented at seminar BIRD in collaboration with IIBM on Micro-finance in North East, 2011, 28th-29th January, Guwahati: 16-21.
42. Centre of Micro-Finance Research (2009). Retrieved from http://www.goggle.com.
43. Sharma, A. (2007). Expanding outreach to underserved regions: Kick-starting Micro-finance in North Eastern Region, *Indian Institute Bank Management*. Retrieved from http://www.shgateway.org.
44. APMAS (2009). Quality and Sustainability of SHGs in Assam. Retrieved from http://www.apmas.org.
45. Sa-Dhan (2003). Quality Parameters of SHGs: A discussion paper. Retrieved from http://.www.sa-dhan.net
46. Reddy, C.S. (2005). SHGs: A Keystone of Micro-Finance in India: Women Empowerment and Social Security. Retrieved from http://www.self-help-approach.com.
47. APMAS (2006). Self-Help Groups in India: A Study of the Lights and Shades, EDA Rural Systems. Retrieved from http://www.edarural.com.
48. Roy, Durgadas (2007). Mid-term Evaluation of the composition and working of Swarnajayanti Gram SwarozgarYojana in 24 Parganas South District (West Bengal). Retrieved from http://www.planningcommission.nic.in.
49. Kumar, Sunil (2010). Centre for Micro-Finance Research and BIRD. Retrieved from http://www.birdindia.org.in.
50. Sahu, Gagan Bihari (2010). SHG Bank Linkages in North-West India: Experiences and Challenges in Financial Access and Poverty Alleviation, *Centre for Micro-Finance (sub-centre) Institute of Development Studies*, Jaipur.
51. Das, S.K. (2012). Best Practices of Self-Help Groups and Women Empowerment: A Case of Barak Valley of Assam, *Far East Journal of Psychology and Business*, Far East Research Centre, 7(2): 29-51.
52. Barnes, Carolyn (1996). *Assets and the Impact of Micro-enterprise Finance Programmes.* Washington DC: Management Systems International.
53. Mayoux, Linda (1997). Impact Assessment and Women's Empowerment in Micro-Finance Programmes: Issues for a Participatory Action and Learning Approach. (mimeo). Washington DC: Consultative Group to Assist the Poorest (CGAP).
54. Goetz, A.M. and Sen Gupta, R. (1996). Who Takes the Credit? Gender, Power and Control over Loan Use in Rural Credit Programmes in Bangladesh. *World Development,* 24(1): 45-64.

55. Schuler, S.R. and Hashemi, S.M. (1996). Credit Programmes, Women's Empowerment and Contraceptive Use in Rural Bangladesh. *Studies in Family Planning,* 25(2): 65-76.
56. Hashemi, S.M., Schuler, S.R. and Riley, A.P. (1996). Rural Credit Programmes and Women's Empowerment in Bangladesh. *World Development,* 24(4): 635-654.
57. Fuglesang, A. and Chandler, D. (1986). *Participation as Process: What We Can Learn From the Grameen Bank*. Oslo: NORAD.
58. NCAER (2008). Impact and Sustainability of SHG-Bank Linkage Programme. New Delhi: National Council of Applied Economic Research (NCAER).

18

Self-Help Groups

A Tool for Women Empowerment: A Case Study

Smti Likha Kiran Kabak

Background of the Study

Women constitute nearly half of the population in India. But major percentage of women particularly of rural areas is poorer than men because of traditional social structure. To achieve the millennium development goal and to claim as developed country, it is mandatory that women are equally advanced and empowered. Gender equality and women empowerment are central to the achievement of different national developmental goals. Various developmental policies and programmes have been initiated to empower women. However, it is a known fact that Indian women are at the crossroad of their destiny. There is a great upsurge in consciousness about their rights among all sections and classes of society in the country. The Ninth Plan document recognises that in spite of development measures and constitutional legal guarantees, women have lagged behind in almost all sectors. Despite tremendous contribution of women to the agricultural sector, their work is considered just an extension of household domain and remains no monetised. Women are deprived of their economic status, especially in rural area. But they do bear sole responsibility for family welfare and household management. Due to societal structured beliefs and norms, barriers in mobility and discrimination in education women are poorer than its counterparts.

SHGs are assumed to play effective role in empowering women in economic, social and psychological dimensions. 'Empowerment' is the implicit goal of the SHG programmes targeting poor women. Several Studies have been conducted in Regional, National and International Level. In State level, only few studies have been attempted to measure empowerment in context of SHGs. The present study examines how far SHGs can generate 'empowerment' of different dimension in women.

Objective

Does participation in SHG empower the women? If so, how far and what extent does the dimension of empowerment achieve through SHG?

Women Empowerment

Very often we talk about empowerment especially women empowerment. What is this empowerment? The Empowerment is about power and about changing the balance of power. In every society, there are powerful and powerless groups. Power is exercised socially, economically and politically by one person over other person or over group of persons. Women usually falls under the powerless group which necessitates the programmes ensured empowerment of women. Power can be defined as the degree or assets fall into five broad categories: physical/material resources (like land, water, forests); human resources (people, their bodies, their labour and skills); intellectual resources (knowledge, information, ideas); social (social capital) and financial resources (money, access to money). This power is dynamic and relational, rather than absolute–it is exercised in the social, economic and political relations between individuals and groups. It is also unequally distributed. In nutshell, any person who have power or have enough confidence to give and take decision and influence other in a particular matter may call as powerful man and the activity is called empowerment.

According to the *International Encyclopaedia* (1999), power means having the capacity and the means to direct one's life towards desired social, political and economic goals or status. Therefore, women empowerment means giving the capacity and means to direct women's life towards desired goals. It does not mean setting women against men. Indeed it means making both men and women realise their changing roles and status and develop a consensus for harmonious living. It means redistribution of work roles, redistributing their values to the changing world and attitudes and evolving new kinds of adjustments, understanding and trust with each other. Empowerment of women is a new ideology for carrying democratic values into the family and society.

Women empowerment is a holistic concept. Over the years, the concept of empowerment has broadened to include the growing concern of women's movement for gender equality and social justice. Accordingly, empowerment is viewed as a process by which the powerless gain greater control over the circumstances of their lives. It includes control over resources and ideology, greater self-confidence, and an inner transformation of one's consciousness that enables one to overcome external barriers (Batlivala, 1994). It is a multi-dimensional in its approach which involves personal, social (social-psychological), economic, and political empowerment (Mayous, 1998a, 1998b, 2001, 2006). Socio-psychological empowerment refers to an increase in people's sense of self and consciousness. It is achieved by creating an enabling environment for interaction among members, awareness creation, leadership training etc. Economic empowerment refers to an increase in net income of individuals, increase in capital stock and also an increase in management skills of individual. The political empowerment refers to the realisation of one's own rights, responsibilities and entitlements. Taking into consideration of all these dimensions of empowerment, the World Bank (2000) defined empowerment as a process of enhancing the capacity of poor people to influence the state institutions that affect their lives, by strengthening their participation in political process and local decision-making. It means removing all kinds of barriers, *viz.* political legal, and social that work against a particular group, and building the assets of poor people to enable them to engage in productive activities.

SHG and Women Empowerment

Self-Help Group (SHG) is a group of persons who have voluntarily become the member of the group to achieve common goal by collective efforts. Goal would be different as per the status of the groups. Suppose for BPL group the goal would be to come above poverty line by venturing into income generating activities with the help of credit facilities from banks and group itself.

Rural women, especially those depend on agriculture for survivals, which may be categorised as poor women have limited access to resources. In this scenario SHGs play vital role for women in accessing, creating and owning the resources. In India, micro-finance is dominated by self-help group-bank linkage programme as a cost effective mechanism for providing services to the "unreached poor" which has been successful not only in meeting financial services to the poor women, but also strengthen collective self-help capacities of the poor, leading to their empowerment. The economic empowerment requires that women have some access to and control over productive resources thus ensuring some degree of financial autonomy. Women empowerment is possible only if they are given opportunity to develop freedom, providing credit and participation in decision-making.

SHGs have become best approach to equip women with the weapons for empowerment in these aspects. SHG becomes best means for achieving the various dimensions of empowerment. The present study examines the impact of SHG in empowerment of women in Joram and Yachuli Village.

Study Area and Methodology

The study was conducted in Phu Joram, a small village but scattered household of 20 numbers and Yachuli village under CD Block Yachuli, Lower Subansiri District, Arunachal Pradesh. Both the villages are located along the NH-52 on the way to District Headquarters, Hapoli which further goes to Upper Subansiri District sharing international border with China. The main source of living is agriculture. Every household have paddy field that is sufficient to feed their family only. Public Distribution System (PDS) are also available throughout the year to meet the shortage of food grain. Being situated along the National Highway, these villages are known to be more advanced than other interior village. They have left the millet cultivation and in place of it, they have adopted commercial cultivation like ginger, vegetables, large cardamom etc.

One group each from Phu Joram and Yachuli were selected for comparative study. One group that is engaged in micro-income generating activities besides having paddy and vegetable garden and other one from Joram villages consisting of farmers only. Focused group discussion was held to find out the role of SHGs in empowering women of these villages. After the discussion, group and individual interview schedule was given to them.

Results and Discussion

Phu Joram SHG from Phu Joram Village and Den Ajin SHG from Yachuli were selected to study the impact of SHG in women empowerment. The distance between two village is about 8 kilometres.

Socio-Economic Profile of Phu Joram SHG: All the eight members of Phu Joram SHG are farmer. Few of them are engaged in some contractual works time to time with their husband. The age group are ranging from 25-50 years. Six of them are educated themselves up to the level of middle school. Two member of Phu Joram SHG could not reach to the door of school. Focus group discussion with all eight members and individual interview schedule formed the primary database for the study. Thrift and credit is the main activity of the group. They save Rs. 800 per month at the rate of Rs.100 per member. Loan is disbursed as per the demands and needs of the members. However, they informed that entire earlier saving has been divided amongst the members for fresh start with few new members because few old members have leaved the group. Therefore, their total saving is just Rs. 2400 up to January, 2014. All the members are Christian.

Socio-Profile of Den Ajin SHG: This group is consisting of 10 members. Maximum of them are farmer like the Phu Joram SHG member except four members who are engaged in meat and vegetable business. One is running the medium size grocery shop and three of them are engaged in meat (chicken) business at Yachuli Market. The age group of the members are ranging from 25-50 years. Thrift and Credit is one of the main activities of the group. They save Rs. 1000 per month at the rate of Rs. 100 per member. All ten members of Den Ajin are Christians. Members of this Den Ajin SHG are earning Rs. 4000–6000 per month from income generating activities.

Member of Phu Joram SHG spends Rs. 15,000 to 1,91,200 in recent year in Food, Cloth, Consumer durable items, Medicine and Health Treatment, Children's education etc. as shown in table 18.1. Maximum of them are earning Rs. 30,000-40,000 in average. They have very limited source of income, i.e. vegetables and MGNREGA.

The expenditure pattern of Den Ajin SHG in recent year varies from Phu Joram SHG which consists of farmers only. Den Ajin SHG are engaged in micro-income generating activities and therefore, they could spend Rs. 72,600 to Rs. 3,36,000 in Food, Cloth, Education etc. as shown in Table 18.2.

The asset position of Phu Joram SHG is average. They owned a *Kuchcha* House, few of them owned semi-*Pucca* House and few acres of agricultural land. Their average saving in a year is just Rs.1200 only. They worked through the year except Sunday and some days of rest during off working season in December and January. Children are studying in private and government schools (*see* Table 18.3).

The asset position of Den Ajin SHG member is good. They owned *kuchcha* and semi-*pucca* houses, few acres of paddy and vegetable field. Some of them owned small shops. Their average income of the year is Rs. 1,60,000. Though the members are very less educated (formal) but their children's are studying in colleges. They are spending in lakhs for their children's education (*see* Table 18.4).

Table 18.1: Expenditure Pattern of Phu Joram SHG in Recent Year (2013-14) (*in Rs.*)

Statistical Tool	*Food*	*Cloth*	*Consumer durable items*	*Medicine and Health Treat-ment*	*Education for Children*		*Entertainment*	*Social responsebilities*	*Home construction and repair*	*Personal Consumables*	*Total*
					Study inside of the State	*Study outside of the State*					
	Upto 25000	*1000-20000*	*Upto 1200*	*1000-30000*	*3000-60000*	*nil*	*1000 - 10000*	*500-2000*	*5000–10000*	*1000–7000*	*15000 – 191200*
Mid-value	12500	10500	600	15500	33000	–	10500	1250	7500	4000	

Source: Field Study in January, 2014.

Table 18.2: Expenditure Pattern of Den Ajin SHG in Recent Year (2013-14) (*in Rs.*)

Statistical tool	*Food*	*Cloth*	*Consumer durable items*	*Medicine and Health Treatment*	*Education for Children*		*Entertainment*	*Social responsebilities*	*Home construction and repair*	*Personal Consumables*	*Total*
					Study inside of the State	*Studyoutside of the State*					
Mid-Value	10000–20000	3000–15000	4000–12000	6000–40000	3000–60000	Nil	600–2000	6000–8000	15000–200000	1000–6000	72600 – 336000
	10500	9500	9000	23000	33000	—	1300	7000	107500	3500	

Source: Field Study in January, 2014.

Table 18.3: Impact of SHG (Phu Joram) on Socio-Economic Variables (*in Rs.*)

Average Income of the house-hold per year	*Asset position of the house-hold*	*Average saving of the house-hold per year*	*Average No. of Days worked in a year*	*Literacy status of the household members*	*Number of household member migrated to other place for job*	*Land Purchase, if any*	*India Tour, if any*
10,000–50,000	*Kuchcha* House, Animals including Mithun	1200	300 days	Husband: Illiterate to Secondary level Sons & Daughters: Studying in Government and Private School	nil	nil	nil

Source: Field Study in January, 2014.

Table 18.4: Impact of SHG (Den Ajin) on Socio-Economic Variables (*in Rs.*)

Average Income of the household per year	*Asset position of the household*	*Average saving of the household per year*	*Average No. of Days worked in a year*	*Literacy status of the household members*	*Number of household member migrated to other place for job*	*Land purchase, if any*	*India Tour, if any*
120000–216000	Average to Good	4000 to 50000	300–317 days	Husband: Illiterate to Secondary level Sons & Daughters : KG to Graduation	nil	nil	nil

Source: Field Study in January, 2014.

Table 18.5: Dimensions of Empowerment achieved by Members of Phu Joram SHG

Sl. No.	*Variables*	*Responses of SHG Members*			*Remarks, if any*
		Yes	*To some extent*	No	
1.	Awareness on benefits of SHGs	6	2		
2.	Better Self-Awareness	6	2		
3.	Decision-making ability				
	(a) Take Decision for self	5	3		
	(b) Give decision for the family	5	3		
	(c) Give Decision for the community/society	2	6		
4.	Excising Power of Authority	2	6		
5.	Ability to face problems	6	2		
	(a) What kind of problems usually face?	Money shortage			Considered as minor problems
	(b) Are you able to solve that problem?	6	2		
6.	SHG helped me personality development	6	2		
7.	Leaderships quality	5	3		
8.	Enhanced knowledge of enterprises	6	2		
9.	Enhance knowledge of rights and legal issues	2	2	4	
10.	Able to read and write	4	2	2	
11.	Able to sign	6	2		
12.	Consciousness about Children Education	6	2		
13.	Consciousness about Voting to right person	6	2		
14.	Consciousness about Better Life Lead	8			
15.	Consciousness about Water and Sanitation Related Diseases	4	4		
16.	Got Confidence	6	2		
17.	Take stand for women's right	4	4		
18.	Interested in contesting in the Panchayat election	2	2	4	

Source: Field Study in January, 2014.

Phu Joram group members are well aware of the benefits of SHGs, conscious on children's education, income generation, voting rights, better life, about water sanitation related diseases etc. They inform that they get motivation from each other in taking decision for welfare of the family and self. They got courage from the SHG to venture into income generation activities as well. However, they are not confident enough to take decision for themselves always. None of them has attended any training so far, except one, who has attended in the training programme organised by SIRD at Yachuli. They are not so aware about women's right or showing interest in politics as well.

Table 18.6: Dimensions of Empowerment achieved by members of Den Ajin SHG

Sl. No	*Variables*	*Responses of SHG Members*			*Remarks, if any*
		Yes	*To some extent*	*No*	
1.	Awareness on benefits of SHGs	10			
2.	Better Self-Awareness	8	2		
3.	Decision-making ability				
	(a) Take Decision for self	10			
	(b) Give decision for the family	10			
	(c) Give Decision for the community/society	5	3	2	
4.	Excising Power of Authority	2	5	3	
5.	Ability to face problems	10			
	(a) What kind of problems usually face?	Income source			Considered as minor problems
	(b) Are you able to solve that problem?	10			
6.	SHG helped me personality deve-lopment	10			
7.	Leaderships Quality	10			
8.	Enhanced knowledge of enterprises	8	2		
9.	Enhance knowledge of rights and legal issues	8	2		
10.	Able to read and write	8	2	2	
11.	Able to sign	8	2	2	
12.	Consciousness about Children Education	10			
13.	Consciousness about Voting to right person	10			
14.	Consciousness about Better Life Lead	10			
15.	Consciousness about Water and Sanitation Related Diseases	8	2		
16.	Got Confidence	6	4		
17.	Take stand for women's right	10			
18.	Interested in contesting in the Panchayat election	2	2	6	

Source: Field Study in January 2014.

From the discussion and schedule it is found that Den Ajin SHG, which is decade old is more empowered than Phu Joram SHG. Den Ajin SHG has taken a loan of Rs. 1,000 from Apex Bank, Yachuli and they repaid it successfully also. In addition to their individual micro-income generating activities, they are earning the income in group also by doing manual fieldwork together by charging nominal fees even from other non-member. They do their cultivation work on rotation basis by depositing nominal fees in the group account. This helps a lot to member because it lessens the burden of manual cultivation work in their respective paddy and vegetable garden. In this way, they do not hire a labour from outside. The leader of the Den Ajin SHG also attends workshops on codification of customary practices of society. This group take strong stand for women's right in the area.

Findings: Den Ajin SHG is achieving common social and economic goal collectively for which it has been voluntarily formed. However, one negative development has occurred. There was one Private company called 'Angel' in Yachuli. This company lured all villagers and groups to invest in their company for a promising and profitable return. This Den Ajin SHG also decided to invest the entire saving and even monthly saving of Rs. 1000 in that company. But after a year of investment, company eloped with the entire amount. This has created hue and cry amongst the villagers, particularly women group. Because of this development, Den Ajin monthly saving activity has halted at present.

The difference in Den Ajin and Phu Joram SHG is apparent in the level of economic and social empowerment. Den Ajin SHG Member is economically and socially more empowered. The reason is participation of member in group process and its activities actively in last 10 years. Moreover, Den Ajin SHG has attended number of training programmes for SHG being motivated by NGO. It reflects that SHG attending training is becoming more empowered in the dimensions mentioned above in Table 18.4. SHG not attending training are limited to thrift and credit activities only. Though they got loan, motivation and confidence from the group, but they are not so enterprising and therefore, not so active in income generating activities. Den SHG become a tool for members of the group for their empowerment.

Conclusion

The study suggest that the empowerment is ensured if the women participate actively in SHG process not only in thrift and credit but also take-up income generating activities by taking loan from the group. SHG is a platform for build herself into confident and aware persons. SHG is the best tool to empower women socially, economically and politically. Capacity Building Training and Skill Development Training is key to the success of SHGs and their empowerment.

REFERENCES

Acharya Meena, and Pushpa Ghimire (2005). "Gender Indicators of Equality, Inclusion and Poverty Reduction-Measuring Programmes/Project Effectiveness", *Economic and Political Weekly*, 29, (October).

Anitha, H.S. and Revankar Ashok, D.: "Micro-credit through Self-help-groups for Rural Development", *Southern Economist,* August 2007, Vol. 46, No. 8, Bangalore.

Balamirthan, P. and Uma Devi, I.V. : "Women SHGs in the Upliftment of Tsunami Victims", *Southern Economist*, December 2009, Vol. 48, No. 16, p. 4, Bangalore.

Bhingardive, Manisha, D. (2014), Economic Empowerment of Rural Women through SHGs, *Southern Economist*, February 2014, Vol. 52 No. 19, p. 9, Banglore.

Schuller, M. (1996), *Empowerment and the Law: Trategies of Third World Women* (Washington: OEF International).

19

Empowerment of Women and Socio-Economic Development of North Eastern Region of India

Paritosh Chandra Dutta

> "Short-changing girls is not only a matter of gender discrimination; it is bad economics and bad societal policy. Experience has shown, over and over again, that investment in girls' education translate directly and quickly into better nutrition for the hole family, better health care, declining fertility, poverty reduction and better overall economic performance".
>
> **Kofi Annan**, *Former United Nations Secretary General*

Background

Empowerment is a process of increasing the capacity of an individual or a group of individuals to make choices and to transform those choices into desired actions and outcomes. Central to this process are actions, which build both individual and collective assets and improve the efficiency and fairness of the organisational and institutional context that govern the use of these assets. Empowerment refers to increasing the spiritual, political, social or economic strength of individuals as well as communities. During the last seven decades, the concept of women empowerment has undergone a sea change from welfare oriented approach of women empowerment to equity approach. It often involves the empowered developing confidence in their capacities. In economic development, the empowerment approach focuses on mobilising the self-help efforts of the poor, rather than providing them with social welfare. Economic empowerment is also the empowering of previously disadvantaged sections of the population. According to the Country

Report[1] of Government of India, *"Empowerment means moving from a position of enforced powerlessness to one of power"*.

The empowerment of women is one of the central issues in the process of development of countries all over the world. It is a process through which women gain greater control over resources-material, human and intellectual like knowledge, information, ideas and financial assets and control over decision-making at home as well as in the community, society and nation, and also gain 'power'. The Government of India has made empowerment of women as one of the principal objectives of the Ninth Five Year Plan (1997-2002) and also declared 2001 as the year of *'Women's Empowerment'*.

"Gender inequality holds back the growth of individuals, the development of nations and the evolution of societies to the disadvantage of both men and women." Gender issues are not simply talking about women's issues. United Nations decided that there should be a conscious effort to involve women in development and give them access to the formal sector of the economy. Prof. Amartya Sen called development as freedom where development is the way to provide capabilities to women to bring out her fullest self. This is to be done through providing literacy, health and nutrition and other basic facilities to change her economic standing in the family and society and thereby improve her position in order to wrest decision-making powers.

Keeping in view the above discussion, the present chapter is an attempt to analyse some of the aspects in relation to the empowerment of women, which play important role in the overall development of the society. The chapter will study the status of women and their empowerment in terms of various indicators such as access to education, health status, employment, financial autonomy, freedom of movement, exposure to media, political participation, experience of violence and crime etc. in the North Eastern region (NER), comprising eight states of India (IND) namely, Arunachal Pradesh (ANP), Assam (ASM), Manipur (MNP), Meghalaya (MGH), Mizoram (MZM), Nagaland (NGN), Sikkim (SKM) and Tripura (TRP) using secondary data obtained from various sources. The chapter is being concluded with valuable suggestions for the policy-makers.

Women and Economy

Women earn only 10 per cent of the world's income. The work participation rate indicates to a great extent the economic empowerment of women in the society. The status of women is intimately connected with their economic position, which in turn depends on opportunities for participation in economic activities. Education along with participation of women in workforce has been universally recognised as an important element in the adoption of small family norms, which is essential for family planning. The average nutritional intake of women is 1400 calories daily. The necessary requirement is approximately 2200 calories. Three hundred women die everyday due to childbirth and pregnancy related causes. Ninty two per cent of women in India suffer from gynaecological problems. The performance of Family Planning (currently married women, age 15-49) in Assam is shown in Table 19.1.

Table 19.1: Family Planning (currently Married Women, Age 15-49) in Assam

		Residence		*Education*					
	NFHS-3 2005-06	U	R	No Edu	< 8 Yrs	8- 9 Yrs	10 yrs & above	NFHS-2 1998-99	NFHS-1 1992-93
Any method (%)	56.5	66.0	54.5	51.2	53.3	63.9	65.2	43.3	43.0
Any modern method (%)	27.0	37.2	24.8	26.7	25.9	29.8	26.3	26.6	19.9
(a) Female sterilization (%)	13.0	14.1	12.7	17.8	11.7	10.2	7.9	15.7	12.2
(b) Male sterilization (%)	0.2	0.2	0.2	0.5	0.0	0.0	0.0	1.0	2.4
(c) IUD (%)	1.3	1.0	1.3	1.0	1.7	1.5	0.6	1.9	0.9
(d) Pill (%)	10.3	15.6	9.1	6.7	11.8	14.8	9.4	6.3	2.8
(e) Condom (%)	2.4	6.5	1.5	0.6	0.7	3.3	8.6	1.8	1.7

Source: NFHS Reports (1992-93, 1998-99, 2005-06).

The *economic participation* of women—their presence in the workforce in quantitative terms—is important not only for lowering the disproportionate levels of poverty among women, but also as an important step towards raising household income and encouraging economic development in countries as a whole.

In recognition of the importance of establishing gender equality around the world, the United Nations Development Fund for Women (UNIFEM) was established as a separate fund within the United Nations Development Programme (UNDP) in 1984. At that time, the General Assembly instructed it to "ensure women's involvement with mainstream activities." In recent years, the Women Leaders Programme of the World Economic Forum has been focused on supporting the advancement of women to positions of leadership in society, and on promoting consideration of other issues affecting women's lives.

Figure 19.2 shows the female Work Participation Rate for different states of NER during the period 1981-2001. A look at the figure confirms the fact that highest participation rate is observed in case of Nagaland (42.45 per cent) followed by Arunachal Pradesh (40.55%) and lowest rate is observed in the state of Tripura (8.95%) followed by Assam (22.8%) in 1981. The scenario has changed in the years 1991 and 2001 when the maximum female participation rate is observed in the state of Mizoram (43.5% and 47.5%) followed by Manipur (39% both in 1991 and 2001) which are above the nation level of 23.1 per cent. It is also to be noted that during the year 2010, highest value is being is observed in Nagaland with 56.5 per cent followed by Meghalaya (51.4%) and Mizoram (45.4%) While lowest rate is observed in the state of Tripura (15.6%) followed by Assam (20.8%) and Manipur (31.5%). It is important to note here that only these three states of NER are below the National Level (35.6%).

According to 55th Round of NSS data, the Rural Female Work Participation Rate (FWPR) was 87 and Urban Female Work Participation Rate (FWPR) was 97 among principal status workers in the state of Assam and were much below the all India average rates of 231 and 117 respectively.

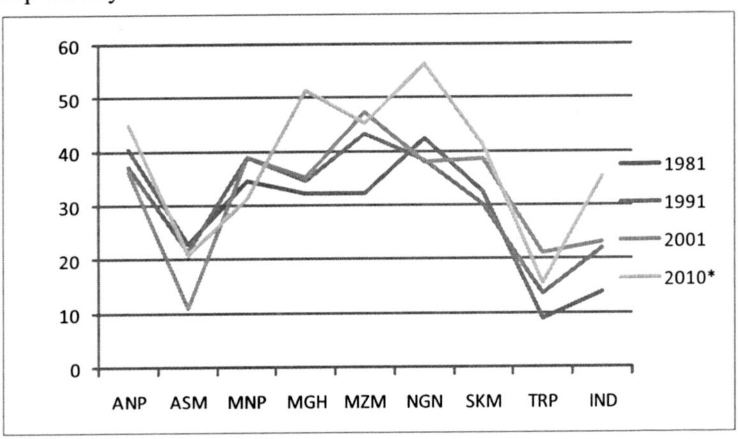

Fig. 19.2: Female Work Participation rate in different states of NER (1981, 1991, 2001 and 2010)

Source: Different Census Data, NSS Reports and Statistical Abstracts.

According to the 58th Round of NSS data (in 2002), the corresponding rates for the state were 116 (rural FWPR) and 101 (urban FWPR) showing an improvement in comparison to 55th Round. But, it is to be noted that both MWPR and FWPR in the State, rural as well as urban, were lower than the corresponding all India rates. However, Percentage of women in the Central Government office is the lowest (6.98%) in the state against the highest women employment of 48.23 in large private sector establishments. In 2000, the proportion of women employed in the private sector in the state was 47.63 per cent in comparison to 14.57 per cent in the public sector. 2001 census data also reveals a large scale variation in the percentage of workers among male and female, the figures being 51.0 per cent and 10.3 per cent respectively.

Analysing the work participation rates with 2001 census data, it has been observed that in the state of Assam, women's participation in administrative and managerial roles is very low. In spite of having a high female literacy rate, the State could produce only lady IAS officers against 216 male IAS officers, the percentage to total being 4.63 against the all India average percentage of 10.4. The percentage of IPS officers was 1.47 with respect to the total of 136 against the all India average percentage of 3.33.

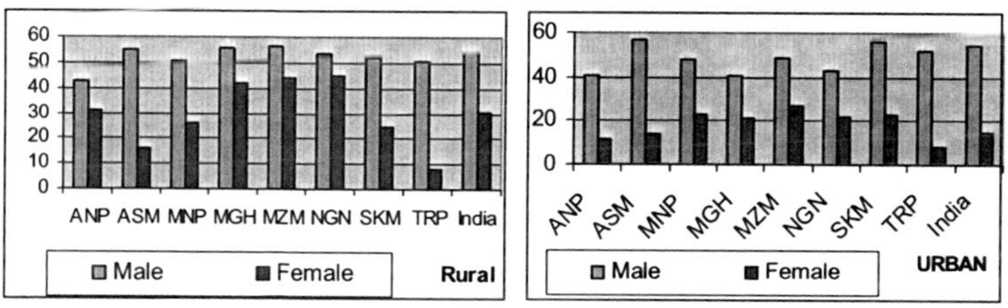

Fig. 19.3A: Labour Force Participation Rates, 1999-2000 (Rural and Urban)
Source: Statistical Abstract 2004 and Other published Reports.

Labour Force participation Rate of different states of NER and India as a whole has been represented through the Figs. 19.3A (Rural and Urban) and 19.3B (Rural and Urban) for the periods 1999-2000 and 2004-05 respectively. It is evident from the figures that in both the periods male labours dominated females in both rural and urban areas and more particularly, the gap is found to be more acute in the rural sectors of the states of Tripura (50.7% for male and 7.6% for female giving a gap of 43.1) and Assam (54.6% for male and 16.1% for female giving a gap of 38.5) in the rural sectors of the period 1999-2000 and for the period 2004-05, the respective gaps are for the states of Assam is 34.4 points (56% for male and 21.6% for female) and for Tripura it is 58.5 points (61% and 2.5% for male and female respectively). Thus for the states of Arunachal Pradesh, Manipur, Meghalaya, Mizoram and Nagaland the participation rates are higher in comparison to the states of Assam and

Tripura. However, almost same pictures are also being observed in urban sectors of different states of NER including the country as a whole.

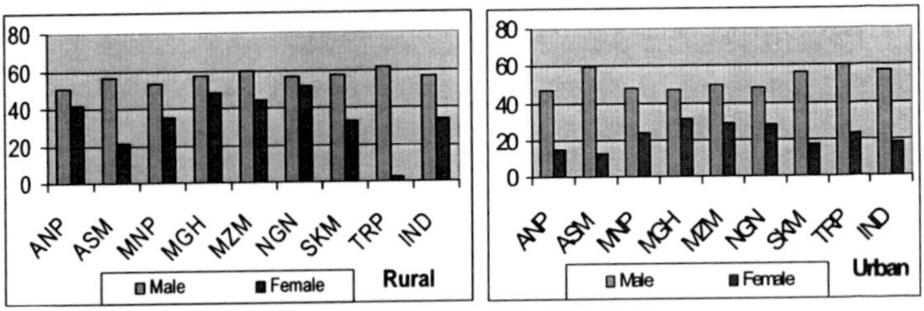

Fig. 19.3B: Labour Force Participation Rates, 2004-2005 (Rural, Urban)
Source: Statistical Abstract 2005-06 and Other Published Reports.

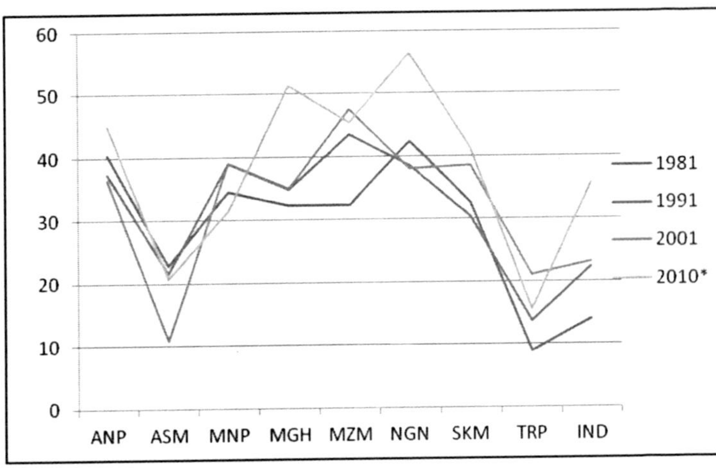

Fig. 19.3C: Female Work Participation Rate in the states of NER during the period 1981-2010
Source: Statistical Abstract 2005-06 and Other Published Reports.

Women and Empowerment

'Leadership' implies 'empowerment'. Empowerment has been generally understood as a process through which existing power relations can be challenged; as a way of gaining and controlling informational resources.[8] Being in a formal position of 'power' is not always equivalent to being a leader. The 73rd Amendment has brought many women into Panchayati Raj Institutions. The Government of India is fully committed to the objective of enhancing the participation of women in key institutions and decision-making structures at various levels. The leadership of women emphasizes reciprocity, mutuality, and responsibility towards others; is collective and participatory; focuses on relationships and empowerment; and highlights outcomes as a central goal of leadership. In the rural environment it was evident that women leader do make a difference. India being a patriarchal society, women are able to identify with a woman more easily. But there is an important distinction between 'effective' leaders and leaders *per se*.

Political empowerment refers to the equitable representation of women in decision-making structures, both formal and informal, and their voice in the formulation of policies affecting their societies. The Inter-Parliamentary Union reports a world average of only 15.6 per cent in combined Houses of Parliament. The statistics by region offer few surprises, ranging from 6.8 per cent in the Arab States to 18.6 per cent in the Americas, and 39.7 per cent in the Nordic states. The United States (17) performs particularly well on educational attainment and only slightly less so on economic participation and political empowerment.

Women have made slow and uneven progress in obtaining a share of managerial positions, which, according to 2002 statistics of the ILO, ranged between 20-40 per cent in 48 out of 63 countries (Wirth, 2004). In addition, women who are in managerial positions often need to make a painful choice between a successful career and family. A study in the United States has found 49 per cent of high-achieving women to be childless, as compared with only 19 per cent of their male colleagues.

Dutta and Pradhan (2007) observed that the number of female persons took part in the political decision-making bodies like Assam that is in Legislative Assembly Election, the percentage of female contestants are being increasing gradually ranges from 2.52 per cent (in 1985) to 6.92 per cent (in 2006). The percentage of number of females wining is also increasing steadily which ranges from 10.0 per cent (in 1991) to 18.87 per cent (2001). However, in the current year the percentage decreased to 18.84 per cent. The number of women candidates contested in the State Assembly polls during 1952 and 1985 ranged between 4 and 20, the percentage to the number of male contestants were 0.99 and 2.18 respectively. The highest number of women contestants during the period was in the year 1978, when 20 women candidates contested, but only 1 won. In the assembly, during these period women legislators were between 7.02 per cent in 1972 and 0.79 per cent in 1978. The position considerably improved in 1996, when 45 women contested and 6 women were elected. In 1999, there were 6 women members in the Assembly comprising 4.92

per cent of the total members as against all India average of 5.63 per cent of women legislators. Women's representation in the Rajya Sabha is also minimal. Out of the seven members from Assam, there was only one woman member in the Rajya Sabha in 1994 and 1996. In the year 1999, 2 women were elected to the Lok Sabha, which comprised 14.29 per cent of the Lok Sabha seats for the State, while in that year, in the Lok Sabha, there were 49 women members, comprising 9 per cent of the total number of members in the Lok Sabha.

The percentage of females took part in the Legislative Assembly Election of Tripura are also being increasing gradually ranges from 1.86 per cent (in 1977) to 5.64 per cent (in 1983). The percentage of number of females wining is also increasing steadily which ranges from 1.67 per cent (in 1977) to 6.67 per cent (1983). These proportions are further increased in the year 2003.

The 73rd Amendment Act of the Constitution has ensured the entry of women in Panchayati Raj Institutions. In the panchayat elections held in 2002, a host of women joined the Panchayats as elected members. In total, 821 women against the total of 2,487, joined as Gaon Panchayat Presidents, 8,210 women against the total of 24,870 joined as Gaon Panchayat members, 821 women against the total of 2,487 members joined as Anchalik Panchayat members and 129 women joined as Zilla Parishad members against the total of 390. This comprised more than 33 per cent women in the Panchayats. Prior to those in 1992 Panchayat elections 8,203 women against 19,143 male members, comprising 30 per cent of total members also had the opportunity of joining The Panchayats. However, during that period, the all-India percentage of women members in Panchayats was 31.32.

Conclusion and Suggestion

Since women comprise the majority of the population below the poverty line and are very often in situations of extreme poverty, given the harsh realities of intra-household and social discrimination, macro economic policies and poverty eradication programmes will specifically address the needs and problems of such women. There will be improved implementation of programmes, which are already women oriented with special targets for women. Steps will be taken for mobilisation of poor women and convergence of services, by offering them a range of economic and social options, along with necessary support measures to enhance their capabilities. In order to enhance women's access to credit for consumption and production, the establishment of new, and strengthening of existing micro-credit mechanisms and micro-finance institution will be undertaken so that the outreach of credit is enhanced. Other supportive measures would be taken to ensure adequate flow of credit through extant financial institutions and banks, so that all women below poverty line have easy access to credit.

In view of the critical role of women in the agriculture and allied sectors, as producers, concentrated efforts will be made to ensure that benefits of training, extension and various programmes will reach them in proportion to their numbers. The programmes for training women in soil conservation, social forestry, dairy development and other occupations allied to agriculture like horticulture, livestock including small animal husbandry, poultry, fisheries etc. will be expanded to benefit women workers in the agriculture sector.

In recognition of the diversity of women's situations and in acknowledgement of the needs of specially disadvantaged groups, measures and programmes will be undertaken to provide them with special assistance. These groups include women in extreme poverty, destitute women, women in conflict situations, women affected by natural calamities, women in less developed regions, the disabled widows, elderly women, single women in difficult circumstances, women heading households, those displaced from employment, migrants, women who are victims of marital violence, deserted women and prostitutes etc.

Globalisation has presented new challenges for the realisation of the goal of women's equality, the gender impact of which has not been systematically evaluated fully. However, from the micro-level studies that were commissioned by the Department of Women & Child Development, it is evident that there is a need for re-framing policies for access to employment and quality of employment. Benefits of the growing global economy have been unevenly distributed leading to wider economic disparities, the feminisation of poverty, increased gender inequality through often deteriorating working conditions and unsafe working environment especially in the informal economy and rural areas. Strategies will be designed to enhance the capacity of women and empower them to meet the negative social and economic impacts, which may flow from the globalisation process.

It will not be prudent on our part to restore the rights of the women belonging to the affluent section of the society only. Therefore, the efforts should be directed towards all-round development of each and every section of Indian women by giving their due share. It is a must to maintain and protect chastity, dignity and modesty of women. What is required is a committed effort to change the existing prejudice against women to enable their entry into areas of activity that would enhance their capacity to influence decision-making in areas affecting their lives.

In recent past, a lot hue and cry is being made over "Women's Reservation Bill" by the different sections of the Indian society, different political or apolitical organisations but nobody seems to be honest in its perspectives. The political empowerment is a must for the all round development of the women. Without academic and social education, the political empowerment of women in certain parts of the country had proved futile. It is the need of the hour to give due share to each and every section of the Indian women. Without removing social stigma, it is not possible to achieve any progress on development of Indian women and more particularly of this region.

The empowerment of Rural Women is crucial for the development of the Rural India. Women engaged in Income-Generation Activity under SGSY economic progress of the community and, bringing women into the mainstream of national development has, therefore, been a major concern of the Government. The Ministry of Rural Development has special components for Women in its programmes and funds are earmarked as "Women's Component" to ensure flow of adequate resources for the same.

For an empowerment approach to be well integrated into health programmes it is important that women's participation is incorporated at each stage of the programme and issues regarding power structures are also dealt with.

Women form a significant portion of labour force. To help women, policies should be undertaken as to increase women's access to computers and internet. There should be provisions for setting up of more women's only access sites. Efforts should be directed towards improving women's skills and usage of new technology. Steps should be taken to encourage women employees.

It may be remarked that women are making men realise that their good lies in women's good and that women's good lies in the entire humanity. Thus, both men and women are complementary to each other not only in household activities but also in other fields. That is why Human Development Index in the states of NER should contain the women development as well

For empowerment, women need to have a voice in decision-making and planning through adequate representation. Reservation of women in the rural and urban local bodies had enabled representation of nearly a million women at the grassroots who play a very important catalytic role in transforming the society. Similar representation in State Legislature and Parliament would further strengthen the process of empowerment of women.

Laws should be gender sensitive and ensure equal provision and access to resources for men and women. Also there needs to be a much broader focus on implementation issues. Many of the existing statutes such as Indecent Representation of Women's Act, Minimum Wages Act, Equal Remuneration Act, and Pre-natal Diagnostic Act, Maternity Benefit Act etc., are implemented more in their violation. A number of these Acts are under review in order to strengthen their provisions.

There is a wide disparity between male and female literacy rates. As per 2001 Census, the literacy rate was 64.4 per cent and 82.4 per cent for females and males respectively in the State. There also exists a rural-urban gender divide in literacy rate across Tamil Nadu. The rate was 76 for urban female whereas it was 55 per cent for its rural counterparts. Compared to urban female literacy rates, the rural rate was lower by 20.71 percentage points, where as the percentage point difference among males in urban and rural areas was only 11.82. The differences in the levels of literacy between males and females were significantly higher in rural areas than in urban areas. This indicates that specific intervention may be required for developing the literacy rates of the female population especially (less privileged classes) in rural areas.

The media needs to introspect upon the role it is playing in spreading the calumny about the victims. Otherwise the female victims of crime in this country will continue to be damned twice—once at the hands of the culprit and once by the norms of our society.

It is very difficult to see the colour of grass distinctly from the sky. The more one comes closer to the ground everything becomes clear and distinct. So, also is the real life situation amongst human beings. To assess the real life of our society one must try to perceive the inner and hidden truth from a close quarter. Problems and challenges are synonymous with human existence whether one is a man or a woman.

But, if we look into the problems of women in one glance than we can notice that women of twenty first century are still not free from their respective problems. We still see how women are being victims of exploitation, violence and all forms of discrimination. But to know the intensity of the problems we must look into those problems and the ultimate solution.

In order to provide justice to women in political and economic fields, the society should stop all kinds of gender based social injustice and create an atmosphere of equality where women can breath, freedom and justice in its true form.

The present status of women in Assam is satisfactory in terms of those women who are blessed enough to avail each and every opportunity of the modern world and they belong to the middle class or upper middle class. On the other hand there are still a major portion of women who belong to the category called "below poverty line." And these women are to be seen anywhere in the urban places as well as villages.

Though, it is gradually rising, the female literacy rate in India is lower than the male literacy rate. Compared to boys, far fewer girls are enrolled in the schools, and many of them drop out. According to the National Sample Survey Data of 1997, only the states of Kerala and Mizoram have approached universal female literacy rates. According to majority of the scholars, the major factor behind the improved social and economic status of women in Kerala is literacy.

Under Non-Formal Education programme, about 40 per cent of the centres in states and 10 per cent of the centres in Union Territories are exclusively reserved for females. As of 2000, about 0.3 million NFE centres were catering to about 7.42 million children, out of which about 0.12 million were exclusively for girls. Currently, in engineering, medical and other colleges, 30 per cent of the seats have been reserved for females. In urban India, girls are nearly at par with the boys in terms of education. However, in rural India girls continue to be less educated than the boys.

In order to make women's movement a success globally, a new approach is to be followed by the leaders of women's movement to set their agenda and women's issues should be sensitised in a non-threatening way by making coalition with men and removing the rural-urban disparity.

To conclude, it can be said that the gender issues and empowerment of women are closely related with the human development of the country and the states of NER should consider it seriously in order to keep pace with the modern world and other regions of the country.

REFERENCES

Dutta, P.C. and B.C. Pradhan (2007): "Gender Issues and Development in North Eastern Region of India", in *Women Emancipation Focus North East India* (ed.) Asok Kumar Ray and Basudeb Datta Ray, Om Publications, New Delhi.

Kapadia, Karin (1997): "Mediating the Meaning of Market Opportunities: Gender, Caste and Class in Rural South India", *Economic and Political Weekly*, December 27.

King, Elizabeth and Anne Hill (1993): *Women's Education in Developing Countries: Barriers, Benefits and Policies*, Johns Hopkins University Press, Baltimore.

Kishore, Sunita (1996): "Urban Women's Employment Trajectories in Ghana and Bolivia", *Occasional Papers, No. 5, Macro International Inc.*, Calverton, Maryland.

Malhotra, Anju and Deborah DeGraff (1997): "Entry versus Success in the Labour Force: Young Women's Employment in Sri Lanka", *World Development*, 25(3): 379-394.

Sen, Amartya (1990): "Gender and Cooperative Conflicts", in Irene Tinker (ed.), *Persistent Inequalities*, Oxford University Press, New York.

Sen, Gita (1992): "Social Needs and Public Accountability: The Case of Kerala", in Marc Wuyts *et al.* (eds.), *Development Policy and Public Action*, Oxford University Press, Oxford.

20

Self-Help Groups

A Paradigm Shift of Women Empowerment

Anusree Krishna Mandal

Introduction

Very often we talk about empowerment especially women empowerment. What is this empowerment? The Empowerment is about power and about changing the balance of power. In every society, there are powerful and powerless groups. Power is exercised socially, economically and politically by one person over other person or over group of persons. Women usually falls under the powerless group, which necessitates the programmes ensured empowerment of women. Power can be defined as the degree or assets fall into five broad categories: physical/material resources (like land, water, forests); human resources (people, their bodies, their labour and skills); intellectual resources (knowledge, information, ideas); social (social capital) and financial resources (money, access to money). This power is dynamic and relational, rather than absolute—it is exercised in the social, economic and political relations between individuals and groups. It is also unequally distributed. In nutshell, any person who have power or have enough confidence to give and take decision and influence other in a particular matter may call as powerful man and the activity is called empowerment. Self-Help Group (SHG) is a group of persons who have voluntarily become the member of the group to achieve common goal by collective efforts. Goal would be different as per the status of the groups. Suppose for BPL group the goal would be to come above poverty line by venturing into income generating activities with the help of credit facilities from banks and group itself.

Women are the nucleus of our civilisation. They have different roles to play in the ever changing social set-up. Women's development is directly related with the nation development. With the dawn of independence our constitution guaranteed gender equality and a large number of schemes and programmes have been initiated for women's development (Mandal, 2012).

Women form a crucial part of human resource. Unless this section of population is given opportunities to prove their capabilities, the development would be imperfect. Women form a vital part of the Indian economy, which constitute one-third of the labour force, and primary members contributing in survival of the family. Women are the backbone of the agricultural sector, comprising the majority of agricultural labourers in India. Indian women are at the crossroads of their destiny. There is a great upsurge in consciousness about their rights among all sections and classes of society in the country. The Ninth Plan document recognises that in spite of development measures and constitutional legal guarantees, women have lagged behind in almost all sectors. Again new economic policy aggravated the problem of women workers in unorganised sectors from bad to worse as most of the women who were engaged in various self-employment activities have lost behind their livelihood, despite tremendous contribution of women to the agricultural sector, their work is considered just an extension of household domain and remains no monetised. Women are deprived of their economic status, especially in rural area. The income earned by them through their hard labour helps to meet their subsistence only. Further, they do not have control over their own income. According to a World Bank study the women in India do 51 per cent of total conventional and non-conventional work. They form about 33 per cent of total agricultural labour and 87 per cent of the labour force engaged in dairy and other animal husbandry activities. They bear sole responsibility for family welfare and household management. Owing to socio-economic factors, the mobility of women are restricted. The lesser mobility results in lesser and limited choices for livelihood, skill upgradation, training, technology, market etc. This restricts the options available to women for income generations and development avenues (Raji, 1999). In India, women earn only 10 per cent of income and own 10 per cent of property and wealth of the country (Karmakar, 1999). They put their entrepreneurial skills in all the activities, but due to poor financial strength they are not able to convert their entrepreneurial dream into reality (Saikia and Deka, 2012).

Rural women, especially those belonging to the weaker sections of the society, have limited access to resources. An employment opportunity that would meet the bare minimum consumption needs. The economic empowerment requires that women have some access to and control over productive resources thus ensuring some degree of financial autonomy. Women empowerment is possible only if they are given opportunity to develop freedom, providing credit and participation in decision-making. The concept of micro-finance through self-help groups has become a major tool for the empowerment of rural women. In India, micro-finance is dominated by self-help group-bank linkage programme as a cost effective mechanism for providing services to the "unreached poor" which has been successful not only in meeting financial services to the poor women, but also strengthen collective self-help capacities of the poor, leading to their empowerment.

Rapid progress in SHG formation has now turned into an empowerment movement among women access in the country. The self-help groups are voluntary associations of people formed to achieve both social and economic goal. SHGs are mostly informal groups that relend their pooled savings within the group on rational of need basis.

The self-help group is a viable organised set-up to disburse micro credit to the rural women for the purpose of making them enterprising and encouraging to enter into entrepreneurial activities. Studies have shown that savings through thrift and credit has been one of the important activities of SHGs and are very popular among the poor particularly among women in rural areas. The money thus saved is used not only for meeting their emergent consumption needs but also for income generating activities (Rao, 1994). The formation of SHGs is not only a micro-credit project, but also an empowerment process. Empowerment encompasses their enhanced status in social, political, and economic spheres. Women's empowerment is to give the power to act, participate, make decision, and raise voice against social evils and fight for their rights. Empowering women is not just for meeting their economic needs, but also for more holistic social development.

Empowerment is a multi-dimensional in its approach and involves a basic realisation and awareness of women powers, potentialities, capabilities and competences, rights and opportunities of all-round development in all spheres of life. Women empowerment is a process which enables women to have access and control over various factors necessary for their economic independence, political participation and social development. Empowerment of women may normally mean equal access to and control over important productive resources. Women empowerment, therefore, may normally describe as a process by which women would be able to develop their confidence level and increase their inner strength and self-reliance to decide and determine their important choices in life.

Empowerment of women also means equal status to women. Women empowerment have mainly five dimensions *viz.*, economic, political, social/cultural, personal and familial. Each dimension is very important because the real empowerment of women is increased access to economic resources, more strength and courage for entering into the power structure, more self-motivation and confidence, and more say in the family matters. Women should be willing to take additional efforts for building a mind-set, which would lead them for their overall empowerment. It is a gradual and consistent process, which requires the support of many persons who are related to them in many ways.

Self-Help Groups as an Instrument for Economic Empowerment: Before getting into the subject matter a clear understanding about what a Self-Help Group is a must. It is key role in gearing up the economic development, various functions and activities, not but the least the problems faced by these Self-Help Groups.

What is Self-Help Group (SHG)?: Self-Help Group (SHG) is a group of village-based financial intermediary usually composed of between 10-15 local women or men. The group may either a registered or unregistered group having homogenous socio-economic backgrounds, wilfully joining together with an attitude to save their money, make use of such funds to contribute to a common fund with an intention to meet their emergency needs on the basis of mutual help.

Origin and Concept of SHGs

***Origin*:** The evolution of Self-Help Group is from Bangladesh, the neighbourhood country of India. SHG originated from the brainchild of Grameen Bank of Bangladesh, which was founded by Mohammed Yunus. In India though the first SHGs was started and formed in 1975, it was started to take off during the year 1986-1987. Self-Help Groups, although initiated in India for the first time in 1984 by the Mysore Resettlement and Development Agency (MYRADA), have caught on rapidly with encouraging support from organisations such as the National Bank for Agricultural and Rural Development (NABARD). Subsequently, at the instance of the Reserve Bank of India (the central banking institution), commercial banks started promoting SHGs.

Concept of Self-Help Group: The concept of SHG is based on the following principles:

One of the most powerful tools among the several that are available for the socio-economic development for the poor is the Self-Help Group coupled with mutual help and highly responsive and efficient participative financial service management; The very vital need for the poor is not only credit support, but they also need savings and other services; Poor can save and are bankable and SHGs as clients result in wider outreach at a low transaction cost with much lower risk costs for the banks; They can create a common fund through contribution as small savings on a regular basis; The working system is highly flexible and democratic in nature; Loaning is done chiefly on good faith with minimum documentation and without any security; The loan amounts are normally very small, reasonable, frequent and for a short period. Default of repayment is very rarely happened and repayment is made in prompt and in time. Periodic meeting is arranged on regular basis. Lending rate of interest is affordable, varies from group to group and loan to loan. But still the interest rate is little higher than the banks, but lower than the money lenders (Saravanakumar and Mamta, 2012).

SHG Movement in India: It was very much difficult and tedious to determine the date of the actual conception and propagation of SHGs, however, the formation of small groups among rural and urban people for the purpose of savings and credit is well established in India. In the earlier periods, NGOs played a crucial role in innovating the SHG model and began to implement the same to develop the process fully. The policy-makers observed and worked with development organisations and bankers and discussed with them the possibility of promoting these savings and credit groups at a larger level in 1980. Out of untiring effort and due to simplicity in the formation of SHGs, it paved a strong platform for the widespread reach across the country. State Governments created revolving loan funds in order to fund SHGs. Later in the 1990s, SHGs were considered as more than just a financial intermediation, but as a common interest group, working on other concerns as well. Due to the widespread of SHGs across the country it paved way for the formation of SHG Federations that are more sophisticated form of organisation that involve several SHGs forming into Village Organisations (VO)/Cluster Federations and then ultimately into higher level federations [called as Mandal Samkhya (MS) in Andhra Pradesh or SHG Federation generally]. The distinction between SHG Federations and SHGs is, the former is a more formal institutions and the latter is an informal one. Many of these SHG federations are registered as societies, mutual benefit trusts and mutually aided cooperative societies. SHG Federations resulted in several key benefits including: Stronger political and advocacy capabilities; Sharing of knowledge and experiences; Economies of scale and Access to greater capital (Saravanakumar and Mamta, 2012).

Need for Empowerment: Every nation across the globe is keen in developing the country as powerful in all dimensions. This could be achieved through empowering its citizens in the country. Empowerment is far away from essentially political; it must be a process involved with personal, economic, social and political dimensions with personal empowerment being the core component in the empowerment process. Micro-financing to SHGs create lot of avenues for the empowerment and in promoting well-being for women. This led to have felt among women as they are strengthened, attained self-esteem and self-worth, instilled a greater sense of awareness about social and political issues leading to increased mobility. Thus micro-finance programmes enabled women to contribute to the household economy, increasing their intra-household bargaining power Micro-financing through Self-help groups had transformed economic power in the hands of women and considerably reduced their dependence on men. Lack of education they had to seek help from their husbands or any other educated man/woman for day-to-day work. The political as well as economic empowerment will not succeed in the absence of women education in skills and vocations they require the most. Therefore, developing countries are under greater thrust and take effective steps to enroll the members of SHGs in the Schemes of open schooling or any other distance mode to impart education. In current scenario SHGs providing micro-credit for economic activities at village level is fast catching up. Many NGOs already operate and are promoted by government sponsored institutions/banks. The most suitable and the ideal form for promoting these SHGs are the village level cooperative institutions. It is mandatory that the policy reforms should include not only co-operativisation, and essential support services, but also the strategic alliance between the state, co-operative sector and the private sector (Saravanakumar and Mamta, 2012).

In the context of Arunachal Pradesh, many SHGs are lending fund to non-members at very high rate of the interest. It is believed that this lending is done for sustenance of the SHG as the members are either not in a position to undertake any economic activity. Many members undertake non-member lending. All such SHGs should try to find ways and means of undertaking economic activity and resist temptation of undertaking external lending. In recent years Self-Help Group has been emerged as an important strategy for economic development in rural areas. The credit of its emergence goes to the efforts of Governmental and Non-governmental Agencies. The groups have attracted the rural poor women to become the members for the benefit not only to them, but also for their families in particular and community as a whole in general through their collective actions.

Objectives

The objective of this chapter is to examine the impact of SHGs, formed by their own effort without the cooperation of others, on the empowerment of rural women socially and economically.

Research Questions: The probable Research Questions are:

1. Are the members of the SHG benefited from its activity?
2. Is there a positive correlation between enhancement of income of enrolled women of SHGs and participation of women in SHG?
3. Is there a significant relationship between awareness of women and enrolment of women in self-help groups?
4. Are the attitudes towards gender disparity changing with the active participation and economic empowerment of women through SHGs?
5. Is there a considerable improvement in the lifestyle of the women after joining the SHG?

Research Methodology

***Geographical Area under Study*:** The study was conducted in three villages namely Upper Cher village, Upper Jumi village and Lichi village under Kimin C.D. Block of Papumpare District of Arunachal Pradesh.

***Status of the SHGs under Study*:** Without co-operation of monitoring authority and also financial help from NGO or Bank, some unregistered SHGs are formed by their own efforts. This is because of lack of cooperation of monitoring authority and also financial help from NGO or Bank. These SHGs have much potentiality to grow up if they are provided a little help. Such type of SHGs was considered here to study.

***Source of Data*:** The primary data so collected was supplemented by secondary data whenever necessary. Primary data pertaining to SHGs was collected in June-August, 2012 from the field study.

***Sample Size and Sampling*:** Five SHGs were selected and studied. Out of 5 SHGs, one SHG of Upper Cher village, two SHGs of Upper Jumi village and two SHGs of Lichi village were considered, as because these SHGs were very active and energetic and also enthusiastic to their duty.

Data Analysis: The various data and information obtained from the field survey were processed, interpreted and analysed through simple numerical calculations, graphical representations to write up the study and also to compare the variables among the SHGs under study.

Tools for Data Collection: The questionnaire subject to our objective relating to individual members was divided into two parts. Part A dealt with the details of members before joining the SHG referred as **Control Group** and Part B with the details of respondents after joining the SHG referred as **Target Group.** The primary data so collected was supplemented by secondary data whenever necessary.

Results and Discussions

The general information of five unregistered SHGs with year of formation, income generating activities, bank linkage, total number of members in each sampled SHG etc. is presented in Table 20.1.

Level of Income of SHG members: It is shown in Table 20.2 that incomes of the members were in increasing trend. However, this income level was not sufficient to lead decent life. They could not fulfil the basic requirement in their daily life. They earnings below the income Rs. 3500 per month had to lead lives hand to mouth. This was due to low level of literacy and lack of skill. Though their overall income level of all respondents was low, but level of earning showed upward trend. Before forming SHG, they were only family workers in their agricultural field. Their agricultural production was used only for self-consumption having no role of money transaction. At least after formation of SHG, they have come in the modern monetised market economy. In Table 20.2 and Fig. 20.1 given below their trend of income are shown for easy understanding at a glance.

Role of SHGs in Promoting Saving Habits: The entire sample groups undertaken for study were saving monthly. Thrift and credit was the main activities of the group which is also the basis of group formation and its sustenance for longer duration. Rural poor women are formed into a group mainly to access credit whenever required from pooled savings. SHG play tremendous role in creating saving habits amongst the women of Arunachal Pradesh. Here the indigenous people do not have the saving habits earlier. In emergency situation, community people come forward and share the crisis of that family. There is no bank in rural areas, therefore, the question of saving habits do not arise. With the opening of banks in the rural areas and opening of bank account by the SHGs, saving habits

Table 20.1: The Names of Five SHGs of the Three villages of Kimin C.D. Block

Name of Villages	*Name of the SHGs*	*Date of Formation*	*Caste of Members*	*No. of Members*	*Income Generating Activity*	*Bank Linkage*	*Literacy*		
							P	U/P	Cl-X
Upper Cher	Chirm-Mollo	2004	Do	15	Poultry, farming	A P Rural Bank & Central Bank	9	5	1
Upper Jumi	Komchi Lela,	2006	Do	12	Contractual work	A P Rural Bank	6	4	2
	Ann-Donyi	2009	Do	10	Contractual work	A P Rural Bank	6	4	–
Lichi	Ann-Gumchi	2006	Do	14	Contractual work	A P Rural Bank	8	4	2
	Huto	2005	Do	12	Contractual work	A P Rural Bank	7	3	2
Total				**63**					

Source: Field Survey, June-August 2012.

Table 20.2: SHG Members in Different Income Level

Income per month (Rs.)	*Total No. of respondents before forming SHG*	*Total No. of respondents after forming SHG*
Up to 500	20	0
500–1000	13	0
1000–1500	12	0
1500– 2000	10	20
2000–2500	5	18
2500–3000	2	15
3000–3500	1	10
Total	**63**	**63**

Source: Field study, June-August, 2012.

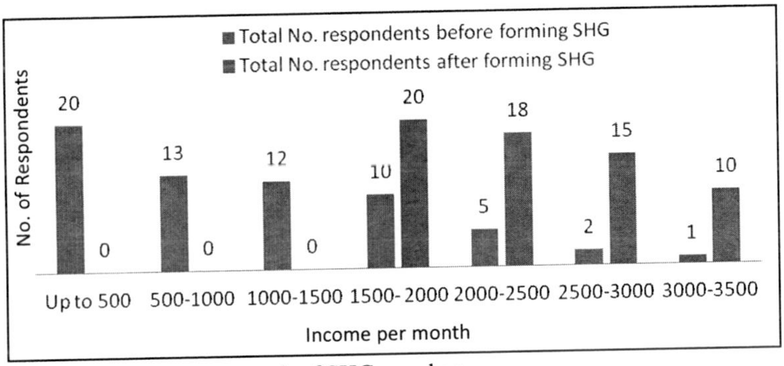

Fig. 20.1: Income per month of SHG member
Source: Field study, June-August, 2012.

are inculcating. As an individual, it is quite difficult for them to open account and save regularly, but as group they are doing. Keeping of money in the banks for unforeseen situation or reaping its benefits after certain period of time was not in their mind before joining the group. From the record of saving amount it is reflected that saving habits were already inculcated amongst the group members of the entire sample group. The total saving till March, 2012 of each group are presented in Table 20.3 and in Fig. 20.2. Figure 20.2 shows that the Ann-Donyi SHG shares highest in savings followed by Ann Gumchi. The Komchi Lela and Huto SHGs share lowest in savings being youngest in time period

***Improvement of Status of Women*:** The attempts of SHG approach are making its impact on the society especially among the women. It is successful in developing sustainable household livelihoods, decreasing household vulnerability and community development up to great extent. This contribution is recognised and valued by other household members

Table 20.3: Savings/Corpus Fund of SHGs

Name of the group	*Total Savings fund*	*% of total savings of each Group*
Chirm-Mollo	117000	17.13
Komchi Lela	100000	14.64
Ann-Donyi	216000	31.63
Ann-Gumchi	150000	21.96
Huto	100000	14.64

Source: Field study, June-August 2012.

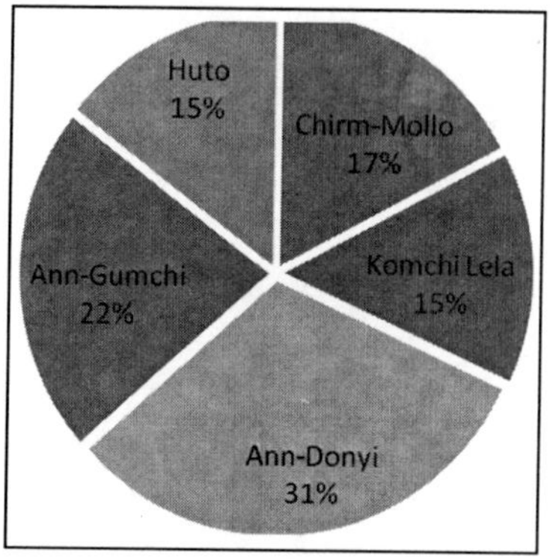

Fig. 20.2: Percentage of Savings of Self-Helf Group
Source: Field study, June-August 2012.

and lead not only to increased household well-being, but women's increased role in decision-making and improved well-being for women themselves. This increased status in the household in itself in turn gives women the support they need to enable them together with men to bring about wider changes in gender inequality in the community.

In addition to the economic empowerment, social and political empowerment too has been attained. The group activities have given them a chance to come out to the mainstream, to realise the potentialities within themselves. This has lead to a change in their outlook towards society. The status of being a woman is no more considered as a curse. All these, in fact, are looked upon as boon to bring them closer, to bind them closer and as a mean to lay the foundation of a new gender equity society. SHG has become an instrument to bridge the gap that exists in the society—the gender gap and the social gap between the rich and poor. By contributing economically, women have gained a pivotal role in the decision-making of the family.

The commonly used statement holds hundred per cent true that "the transformation of any society has to begin from women, because women are the centre of a family—the foundation stone on which the family is built. When a woman is changed, the family is changed and a change in the family brings changes in the society. The impact of past seventy years of efforts by the Central and State Governments to eradicate poverty from the society was not up to the expectation in spite of the better educational, economic, political, cultural and social environment. Again almost all the programmes failed to include women in eradication of poverty. It is in this decade the women empowerment policy (2001) has been introduced and women become integral part of the development strategy. Therefore, SHG is a silent revolution—a revolution that has all the potentiality of bridging the gender gap and building a world where poverty and gender discrimination with its all evils will be uprooted.

Level of Empowerment: An attempt is made to analyse the extent of empowerment achieved by SHG members after joining SHGs or through SHGs. In order to measure the degree of empowerment, 8 variables shown in table given below were identified and analysed. Table 20.4 and Fig. 20.3 reveal that SHG has contributed significantly for the members in response of the variables and also we verified the position of the variables before and after forming SHGs i.e. in Pre-SHGs, and Post-SHGs in responses to the respondents. We can see the level of empowerment of women in pre-SHGs and post-SHGs.

Findings in Second Time Field Visit: The role of SHGs on women empowerment in second time field visit is shown in Table 20.5 and in Fig. 20.4. After joining a SHG, though the returns from income earning activities taken up under it remained unstable, they would make a lot of difference to the lives of the poor. According to our respondents, women Contribution to Household such as financial help, education of children, decision-making in loan arrangements, purchasing of assets etc.; Contribution to Community such as helping neighbours, give suggestion to the villagers and leadership in the community or in the meetings of the community and interaction with own family members, neighbours and community leaders etc. had increased to the greater extent since most of the decision were taken by male-female jointly.

Therefore, from Table 20.5 and Fig. 20.4, it is observed that majority of the members now experienced better treatment in their family than that of pre-SHG situation. They also expressed their mobility and recognition in family and community. The women reported that they were more sensitised and aware of nutrition, family planning, health and

Table 20.4: Number of Respondents in Level of Empowerment in Pre-SHGs and Post-SHGs

Variable	Post-SHG Situation		Pre-SHG Situation	
	Yes	To some extent	Yes	To some extent
1. Awareness of benefits of SHGs	63	0	0	0
2. Better Self-Awareness	49	14	0	0
3. Decision-making ability	48	10	3	2
4. Ability to face problems	30	19	5	9
5. Helped in personality development	40	15	3	5
6. Leaderships Quality	30	20	3	10
7. Enhanced knowledge of enterprises	40	23	0	0
8. Enhance knowledge of rights and legal issues	30	33	0	0

Source: Field Study in June-August 2012.

participation in development programmes. The respondents expressed high level of self-confidence because of their ability to contribute to their household (Saikia and Deka, 2012). Therefore, all the research questions were satisfied and we got positive results.

***Problems Faced by SHG*:** The major problem faced by SHGs was the lack of transaction and getting linkage with the financial institutions and legend agencies. The reason was that most of these SHGs in the state were not formal but wit unregistered status. Some of them were not attached with formally registered NGOs in this regard. There was lack of motivation and information about the programme. In most cases, NGOs involvement in facilitating and linking the SHGs with banks were nil. SHGs also did not have their own business models for the purpose of promoting themselves in the market and get the support from other agencies and other institutions. Though it was found that the performance and growth of SHGs were rapidly increasing, it was also found in certain critical areas where information was not lacking to a major extent. Although several statistical information of others SHGs under not study here disclosed that the credit availed by SHGs from banks and other financial institutions were increasing year after year, nothing was mentioned about the purpose and the nature of enterprises for which such loans and credit were received by them. It was also observed that there was an unclear lending norm and practices being practiced and hence all these led to a difficult situation for the assessment of SHGs. In addition to their routine work, women faced problem to travel and spent time and

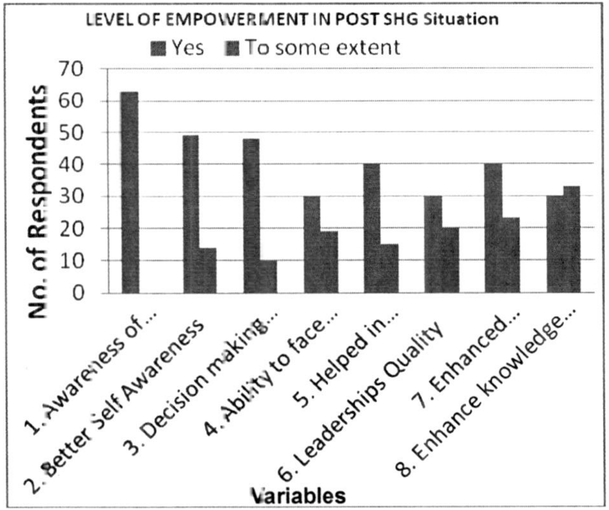

In this figure, it is clear that after forming SHG the level of empowerment of the all the members are increasing in comparison to before forming the SHG.

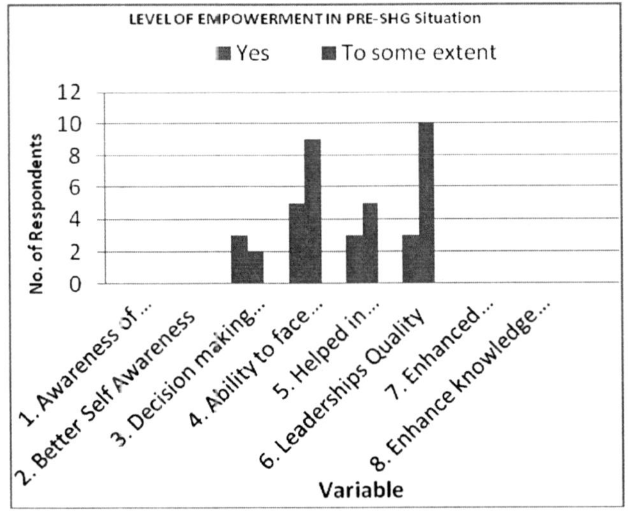

In this figure, it is seen that before joining SHG, the level of empowerment of the SHG members was very poor or nil.

Fig. 20.3: Level of Empowerment in Pre- and Post-SHG Situations.

Source: Field Study in June-August 2012.

Table 20.5: Empowerment of Women Self-Help Group Members

	Indicators	*Post-SHG Situation*	*Pre-SHG Situation*
Contribution to Household	Financial help	55(83.33)	20
	Education of children	45(68.18)	10
	Takes decision	50(75.75)	13
Contribution to Community	Helping neighbours	40(60.60)	11
	Give suggestion	35(53.03)	9
	Leadership	40(60.60)	5
Interaction	with own family members	60(90.90)	21
	with neighbours	56(84.84)	20
	with community leaders	51(77.27)	7

Source: Field Study in October 2012.

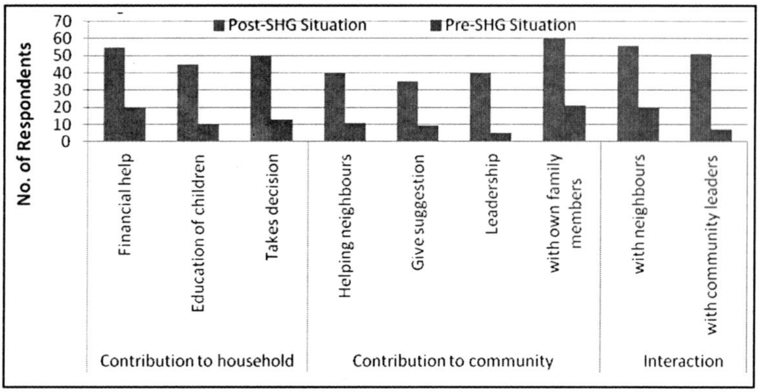

Fig. 20.4: Empowerment of Women Self-Help Group Members
Source: Field Study in October 2012.

money for bank transaction. The findings are subject to error as it is based on the information received in short time field study by my non-trained student.

Weaknesses of SHGs

Following are the weaknesses of SHGs realised throughout the study:

1. Many respondents are inclined towards SHGs only for the monetary benefits; otherwise they will not get from the bank.
2. Many respondents have cited that they have to pay the interest from their own pocket.

3. The loans are not released in time by the banks.
4. Women faces problem in accessing the bank credit due to lots of paper work.
5. Due to unaware about the bank credit, members of SHGs think that they may fall in vicious circle of indebtedness due to late repayment.
6. There is lack of motivation and information about the programme.
7. NGOs involvement in facilitating and linking the SHGs with banks are small.
8. Many times the women of the SHGs are victimised by their male counterpart.

Suggestions

Attitudinal Change: To bring about gender equity society, it is important that any move to enforce laws must be accompanied by a movement to bring about an attitudinal change in our society. The existing laws and rights for women need to be strengthened and more vigorously implemented. Where policies and programmes do not serve the special needs of women, they need to be amended or recast. Where benefits do not reach to our women in general and rural women in particular, there is need for special intervention to enhance accessibility. Attitudinal change is possible only through the empowerment of women and empowerment of women may come by the formation of more and more SHG. Basic education and training among the members of the self-help groups is essential, so that they have the same level of expertise or understanding capacity which empowers the group members. More number of women should encouraged to join SHGs by Government to fulfil the objective of "Microfinance Vision–2011" of Arunachal Pradesh Government to promote 5000 women SHGs which was far lagging behind it. The authorising Agencies should organise various campaigns to create awareness of SHGs and should also spread information about various schemes available to the members and training to the women entrepreneurs can be provided for the better performance of their business activities. The field officers at the Government level and NGOs have to participate actively in improving the economic and social conditions of the women entrepreneurs at each district.

Conclusion

It is seen that the SHG strategy provides women with a chance for educative programme, awareness creation on issues such as drinking water and sanitation, family planning and literacy. Moreover, the group helps women to interact among themselves and enhance their participation in different developmental activities. As women are empowered with information resources, it enables them to initiate social action against alcoholism, illiteracy and other social evil issues.

It is matter of fact that amending laws and rights is not enough. A change of attitude within each individual towards gender equality is must for empowerment of women. It is found that SHG approaches are playing tremendous role because of its process oriented approach, member of the SHG are automatically becoming assertive after joining into the SHGs. In the process, awareness is created on rights and many other welfare aspects in the group. Their confidence level increases in manifold and they are confident enough to take up the challenge that comes in their life. It is proven in the study that SHG has played significant role in increasing the income, awareness, confidence and solidarity. They have ventured into various income generating activities. They have challenged the social structure for their justice and rights. Economic and social vulnerability have been reduced considerably.

In particular, empowerment of women and the inculcation of financial training and discipline amongst the poor will undoubtedly have long-term socio-economic benefits. The principles of self-help and micro-credit thus hold the key to economic and socio-cultural freedom for state's lakhs of poor, opening the gates of a hitherto untapped reservoir of human enterprise. Therefore, SHG is a new tool for poverty alleviation through social and economic empowerment of women. The Government should encourage heart and soul in order to achieve the micro-finance Vision of 2011 of the State. Therefore, we can conclude that—

1. SHGs are important tool for socio-economic empowerment of poor rural women.
2. SHGs are in instrumental in setting up a number of micro-enterprises which rendered them monetary benefits.
3. Women can be motivated through proper training and education under SHG programme which is helpful for changing their social attitude and outlook.
4. Effective functioning and implementation of SHGs can lead to overall development of poor women.

Acknowledgement: The author acknowledges the co-operation of her father Dr. Ram Krishna Mandal for the field survey of the study area and to develop the text of the study.

REFERENCES

Gangaiah, C., Nagaraja, B., and Vasudevulu, C. Naidu (2008): "Impact of Self-Help Groups on Income and Employment: A Case Study," *Kurukshetra*, Vol. 54, No. 5, pp. 18-21.

Kamararaja, K. (2009): "Performance of Self-Help Group in Tamil Nadu", *Southern Economist*, November, Vol. 47, No. 19, p. 14, Bangalore.

Karmakar, K.G. (1999): *Rural Credit and Self-Help Group: Micro-Finance Needs and Concept in India*, Sage Publications, New Delhi.

Mandal, R.K. (2012): Women Empowerment through Self-Help Groups in Socio-Economic Development: A Study of Papumpare District", *The Arun Information: A Weekly Newspaper*, Vol. 1, Issues 1-4, August.

Nallabelli, R. N. (2012): "Microfinance—Women Empowerment: A Case Study of Warangal District, Andhra Pradesh", *Journal of Global Economy*, Vol. 8(3), July-September.

Raji, Gian, T.S. (1999): "Access of Women to Banking", *Banking Finance*, Vol. 12(7).

Rao, Dinkar K. (1994): "Self-Help Group and Credit", *Arthvijnana*, Vol. 36(3): 194-208.

Saikia Brajendra and Deka Anamika (2012): "Women Empowerment through SHGs—A Case Study", *Governance Issues and Gender Aspects in Development: A North East India Perspective*, Papyrus, Guwahati.

Saravanakumar and Mamta, S. (2012): "Self-Help Group in Socio-economic Transformation with Special Regerence to Coimbatore", *International Journal of Research in Commerce, Economics & Management*, Vol. 2(9) September.

Subrahmanya, Susheela (2005): "Women and Development: A Proactive Perspective" in Subrahmanya, Susheela (eds): in *Women in Nation Building*, A Southern Economist Publication, Bangalore.

Vasanthakumari, P. (2000): "Women Empowerment through Micro-Enterprises Development", *Southern Economist*, December, Vol. 47, No.15, p. 31, Bangalore.

21

Women Education in Special Reference to Rural Areas of North East India

Ritwika Rajendra

Introduction

Education is essential to advancing human capital by enabling individuals to develop their knowledge and skills throughout their lives. Relatively high levels of education are often related to higher earnings and productivity, better career progression, health, life satisfaction as well as to better investments in education and health of future generations. Education is one of the most important means of empowering women with the knowledge, skills and self-confidence necessary to participate fully in the development process in today's world, education tends to become the master determinant of social mobility and social transformation because it alone leads to higher occupational achievements. Provision of education is key to the development of human resources just like the provision of other basic amenities like safe drinking water, adequate shelter, health care and optimal level of nourishment. In a democracy, it is the most important that equality of educational opportunities showed be available to all. The more the people of a nation are educated, the more the nation tends to progress in the right direction. It is, hence, extremely important for the government to give utmost stress on the various aspects of education. While imparting education, another important point which should be kept in mind is the education meant for women. Investing in formal education is essential to promote equality of employment opportunities and strengthen economic growth. It increases cognitive and non-cognitive skills, it improves productivity and it provides individuals with a greater ability to further develop their knowledge and skills throughout their lives. Increased education participation is also associated with better health, and more investments in the education and health of children—especially among women and particularly in developing countries.

Gender equality in terms of participation in, and attainment of education has been achieved in most countries: girls have on average better grades and often out number boys among new college graduates. However, in many developing countries, girls still have poorer educational attainments, especially at the secondary and tertiary levels. Achieving gender equality in education in these countries will not only promote greater equality in employment outcomes, but also help postpone early-marriages, reduce infant mortality rates and improve health and education of future generations. Gaps in cognitive skills of boys and girls around age 15 are similar across countries: boys perform better than girls in mathematics in most countries, and girls out perform boys in reading in all countries. In terms of science literacy, there are no significant gender differences. But young women are much less likely than young men to choose Science, Technology, Engineering, or Mathematics (STEM) as field of study at graduate level; the share of women in these fields further declines at the post-graduate level. Gender differences in educational choices appear to be related to student attitudes (motivation, interest) in studying a particular subject rather than their ability and school performance. Gender gaps in performance are smaller than gender gaps in fields of tertiary study, indicating that young women often do not translate their good school performance into field of studies for higher education that offer better employment prospects. In developing countries in 2008, 78 per cent of girls in primary school age were enrolled in primary education, *vis-à-vis* 82 per cent of boys. However, enrolment rates in primary education are more unequal in many developing regions (OECD/UNESCO, 2004).

North East India—A Brief Profile

Consisting of eight states, the North Eastern part of India is bounded by China in the North, Bangladesh in the South-West, Bhutan in the North-West and Burma in the East. Isolated from the rest of India, both geographically and economically, this region is tenuously linked to the rest of the country by a narrow corridor running 56 km though the foothills of Bhutan and Sikkim to the state of West Bengal. Total area of the North East is 2,62,230 km. One of the most ethically and linguistically diverse regions in Asia, each state has its distinct culture and traditions. North East India refers to the easternmost region of India consisting of eight states (i.e. Arunachal Pradesh, Assam, Manipur, Mizoram, Meghalaya, Nagaland, Tripura and Sikkim). From times immemorial, India's North-East has been the meeting point of many communities, faith and cultures. A place of North East India is the home for more than 166 separate tribes speaking a wide range of languages. Some groups have migrate over the centuries from places as far as South-East Asia. But they retain their cultural traditions and values, but are beginning to adapt to contemporary life style. The lushness of its landscape, the range of communication and geographical and ecological diversity make the North-East quite different from other parts of the subcontinent. In winters, mist carpets the valleys but swirls around the travellers in hills during summer rains. The festivals and celebrations in the North East States of India are a colourful reflection of the people and their lives. Most of them centring on their modes of living and livelihood. So far as socio-geographical and demographic characteristics are concerned, North East India is not evenly distributed. Some places are purely hilly areas whereas some are purely plains. Assam occupies the lush lowland of the Brahmaputra Valley land which is the most densely populated. Arunachal Pradesh occupies the densely forest and sparsely populated foothills of the Himalayas and one of the major tourist attractions because of its Buddhist influence. Meghalaya with its pine clad hills and lakes, is famous for the wettest region of the world. Nagaland has rich war history that attracts tourists. The other four states, Manipur known as the land of jewels, Mizoram and Tripura make up a fascinating area of green valleys, Lush hills with variety of flora and fauna.

Present Scenario of Women Education

In the developed world, women have surpassed men at many levels of education. For example, in the United States in 2005-06, women earned 62 per cent of Associate's degree, 58 per cent of Bachelor's degree, 60 per cent of Master's degree, and 50 per cent of Doctorates. But, in the developing and underdeveloped nations, women education is yet to achieve the desired results. In India, specially rural areas, gender discrimination still persists and a lot more needs to be done in the field of women education as it is the only indicator of improving women's position in the society. The population while resided in rural areas is known as rural population. According to the 2001 Census, 74.5 per cent people resided in rural areas in India. In rural areas, the educational level is very low, particularly for women; the national literacy rate in the country was 64.8 per cent (75.3% for men and 53.7% for women)

North East and Women Education

Geographically, men and women share the same space, but everywhere in the world, women are accorded a lower status than men. The North Eastern Region of India has been considered as a backward region in terms of growth in per capita income. However, there is a perception that the status of women is higher in the North Eastern Region of the country in comparison with the status of women in all India average. In this study, an attempt has been made to examine the status of women in the North Eastern Region in comparison with all India average. It is found from the analysis that the status of women in the region is comparatively better than the rest of the country only in some selected indicators. The indicators reveal that women have a very low degree of freedom of movement and low level of control over themselves in North Eastern Region.

Status of Women refers to the position of women in society in relation to men. Although, geographically, men and women share the same space, yet they are not treated equally in the world. In reality, there exists inequality in women's access to education, health care, physical and financial resources and opportunities in the political, economic, social and cultural field. Everywhere in the world, women are accorded a lower status than men. According to Mohiuddin (1995), women's lower status is manifested in women's low wage rates than men in all occupational fields and industries, in their limited upward mobility, and in their greater family responsibilities due to divorce, abandonment etc. in the developed countries. In the developing countries, women's lower status is reflected not only in their work being underpaid, unrecognised, but also in their limited access to productive resources and support services such as health and education.

The North Eastern Region (NER) consists of Arunachal Pradesh, Assam, Manipur, Meghalaya, Mizoram, Nagaland, Tripura, and Sikkim. The NER of India has been considered as a backward region in terms of growth in per capita income. Pandey, Das and Joshi (2011) point out that time to time and very frequently media has advocated for women education through the popular advertisements such as "Padhega India, Tabhi toh badhega India", "School Chalein hum of Sarva Shiksha Abhiyan" (SSA), National Rural Health Mission (NRHM), National Rural Employment Guarantee Act (NREGA) to enlighten the various schemes of government for the development of women, children and girl child. Gyan Vani, FM Channel by IGNOU, telecast programmes on gender disparities, train women for future.

Women Education in Rural Areas of North East India

Over the years, the North East region has made considerable progress in the education. The UGC Chairman said the North Eastern states would have to address the rural urban and male female disparities in access to higher education. The male and female enrolment percentage of North East region is 10.81 per cent and 8.14 per cent respectively. The national average as whole is 15.56 per cent for male and 11.46 per cent for female. The following table illustrates the low literacy rate of women in comparison to men in the rural areas of North East India.

(in %)

States	*Male*	*Female*
Arunachal Pradesh	73.69	59.57
Assam	78.81	67.27
Nagaland	83.29	76.69
Manipur	86.49	73.17
Tripura	92.18	83.15
Mizoram	93.72	89.40
Sikkim	87.29	76.43
Meghalaya	77.17	73.78

Source: Government of India, Provincial Census Report, 2011.

Table shows that there is low female literacy rate in all the states of North East region among all the eight North East states, Arunachal Pradesh has the lowest female literacy rate and Mizoram has the highest female literacy rate.

Issues and Challenges of Women Education in Rural Areas of North East India

In Indian North East Region, there are many issues facing by women and although many of them are now recognised and are improving, but there is still a long way to go. Although, the literacy rate for women is gradually increasing, almost half the women are still illiterate.

Klasen (1999) pointed out that gender inequalities in education have direct impact on growth, and through distorting incentives and indirect impact on investment and population growth. The following issues and challenges are addressing the women education now-a-days in the rural areas of North East Region.

Economic Backwardness of the Rural Community: In the rural areas, Girls have to help their mothers in the household work, look after the siblings, and fetch driving water from distant taps and wells. For them continuing education or going to educational institutions is an unaffordable luxury.

Unfavourable Social Attitude: In the rural areas of this region, women are still in *purdah*. Besides, there are many superstitions and unfavourable attitudes towards women. In some rural areas, there is the practice of female foeticide to avoid dowry.

Lack of Personal Guidance and Supervision: In this male dominated world, there is the absence of women in all stages of educational management and administration. As a result of this, the female participants do not get the guidance and counselling that she deserves.

Inappropriate Curriculum: Our general curriculum cannot cater the needs, interests, tastes, abilities and aptitudes of the female students. Many of them find education totally irrelevant to life and as a result, they drop out from educational institutions. Due to inadequate curriculum, the women in rural areas do not have faith on education. From their point of view, education is not life related and waste of time.

Discrimination Against Women in Education: Much of society is still geared towards thinking that women should ultimately become mothers, and therefore be responsible for looking after the children. Many women, therefore, pursue an education, which leads to an occupation allowing for long periods of absence, to give them the opportunity to stay at home and be full time moms. This ultimately leads to many women being unable to learn.

Lack of Confidence: Many women lack the sheer confidence to compete with men in this culturally male dominated profession.

Impact of Globalisation: Major aspects of globalisation that relate to rural development include the commercialisation of agriculture and expansion of agro-industries, the liberalisation of international trade and the wider use of information and communication technologies. The implications of globalisation for rural women are complex and data remain sparse and unindicated. For some women, in rural areas, the ongoing changes present new opportunities. But, they ignore educational opportunities and gives more importance in family livelihood due to their poverty.

Decision-Making: In North East Region, it is found that after marriage, a woman is under the authority of her husband and generally has little autonomy in decision-making, even regarding her own fertility.

Female Age at Marriage: There is high association of female literacy with female age at marriage. By and large the female age at marriage of 18 (recently 21 years) as prescribed by various legislations not at all followed in rural areas of Indian North East Region. It is very much ignored and neglected by the families of parents with low literacy and illiteracy background.

Demographic Factor: The high population growth rate, rapid urbanisation, migration etc. also attribute immensely the poor literacy level of women in rural areas in North Eastern Region. Social Assistance and the provision of public services to households determines a significant part of the observed differentials in employment, as well as civic development and gender-based discrimination. Contrary to what frequently assumed, pure macro-economic variables, such as GDP growth or the extent of the Services Sector, seem to significantly affect only men's employment. These two findings suggest that no reliance can be put on self-correcting mechanisms of economic growth to automatically address gender unbalances in the labour market, and that women's full inclusion requires the provision of effective public services as well as the pursue of wide-ranging regional development policies, well beyond strictly focused labour market interventions.

Geographical Factor: The considerable spatial disparity, and in some cases incompleteness, of institutional provision (even at primary level) relates directly to difficulties of physical access which adversely affect girls more than boys; there is an overall and profound urban/rural dichotomy which favours towns and cities, especially in respect of secondary school (and especially single sex) provision for girls; patterns of transportation and migration affect educational provision and take up, again normally disadvantaging females and in some cases extreme physical difficulties, such as flooding and other hazards act in the same way. The influence of this factor can only be overcome by more sophisticated and multivariate spatial analysis of educational needs and the planning and implementation of integrated development projects as a result. Educational planning on its own would be futile.

Socio-Cultural Factor: A major deterrent to female take up and follow through of educational opportunities (even when these are available) is a near universal fundamental cultural bias in favour of males. The widespread operation of patriarchal systems of social organisation; of customary early marriage; of the incidence of early pregnancy (in and out of marriage); of heavier domestic and subsistence duties of females (especially in rural areas); a generally lower regard for the value of female life, all combine though differentially in each case, to adversely affect the participation of girls and women in formal education. To this list may be added problems of seclusion and security in some areas. Such long standing constraints result in a dearth of female role models that could challenge the traditional one that is clearly acquired by both sexes at a very early age. The influence of this factor can only be overcome, *inter alia* by a profound change of attitude on the part of influential males, and in some countries of traditionally minded powerful females in key family positions.

Health Factor: In general the effect of poverty and malnutrition on the health of school age children falls harder on girls than boys. Boys may get preferential feeding, while girls (who have a heavier domestic work load) are more likely to be undernourished. Even if they get to school, this adversely affects their performance and therefore, retention rate. Health problems associated with pregnancy, especially for adolescent girls, obviously have a negative effect, as do rising trends of sexual activity in the younger generations where these occur. Problems associated with family size and family planning are widespread in relation to possible participation in education and imply the need for sex/health education at school level. It is clear that the health factor, though partly hidden and indirect in effect is a very significant one in respect of the quality of (young) female participation in education as well as the quantity of it.

Economic Factor: Together with the fundamental socio-cultural bias in favour of males, the economic factor, especially in terms of grinding poverty and hunger, is probably the most influential in adversely affecting female participation in education, especially in rural areas. In such harsh economic circumstances, both direct and hidden costs to a family of sending daughters to school are perceived by parents to be prohibitive in terms of the provision of books, paper and uniforms/clothing (important for social reasons) as well as the loss of vital help at home and on the land. In most cases the contribution of females is unpaid and they may have little or no experience of the handling of money which further reduces their status and power, but increases their vulnerability. Because of the patriarchal and patrilocal predominance, investment in a girl's schooling is wasteful since it benefits the family into which a girl marries rather than her own. In the more privileged classes investment in the education of females may be an advantage in 'marrying well'. This further increases the urban/rural gap. Vocational education which might relate to employment prospects, is everywhere weak and under-valued, but especially so in respect of the interests of girls. The apparent inability of some countries to resource their schools and even to pay their teachers regularly leads to low morale, teacher absenteeism and parental disenchantment.

Religious Factor: Although in general acting indirectly, the religious factor is on balance a positive one, though it is often overcome by the fundamental socio-cultural bias in favour of males. The fact that most religious practitioners and leaders are male makes for a powerful image in favour of that sex, and it would be a very helpful move if religious leaders of all faiths and denominations were to speak out strongly in support of the female cause. Christian missions have, in various areas, had a most positive effect on female education and literacy levels, though some have a legacy of harsh sanctions in respect of early pregnancy. In Islamic areas the situation is generally not so supportive but a number of positive trends were apparent. The religious significance of sons in the Hindu family, while still operative, no longer seems in itself to disadvantage daughters. Often in contrast to the state system, and especially—at secondary level, denominational schools are well organised and resourced, attracting stable, well qualified staff. This weighs heavily with parents when deciding whether or not to send their daughters to schools, especially since boarding facilities tend to be more favourable and secure.

Legal Factor: Again this factor acts mainly indirectly. Most countries have now legislated for equal status in respect of sex, but this is usually a recent innovation and traditional sanctions often still operate unchallenged. So, there are still important areas where the law could be reformed further to encourage compliance and the system of justice strengthened to ensure that this actually happens. In many rural areas long standing societal rules constraining females are still operative, as is the case with condoning early marriage. The acquisition of minimum legal knowledge and support in such areas as: gaming justice and compensation for assault; understanding letters and contracts; arguing for educational provision according to the law, and challenging disadvantageous pressures in respect of marriage, divorce and inheritance could be very helpful to the female cause. There must be concern over the legality of the employment of (young) children, particularly girls, and the dominance of males in the legal profession. The encouragement and support for more females to seek and develop careers in various areas of this profession could be a very significant development in respect of female participation in education.

Political/Administrative Factors: Although policies exist in most cases for such developments as universal primary education, equal educational opportunities in terms of gender and the eradication of gender bias from texts and other materials, the political will to carry these through seems to be weak in the face of severe economic constraint. The creation of Ministries or Bureaux of Women's Affairs appears to be counter-productive, and the poor quality of local administrative/advisory staff and resources renders such Government initiatives as do occur, relatively ineffective. The record of NGOs is markedly better, and those governments that enable NGOs to operate in favours of increased female participation are to be commended. In some cases where strong political dichotomies or other such disparities exist even elite females may be disadvantaged by being in the 'wrong' camp, and their potential contribution to national development and the role of females in general to that end may be lost. Language policies can adversely affect female participation in that where vernaculars have no status, and schooling is either absent or very poor, women and girls remain 'trapped'. As with the churches, political leaders are almost always male, and until considerably more women break into the most influential echelons of power, the question of low female participation in education and its implications for national development may well remain on the sidelines.

Educational Factor: This factor itself can be a deterrent to female participation in schooling. Difficulties of accessibility, lack of resources and low teacher quality and morale are widespread. In particular the lack of female primary teachers in rural areas is a real problem. Parents are, in some countries, very reluctant indeed to send daughters to school if there is no female teacher and the facilities for the accommodation and security of such teachers are usually absent or inadequate. The organisation of schooling in terms of the daily and seasonal imperatives of local economies usually renders it dysfunctional, and the curriculum is often unattractive in instrumental terms. At secondary level, in addition to the lack of (accessible) places, problems of cost, direct and hidden are acute, and there is a considerable need for more single-sex (girls) schools, some with secure boarding facilities and scholarship schemes to enable participation. Vocational education is weak and schemes open to girls in this field are particularly useful. There is still a widespread problem of gender bias in books and materials.

Suggestions

The benefit and potentials of women education far outweigh its challenges.

Thus, it is imperative that institutions and government come together to resolve the issues discussed above. Some of the suggestions that can be adopted are listed below:

- Strengthening legal systems aimed at elimination of all forms of discrimination against women.
- Changing societal attitudes and community practices by active participation and involvement of both men and women.
- Creating an environment through positive educational policies for full development of women to enable them to realise their full potential.
- Equal access to participation and decision-making of women in social, political and economic life of the nation.
- Elimination of discrimination and all forms of violence against women.
- Building and strengthening partnership with civil, particularly women's organisation.
- The poverty stricken families can be identified through proper research and necessary poverty alleviation services be provided to strengthen the income thereby to enable the families to send their female members to schools and colleges without much financial difficulties.
- Increased support to be given to NGOs involved in (non-formal) primary education projects which positively discriminate in favours of the participation of girls.
- Wherever possible, schemes for the enhancement of female participation in schooling, especially in rural areas, be part of an integrated and coordinated development including such other aspects as health, environment and economy.
- Projects to be developed and supported that address pre-school child care needs and adult literacy/skills development needs, in an integrated and coordinate way.
- Aid to be considered for the provision of books, other learning materials, uniforms (or other necessary clothing) and fees to enable more girls to participate in schooling at both primary and secondary levels.
- Support should be given to the construction of more single-sex schools for girls with adequate residential facilities for pupils and female teachers in those locations where this is necessary for either environmental or social or cultural reasons.

- Aid should be provided for more scholarships to enable girls from poorer economic backgrounds to attend secondary school, whether boarding or otherwise.
- Positive incentives, such as more secondary scholarships for girls might be considered to go along with the present expansion of the junior secondary sector.
- NGOs be encouraged to submit schemes for aid approval that would have the effect of improving the rate of progression of girls from primary to secondary schooling.
- Funding to be considered for improvements in the provision of teachereducation and training especially for primary school work, that would encourage greater female participation and include more residential accommodation for female students.
- Aid should be considered for the upgrading of technical and vocational education for both sexes, partly (though not exclusively) as a 'second chance' opportunity of dropouts from the formal system. In some cases this could be part of a community based skills development programme.
- Support to be given for feeding schemes in primary and secondary schools where such a facility might encourage and enable the poorest families to send their boys and girls to school.
- Aid to be provided to improve the level of educational policy implementation at the local level through the training of significant numbers of personnel in systems of implementation and delivery. Their role would be a practical one of animation, advice and support rather than mere administration. The opportunity should be taken to include a considerable number of women in such programmes of training and subsequent employment that assistance be provided to enable the school day and the school year to bead justed to the realities of rural life and the demands of rural economies on child labour.
- Aid be given for resolving the urgent and particular problem of the security of female teachers especially in rural areas, by providing adequate accommodation and protection.
- Reducing user fees, providing school materials, uniforms and meals, making (travel to) schools safer for girls (e.g. through safe transport, the provision of restrooms and training of teachers).
- Making cash transfers to poor families conditional on them investing in the education and health of their children.

- Effective policies need to be multifaceted because infrastructure, health issues, laws, social norms and cultural practices can also influence the ability of girls to attend and complete school.
- Support the design and implementation of specific financial education programmes for men and women (and particularly vulnerable groups) to enhance their level of confidence and knowledge on financial issues, to encourage higher savings and to improve the quality of their investments in order to promote a financially secure retirement and to improve their ability to participate more dynamically in economic activities.

Conclusion

The women education in North East India presents a broad spectrum with gender biases leading to poor education and health of women and development constraints. However, in order to realise the full potentials of women education, the government needs to play a more active role in promoting and supporting the women education in the rural areas of North East India. While acknowledging that our study confirms the near universal, and especially in rural areas, deeply rooted incidence of female disadvantage in education, the researchers would also wish to mention the numerous efforts being made in all case countries to confront the problem. We hope that the recommendations made above will be helpful in maintaining and increasing the effort to assist increased female participation, especially at primary and secondary level, and we would like to see more research carried out with.

REFERENCES

Ahmed, M. and M. Ahmed (2002), *Bangladesh Education Sector Overview,* Japan Bank for International Cooperation (JBIC), Tokyo.

Banbeis (2003), "Statistical Profile on Education in Bangladesh", Bangladesh Bureau of Educational Information and Statistics, Dhaka.

Colin Brock & Nadine Cammish, "Factors Affecting Female Participation in Education in Seven Developing Countries", Education Department for Research Paper No. 9, 1993, p. 96, Universities of Oxford and Hull 1997 (Second Edition).

Directorate of Census, 2011, Provisional Census Data, Government of India, New Delhi.

Flabbi, L. (2011), "Gender Differentials in Education, Career, Choices and Labour Market Outcomes on a Sample of OECD Countries", mimeo, forthcoming.

IFAD Experience with Indigenous Women in Latin America and Asia.

Kiran (2010). Globalisation and Indian Higher Education. *University News*.

Magrotra, R. (2007) Higher Education in the context of Globalisation. *University News*.

National Commission for Women, New Delhi (2004). Report of the North East Network.

Pandey, P.G., Das, Payel & Joshi, Charu (2011). Education, Media and Women Empowerment from Feminist Perspective. *University News*.

Rymbai, Bazeley Brinda (2011). Interview with Kaiming Cheng: Humanities and Social Science Education in Hongkong and East Asia. The CIHE Podcast Initiative.

World Bank (2008), Girls' Education in the 21st Century, the World Bank, Washington DC, USA.

22

Status of Women and Their Role in Socio-Economic Development of Ilam District in Nepal

Sudarshan Prasad Regmi

Background

Nepal is a small country having area of 1,41,181 square kilometre, which is a landlocked between two giant Asian countries, *viz.* China and India. Nepal occupies 0.03 percentage of area of the world and 0.30 percentage of area of Asia. Nepal ecologically has three belts or regions, namely mountain 35 per cent, hill 42 per cent, and terai 23 per cent; and is lengthily distributed from east to west. Administratively, country is divided into five development regions and 75 districts of which Ilam falls to Eastern hill district adjoining to West Bengal State of India.

Nepal has been always an independent and sovereign country with glorious history, culture and tradition which dates back to time immemorial. Nepal is famous in world for its unique features among these the major three important features are: the highest peak mountain—Everest (*Sagarmatha*); the birth place of Lord Buddha—Lumbini; and Pashupatinath—the Hindu's biggest temple listed under the world heritage lies in Nepal.

Ilam falls under hill ecology and is famous in the region for production of the milk; ginger; the broom grass; the potato. The district experiences temperate in the northern part and sub-tropical climate in the southern part with an average precipitation about 1400 mm to 1500 mm annually and about 85 per cent or more during months of May to September. Basically, Ilam is considered as pioneer head in agriculture and livestock husbandry, especially cash crops as mentioned above. In livestock, cattle farming for milk production are highly integrated with agro-forestry and agricultural practice.

Ilam has spread over an area of 1,71,725 hectare that is only about 12.14 per cent of area of Nepal. The district is divided into three electoral constituencies, nine *Ilakas*, with households 64,435 in 2009, average household size being 6.0. Ilam district ranks to 12th out of 75 districts for its overall composite index with a farm size 0.98 ha and about 5.56 livestocks' density per household (*see* the Annex Table A-22.1). Demographic trend indicates there is increasing in both population size household size and literacy from 1981 Census to the projected till 2011. People are more influenced and affiliated development activities with the neighbouring state of India.

Women make up about 40 per cent of world's workforce in agriculture, a quarter in industries and a third in services. Women farmers in developing countries grow at least 50 per cent of world's food, for example 80 per cent in some African countries. In addition to income generating activities (in cash and kind), women's household activities include caring for sick, house maintenance, and such vital work as caring for children, prepare food, and fetching water and firewood. Yet women's productivity remains low—both in income generating work and in home production.

According to the population Census 2001, women's contribution in agriculture is 60.5 per cent, but economically they rely on men. Women's ownership of land is 10.83 per cent and house ownership is 5.51 per cent only. Though the women constitute half the population in Nepal, their share in the national economy is insignificant. The population Census 2001 shows that only 8.55 per cent women are in government jobs, 26 per cent are involved in the teaching profession, 12 per cent in the media, 10.5 per cent in foreign employment and only 2.05 per cent are judges.

Improving women productivity can contribute to growth, efficiency and poverty reduction, which are the key development goals everywhere.

Gaps and Constrains

The gaps and constrains observed worldwide and related to Nepalese context were reviewed:

- Girls' school enrolment rate lay behind those of boys, dropout rate are higher for girls than for boys.
- Many more women than men are low-paying, low skilled informal activities.

- The combination of poor education and lack of access to services, like family planning can be—as prevailing higher maternal mortality rate testify.
- Social and institutional factors such as lack of access to land and information often undermine women's ability to maintain environmental quality and sustainable use of the resources.
- Lack of access to credit for female entrepreneurs' limits the profitability and growth of their enterprises. This relates to the limited education and mobility and, in some cases, cultural barriers restrict women's contact with institutions that offer financial services as do the high transaction cost and collateral requirements associated with making small loans.
- Legal and regulatory barriers that do not apply to men exacerbate the inefficiencies of inequality. Especially, property, like land (the universal collateral) is usually registered in men's name.
- Some countries have laws that prevent women to register the land in their own name or from owning or selling it; also restriction prevents women from participating in the labour force on equal term with men.
- The need to balance home and market responsibilities is a major constrains on women's earning, productivity and accumulation of human capital.

Research Methodology

Random sample survey technique was used for collecting the primary data. The primary data were collected from each Village Development Committee (VDC) and Municipality of the district. The format was structured to get information in both closed and open ended questions patterns. Demographic information; use of materials for the family planning by both gender and short term or permanent; involvements to some saving and credit or some other organisation; income generating activities for different categories; awareness about household conflicts observed and causes of the conflicts and so on were captured in the primary data collection. All data were analysed using Microsoft access programme in computer. During data entry two VDCs, viz. *Chisapani*, and *Gorkhe* were having distorted data, and so were excluded from the analysis.

Review of Literatures

Some Facts and Figures on Status of Women

Following are some facts and figures found in related publications on the worldwide as well as some country or region specific on the status of women.

A. Health Status of Women and Girls

- More than a half of women die from complications related to pregnancy and child birth every year. Ninety-nine per cent of these deaths occur in developing countries (WHO, 2004).
- Providing basic maternal and new born health service to developing nations would cost an average US$ 3 per capita per year. However, once complication developed, saving the life of a mother or infant costs about US$ 230 (United Nations Population Fund, 2003).
- There are 50 million abortions worldwide annually, 30 million of them are illegal (Alan Guttmacher Institute, May 1998).
- More adolescent girls than boys are diagnosed with HIV positive, 90 per cent of AIDS cases under age of 20 are girls (US Centre for Disease Control, 2002).

B. Access to Education

- Of an estimated 115 million children who currently do not attend school, girls make up 57 per cent (United Nations, 2003).
- Of the world's 979 million illiterate adults, two-thirds are women (UNDP Human Development Report, 2003).
- A recent study shows that increase in women's education made the greatest contribution to reducing the rate of child malnutrition, accounting for 43 per cent of the reduction (UNPF, 2002).
- On an average, by age 18, girls receive 4.4 years less education than boys.

C. Political Power

- In 2003, at least 54 countries had discriminatory laws against women (Amnesty International, 2003).

- Some countries still do not have universal suffrage. Among these are Brunei, Kuwait, Oman, Saudi Arabia, and UAE (Women in Politics, 2003).
- Of more than 180 countries of the world, only 12 are headed by women (Women in Politics, 2003).
- Women hold only 6.4 per cent of seats in Arab States' Parliaments, 14.4 per cent of seats in Sub-Saharan Africa, 17.6 per cent of seats in Europe and 18.5 per cent seats in the Americas (Women's Learning Partnership, 2002).
- In Nepal, under the interim assembly, it is about 33 per cent seats in the parliament occupied by women.

D. Economic Status

- More than US$ 7 trillion worth of women's work goes unpaid.
- Only one per cent of the world's assets are in the name of women. This percentage may be more in case of Nepalese context only (Women's Learning Partnership, 2003).
- 2.1 billion women live on less than US$ 2 a day, and 330 million women live on less than US$ 1 a day (Centre for Women Policy Studies, 2003).
- In the Middle East, North Africa and South Asia, only 40 women per 100 men are economically active in the formal economy (US News Centre, 2004).

E. Violence Parameters

- During the past 30 years, 30 million women and children have been trafficked for sexual exploitation (United Nations, 2003).
- Gender based violence against women (like female infanticide, sexual trafficking and exploitation, dowry killings and domestic violence) causes more death and disability among women in 15-44 age group than other casualties (like cancer, malaria, traffic accident and war combined) (Centre for Women Policy Studies, 2003).
- Up to 47 per cent women reported that their first sexual intercourse was forced (World Health Organisation, 2003).
- An estimated 130 million women worldwide have under gone female genital mutilation and 2 million more are mutilated every year and 98 per cent of Somali women have been mutilated.

Nepalese Context

Women Representation

Trade Unions

Trade unions are primarily labour advocacy NGOs often promoting worker's interests and are directly concerned with the workers' well-being and women constitute a substantial proportion among the workers. However, no data are available on the female membership of the trade unions, although of the 3.5 million wage earners, 6,21,000, about 18 per cent have been reported to be organised (GEFONT, 2001).

Table 22.1 below revealed that women constitute about 12 per cent of the central leadership of women in the three largest unions. The Labour Act and Labour Regulations (1993) has provisions of 52 days of paid maternity leave up to two pregnancies, only day time employment, limitation on the loads larger than their own body weight etc.

Table 22.1: Women in Policy-Making Bodies in Trade Unions in Nepal

Institutions	*National Committee Members*		*Central Leadership*	
	Number	*Female %*	*Number*	*Female %*
GEFONT	35	8.6	206	6.3
NTUC	21	23.8	239	14.6
DECONT	21	9.5	141	15.6
Total	**77**	**13.97**	**586**	**12.16**
Committees under GEFONT affiliates	9203	11.58	—	—

Source: GEFONT, 2001.

Media

There has been much progress in women's participation in media channels, particularly in electronic media, with the democratic changes of 1990 and since opening up of the sector to the private sector. Women constituted 12.3 per cent in 1991 and 12.9 per cent of media personnel in 1991. At that time sole electronic media were Nepal Radio and Nepal TV. With the proliferation of FM radios and private TV channels, women's participation as media workers has increased significantly in 2002 as reflected in Table 22.2.

Table 22.2: Percentage of Women involved in Media, Nepal 2002

Media/Year	*2002*	*Media/Year*	*2002*
Print	9.1	TV	30.8
— Public	4.2	— Public	31.8
— Private	11.2	— Private	68.2
Radio	29.1	**Total**	**19.4**
— Public	16.5	— Public	4.2
— Private	37.9	— Private	18.6

Source: Asmita Publishing House, 2003.

Similarly, there has been a substantial progress in media coverage of women's issues (Asmita Publishing House, 2003). This positive development, nevertheless, has not been accompanied by a changed attitude towards a need for inducting women in this sector by social consciousness for promoting women, but for commercial gains only as accepted by the management in interviews (Asmita, 2003).

Political Status

Women's access to positions of power, political or otherwise has not improved much in the last 10-15 years except at the grassroots level; the 20 per cent reservation by the LSGA-2055 Act has made a difference. One female member in 20-45 ministers has been the rule. Still today women constitute less than 10 per cent in the Central Committees of the major politically parties.

Only reservation since 1997 has been able to bring out women into politics in significant proportions, 20 per cent at the grassroots level. Compared to 1978, the proportion of women in the government administration has almost trebled. At officer and higher levels it has doubled. Still women constitute less than ten per cent of the government staff.

The proportion of women even among the professional and technical group in the occupational classification had declined in 1991 as compared to 1981, but the trend has fortunately reversed as per the 2001 Census (Table 22.3). The trend of increasing proportion of women in administration and management is more encouraging. During the 1990s, women's awareness and women have been mobilised extensively into groups by various NGOs/INGOs and the government programmes.

Women's political consciousness is also increasing. The proportion of rural women who knew about women's organisations had more than

Table 22.3: Access to Positions of Power: Per cent Women in Various Positions of Power during Pre-democratic Situation, Nepal (1986-87 to 2000)

Details	*1986-87*	*1991-92*	*2000*
Parliament[3]	5.70	3.80	6.4
House of Representatives	—	3.4	5.8
Upper House (Rastriya Shava)	—	5.0	15.0
Number of Women in the Cabinet	1	2	2
Executives of the major political parties[2]	—	7.8/2	8.3/3
LSG Structure	0.58	0.54	—
District Councils	na	na	1.5
DDCs	0.74	0.75	6.7
Municipalities	1.13	0.38	19.5
VDCs	0.60	0.58	7.7
Village Councils	na	na	2.1
Ward Committees	na	na	20
Government Administration[1]	2.87	na	7.8
Of which: Officers	3.23	4.39	6.2
High Government Position—First and Special Class	1.10	2.46	2.4
Professional and technical human power (All sectors—Census, 2001)	16.6	15.1	19.0
Administration and Management (All sectors—Census, 2001)	6.6	9.3	13.8

Source: Acharya 1994; CBS/MGEP, Asmita Publishing House, 2002: 1. Figures relate to 1978, 1993 and 2000. 2. Five nationally recognized parties (NC, UML, RPP, SJN, and NSP). 3. Seven Parties in the Parliament (NC, UML, RPP, SJN, NSP and NPWP).

trebled between 1978 and 1992 (from 4.7% to 14.9%). But still only 15 per cent of rural women know about women's organisations and less than one per cent participated in them. Slightly more than 20 per cent knew about the new constitution, but only 6.2 per cent was aware of its discriminatory features. Awareness in urban was higher (Acharya, 1997) at 29.2 per cent.

In contrast to one per cent women reporting any women's organisation membership, a recent survey conducted by GEFONT among women/men workers reports (GEFONT, 2003) that 27 per cent of the women workers interviewed had ever joined one or other woman's organisation.

Social Status

Achievements in terms of social development indicators have been significant for both women and men in the last two decades. Access to social services in terms of schools and health posts and hospital beds has increased significantly.

Table 22.4: Social dimensions of Gender Status, Nepal 2001

Indicators/Census Years	*1981*	*1991*	*2001*
Health			
Sex-Ratio (Males per 100 Female)	105.0	99.5	99.8
Mean Age of Marriage (Years)	–	–	–
– Male	20.7	21.4	22.9
– Female	17.2	18.1	19.5
MMR per 1,00,000 delivery (Number)	850	539	–
TFR (15-49 ages, 1995-2000 period) (Number)	5.1	5.1	4.1
Life Expectancy at birth (Years)	–	–	–
– Male	50.9	55.0	60.8
– Female	48.1	53.5	61.0
Education			
Literacy in 6 years+ age group (%)	–	–	–
– Male	34.0	54.1	65.1
– Female	12.0	24.7	42.5
– Literacy Ratio (Literate female/100 literate Male)	33.8	46.3	65.8
Female in school enrolment (%)	–	–	–
– Primary	–	37.2	44.1
– Secondary	–	31.5	41.5
– Higher Secondary	–	28.7	40.6
Female per cent among full time students	27.2	34.7	43.1
SLC and Above (Females/100 Male) (Number)	21.0	28.2	43.2
Graduates (Females/100 Male) (Number)	18.4	22.5	22.9
HDI Index	**0.328**	**0.416**	**0.490**
GDI Index	–	**0.312**	**0.470**

Sources: (1) Population Census, 2001;
(2) HDR, 1995 and 2002; and
(3) Population Monograph, CBS 1995.

Human development indicators have improved significantly for both men and women. In literacy and education gender disparities are decreasing very slowly. Girl's enrolment has not attended parity even at the primary level. The number of women with SLC and higher degrees still constitute only 43 to 100 men with such qualifications.

Similarly, the number of women, with graduate and higher degrees, is still less than 20 to 100 men with such degrees. What is more, this ratio has declined as compared to 1991 figure. The male female ratio of full-time students is still only 43:57. Further, these achievements are very unequally distributed as between the regions, rural and urban areas, among castes and various ethnic groups.

In the health sector the improvement is visible in terms of a substantial improvement in MMR, fertility behaviour and ultimately life expectancy. The mean age of first marriage for both the girls and the boys are increasing. It is well recognised by now that there is a large variation between the Indo-Aryan and the Tibeto-Burman groups and even within each of these groups in terms of social relations governing gender relations. In spite of this diversity, land is inherited universally in all communities from the father to the son and women lag far behind men in access to knowledge, economic resources and modern avenues of employment.

Marriage is compulsory and seen as a primary means of livelihood for women in all most all communities (Acharya and Bennett, 1981; Gurung, 1999).

Women Violence

Violence against women is also widespread in all communities. Violence, both in the domestic as well as in the public arena is still used extensively by the patriarchy to establish domination over women.

As per the 2001 Census more than five hundred fifty-five thousand women are living in polygyneous marriages. Alcohol and polygyny related violence in the domestic arena is reported high all over Nepal and across all communities (New ERA, 1998).

Dowry related violence was reported to a lesser extent, but it does exist. A large group of young widows, particularly, in the Indo-Aryan community, are subject to covert and overt violence and face both psychological (as forerunners of misfortune) and physical violence, often for her share of property.

Trafficking is widely reported but hard data are impossible to collect. Police estimate trafficking of about 5000-7000 women for commercial sex work annually. In the past, girls and women from the Tibeto-Burman groups, coming from poor rural areas were prone to trafficking.

The patriarchal socialisation, which establishes marriage as a respectable livelihood option for the girls, is one of the causes of girls falling to trafficker's traps. The Maoist insurgency has compounded the problem of violence against women and children.

Result and Discussion

Involvement in the Local Cooperatives

Data indicated that there were on average 41.33 per cent women involved in different cooperatives of which more that 60 per cent VDCs reported to be more of the average. The highest involvement of women were in cooperative has from Shakhejung, 53.42 per cent; Mahamai, 53.13 per cent; and Fikkal, 52.53 VDCs. However, lowest participation was from Smalbung, 8.54 per cent and Banjho, 9.64 per cent.

Domestic Violence and Conflicts at Home

Under the three categories of closed answers to the domestic violence's, women of Ilam responded that only 210 (06.19%) women out of 3394 know well about domestic violence's and 1814, (53.45%) women know only a little of violence's; whereas 1370 (40.36%) women were not knowing about the domestic violence. Knowing did not at all mean that there were no violence at their house, but they were basically doing not relate about the hostility. It indicates that most of the women about 96 per cent were not fully know about the different violence.

Table 22.5: Perception of Domestic Violence by Women of Ilam, 2010

Particulars	*No. of Respondents*	*Percentage*
Better known	210	6.19
Little known	1814	53.45
Not known at all	1370	40.36
Total	**3394**	**100**

Source: Field survey.

The cases of violence were also recorded. These were categories under 4 categories of reason of violence and of which highest number of cases were less education of women and polygamy of man and both 620 (43.24%); followed by the reason of drinking habit of husband, 393 (27.41%); and third highest was due to facial beautiful, disease, and disability of women and all together.

Table 22.6: Reason of Domestic Violence of Women of Ilam, 2010

Category	*Particular*	*Number of Respondents*	*Percentage*
I	Dowry (*Daijo*), birth of female child and both	176	12.27
II	Face beautiful, disease, disability and all	245	17.08
III	Less education, and polygamy and both	620	43.24
IV	Drinking habit of husband	393	27.41
	Total	**1434**	**100**

Source: Field survey.

As we interpreting data the reason behind the violence is male born in both highest interrogation goes to male as he is the boss to the house. It is human born reason acceptability and responsibility of male in the society.

Conflict in home environment and condition as women of Ilam reported those only 218 cases of husband beating, 129 cases of family discrimination (*hela*) and 68 cases of polygamy. Highest conflicts were reported from Mahamai, 26; and Kanyam, 23; whereas no conflict was reported from Barbote, Dhuseni, Fikkal, Sagfara, Januna, Panchkanya, Pashupatinagar. Here again it is male partner of the household has been responsible for conflict.

Table 22.7: Number of Conflict Cases in Household in Ilam, 2010

Particular	*Number of Cases*	*Per cent*
Beaten by Husband	218	52.53
Polygamy	68	16.38
Family Discrimination	129	31.09
Total	**415**	**100**

Source: Field survey.

Works and Working Hours of Women

Works under nine categories and rest period were responded and found that women of Ilam district spent about two and half hours working with care and management of animals in the shed. They spare only one third of an hour for care of old members of house. Women spent almost two hours in making food for the family and take similar time for as leisure time. It is observed that about two-third of an hour in collection/fetching of water. Women spent about one and quarter hours in children care, home cleaning, cloth washing, and wood collection for the household everyday (*see* Table 22.8).

Although, there were out layers in the data for Lumde and Shantidada VDCs for their externality of data and were excluded. It is also observed that women of Puwamajhuwa and Phakphok VDCs were spending more hours, 14hrs in household works and enjoying a two hours of leisure that was followed by women of Sumbek, Maipokhari, Sangrumba, Lumde, Phuyathappa and Nayabajar, 13 hrs. VDCs. Similarly, women of Danabari, Barebote, Panchkanya, were spending only about 7 hours in work and having only one hour of rest.

Table 22.8: Time Spent on Different Categories of Household Works by Women of Ilam, 2010

Type of Work	*Time spent (Hr)*	*Percentage*	*Type of Work*	*Time spent (Hr)*	*Percentage*
Animal care in shed	2.5	20.83	Water Fetching	0.6	5.00
House Cleaning	1.1	9.17	Wood collection	1.2	10.00
Food Preparation	1.8	15.00	Cloth Washing	1.2	10.00
Care of children	1.2	10.00	Care of old persons	0.3	2.50
Leisure period	1.9	15.83	**Total**	**11.8**	**100**

Source: Field survey.

Income Generating Activities

Respondents were asked to express their income generating activities in three categories of which poultry, goat keeping and agricultural; retail shop keeping, cottage industries, and doll making; and business, driving and other technical activities were listed. Out of 2921 women respondents 2569 (87.95%) expressed their source of income highest from poultry, goat keeping and agriculture activities and 234 (8.01%) expressed retailing, cottage industry and doll-making as second income generating activities. Women in Ilam are more preferred to raise animals in their household as they are dedicated to have some animals in their house. Now-a-days, they are diverting their substantial animal husbandry to commercial one along with some NGOs involvement by forming user groups, committees and farming improve breeds and suitable variety of crops (*see* Table 22.9).

Table 22.9: Involvement in Income Generating Activities by Women of Ilam, 2010

Type of activities	*No. of Respondents*	*Percentage*
1. Goat, poultry raising, and agriculture	2569	87.95
2. Retailing, Cottage industries and doll-making	234	8.01
3. Business, Driving and other technical jobs	118	4.03
Total	**2921**	**100**

Source: Field survey.

It was observed that activities related to agriculture and livestock were higher in Fikkal (111) and Mahamai (108) whereas, retailing shops and cottage industries were higher in Chulachuli VDCs. Similarly,

Business and other technical jobs were highly concentrated in Ilam municipal, but overall the income generating activities were highest in Chulachuli VDC, it may be due to more near to Jhapa. Here, it can be related that all shorts of income activities can be cashed through nearest market, which is Jhapa.

Sources of Information and Entertainment

The information and entertainments are the basic need of any life style in the context of twenty first century. These facilities were captured through availability of radio, television, telephone, mobiles and newspapers to the women of Ilam. It was found that radio was the prime source of information and entertainment which accounted, 3862 (95.26%) and the second facility they have mobile, 1858 (45.83%) and the third entertaining facility was visual television, 1570 (38.73%).

Though newspaper availability were less than 5 per cent, but use of mobile had exceeded to 5 times than telephone, which may be due to unavailability of telephone line distribution and cheaper to landline telephone in context to its technology.

Table 22.10: Information and Entertainment Facilities of Women of Ilam, 2010

Facilities	*No. of Respondents*	*Percentage*
Radio	3862	95.28
Television	1570	38.73
Telephone	347	08.56
Mobile	1858	45.83
Newspaper	196	04.83
Total	**7833**	**100**

Source: Field survey.

Although, highest newspapers were read by Pyang, Kolbung and Ilam municipal women but almost all women in Ilam district have radio with them. It seems that facilities of mobiles ranked first by women of Fikkal VDC, 74.3 per cent and Ilam municipal, 72.12 per cent but women of Jitpur responded zero to mobile facility.

It has observed that 14 VDCs out of 47, i.e. 29.78 recorded were not enjoying reading newspaper, which may be an opportunity to promote newspaper distribution and marketing to those VDCs, viz. Danabari, Gajurmukhi, Jirmale, Jitpur, Lumde, Santipur, Sri Antu and so on.

Family Planning

The family planning concept was bifurcated with two categories, *viz.* permanent and temporary family planning and in both the sexes. It is interesting that in both categories female were doing more practice than male. Males were still behind to go forward for uses of contraceptives in family planning. It has drawn attention that females' responsibility to tackle the sensitiveness of reproducing and giving birth to children in that family.

Table 22.11: Use of Temporary and Permanent Means of Family Planning by Both Male and Female of Ilam District, 2010

Categories	*No. of respondents*	*Female : Male Ratio*
1. Temporary		
Male	44	36.4 : 1.00
Female	1600	36.36 : 1.00
2. Permanent		
Male	154	03.6 : 1.00
Female	557	03.62 : 1.00
Total	**2355**	**10.89 : 1.00**

Source: Field survey.

Women from Shakhejung, Fikkale, Mahamai and Maipokhari VDCs were reported higher number of female contraceptive users than women of Banjho, Jitpur, Samalbung and Sidhithumka, Similarly, permanent family planning were higher in the women of Ilam, Pasupatinager, Pyang and Sri Antu. Among the males use of condoms has reported as minimal, but the permanent family planning was observed in Santipur, Namsaling and Shidhithumka.

It is observed that nearer to capital city or where sub-health centres or the highways the use of temporary means as well as permanent means of female family planning are more as it is in the remote villages, which may be due to access of means to the community. Whereas, permanent family planning is more prevalent in the remote area of Ilam as compared to sub-city area.

Social Inclusion

In regard to social inclusion it was asked whether women of Ilam know about the social inclusion and what would be the inclusion of women in the society at three categorical contexts. Although, only 41.47 per cent women were knowing social inclusion the result indicated higher towards covering all casts groups and gender in social inclusion, 1546 (78.12%) whereas minimal responded to work only by women. It is highly appreciable that women are conscious about inclusion and want to significantly cover all caste groups and gender issues.

Table 22.12: Inclusion of Women in Social Aspects of Women of Ilam-2010

Category	*No. of respondents*	*Percentage of inclusion*
1. Cover all casts groups and sexes	1546	78.13
2. Works only by women	108	5.45
3. Include women in some cases	325	16.42
4. Knowing the social Inclusion	1979	41.47
Total respondents	**3958**	**100**

Source: Field survey.

It has been observed that women of Ilam municipality and Sulubung VDC knew higher regarding social inclusion of women and least by Banjho, Jirmale, Jitpur and Santidanda. The least known were the women of remote and rural area of the district.

Involvement of Social Organisation

It has been observed that only 13.99 per cent of women were involved and had activist in different organisations. The more percentage goes to farmers groups and committees directly handled under different line agencies of government at district level.

It was found that women of Fikkal, Jogmai were highly involved in NGOs, however Panchkanya and Pashupatinagar VDCs' women had shown higher involvement in Governmental organisations.

Disabilities

The conditions of disabilities were responded (Table 22.14) and about 56.37 percentage of women recorded only 20.66 per cent of disabilities under seven different types of disabilities. The number of disability found were higher in physical disability, 308 (31.23%) which were followed by listing disability of both ears, 216 (22.00%) of the disability, 986 reported.

Table 22.13: Involvement of Women in Different Organisations at Local Level Institutions of Ilam, 2010

Organisations/Institution	*No. of respondent involved*	*Percentage of involvement*
Non-governmental organisations (NGOs)	182	27.24
Red cross	74	11.07
Governmental organisations (GOs)	261	39.07
Youth Clubs	55	7.99
Children Committee	73	10.93
Labour Committee	20	2.99
Others	3	0.40
Total involvements	**668**	**14.00 (100)**
Total respondents	**3958**	**100.00**

Source: Field survey.

The disability varies from their types. It is observed that females were more prone to vision, 56.73 per cent than male, 43.27 per cent and it is seen also in listening irrespective of age. Though the mental problems rank fourth of the disability, but more percentage is observed in youth age than the others age. Listening by single ear and the abandoned problems are less than ten per cent in total.

Table 22.14: Summary of Categorical Disabilities of Ilam-2010

Type of Disabilities	*No. of Observation*	*Percentage of observed*	*(Male and Female) & their percentage*
Physical	308	31.23	Female: 559
Listening (both ears)	216	22.00	(56.70%)
Listening (single ear)	069	07.00	
Vision (Blindness)	171	17.34	
Mental	102	10.30	
Multi-disability	97	09.80	Male: 427
Abandoned	23	02.33	(43.30%)
Disabilities	**986**	**20.66**	
Respondents	**3958**	**100**	

Source: Field survey.

Annual Saving and Income

Annual savings as the net income of the household were reported by four ranges of income groups as well as four categories of age distributions for both male and female member of the family. There were 3673 respondents accounting 67.97 per cent of total of which 2079 females reported higher by 19.93 per cent as of 1592 males under different categories.

The actively participation in saving for future indicates some favours towards self-help attitude in women of the district. This might be related to saving and credit co-operatives active in the village premier. Although, women exceeded in saving the income both in numbers and amount, but the per capita annual saving is lower for women NRs. 8488.70 as compared to men NRs. 9252.51 and together average of NRs. 8819.76.

Table 22.15: Annual Savings of Household at Different Ranges of Income and Age Groups for Both Female and Male, Ilam, 2010

Amount of savings and age group	*No. of respondents and percentage*		*Total*	*Average Savings NRs.*
	Female	*Male*		
1. One to five thousand				
- Children	103 (05.1)	032 (01.6)	2020	10100,000
- Youth	820 (40.6)	560 (27.7)	(54.99)	
- Adults	282 (14.0)	160 (08.2)		
- Older	027 (01.3)	030 (00.2)		
2. Six to ten thousand				
- Children	032 (03.8)	005 (00.6)	842	8420,000
- Youth	288 (34.2)	287 (34.4)	(22.93)	
- Adults	105 (12.5)	106 (12.6)		
- Older	009 (10.7)	010 (01.2)		
3. Eleven to Twenty thousand				
- Children	007 (01.5)	004 (01.2)	469	7035,000
- Youth	127 (27.1)	158 (33.7)	(12.76)	
- Adults	085 (18.1)	072 (15.4)		
- Older	006 (01.3)	008 (01.6)		
4. More than Twenty thousand				
- Children	003 (01.0)	003 (01.0)	342	8640,000
- Youths	129 (37.7)	100 (29.0)	(09.32)	
- Adults	047 (13.7)	042 (12.3)		
- Older	009 (02.6)	009 (02.6)		
Total	**2079 (56.7)**	**1592 (43.3)**	**3673 (100)**	

Note: Figures in the parentheses indicate percentage in those categories.
Source: Field Survey.

Recommendations/Conclusion

It is the demand of time to rupture the walls of confinement and set into

Table 22.16: Summary of Total Annual Savings by Gender and their Per Capita Savings

Gender Category	*One to five thousand @NRs 5,000*	*Six to ten thousand @NRs 10,000*	*Eleven to Twenty thousand @NRs15,000*	*More than Twenty thousand @ NRs 20,000*	*Total*
Female					
– Respondent	1232	434	227	188	2079
– Amount	6160,000	4340,000	3405,000	3760,000	17665,000
Male					
– Respondent	788	408	242	154	1592
– Amount	3940,000	4080,000	3630,000	3080,000	14730,000
Total					
– **Respondent**	2020	842	469	342	3673
– Amount	10100,000	84200,000	7035,000	6840,000	32395,000
Per capita Annual saving	**Male: NRs. 9252.51; Female: NRs. 8488.70; and Average: NRs. 8819.76**				

Source: Field survey.

motion women's talent for equal opportunities and rights. They should demand education and equal rights and opportunity. Women have secured at least 33 per cent seats in the Constituent Assembly, this is positive but changing the traditional patriarchal values prevalent in the society is of outmost. Followings are some of the policy implications which could be done:

1. Educate the half population, that is, women of your society and policy should not forget to maximize this in relation to increase in knowledge and skill so that they could do for their own development in the socio-economic perspectives.
2. Provide soft loan and credit facilities to women, improving women productivity can contribute to growth, efficiency and poverty reduction.
3. Make use of recent technology like mobile and facilitate women to access new technology as well as their right to inform and develop themselves. Government may develop a system to inform them by mobile service about different types of notice and massages for their personal development and any type of agricultural/livestock or entrepreneurial development perspectives.

ANNEX

Table A-22.1: Rank of Ilam District as Compared with All 75 Districts in Nepal for the Health, Education, and Socio-Economic Indicators

Sl. No.	*Indicators*	*Data value*	*Rank (Out of 75)*
1.	Access to electricity facilities, per cent	43.1	22
2.	Access to having radio facility, percentage	56.8	31
3.	Access to improved toilet facility, percentage	76.4	6
4.	Access to improves source of drinking water	78.3	42
5.	Access to telephone per1000 population, number	2.92	26
6.	Access to using solid fuels for cooking, percentage	79.5	20
7.	Adult gender imbalance rate in literacy status, per cent	0.71	na
8.	Adult gender imbalance rate in non-agri. Occupation, per cent	0.36	na
9.	Agricultural credit, per cent	11.65	na
10.	Bank density, in 1000 persons	0.23	56
11.	Child dependency ratio, percentage	66.5	10
12.	Child economic activity rate, per cent	9.4	na
13.	Child illiteracy rate, per cent	8.45	na
14.	Contraceptive prevalence rate, per cent	52.06	11
15.	Cooperative density, in 1000	7.48	12
16.	Farm size, ha/household	0.98	11
17.	Forest user household, percentage	44.28	46
18.	Health institution density, per 1000 person	2.23	45
19.	Incidence of ARI per 1000 children <5yrs	198	38
20.	Incidence of diarrhoea per 1000 children <5yrs	209	49
21.	Literacy rate of population 15-24 yrs, per cent	87.6	4
22.	Livestock per farm household, number	5.57	na
23.	Malnourished children <3yrs, per 1000	13.6	26
24.	**Overall composite index**		**12**
25.	Per capita development budget expenditure, NRS	732	43
26.	Per capita food production	3404	35
27.	Per capita regular budget expenditure, NRS	971	44
28.	Percentage of educationally disadvantaged population	0	1
29.	Percentage of Irrigated area,	16.27	53
30.	Percentage of marginal farm household	26	18
31.	Percentage share of female in non-agri. Occupations	26.19	18
32.	Post office density, in 100 sq. km	2.34	na
33.	Primary School net enrolment ratio, per cent	93.8	15
34.	Proportion of child marriage, per cent	0.17	na
35.	Proportion of urban population, per cent	6.7	37
36.	Rank according to child deprivation index	na	3
37.	Rank according to infrastructure Development	na	36
38.	Rank according to primary sector development index	na	26
39.	Rank according to socio-economic and infrastructure deprivation index	na	11
40.	Rank according to the gender discrimination	na	3
41.	Rank according to the health development	na	8

(*Contd.*)

Sl. No.	Indicators	Data value	Rank (Out of 75)
42.	Rank according to women empowerment index	na	19
43.	Ratio of girls to boys in primary education, per cent	96.8	12
44.	Ratio of literate female to male 15-24 yrs, per cent	92.7	3
45.	Ratio of Student to teachers in secondary education, per cent	34.4	64
46.	Reported death per 1000 population	5.102	40
47.	Road density, length/sq.km area	0.221 05	18
48.	Simulated mean age at marriage female, years	21.7	6

Note: na indicates data not available.
Source: Statistical Abstract, Government of Nepal.

Table A-22.2: Demographic Trend for Ilam District

Particulars	1981 Census	1991 Census	2001 Census	2011 projected
Population	178356	229214	282806	348066
Male	92031	115377	142434	174933
Female	87325	113837	140372	173133
Sex-Ratio			101	101.04
Household	31330	41450	54565	71824
Average Household Size	5.7	5.5	5.18	6.0
Literacy Rate	33.0	52.5	66.23	67.0
Population Density (per sq. km)	104.7	134.6	166	211

Source: Census Report.

Table A-22.3: Religious Population of Ilam during Census 2001

Particulars	Numbers	Percentage
Hindu	133718	47.28
Kirat	102302	36.17
Buddha	44354	15.68
Chritrian	1601	0.57
Sikha	287	0.10
Islam	127	0.04
Jain	27	0.01
Others	390	0.14
Total	**282806**	**100.00**

Source: Census Report.

Table A-22.4: Linguistic Population of Ilam during Census 2001

Mother Tongue	Numbers	Percentage
Nepali	152804	54.03
Bantawa	50048	17.70

(Contd.)

Mother Tongue	Numbers	Percentage
Limbu	35868	12.68
Tamang	14145	5.00
Magar	10786	3.81
Sherpa	3766	1.33
Gurung	3407	1.20
Sunuwar	2215	0.78
Others	9767	3.45
Total	**282806**	**100.00**

Source: Census Report, 2001.

REFERENCES

Acharya, Meena and Acharya, Pushpa (1997a) *Gender Equality and Empowerment of Women, A Status Report*, UNFPA, Kathmandu.

Acharya, Meena and Bennett, Lynn, (1981) *An Aggregate Analysis and Summary of 8 Village Studies. The Status of Women in Nepal*. Vol. II, Part 9. CEDA, Kathmandu.

Acharya, Meena, (2000) *Labour Market Developments and Poverty: With Focus on Economic Opportunities for Women*, TPMF and Friedrich-Ebert-Stiftung, Kathmandu.

Asmita Publishing House (2002): *Patrakarita ma Mahila Prashna* (Nepali).

Central Bureau of Statistics, (1995) *Population Monograph of Nepal*, Kathmandu.

Central Bureau of Statistics,/NPC/HMG (1996) *Nepal Living Standards Survey, 1995/96. Main Findings*, Vols. I. & II. Kathmandu.

GDS\FES (1997): *Women in Garment Industries*, Kathmandu.

GEFONT (2001): *Woman Participation in Nepali Labour Movement*, Kathmandu.

GEFONT (2003): *Search for Alternatives*, Kathmandu.

Gurung, Jeannette, D. (1999) (Ed.) *Searching for Women's Voices in the Hindu Kush Himalayas*, ICIMOD, Kathmandu.

HMG\N (1997): Local Self-Governance Act, 1997, Kathmandu.

INSEC (2002): *Human Rights Report*. Kathmandu.

National Planning Commission/HMG (1996) *Nepal Multiple Indicators Surveillance (NMIS): Primary Education Second Cycle*, April-June 1995.

National Planning Commission/HMG *Sixth Five Year to Tenth Five Year Plans*.

New ERA (1998) *A Situation Analysis of Sex Work and Trafficking in Nepal with Reference to Children*, October 1996. Submitted to UNICEF, Nepal.

SAATHI and The Asia Foundation, (1997) *A Situation Analysis of Violence Against Women and Girls in Nepal*. Kathmandu.

UNDP (1998): *National Gender Analysis on Elected and Nominated Women Ward Representative*, Kathmandu.

United Nations (1995, 2002): *Human Development Report*.

Viktoria Walter (2003): *Practicing Gender: The Tool Book*, Friedrich-Ebert-Stiftung, Germany.

23

Empowerment of Indian Women in the 21st Century

A General Perspective

V. Ramabrahmam

Introduction

"Women entrepreneur according to Government of India is an entrepreneur, who runs an enterprise owned and controlled by her and having minimum financial interest up to 51 per cent of the capital giving at least 51 per cent of the employment to women." Women entrepreneur is one, who initiates, organises and operates a business enterprise. In developing countries like India such Innovations are found less in number when compared with advanced countries.

Entrepreneurship is not related to sex of an individual. Women can be as successful entrepreneur as men. The entry woman in business is only a recent development in the orthodox, traditional, social and cultural environment of our society. Our society has not allowed women to think independently in the past. But in last decade, economic compulsions have led more and more young girls to take up employment and potential source of women entrepreneurship has emerged.

The following are some of the reasons for emerging women entrepreneurship:

(i) Not finding a job.
(ii) Unable to work in her house.
(iii) New challenges and opportunities for self-fulfilment.
(iv) Proving their innovative skills.
(v) Need for additional income.

Swami Vivekananda observed that lack of education weekened the self-confidence of majority of women in India. He drew pointed attention of the people towards the fact that self-confidence was more than half of the "Secret of Success" in life. Women education of the right type which leads to characters, foundation, strengthening of mind, development of the intellect and self-reliance.

According to Rammanohar Lohia, the emancipating of women was the foundation of social revolution, without this there can be no prosperity. Mahatma Gandhi was a strong advocate of women's rights. His successful call to women to join the national movement served as a catalyst for the wider participation of women in public affairs.

Historical Background of Women Empowerment in India

The status of women in India has been subject to many great changes over the past few millenium. In early Vedic period women enjoyed equal status with men. *Rigveda* and *Upnishads* mention several names of women sages and seers notably Gargi and Maitreyi. Later the status of women began to deteriorate approximately from 500 B.C. The situation worsened with invasion of Mughals and later on by European invaders.

Some reformatory movements by Guru Nanak, Raja Rammohun Ray, Ishwarchandra Vidyasagar, Pandita Rama Bai and others did give some relief. It is not that Britishers did not do anything for improving the condition of women. Some laws were enacted such an "Abolition of Practice of Sati", Widow Remarriage Act, 1856 etc.

The real change came after independence. Constitution of India guarantees equality to women (Article 14). There are other Articles too which ensure rights of women, e.g. no discrimination by the state [Article15 (1)] equality of opportunity (Article16) etc. Feminist activism picked up momentum in India during later 1970s. Later on many groups and NGOs have been working for the Empowerment of Women. We are proud that in India Women got voting right much before USA and some other European countries.

Women Associations

1. The International Council of Women convened its first meeting in Washington in 1888 to advance to women's social, economic and political rights.
2. The founding members of women Indian Association in 1917 were Mrs. Annie Besant, Mrs. Margaret cousions and Dorothy Jinarajadasa.

3. The National Council of Women in India was renamed as All India Women's Organisation established in 1925.
4. The eighth session of the Andhradesa Constituency Conference was held on 17th November, 1934 at the Besant Hall, Madanapalle under the presidency of Srimati G. Durgabai Deshmukh.

Empowerment—Conceptual Framework

The origins of the concept of empowerment go back to the civil rights movement in the USA in the 1960. The empowerment of women is located within the discourse and agenda of gender equality and is increasingly being taken in the agendas of international development organisations, perhaps more as a means to achieve gender equality than as an end in itself. At the Social Summit in Copenhagen in 1993 and the International Conference on Population and Development in Cairo 1994, Governments committed themselves to the empowerment of women. This commitment was operationalised and formulated into a clear action plan at the Fourth World Conference on Women in Beijing 1995 where Governments committed themselves to the "empowerment and advancement of women, including the right to freedom of thought, conscience, religion and belief, thus contributing to the moral, ethical, spiritual and intellectual needs of women and men, individually or in community with others and thereby guaranteeing them the possibility of realising their full potential in society and shaping their lives in accordance with their own aspirations."

Constitution of India

The Constitution of the country provides for equality of opportunities to all citizens irrespective of race, sex, caste and communities. Recently, the Supreme Court has highlighted the right of the women in India to eliminate gender based discrimination particularly in respect of property so as to attain economic empowerment.

The Constitution Framers were very much conscious of the problems of women empowerment hence they ensured that the Principle of Gender Equality is enshrined in the Constitution of India in its Preamble, Fundamental duties and Directive Principles. The various articles mentioned in the earlier paragraph are meant for ensuring gender equality. Moreover, the Constitution also empowers the States to adopt measures of positive discrimination in favour of women. The real impetus for this movement was gained when under the then Priministership of Mrs. Indira Gandhi, a scheme known as Indira Mahila Yojana was launched, UNDP also incorporated issues of women upliftment as Primary objective. Various Schemes were later on launched for the empowerment of women such as Rashtriya Mahila Kosh, Mahila Samridhi Yojana, Self-help groups at Panchayat level and many more. The establishment of National Women's Commission and State Women's Commissions were important milestones in the direction of Women Empowerment in India.

National Commission for Women Act, 1990

The Union Government of India under the leadership of V.P. Singh in 1989 felt that the task of the development of women through their empowerment would not be possible in the absence of a commission for women who act as a nodal agency—a watchdog to safeguard the interests of women and advise government on all issues concerning women.

National Policy for the Empowerment of Women, 2001

The National Policy (2001) was formulated with a view to bridging the gap between the goals enunciated in the Constitution, legislation, policies, planning, programmes and related mechanisms on the one hand and situational reality of the status of women in India, on the other.

Some of the important features of the policy include their active participation in decision-making including the political process at all levels, adopting a gender perspective to ensure main streaming of women in all developmental processes, as catalysts, participants and recipients.

The policy was aimed at ensuring women empowerment through positive economic and social policies for the full development of women. So, that they could realise their full potential. The policy assured equal access to women to health care, quality education, participation and decision-making in Social, Political and Economical Life of the Nation. The National Policy also aims at strengthening legal system for eliminating discrimination against women. It also visualises strengthening partnership with Civil Society, particularly Women's Organisations.

Education and Women Empowerment

Education is a powerful tool of social transformation. Hence, education for women has to be paid special attention. Greater access for women to education must be ensured in the educational system. Gender sensitivity must be developed. A watch has to be kept on dropout rate of girls and corrective measures should be taken to check the dropout rates.

Role of NGOs in Women Empowerment

Governmental Organisations are formal agencies working for the empowerment of women. But this work requires multi-dimensional approach and hence a large number of voluntary organisations/NGOs have gained increased attention in the field from grassroots level to national and international level. Their role is so impressive because they work with missionary zeal and commitment. The working style of NGOs is open, transparent and personal. So, they are more effective in this direction. They organise seminars, conferences and workshops for the awakening of the masses. Their mass appeal-style contributes to a better understanding of women's rights and of the means to ensures the enjoyment of those rights and the elimination of discrimination. They prepare urban and rural uneducated women for self-employment, which is vital for the economic empowerment of the women. In short, all these programmes and functions of NGOs contribute towards the realisation of sustainable community development and hence women empowerment.

Women Welfare and Empowerment in India

In India, policies and programmes at different levels of the government cover various dimensions and strategies in gender development. Over the years, efforts have been made to empower women socially, economically, and politically. However, due to a lack of synergy and coordination, the achievements are not satisfactory. It is imperative that an integrated policy and strategy be formulated to address the economic, social, and political issues related to women, along with the requisite programmes and schemes. Though India has created protective legislations for women, the enactments have not been easy to implement. The vastness of the country, the scattered nature of women workers, their lack of education and legal literacy, and the indifferent attitude of government bureaucracy have all contributed to the continuing vulnerability of women. This is true not only for unorganised rural women, but also for urban women workers. Although the constitutional commitments to women find reflections in the planning processes, legislation, policies, and programmes of the Central and State Governments, the current socio-economic status of women is unsatisfactory in terms of almost all important indicators of human development.

January 4-10, 2010 is Women's Self-Empowerment Week

The national recognition of women's self-empowerment is intended as an opportunity for women (and men) to reflect on the important roles that women occupy in society. Another intended goal is that women recognize and observe the variety of ways we contribute to making our families and communities better. More specifically, "women's self-empowerment" or "female empowerment" has become synonymous with "feminism" or "women's liberation"—which is not the case.

Influential Women of 21st Century

Indira Priyadarshini Gandhi (19 November, 1917–31 October, 1984) was the third Prime Minister of India and a central figure of the Indian National Congress Party. Gandhi, who served from 1966 to 1977 and then again from 1980 until her assassination in 1984, is the second-longest-serving Prime Minister of India and the only woman to hold the office. Indira Gandhi was the only child of Indian Prime Minister Jawaharlal Nehru. She served as the Chief of Staff of her father's highly centralised administration between 1947 and 1964 and came to wield considerable unofficial influence in government. Elected Congress President in 1959, she was offered the premiership in succession to her father. Gandhi refused and instead chose to become a Cabinet Minister in the government. She finally consented to become Prime Minister in succession to Lal Bahadur Shastri in 1966.

As Prime Minister, Gandhi became known for her political ruthlessness and unprecedented centralisation of power. She went to war with Pakistan in support of the independence movement in East Pakistan, which resulted in an Indian victory and the creation of Bangladesh, as well as increasing India's influence to the point where it became the regional hegemony of South Asia. Gandhi also presided over a state of emergency from 1975 to 1977 during which she ruled by decree and made lasting changes to the Constitution of India. She was assassinated in the aftermath of Operation Blue Star. In 2001, Gandhi was voted the greatest Indian Prime Minister in a poll organised by India Today. She was also named "Woman of the Millennium" in a poll organised by the BBC in 1999.

Meirakumar (born March 31, 1945) is an Indian politician and a five time Member of Parliament. She was elected unopposed as the first women Speaker of Lok Sabha on 3rd June, 2009. She is a lawyer and a former diplomat. Prior to being a member of the 15th Lok Sabha, she has been elected earlier to 8th, 11th, 12th and 14th Lok Sabha, wherein she remained Cabinet Minister in the Ministry of Social Justice and Empowerment (2004–2009).

Mamata Banerjee (born January 5, 1955) is the leader of the Trinamool Congress and Leader of the Opposition in the state of West Bengal. She is the founder and Chairperson of the party and held the position of Union Minister for Railways in the Republic India. Mamata is popularly known as "Didi"—the elder sister to all her followers in West Bengal. Now, she is the present Chief Minister of West Bengal.

Jayalalitha Jayaram (born 24 February, 1948–death 5th December, 2016), commonly referred to as **Jayalalitha**, is an Indian politician who has been the Chief Minister of Tamil Nadu, a state in southern India, since 2011. Previously she served as Chief Minister from 1991 to 1996, briefly in 2001, and from 2002 to 2006. She was a popular film star in Indian cinema before her entry into politics, having appeared as main female lead heroine in over 140 films, which includes films in Tamil, Telugu, Kannada and worked in one Hindi film. She is the incumbent General Secretary of All India Anna Dravida Munnetra Kazhagam (AIADMK). She is called *Amma* ('Mother') and sometimes *Puratchi Thalaivi* ('Revolutionary Leader') by her followers.

Indu Jain belongs to the Sahu Jain family and is the current chairperson of India's largest media group, Bennett Coleman & Co. Ltd., which owns the *Times of India* and other large newspapers. Her net worth is said to be US Dollar 4.4 billion, making her the 17th richest Indian in the world.

Lalita D. Gupte, Joint Managing Director of ICICI Bank (India's second largest Commercial Bank), until October 31, 2006, is an important figure in India's banking and financial services sector. An INSEAD alumnus, Gupte was listed by the Fortune "as one of the fifty most powerful women in international business." She is currently the Chairperson on the Board of ICICI Venture and a Board member of Nokia Corporation. On 22nd June, 2010 she was appointed as member of Alstom's Board of Directors.

Priya Paul (born 1967), is a prominent woman entrepreneur of India, and currently the Chairperson of Appeejay. The Park Hotels chain of boutique hotels. She joined the company, after finishing her studies in

Economics at the Wellesley College (US) working under her father, as Marketing Manager at the Park Hotel, Delhi, at the age of 22.

Conclusion

The Empowerment of Women has become one of the most important Concerns of twenty first century not only at national level, but also at the international level. Efforts by the Government are on to ensure Gender equality, but Government initiatives alone would not be sufficient to achieve this goal. Society must take initiative to create a climate in which there is no gender discrimination and women have full opportunities of self-decision-making and participating in the Social, Political and Economic life of the country with a sense of equality.

REFERENCES

Chandrababu, B.S., Thilagavathi, L., 2009, *Women: Her History and her Struggle for Emancipation,* Chennai, p. 27.

India: Woman Wins Post of Speaker, *New York Times*, June 4, 2009.

Indira Gandhi "greatest woman *BBC News*." 1999-12-01. Retrieved 31 July, 2013.

Indus Grover, Deepak Grover (Ed.), *Empowerment of Women*, pp. 14-17.

Ramabrahmam, V., & Gangaiah, K., "Women Entrepreneur and Empowerment of Women", 2013, in P. Venkatarao (ed.), *Social Work Intervention in Policy Making*, New Delhi, p. 189.

Srinivasaraju, Sugata (2011). "The Road To Ammahood", *Outlook India*. Retrieved 10 November, 2013.

24

Constraints Faced by the Tribal (Santal) SHG Members in the Process of Empowerment

Amitava Dutta and *Paulami Das*

Introduction

Women in ancient India (Vedic period) enjoyed equal status with men in all aspects of life. Women's position in society further deteriorated during the medieval period. During the British Raj, many reformers such as Raja Ram Mohun Ray, Ishwarchandra Vidyasagar fought for the betterment of women. But, still in modern time the women's status is not in a better position. According to FAO, the most disadvantaged section of society is the women; they are the 'silent majority' of the world's poor. Seventy per cent of the world's poor are women. They face peculiar social, cultural, educational, political and allied problems. Women constitute almost half of the total population in the world and out of which two-third of world's adult illiterates are women. Tribal community constitutes a significant percentage (8%) of Indian population and 90 per cent of tribal population is living in rural areas. The tribes, particularly womenfolk, are suffering due to non-availability of transportation, medical, education, electricity and infrastructure and suffering with malnutrition, low literacy, poverty and lack of information on government activities and welfare schemes. To overcome the sufferings Government has taken various scheme, policies, for upliftment of tribals, specially for women. Not only tribal women but also women of all caste and creed have been granted for upliftment through the process of empowerment. Empowerment in the context of women's development is a way of defining, challenging and overcoming barriers in a woman's life through which she increases her ability to shape her life and environment. It is an active, multidimensional process which should enable women to realise their full identity and power in all spheres of life. empowerment as a concept was first brought at the International Women's Conference in 1985 at Nairobi. It is one of the Eight Millennium Goals to which world leaders agreed at the Millennium Summit held at New York in 2000 (Bhagyalakshmi, 2004). In various national policies and developmental programmes, emphasis has been given on organising women in Self-Help Groups and thus, marks the beginning of a major process of empowering women. SHG is an organisation of rural poor. The objectives of the SHGs go beyond thrift and credit—and include the overall development of members in the social, political, cultural and economic arena; thus the SHGs are 'credit plus' institutions (Fernandez, 1998). Involvement in SHGs has enabled women to have a voice in the community affairs and they have been able to tackle problems such as a lack of drinking water and electricity, access to health services and children's education. Though women face handicaps to their involvement in politics, their participation in SHGs has altered them, and these women can be prospective leaders in the local political field. Kiranmayee (1996) revealed that contraints by women as lack of cooperation among members, irregularity in repaying loan, illiteracy, lack of knowledge, lack of marketing facilities. They are facing various constraints in the process of their employment. Majority of women are engaged in traditional household industries because of uneconomic holdings, restrictions of women's access to resources like land, credit, technology, illiteracy, in adequate training, household and childcare responsibilities (Seetaram, 1992).

Rationale of the Study

Tribal community represents a significant percentage (8.6%) of Indian population. At the same time the tribal community is considered as the most backward, underprivileged group of people who are still suffering from hunger, poverty, illiteracy, poor health etc. A separate ministry named as Ministry of Tribal Welfare and Development renders its continuous effort for the welfare and well-being of the tribal living in India. In spite of such effort tribal people still considered as the most neglected, uncared segment of Indian society. Almost all the tribes in India are living in a isolated places like jungle, hill tracks, coastal belt which are considered as the part of India. The researcher enjoy the opportunity of studying tribal people since undergraduate studies and have the information about the life, livelihood pattern and sufferings of such ethnic groups. Being a rural development worker the present researcher feel urge of overall development of tribal people of India. Tribal women are mostly illiterate and unaware of many sort of positive changes. The literacy rate of tribes in the year 1991 was 29.60 per cent, where general literacy rate was 52.21 per cent. In the year 2011 total literacy rate of India is 73 per cent, where female literacy rate is 64.6 per cent but tribal women literacy rate 49.4 per cent specially incase rural tribal the rate is 46.9 per cent. The health and nutritional status of tribal women became inefficient by giving extreme toil in doing domestic work, economic processes and reproduction. Malnutrition, anaemia, early marriage, conceives in early age are the common phenomenon among the tribal women (Biju, 2006). Most of the tribal women are working in unorganised sector, usually get fewer wages as compare to men worker. They are getting less opportunity in political processes, less access and opportunity in making views on political aspect instead of 73rd Amendment. Moreover, the superstitious belief and prejudices affect their lives where from their sufferings are unaccountable which is evidenced.

Objectives of the Present Study

1. Specific objectives:
   - To understand the constraints faced by SHG women in the process of empowerment.
   - To identify the reasons behind such problems.
   - To understand how the constraints further affect the process of empowerment.
2. Broader objectives:
   - To minimize the problems and make the process of empowerment meaningful and effective in the future.

Methodology

The present study was carried out in a purposively 5 selected villages of Palojori block of Deoghar district of Jharkhand. Five villages' *viz*. Simla of Matiara Gram Panchayat Dumarkala and Kachuasholi of Kochuasholi Gram Panchayat and Nawadih. And Chalbali of Bhunkundi Gram

Panchayat, were the study area. For the present study exploratory design of social research was used. The study was conducted to find out the constraint faced by the tribal SHG women in the process of empowerment. In the study, constraint means, repression or control of natural feeling or impulse; a forced unnatural manner or inhibition; restrictive condition; something that limits your freedom to do what you want (*Harper Collins English Dictionary*), empowerment means, the expansion of assets and capabilities of poor people to participate in, negotiate with, influence, control and hold accountable institutions that affect their lives (The World Bank, 2002). In the operational definitions were SHG and tribe woman. SHG and tribe was operationally defined as Self-Help Group are small homogeneous group of individual members who voluntarily come together and form an association for the purpose of solving their common problems through self-help and mutual help and for achieving a common objective. In the study, the tribal SHGs that are connected with NEEDS are selected. Woman was referred, in the study, to those, adult female human being, as contrasted to men, an adult male, and a girl, a female child. The term woman (irregular plural: women) is used to indicate biological sex distinctions, cultural gender role, role distinctions, or both (Wikipedia, 2005:1. With the help of Quota Sampling 2 SHGs in Nawadih, 2 out of 3 SHGs in Kachuasholi and 2 out of 3 SHGs in Dumarkala, 3 SHGs out of 4 of Simla, 1 SHG of village Chalbali had been selected for the present study. So, there were total 10 SHGs were selected for the study.). The sample for study comprised 60 SHG women. From each SHG, 6 SHG members of those selected SHG members had been selected for the present study and thoroughly inquired and interviewed for completing the questionnaire.

Selection of Variables

There are mainly two types of variables, *viz.* independent and dependent variables which were selected on the basis of:

- Extensive review of literature (Ministry of Tribal Affairs; Chandra, 2008, 2005, Talukdar & Dutta, 2009).
- Expert consultation.
- Case exploration during phase of data collection.

Types of Variables	*Variables*	*Description*
Independent variables	Age	Chronological Age
	Educational status	Education received in formal education system
	Family size	Numbers of person in the family
	Family occupation	Main occupation of the individual members of the family was taken into consideration
	Family income	The monthly income of the all family member of respondent from the main and subsidiary occupation.
Dependent variables	Constraints faced by SHG members in the process of empowerment	Problems and sufferings of the SHG women regarding to the role in society (within family and outside the family), economy (subsistence pattern), political, entrepreneurial, health-hygiene and family planning.

Data Collection Methods and its Analysis Process

The researcher has applied PRA methods (Resource map, Trend analysis), daily routine (both for male and female). Simple ranking method and interview schedule. The researcher also arranged FGD (Focus Group Discussion) with the SHG members. The collected data and information were analysed in the form of percentage.

Results and Discussions

1. Demographic Status of Members

The independent variables which were taken for measuring the findings of the research were age, marital status, family size, family occupation, family income, educational status of individual SHG members.

Discussions

The results of the selected characteristics of respondents have been presented in Table 24.1. The data in Table 24.1 revealed that most of the respondents, i.e. 40 per cent (24) belonged to 20-30 years and again 40 per cent (24) respondents were in the age group of 30-40 years. The numbers of women were equal the age group in 20 to 30 and 30—40 are in equal which further represented the maximum number of representatives than the other age groups. It indicated that this age group has that much of motivation to join the group, The women belonged to that age group are physically active. They were not fully but to some extent got liberty, freedom to take decision for valuable contribution in family. Before, they were not allowed or hardly allowed to take decision by themselves in any

Table 24.1: Distribution of Respondents according to their Selected Characteristics (Independent Variables)

Sl. No.	*Category*	*Repondents*	
		Number	*Percentage*
Age in years			
	Young (20–30)	24	40
	Middle (31–40)	24	40
	Matured (41–50)	11	18.33
	Aged (Above 50)	1	1.66
Marital status			
	Married	60	100
	Unmarried	0	0
	Widow	0	0
Family size			
	Small (up to 4 members)	19	31.66
	Medium (5 to 8 members)	37	61.66
	Large (Above 8 members)	4	6.64
Educational status			
	Cannot sign	31	51.66
	Can sign only	16	26.66
	Class I to IV	6	10
	Class V to VIII	4	6.66
	Secondary	2	3.33
	Higher secondary	0	0
	Graduate	1	1.66
Family occupation			
	Agriculture	1	1.66
	Agriculture, agricultural labour	17	28.33
	Agriculture, agricultural labour, daily labour	27	45
	Agriculture, daily labour, basket making	10	16.67
	Agriculture, basket-making	5	8.33
Family occupation			
	Others	1	1.66
Family income			
	Rupees 2000–3000	43	71.66
	Rupees 3000–4000	12	20
	Rupees 4000–5000	2	3.33
	Rupees 5000–6000	1	1.66
	Rupees 6000–7000	1	1.66
	Above Rupees 7000	1	1.66

Source: Field survey.

matter of family or outside the family. The lowest percentage has gone to the age group of above 50, i.e. 1.66 per cent. A significant percentage of women, i.e. 18.33 per cent were in the age group of 40–50 years. The lowest percentage has indicated that these groups were not very eager to accept any change.

Table 24.1 revealed the distribution of the respondents according to the marital status. It has very interestingly been observed that 60 (100%) respondents were married. Not a single case was identified as unmarried or widow. When the reasons for such representation were enquired, it was found that almost all the representatives were married, because this tribal group still practiced remarriage, widow marriage and polygamy.

The present Table 24.1 depicted that the members of SHG belonged to different family sizes, *viz.* small, medium, and large. The maximum SHG members, i.e. 61.66 per cent belonged to medium family size. The members have more than 3 children. They did not maintain family planning measures. A significant number of respondents, i.e. 6.64 per cent, belonged to the large family size. 31.66 per cent respondents belonged to the small family size. It indicated that the respondents' first or second issue was male child.

This table unfolded that maximum number of respondents, i.e. 51.66 per cent of total respondents could not sign. It indicated that there was a practice of early marriage in those villages where they had come from. As well as their economic condition was poor, so, they could not get opportunity for formal education. But, a significant number of respondents, i.e. 26.66 per cent could sign. It means that there was a intervention of local NGO, who started "Adult education." The researcher found a good number of respondents were able to sign their names. It indicated that the children of the respondents have started education and they took initiatives to teach their mother how to sign. 6.66 per cent respondents continued their education till secondary. No higher secondary passed respondent was found. It indicated that SHG has a lot of things to do in the field of women literacy.

The distribution of the respondents according to the family occupation was represented through the above table. The present table has shown, that maximum number of respondent, i.e. 27(45%) were engaged with more than three types of occupations. It indicated that most of the respondents had low amount of land. A good number of respondents could cultivate for once (rainy season) in a year due to lack of irrigational facilities in other seasons (*Rabi*, summer). The earned income was not sufficient for family consumption. They were compelled to work as daily labour in others states. Even after income from daily labour work, could not make to satisfy their basic needs properly. Further they were engaged with MGNREGA activities. Another significant number of respondents, i.e. 17 (28%) were engaged with agriculture and as agricultural labour. It revealed that they had enough land and the produced from the land could satisfy their basic needs or the respondents belonged to the small or medium family size. 10 (17%) respondents were engaged with cultivation, daily labour work along with basket making. 5 (8%) were engaged with agriculture and basket-making. It depicted that they had not sufficient land by which they could fulfil their basic amenities. On the other hand, the basket-making was the traditional cottage business of them. Except cultivation they were easily accustomed with the basket-making than any other work. On the other hand they got training on it. They thought the basket-making easier to them. So, they were engaged with basket making with the combination their inborn skill along with learnt advanced technology. It had been found that only 1 (2%) of total respondents was engaged with only cultivation. It can be said that the respondent was the owner of sufficient amount of lands which could mitigate the needs of all members of the family or the respondent belonged to the small family or the family members of respondent were not able to do any work except cultivation.

The researchers found that most of the villagers were poorest of the poor who worked throughout the year for earning breads for families. Though they practiced agriculture, it was not sufficient to fulfil their basic needs and that was why they were working as daily labour in other hand and also joined with MGNREGA programme. For their survival they had to depend on various earning sources. Only 1 (1.66%) worked as '*saiya*' (Health worker). It indicated that she was educated and also had the family support.

The above Table 24.1 has shown that 43 (71.66%) respondents had income between rupees 2000–3000 per month. 12 (20%) had income between rupees 300–4000. 2 (3.33%), 1 (1.66%), 1 (1.66%), 1 (1.66%) had income between rupees 4000–5000, rupees 5000–6000, rupees 6000–7000, above 7000, respectively.

The present study has been based on the objectives, i.e. to find out the constraints faced by the tribal SHG in the process of empowerment and reasons behind of those. To support the objectives the some findings have come out from the research work. These are as follows:

Low Attendance in Group Meeting

Yes	No
37	23

Reasons Behind Irregularities (Multiple Responses by the Respondents)

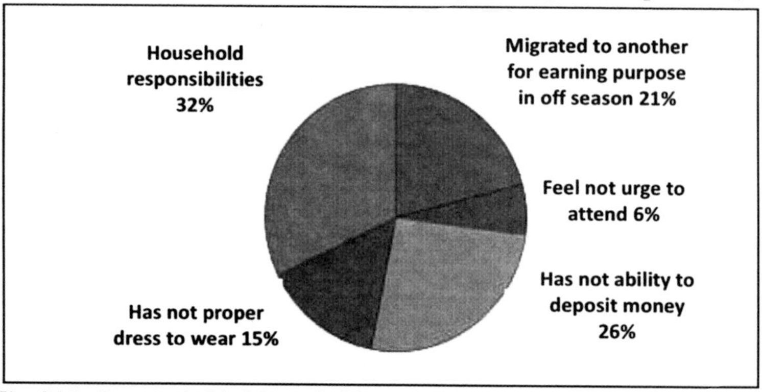

Fig. 24.1: Reasons behind Irregularities.

Analysis

The above figure has shown the reasons for low attendance of the SHG members in their regular meeting. Several causes have been identified for their low attendance in regular meetings. According to the figure, maximum number of responses 37 (32%) supported the reasons for not coming to the meeting was the household responsibilities of the women. The next reason was the inability of depositing money or irregular subscription. 30 (26%) responses supported the reason. 24 (21%) responses supported that the migration for earning was the another reason for their inabilities of attending the meeting regularly. 17 (15%) of total responses supported the view of "has not proper dress to wear" was also another significant reasons for their low attendance and only 7 (6%) responses supported the reason like "feel no urge to attend". It can be concluded from this discussion that women were very much engaged with household activities and were unable to attend the meetings. It was also found that the poor Santal women were unable to accumulate their regular subscription at the end of the week because of their extreme poverty. The next cause was again related to poverty where the respondents shared that due to migration for earning of wages they were unable to attend a meeting. It indicated extreme poverty stricken condition of these tribal women who were compelled to migrate (seasonal) to different places for earning breads in a regular manner. The next reasons for absenteeism from attending meeting was again directly related to poor and helpless situation of the tribal women, where the women shared that due to lack of proper cloths, they were compelled to absent from this SHG meetings. They shared the truth that they possessed only "*gamcha*" (towel) for covering their bodies and that is why they were unable to attend the meetings. Lastly, only 6 per cent respondents shared the view of lack of interest for attending the meeting. Thus, at the end, it can be said that 'poverty' was the root cause and acted as a constraint for low attendance of the beneficiaries in their SHG meetings.

Inabilities to Understand the and to Manage the Duties and Responsibilities

Yes	*No*
30	30

Reasons behind unable to understand and to manage the duties and responsibilities (Multiple responses of the respondents)

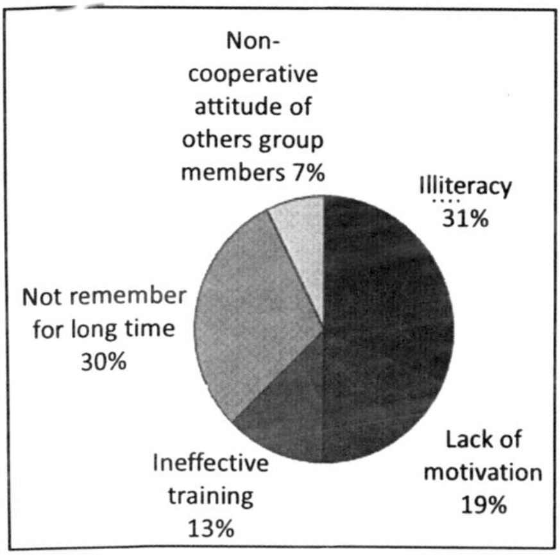

Fig. 24.2: Reasons behind unable to understand and to manage the duties and responsibilities.

Analysis

It was observed that when the reasons for their poor performances of duties and responsibilities were asked through multiple responses, the respondents shared the causes, where illiteracy was responded by maximum number 30 (31%) of respondents as the reasons for not understanding and managing the duties and responsibilities of SHG members. It was followed by the reason "not remember for long time" as responded by 29 (30%) of respondents. Lack of proper motivation was considered as another reason for the same as responded by 18 (19%) responses and ineffective training by 12 (13%) responses. "Non cooperative of other group members" was considered by 7 (7%) of total responses. It can be said by analysing the above mentioning data that illiteracy was the root cause for the low, poor performances of the tribal women in their SHGs, in relation to their duties and responsibilities. Lack of memory was immediately followed by illiteracy, which again supported the reason 'illiteracy' and immaturity and lack of confidence of the members. Moreover, there was lack of motivation and ineffective training on behalf of the organisers where accelerated the low, slow and poor performances of tribal SHG members. Moreover, the non-co-operative and non-supportive attitudes were also prevailed among the group members who were also considered as one of the cause for their poor performances.

Inabilities or Facing Constraints in Relation to Membership Subscription

Yes	No
35	25

Reasons behind the Constraint (Multiple Responses by the Respondents)

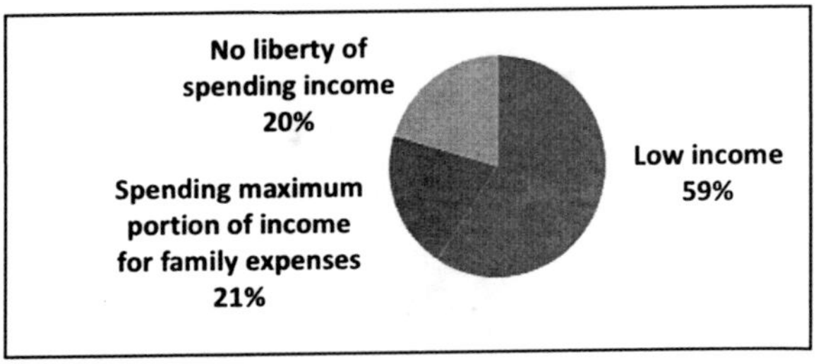

Fig. 24.3: Reasons behind the constraint

Analysis

The figure represented that respondent felt difficulties to pay monthly subscription. 35 (59%) responses revealed that the respondents have hardly any money to pay the minimum membership subscription due to the low income. It has been found that they were belonging to below poverty. They hardly maintained the expenditure of the families. They faced hurdle to pay the minimum monthly subscription. "Spending maximum portion of income spending for family expenses" was considered as another reason for the same as responded by 12 (21%) responses and "no liberty of spending income" by 12 (20%) responses. It can be concluded that they preferred to take decision together for their family expenditure which further made them happy. The prime motto of such Santal groups was to maintain happiness in family and that was why they preferred to take decisions together for spending their earnings as for family. The major portions of their income were spent behind their families and that was why they were unable to pay their membership subscriptions in group. Further, it can be also said that due to the low self-image, low self-esteem, women had hardly any power to say against their husbands.

Inabilities or constraint regarding training

Yes	*No*
35	25

Reasons behind the inabilities

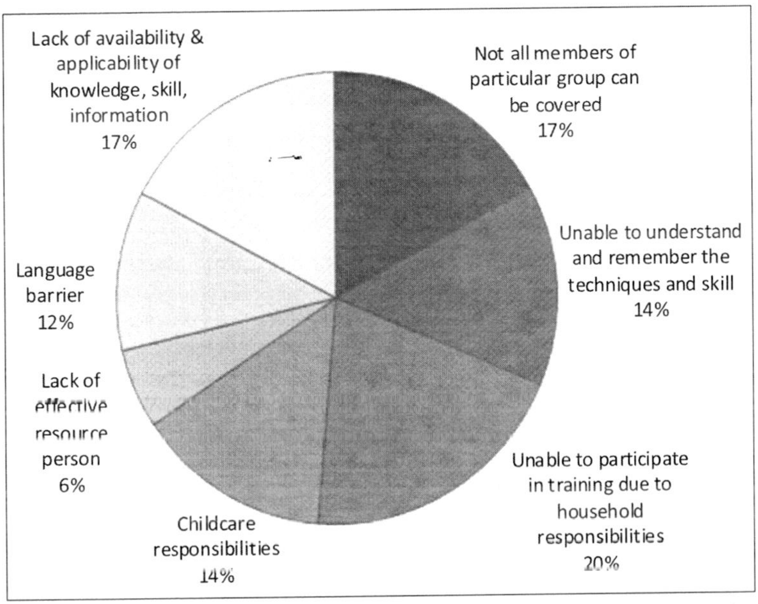

Fig. 24.4: Reasons behind the inabilities or constraint (Multiple responses by the respondents)

Analysis

Though training was imparted among the SHG members with the objectives of enhancement of potentialities of the SHG members but most unfortunately it was observed that the training was never proved effective and meaningful due to following reasons. According to 35 (20%) responses, the group members were unable to participate in training due to household responsibilities. The tribal women gave more importance to look after their families rather than attending SHG meetings. 30 (17%) of total responses expressed the views that it was not possible for them to apply and effectively implement the skill, knowledge, information, they usually gathered from the training, but they hardly got opportunities for the meaningful application of their knowledge and skill, which they gained from the trainings. For example—they came to know about scientific way of irrigation but due to lack of water supply they could not apply properly the knowledge. They received kid (young goat) for rearing, but most unfortunately kid had been died. Because, the kid had been provided without giving any rearing (including vaccination, treatment) knowledge. So, it was not possible for them to rear the goats scientifically. The SHG members did not maintain the knowledge due to lack of motivation.

It was also responded a significant number 30 (17%) of respondents of all members of the group were not enrolled in the training. A considerable number of SHG members never got the opportunities of attending the training. Thus, it was acted as a constraint against them for their meaningful participation in SHG. Childcare was another reason for not attending the training and it was supported by 25 (14%) of total responses. Language was considered as a reason for not effective training by 20 (12%) responses. Language acted as a barrier against effective communication between trainer and trainees. And, lastly, 10 (6%) expressed their views that lack of resource persons was a reason against effective and fruitful training.

Frequency of bank visit by the SHG members

Types of SHG members	*Times of visit*			
	Never	*One*	*Two*	*Several*
Group leaders (30)				✓
Others group members (30)			✓	

Reasons behind for not going to bank more than two times

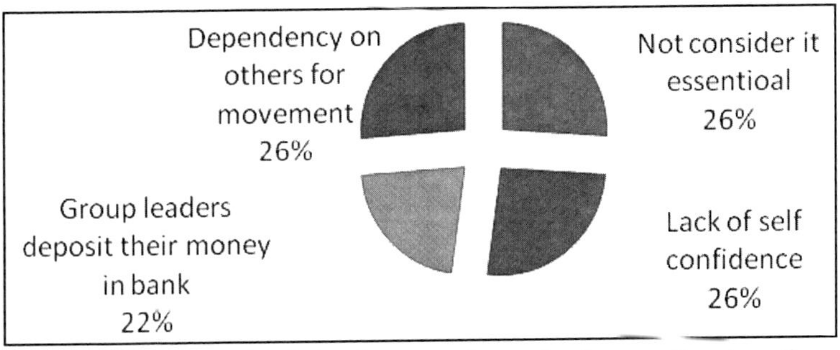

Fig. 24.5: Reasons behind the for not going to bank more than two times (Multiple responses by the respondents)

Analysis

The present table represented that the group leaders had visited the bank for several times (20 times) in a year where as the others group members of SHG never visited the bank more than two times. They went for opening of the group account and second time for receiving the provided loan from bank to group. The group leaders had the idea of banking services for going several times in bank. But most of the members of the groups were unable to understand the service of bank. The below figure revealed the reasons for not going the bank more than two times. According to the figure, 30 (26%) respondents did not consider to go to bank at regular interval as necessary activities. Lack of self-confidence was considered as another reasons for less visiting bank and it was shared by 30 (26%) of responses. 25 (22%) responses have claimed that the group leaders deposited the money in bank so why they would go. Again 30 (26%) told that they are dependable on others for movement. Above all these reasons acted as limitation or constraints against the effective promotion and implementation of the SHG.

Facing problem of refunding loan in proper time

Yes	*No*
36	**24**

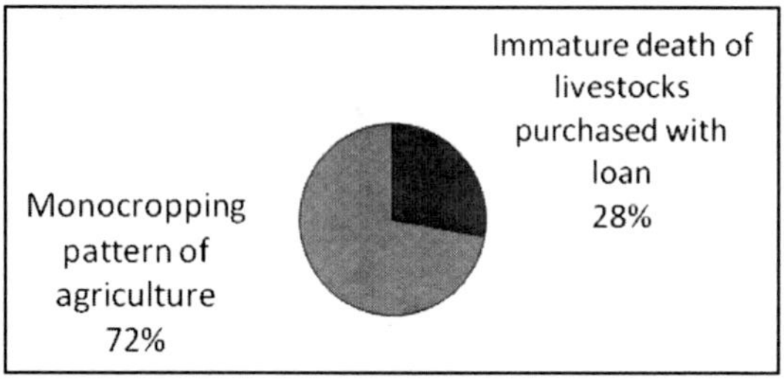

Fig. 24.6: Reasons behind the problem or constraints (Multiple responses by the respondents)

Analysis

It was observed that when the reasons behind the problems of loan refund were asked through multiple responses, the respondents shared the causes where mono cropping cultivation was responded by maximum number 26 (72%) of respondents as the reason. "Immature death of the provided livestock" was considered as another reason. Lack of motivation was the cause of premature death of livestock. The SHG members were not at all motivated properly and attended the training for rearing kids effectively and that was why the premature death of the livestock had been occurred. In that case the provided loan had been utilised properly or further it could not help them to generate income. The provided loan became a burden to them. So, they had to return the money from their home. All these acted as hindrance against the proper, effective growth of SHG as well as the SHG members.

Inabilities of decision-making for not utilisation of the loan amount for self-interest

Yes	*No*
36	**24**

Reasons behind the constraint

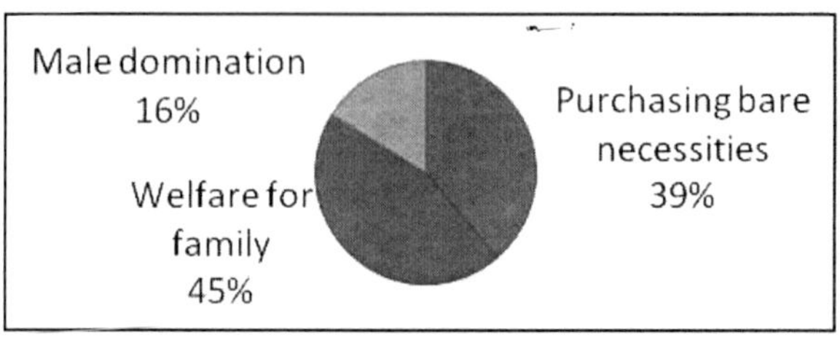

Fig. 24.7: Reasons Behind the constraints.

Analysis

The constraint faced by SHG members was directly related with utilisation of borrowed loan for their self-interest. The figure has shown that after borrowing the loan the maximum number 36 (45%) of SHG members spent money (loan) behind the welfare of their families and another significant number 31 (39%) of respondents spent their money for purchasing bare necessities. Another 13 (16%) respondents shared that due to male domination; they were never allowed to spend money for their own purpose. It further revealed and unfolded the helpless and powerless condition of the tribal SHG members who had directly involved with the empowerment process, but they were exploited by their families. They never got the opportunity to utilise a single rupees for their self-interest rather they were compelled to spend the money for others. It again proved that, even, loan acted as a constraint against the empowerment of women through SHG.

Feel hesitant to speak in front of all (within group and outside the group)

Yes	*No*
24	**36**

Reasons for the constraint (Multiple responses by the respondents)

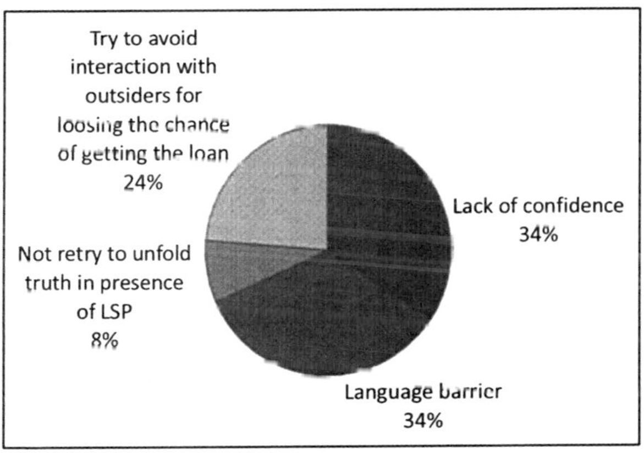

Fig. 24.8: Reasons for the Constraint

Analysis

The present figure represented that 26 (34%) respondents felt hesitant to speak due to lack of confidence and again 26 (34%) respondents felt hesitant due to lack of language barrier. It further indicated their introvert nature which was affecting their activities. They never opened truth for their shyness. Due to language barrier they hardly speak. It was found that a significant number of respondents, i.e. 18 (24%) were trying to avoid interactions with outsiders for losing the chance of getting loans. 6 (8%) responses supported that the presence of LSP was another cause of their inabilities to speak in front of all. Because the external loan was provided on the basis of the performance of the group members. During the conversations with outsiders with or without the presence of the NGO personnel or LSP, they felt insecurities that if they would say something abnormal about the group performances, it would be become a hindrance against the chance of getting loan. Above all these created severe constraints for promotion of SHGs. They could not understand their weaknesses as well as good qualities. All these acted as constraints against effectiveness of SHG.

Dependency on others for movement

Yes	*No*
20	40

Reasons of that Constraint (Multiple Respondents by the Respondents)

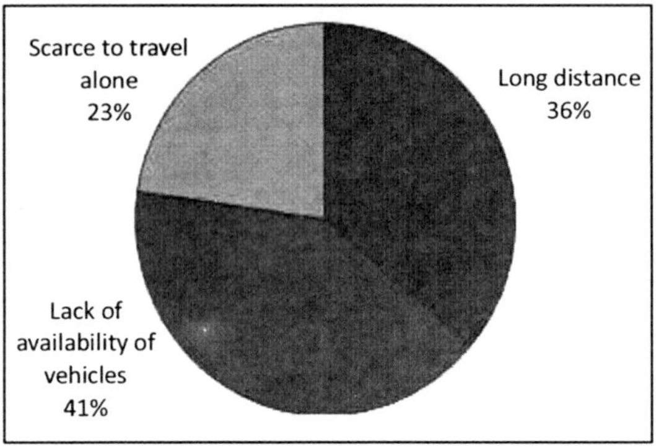

Fig. 24.9: Reasons of that constraints

Analysis

The figure represented that 18 (41%) of respondents had to depend on others (male members) for their movements due to lack of availability of vehicles. Lack of communication facilities restricted the mobilities of the women which further affected their self development as well as the development of the SHG. The figure represented that 16 (36%) respondents faced hurdle for going anywhere alone due to long distance. 6 (23%) claimed that they felt insecure to travel alone due to the probability of physical harassment, sexual assault. This matter further stopped the effective growth of the women as well as the group.

Lack of Participation on Community Affairs

Yes	No
54	6

Reasons behind the constraint (Multiple responses by the respondents)

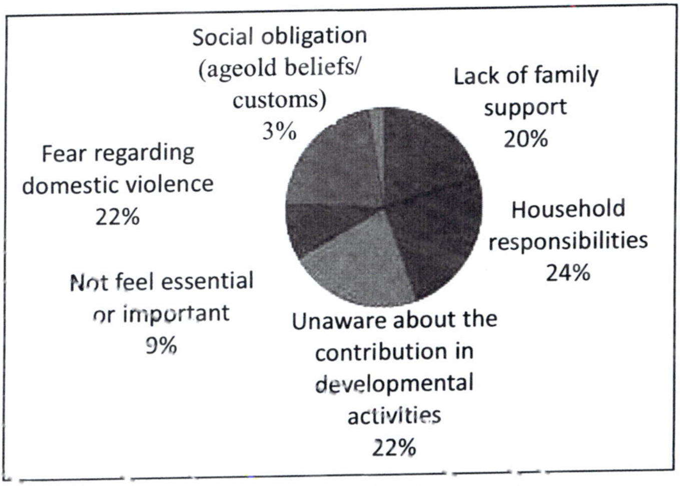

Fig. 24.10: Reasons Behind the constraint

Analysis

The empowerment process of the SHG members was not at all effective which was reflected through the causes of lack of participation in community affairs. It was found that due to several causes, the participation of community members was not ensured and these were household responsibilities as responded by 54 (24%) responses. Ultimately, it can be concluded that the SHG members were suffering from several social obligations against their effective participation in community affairs. It was found that the maximum number of respondents were unable to participate in community affairs due to their day long toilsome never-ending household responsibilities. It was very difficult for them to get rid of such responsibilities. Another significant number of respondents, i.e. 48 (22%) shared their views that they were the prey of domestic violence and it was very difficult for them to overcome such problem and to participate in community affairs. Another 48 (22%) of responses came out from the SHG members where they shared that they did not know their roles, responsibilities or meaningful contribution in developmental activities and that was why they hardly be able to participate in community affairs. Lack of family support was always acted as a constraint against their participation in community affairs, as expressed by 45 (20%) of respondents. 20 (9%) of respondents never felt it essential to participate in community affairs and 6 (3%) of respondents believed in age-old belief and customs where they never allowed to participate in such affairs of communities. The present researcher perceived that empowerment of tribal women was not effectively possible because of such above mentioned reasons.

Inabilities to create any assets

Yes	*No*
48	12

Reasons behind the inability (Multiple responses by the respondents)

(*see* Fig. 24.11 on next page 347).

Analysis

The present figure has shown the causes of inabilities of the SHG members to create any assets (movable and/or immovable). Several causes had been identified of their inabilities. According to the figure, maximum number of responses 36 (44%) shared that they borrowed internal and external loan and gave it to their husbands. The money was utilised for

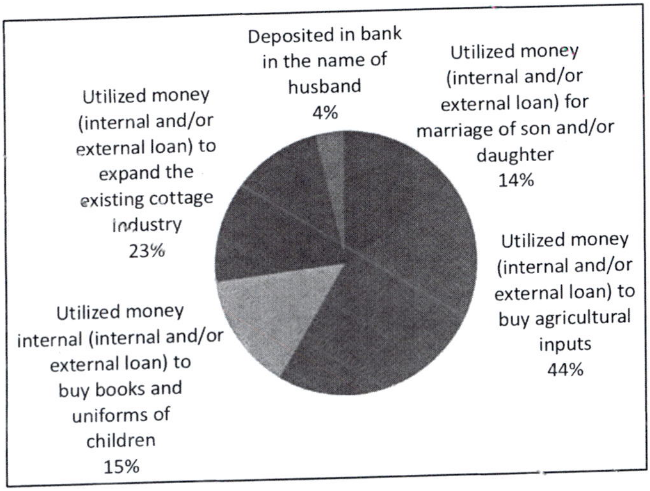

Fig. 24.11: Reasons behind the inability (Multiple responses by the respondents)

purchasing agricultural inputs. Next, 19 (23%) had utilised money of internal and/or external loan for expanding and developing the existing cottage industry of them. The money was utilised to generate income but the earned money from the business was generally spent for fulfilling their basic needs. After mitigating the basic amenities, there was hardly any money left for buying any assets. 12 (15%) respondents expressed that they utilised money to buy books, uniforms of their children. It further unfolded the fact that there was a tendency of increasing of enrolling the name of the children of SHG members in to school. The motto of the saving of money to the group that the women could get money for their necessary especially for their own socio-economic development. But most of times the money utilised just for mitigating the family needs. 12 (14%) of total responses shared that they utilised money for the marriage purpose of their sons and/or daughters. It was found that the respondents were overburden for borrowing loans from various sources for overcoming financial crises in relation to occasion like marriage. Most of the cases they felt difficulties to repay the loan borrowed by different sources and that are why they were unable to think for creation of assets. A significant number, 3 (4%) of respondents expressed their views that they deposited to bank in the name of their husbands. It further indicated the vulnerability or lower status of the women who still deposited their money in the name of their husbands instead of opening own accounts. Above all these reasons acted as constraint against effective growth and development of the SHGs as well as the group members.

Not having any Freedom for joining any Sort of Employment

Yes	No
24	36

Reasons behind the Lack of Freedom (Multiple responses by the respondents)

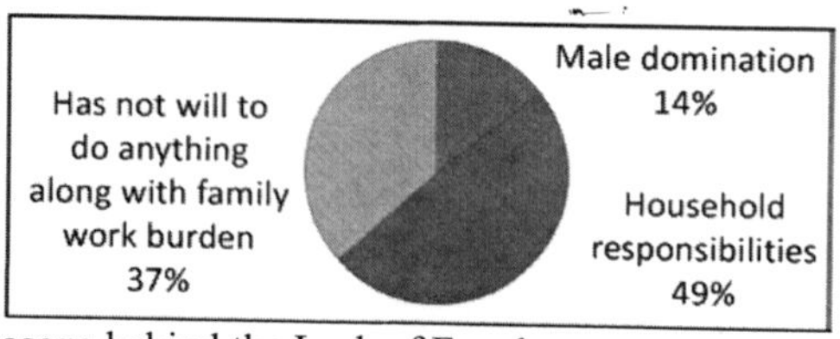

Fig. 24.12: Reasons behind the Lack of Freedom

Analysis

The figure represented that 24 (49%) of respondent could not join any sort of employment due to the household responsibilities, family liabilities. 18 (37%) responses supported that unwillingness to do any work along with family work was another reason behind for not joining any sort of employment. Illiteracy or low literacy, poor self image, lack of self confidence made the women unable to contribute anything outside the home environment. The figure depicted that still then 7 (14%) women were dominated by the male members of their houses. When they were suppressed in their own houses and could not protest against anything, it was impossible for them to contribute anything for their own development and for the society at large.

Absence of Controlling Power

Yes	No
60	0

Reasons behind the absence of Controlling Power (Multiple responses by the respondents)

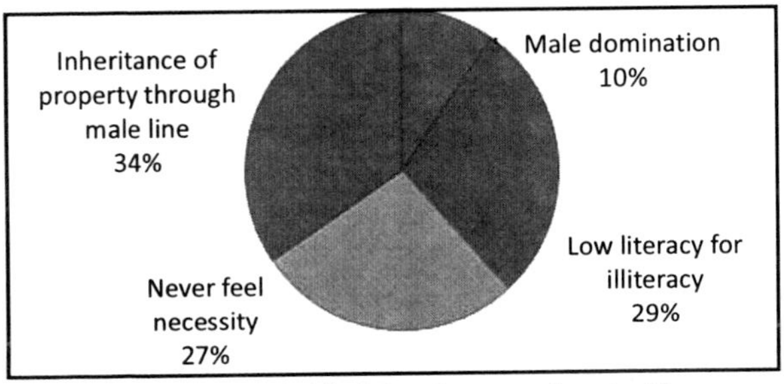

Fig. 24.13: Reasons behind the absence of controlling power

Analysis

According to figure, it was found that the women SHG members never enjoyed the power or they never had any power. When they were asked about the reasons behind such inability, the maximum responses 60 (34%) supported the view that the male were the owner of the property as inheritance of property through male line was in practice. That was why women never got the right or ownership to their properties and thus never got any power. Another significant number of responses, i.e. 50 (29%) favoured that "low literacy rate or illiteracy" was responsible for the absence of controlling power among women. Due to the illiteracy or low literacy, they were hardly in the position to understand the positive or negative aspects of any issues and that's why they preferred to keep quiet and lost their powers. Another important responses was "never feel necessary" as responded by 48 (27%) of the respondents and it again unfolded the low self-image and poor self-esteem of the tribal women. They never thought to enjoy the power for dominating others, but they were always dominated, uncared, neglected and that why the enjoyment of power was not considered as an essential achievements to them. Thus, it can be concluded that the women SHG members had no controlling power due to the above mentioned reasons and it further expressed their helplessness, vulnerabilitics which acted as the constraints against empowerment of women through SHG groups.

Inabilities of Casting Vote

Yes	*No*
57	3

Reasons behind the Inabilities (Multiple responses by the respondents)

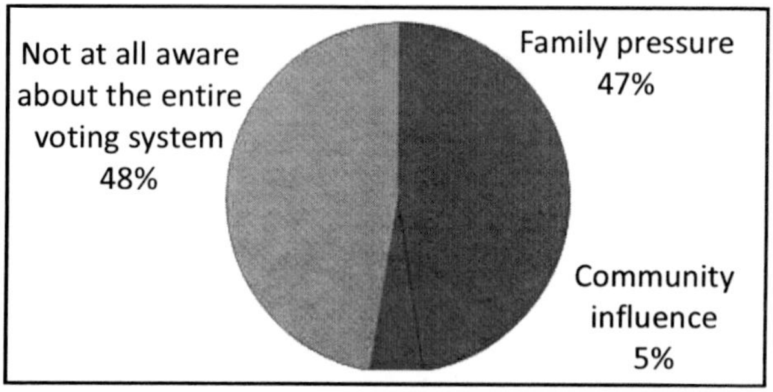

Fig. 24.14: Reasons behind the Inabilities

Analysis

The present figure has shown the reasons behind the inabilities of the SHG members to cast vote independently with own opinion. Several causes had been identified behind their inabilities. According to the figure, 57 (48%) responses responded that unawareness or lack of awareness was the reasons behind their inabilities to cast vote independently with own opinion. Next, 57 (47%) responses supported the family pressure as a reason of inability. 6 (5%) responses expressed that they could not cast vote with own opinion due to the community pressure. Above all these together proved their inabilities in decision-making for casting vote which further revealed their helplessness. Thus, it can be said that the SHG members who were unable to cast their votes independently with own opinion; they were hardly be in a position to contribute for the promotion or effective growth of SHGs.

Age-wise distribution of mother and number of their children

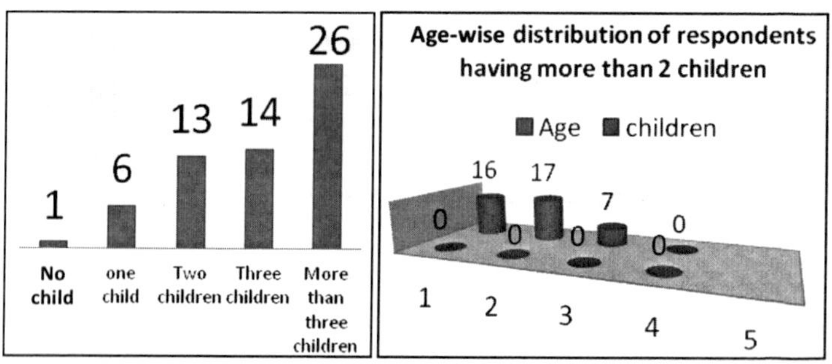

Fig. 24.15: Age-wise distribution of mothers and number of their children

Analysis

The present Figure revealed the age-wise distribution of mothers and number of their children, they possessed. According to this figure maximum number of respondents had more than three children. It was found that 26 (43.33%) of respondents had more than three children Then it was observed that 14 (23.33%) of respondents had maximum three children and 13 (21.66%) had maximum two children. It expressed the tendency of having more children among such tribal group due to the several socio-religious causes. High rate of child birth had been found within such community. The researchers had observed that the excess number of children affected not only the health of mothers, but it further became reason for poor health and nutritional status of children, lack of opportunities for education along with scarcity of space for living, cloths for wearing, poor sanitation, even lack of availability of safe drinking water. Almost all the SHG members who were considered as the agent for bringing positive changes were unfortunately suffered from poor health, huge family liabilities, extreme poverty. The women were hardly in the position to contribute their families and for the growth of SHGs. It was very unfortunate that SHG members of that community never adopted family planning measures in spite of their sufficient knowledge and information about the effectiveness of family planning measure. Thus, it can be said that, SHG members still possessed not only poor socio-economic status but also poor health status, which was acted as a hindrance against their meaningful contribution for their growth and development of SHG and for their empowerment.

Recommendations

- Care should be taken of forming those groups which were workable. Pressurising on formation of groups does not help their continuity. Such groups will stop functioning at latter stage.
- The members of SHG should be properly trained in maintaining various accounts and books, as they become instruments of guide and monitoring the functions of SHG.
- The savings of SHG should be properly utilised by the members to enhance their financial resources. The initiators should guide them.
- The initiators should take special interest in educating the members and make them literate through non-formal education.

- The members should be guided to go to banks and should be familiar with different types of banking functions, particularly deposits and loans.
- The initiators should tell the members of SHG about the insurance schemes of Government for the protection of life, property and liability of the tribes, specially Tribal Welfare Schemes, programmes as Adivasi Mahila Sashaktikaran Yojana, Rajiv Gandhi National Fellowship, Post Metric Scholarship etc. These schemes should be highlighted to them.
- The initiators should take special interest in educating the members and make them literate through non-formal education. Special importance should be given to educate them.
- To promote women empowerment SHGs should pay importance in gender sensitisation, awareness programme on rights of women. Detailed discussions with the women about the rules, regulations, opportunity, their roles and responsibility should be done in their own language.
- The initiators should be well-versed in health facilities so that they can propagate the health campaigns, family planning, nutrition, house-keeping, medical treatment etc.
- The initiators should take serious interest in transformation and empowerment of tribal women through attitude change, preference development, social consciousness and resource generation.
- The constraints of empowerment should be avoided effectively by developing confidence, dissemination of information and deciding the priority for empowerment.
- The members of SHG should be motivated to undertake sensitive and advance training. The government officials should come forward to provide them at the spot training.
- Socio-economic empowering was built and developed through social interaction. The initiators should provide them adequate opportunities for interacting with developed SHGs and model villages.
- The members have not properly perceived the importance of political citizenship. Power of assertiveness, protest and firm determination to get work done by the Government Officers should be developed gradually by the initiators.
- Effective empowerment is possible if the members develop their knowledge, confidence, self-esteem, leadership qualities under the supervision of initiators.

- SHG should be helped by panchayat to find suitable economic activities. The Pradhan should come forward to diagnosis their problems and provide suitable helps to them.
- The infrastructure such as road, electricity, energy, water, school and health centres can effectively be developed, if panchayat takes the help of SHG.
- The political empowerment was very much linked with panchayat. The president and treasurers of SHG should be invited by Panchayat Pradhan to participate in the meeting.
- Only distribution or disbursement of Government money does not help poor. The officers should come forward to guide them how to use the funds effectively and get a feeling of empowerment through SHG.

Conclusions

At the end of the study, the researchers wanted to conclude that though SHG always considered as an instrument for bringing positive changes and empowering women but their present experience revealed that it was really difficult to bring positive changes among the tribal women through the promotion of SHGs. Empowerment of women through SHGs faced a lot of barriers or constraints, which was further reflected in the entire study.

SHGs formed the groups which helped the women to save their money and also helped them to take part in their own development process, but the integrity, the urge of savings, thinking about the future of children were some areas, where the SHG members successfully participated, but still a long way they have to go. It was found that these poor tribal women still then were deprived, under-utilised, neglected, uncared and unprotected where they compelled to tolerate the male domination. At a halt, they were guided by the age-old traditional beliefs, practices where superstitions, prejudices guided them towards the uncertain destinies. The evil practices like physical torture, sexual molestation, alcoholism, were motionlessly in practice, where they were hardly in the position to raise their voice against such inhuman behaviour. The researchers perceived the idea at the end of their studies that formation and promotion of SHG should only be possible when the societal attitude and self-image of women will be uplifted. Until and unless the societal attitude will be changed and the negligence, torture against the women will be stopped, the empowerment of such women will never be possible. SHGs field, on the preach, as an effective instrument for empowering the women, when the other support, cares and welfare measures will be ensured by the family members, community members and the nation. Moreover, the involvement and participation of CBOs, NGOs, VOs along with the development workers should be encouraged for meaningful implementation and promotion of SHGs which further can ensure the women empowerment and be considered as the change maker of the society.

REFERENCES

Biju, R. (2005): *Women's Empowerment*, New Delhi: Mohit Publications.

Census.gov. in

Cynthia Panadian (2006): Role of University in Empowering Weaker Sections of the Society, *University News*, April 17-23, pp. 29-30.

Dhamija, Neelam and Panda, Sushant Kumar (2006): Women Empowerment Through Education, *University News*, July 3-9, pp. 12-15.

Dutta, Subhabrata and Ghosh, Bholanath (2008): *Women Speak*, New Delhi: Mittal Publications.

Kumar, Somesh (2009): *Methods for Community Participation*. Vistar Publication, New Delhi, pp. 22-42.

Macaulay, Fiona (1998): *Localities of Power in Chile and Brazil: Women and Empowerment*, MacMillan Press Ltd., pp. 93-104.

Narayanaswamy, B., Samanta, R.K. and Gowda, K. Narayan (2007), *Self-Help Groups—Key to Empowerment*.

Ray, G.L. and Mondol, S.: *Research Methods in Social Science and Extension Education*, Kalyani Publishers, New Delhi, pp. 77-92.

Sabala and Kranti (2000): *Self-Help Groups and Reproductive Health: Lessons on Capacity Building for Women Empowerment*, Sage Publications, New Delhi, pp. 47-66.

Samanta, R.K. (2001): *Empowering Rural Women*, New Delhi: Mohit Publications.

www.maps of india.com

25

Women Environment Interaction and Traditional Ecological Knowledge

Concerns in Mountain Region

Bal Krishan Choudhary, Kaushik Majumder and *Badal Kumar Datta*

Introduction

In all civilisation of the world, women have been noted as symbol of power and devotion. She creates and nurtures the creation to bloom. She signifies the "*Shakti*" the power that drives the system. Globally, from beginning women have been recognised as agents of change for environment and crucial factor for sustainable development, but in recent time this role in becoming more prompt. Women particularly those living in rural areas or mountain areas have special relationship with the environment. They are more close to the nature than men and this very close relationship makes them perfect managers of an ecosystem. This has resulted in a gender-specific approach in environment and sustainable development policies and practices. Mountain habitats possess both biophysical and cultural characteristics which required special consideration and treatment in the matter of preservation and conservation. The life of mountain women is so much intertwined with the environment that whole ecosystem revolves around her and she can not even think of her survival without it. For her forest is her mother's home as she is entirely dependent on the forest to meet her daily needs, such as water, fodder, fuels, minor forest product etc. Both mountain and women have begun to receive more global attention in last two and half decades but they are not yet optimistically on the conservation agenda. Throughout the history, men have looked at natural resources as commercial entities or income generating tool, while women have tended to see the environment as a resource supporting their basic needs. In developing areas of the world, women are considered the primary users of natural resources, because they are the one who are responsible for gathering food, fuel and fodder. Women's and men's environmental perceptions, their interests and rights in the natural environment, and their environmental awareness and knowledge are significantly different from one another. Their different perception is outcome of particular cultural traditions, various experiences of colonial rule, specific impacts of the global economy, and other locally relevant factors, such as climatic patterns. They are reflected in the prevailing gender-based division of labour; in the various responsibilities and rights that women and men have in the use and ownership of land, trees, animals, plants, and water; and in the different knowledge that women and men may have about the sustainable management of particular natural resources and ecological zones. There is growing recognition of the need to strengthen women's capabilities to participate in decision-making affairs related to environment.

Environmental Perturbations and Women Health

For the same magnitude of environmental perturbation, men and women reacts differently, women are more sensitive to environmental degradation than men because of their delicate emotional and mental make up. Women have the responsibility for managing household resources, but they typically do not have managerial control. Women throughout the world, engage a substantial portion of their life in cooking. Pollutants like noxious gases and particulate matter, released by burning of fire woods and coal affect their health and hygiene. Deforestation and contamination increases the time women must spend for gathering fuel wood or collecting safe and clean water. Contaminated water and prolong exposure also increase the women's risk of water-borne disease. The persistent chemicals and organics enter in her body tissues and breast milk and they are passed on to infants, leads to various complexities. There are plenty of examples regarding ill effects of environmental degradation on women health. In a village in China's Gansu province, discharges from a state-run fertiliser factory have been linked to a high number of stillbirths and miscarriages. Water pollution in Russian rivers is a factor in the doubling of bladder and kidney disorders in pregnant women. In Sudan, a link has been established between exposure to pesticides and prenatal mortality with the high risk among women farmers. In urban settings in particular, air and water pollution is extreme, which leads to poor ventilation and sanitation. Poor or non-existing waste treatment facility is presenting new threats to health, particularly for women, who have the highest levels of exposure. Studies have shown the direct effects of chemicals and pesticides on human health. According to *United Nations Chronicle Journal*, researchers have found an association between breast cancer and the pesticide DDT and its derivative DDE. Study by the World Health Organisation (WHO) has found that women who are exposed to pesticides face a higher risk of abortion. These kinds of health problems cause women to feel more responsible regarding environmental issues. Degraded environments mean that women must spend more time and effort to find fuel or produce food, but their other responsibilities, for meeting household needs and ensuring family health. Gendered divisions of labour have so far resisted real change. In many countries, women already work 12 hours or more a day in and out of the home; in Africa and Asia, women work an average of 13 hours more each week than men. Women are becoming AIDS victim by engaging themselves into multiple sex works due to increase in poverty level. Poor one are bound to adopt such risky and indecorous profession and starving condition forcing them to fall back on natural resources to meet their basic needs. Health problems like anaemia is common among ill-nourished girls and women and can affect the age at menarche. Frequent child bearing intensifies the incidence and severity of anaemia. In many communities environmental damage has greatly increased the distance to be covered by women for collecting fuel or water. Women often carry heavy loads in terms of water and fire wood (in hilly areas work become more intense). In addition to their general effect on health and the possibility of injury, these heavy loads contribute to low weight and proportions of body fat among women. Below certain levels low body weight contributes to the cessation of menses and reduced fertility. Women weakened by general ill-health, and by infectious and respiratory diseases, are much more vulnerable during pregnancy and childbirth, especially if they are very young, near the end of their reproductive years, or have had many children. Climate change is the hot topic of discussion and will be continuing in the future is severely affecting the mountain environment and the hill women. Higher temperatures will encourage insect hosts to breed and to move further up hillsides and mountains and will ultimately lead to various insect borne diseases among the hill dwellers. Disasters like land slide, earthquake and flood are very frequent in the mountain region and it disrupts the health services in terms of infrastructure, equipment and drugs. Access to affected areas become more difficult, and other immediate priorities will suffer. Reproductive health, including safe motherhood, is totally ignored, since pregnancy is not regarded as an emergency and contraception is not given priority in relief efforts. Extended settlement in temporary shelters or refugee camps exposes women and girls to sexual abuse, sexually transmitted diseases and unwanted pregnancies.

Role of Women in Environment Conservation

Traditionally, women have been responsible for subsistence and survival for water, food, fuel, fodder and habitat, though they rarely get the credit for nurturing these life support systems. Added to these environmental destruction, exacerbates women's problems in a way very difficult from that of men. The challenge is to re-establish the symbiosis between communities, women and natural resources and reverse the trend of the negative impact of existing developmental paradigms. Women have always been the principal conservers of bio-diversity. Even today they perform duties such as seed selection, multiplication and preservation for future use. The on-farm conservation traditions of rural and tribal women, with reference to agro-biodiversity are well known. Unfortunately, current food security systems depend on few crops. It is important to expand the basis of food security by including large numbers of species and varieties of food plants still maintained by tribal and rural families. Traditionally, women have dealt with non-monetised biomass based subsistence economy of the household, i.e. firewood, cow dung, crop wastes, organic manure etc. Men mostly tend to destroy nature to earn cash even if it means creating hardship in their own families. Most of the time, they collect fuel and fodder, e.g. sale of herbs and wood in destructive manner. In developing countries, women mostly can not own the land and farms outright, but they are the ones who spend most of their time working on the farms to feed the household. Shouldering this responsibility leads them to learn more about soil, plants, and trees and not misuse them. Although, technological inputs increase male involvement with land, many of them leave the farm to go to cities to find jobs; so women become increasingly responsible for an increasing portion of farm tasks. These rural women tend to have a closer relationship with land and other natural resources, which promotes a new culture of respectful use and preservation of natural resources and the environment, ensuring that the following generations can meet their needs. Besides considering how to achieve appropriate agricultural production and human nutrition, women want to secure access to the land. Women's perspectives and values for the environment are somewhat different than men. They give greater priority to protection of and improving the capacity of nature, maintaining farming lands, and caring for nature and environment's future. Repeated studies have shown that women have a stake in environment and this stake is reflected in the degree to which they care about natural resources.

Ecofeminism

The term "*ecofeminism*" was coined in 1974 by French feminist Francoise d'Eaubonne. It is also called as "*the third wave of the feminist movement*". The word "ecofeminism" is the combination of ecology and feminism. Ecology is the study of relationship between living organisms and their physical and social environment, whereas feminism can be defined as the thought and movement towards the political, economic and social environments. The ecofeminism conceive the idea that the oppression of woman and the oppression or destruction of nature is closely connected. Another definition suggests that discrimination and oppression based on gender, race and class directly related to exploitation and destruction of the environment. Ecofeminist claim that both environment and women share a common inferior position. Male are more related to culture and women are more related to environment and culture has been seen as superior to environment and hence both women and environment have been dominated by men. Thus, women have responsibility to cease male domination over both. Elements of feminist movement, the peace movement and the environmentalists and green movement can be seen in ecofeminism. The reason that the term includes feminists is that the movement uses gender equality as a starting point for working to end oppression. Because of close ties of nature and spirituality, goddess worship and the divine female are often tied to ecofeminism. Academics and activists like Vandana Shiva (India), Ariel Salleh (Australia), Maria Mies (Germany) and Gloria Goldstein (USA) are often seen as important representatives from ecofeminism. *Ecofeminist* address issues like water pollution, deforestation, toxic waste dumping, agricultural development and sustainability, animal rights and nuclear weapons policies. The person associated with the study state that the people will continue to exploit women and nature because man sees both as eternally fertile and endlessly capable of providing life. Bina Agarwal (1998) suggests '*feminist environmentalism*' as an alternative concept. This concept insists that the link between women and the environment should be seen as "*structured by a given gender and class/caste/race organisation of production, reproduction and distribution*". She speaks of class-gender effects of environmental change, and underlines the need to transform the actual division of work and access to resources.

Ecofeminism also refers to women's and feminist perspectives on the environment—where the domination an exploitation of women, of poorly resourced people and of nature is at the heart of the ecofeminist movement. Today, women struggle against alarming global trends, but they are working together to effect change. By establishing domestic and international non-governmental organisations, many women have recognised themselves and acknowledge to the world that they not only have the right to participate in environmental dilemmas, but they have different relationship with environment including different needs, responsibilities, and knowledge about natural resources. The ecofeminist approach takes a number of forms, but two can be distinguished in general terms: social ecofeminism and cultural ecofeminism (Plumwood, 1992). Cultural ecofeminism has an important influence on the work of activists promoting the subject of women and the environment inside both the feminist and the ecology movements. The distinguishing feature of ecofeminism is the way it conceptualises the relationship of women with nature, maintaining that there is a strong link between the two, and defending a return to a "femininity principle" involving harmony, sustainability and diversity. It is globally getting attention that the experiences of women, be they biological, as determined by the female body and its functions (pregnancy, childbirth, lactation, menstruation), or cultural (the care and bringing up of children), give them a different "natural mindset". In turn, the closeness of women to nature supposedly gives them a "special" knowledge that will enable them to save the planet. Their "natural" propensity to protect the environment is an extension of their role as careers in the family group and the community. Again, from ecofeminism comes the contention that the assertion of control over nature and over women has been an integrated, parallel process, historically connected (Mies and Shiva, 1993). This, it is maintained, is due to the effects of the patriarchal structure and the perceptive dualism that subordinates nature to culture and the feminine to the masculine, so that women are socially perceived as being close to nature, and as a result there are connections of an ideological type, based on a system of ideas and representations, values and beliefs, between the oppression that they experience and the exploitation of the natural system. With this approach, women are cast as "victims" of development (Shiva, 1989). This strand of thought is also defined as a movement arising spontaneously from groups made up of ordinary women, which links and integrates theory and practice, on the basis of what is called the survival approach. The origin of what is called "bad development" is pinned down to the Western patriarchal system and its reductionist science; traditional societies are often idealised and prominence is given to respect for cultural diversity. This latter characteristic is a valuable contribution in so far as it means that priority is given to considering the cultural dimension of sustainability. Although this line of thinking has had a great impact in highlighting the interrelationship between women and the environment, it is not clear what contribution it has made, beyond the debate, to the development of public policy aimed at improving the situation of these. The concept ecofeminism has been criticised for failing to embrace diversity among women and it is academicise itself, seems to have stuck in the cloud of theoretical debate.

Women's Movement and Environment

The first documented expression of a woman, who gave her life to safeguarding the environment, goes back more than three hundred years ago, when Amrita Devi, member of *Bishnoi* community along with villagers protested against the exploitation of forest by Maharaja of Jodhpur. The Chipko movement is particularly known because of its actions to resist the destruction of the land of locals and their livelihood in 1974. In that year, the Government of Uttar Pradesh (now Uttarakhand) in the Himalayan foothills diverted the men of Reni village to a fictional compensation payment site. Under the leadership of Gaura Devi, a 50 year old illiterate woman, women rushed from their homes to hug the trees ('*Chipko*' means hugging) and prevent them from being cut. A four-day standoff ended in victory for the villagers. The actions of the women of Reni were repeated in several other places in the region, as hill women demonstrated their power as non-violent activists. When we look into the history of environmental activism and contribution of women, the first name come in our mind is Rachel Carson. She focused the issues that while human beings are small part of nature, they have enormous ability to alter it. Carson was deeply troubled by the use of synthetic pesticides (DDT) and their potential long term negative effects. Her 1962 book "Silent Spring" asserted the detrimental and environmental effects of the pesticides. Carson wrote in *Silent Spring:* "Man's attitude toward nature is today more critically important, simply because of his new found power to destroy it... We now wage war on other organisms, turning against them all the terrible armaments of modern chemistry, and we assume a right to push whole species on the brink of extension...." Carson's work resulted in strong legislation and the establishment of environmental institutions in the USA and throughout the world. In Japan, in the 1950s, the "*Nakabaru Women's Society*" and "*Sanroku Women's Society*" protested loudly against pollution from industries and power plants in the Tobata region. While industrial development had made the society richer, the environmental destruction began to threaten the health of local citizens. Women started to raise their voices in opposition and organised an increasingly powerful movement. They discussed how to prevent pollution, while holding basic study meetings on pollution and conducting field surveys, collecting scientific knowledge through several years of action. From the authorities and companies, the women claimed the right to live in a safe and healthy environment. This resulted in major pollution prevention measures taken by the local government and corporations. If we only look in the field of biodiversity, numerous examples are available about women's knowledge of local ecosystems and species, and their commitment and practices to conserve these. Particularly indigenous women, in all regions of the world, are custodians of local biodiversity. They know the optimum use, conservation and characteristics of natural resources by their own traditional knowledge system. Ruth Lilongula from the Solomon Islands noted, "Biodiversity is the very core of our existence within our communities". We can not say how many dollars this is worth because it is our culture and our survival. On the issue of women, economy and environment nicely quoted by the Nobel laureate Amartya Sen that "Advancing gender equality, through reversing the various social and economic handicaps that make women voiceless and powerless, may also be one of the best ways of saving the environment and countering the dangers of overcrowding and other adversities associated with population pressure. The voice of women is critically important for the world's future—not just for women's future." Women have contributed greatly to the conservational movement of the world. All wild animals are nourished with the food and protected from the intruders by women of *Bishnoi* community. Women are providing leadership in different conservation movement of the world. Vandana Shiva is engaged in conservation movement relating to biodiversity, seed bank etc. Women also actively take part in propagation and protection of seed, which is very important from conservational point of view. Sunita Narain is engaged in the field of environmental information and activism. Maneka Gandhi has been working to prevent cruelty to animals.

Women in Hill Environment

Traditional societies of mountains often referred as indigenous people, have accumulated a whole lot of empirical knowledge on the basis of their experience whilst dealing with natural problems and natural resources. This traditional wisdom is based on the intrinsic realisation that human being and nature form part of an indivisible whole. Therefore, both should live in partnership with each other. Women of the tribal communities know the best use of wild life, especially for food and medicine. They sustain the economic condition by using their own skills, i.e. weaving of natural fibres, is an important rural enterprise for all traditional societies in North East India. By using traditional water harvesting system women are able to solve the problems of drinking water and irrigation in the difficult terrain and sprinkled settlement of region. In the mountain state of North East India, women now spends more hours a day for collecting fuel wood, where previously they would have done so once every four to five days. Women particularly in hill environment carry heavy loads (water and fuel wood) in mountain environment rigorously contribute to the ill health. They feed their husbands, children and other family members. So, the economic development of the family and region entirely depends upon the status of women. Soil erosion, water shortage and crop failures reduce harvest yields; soil exhausted from over-use reduces the productivity of kitchen gardens. Due to *jhum* cultivation the productivity from land is declining hence the pressure on women for income generation is increasing day by day. Hill women generally used fire wood for cooking, smoke coming out of it may led to various respiratory disease. This condition may further deteriorate if the location is poorly ventilated. Toxic chemicals and pesticides in air, water and earth are responsible for a variety of women's health risks, although such risk are still irrelevant in hill environment. Due to continuous exploitation of resources by foreigners the locals are deprived of the use of resources for their betterment in long term. The common practice of disregarding the traditional rights and practices of local dwellers in order to establish new conservation area has been termed as "*ecocolonialism*" because its similarity with the historical abuse of native rights by colonial power of past eras. Cultural diversity is strongly linked with the genetic diversity of crop plants. Mountain women help maintaining the traditional form of agriculture system. In mountain areas in particular, inaccessible terrain often leads to the development of diverse tribes. The women of these communities develop local plant varieties know as "*landraces*". These landraces has global significance to conservation and improvement of crop species. After the inception of Western culture and its adoption by the tribal women of hilly areas of North East, the various environmental and health abuse are flourishing. The women are now more vulnerable to HIV infection and drug abuse, especially when they are not aware of the causing factor and preventive measure of such infectitious and addictive phenomenon.

Women and Climate Change

It is well stated in Principle 20 of the 1992 Rio Declaration on Environment and Development, "women have a vital role in environmental management and development ... and are therefore essential to achieve sustainable development." Gender is a significant aspect to be taken into account when considering actions both to adapt and mitigate climate change. Climate change impacts are not only physical and economic, but also social and cultural. Because of gender differences in social and economic roles and responsibilities, the effects of climate change affect men and women in varied ways, and often women more severely. At the same time, women generally advocate a wider set of actions than men for addressing climate change. Women tend to be affected differently, and more harshly, by climate change because of their social roles and more impoverished status in both develop and developing countries. In developed countries, women are among the most vulnerable groups owing to a reduced ability to access finance, technology and information needed to adapt to climate change impacts. In poorer countries, climate change can adversely affect crop yields and thus the livelihoods and food security of women who are largely responsible for food production as well as family nutrition. Supplying water and fuel for families, which is typically the responsibility of women, becomes more difficult as environmental changes negatively affect clean water supply, existing infrastructure, and urban and rural settlements. Coping with the damage of extreme weather events such as storms, floods, and cyclones may also fall more on women who hold together families and households. Climate change can lead to shortages of resources and unreliable job markets, causing male emigration in the search for work and increasing the agricultural and household duties of women. Women and children are far more likely to die than men during extreme weather events linked to climate change owing to their greater vulnerability (Mirza, 2003). In the 2004 Asian tsunami, 70 per cent–80 per cent of all deaths were women. In the 1991 cyclone disasters in

Bangladesh, 90 per cent of victims were women. In Europe, more women than men died during the 2003 heat wave. For mitigating climate change, women propose more comprehensive approaches to those advocated by men, but they have less power and influence to affect public policy. Women tend to focus more on lifestyle and social changes to reduce greenhouse gas emissions, including reducing the impact of unsustainable consumption and production patterns on the environment and promoting actions such as energy-saving and greener purchasing. Women have greater doubts than men that technological solutions alone will solve the problem of global warming and support initiatives to induce changes in personal behaviour.

Traditional Environment/Ecological Knowledge (TEK)

TEK refers to the body of environmental or ecological knowledge that indigenous people have that has sustained them over thousands of years (Johnson, 1992; Lewis, 1993; Nakashima, 1993). The concept was coined in the early 1980s by academics to describe the knowledge held by indigenous people relating to the environment. Although Indigenous ecological or environmental knowledge has long been of interest to academics (and often considered in areas of study such as ethnobotany or ethnozoology), it was not until the recognition of the environmental crisis. In Tripura, suitable tropical climate support luxuriant growth of various types of medicinal plants and other forest resources spread all over the hilly and plain areas. There are about 19 ethnic groups (Tripuri, Mog, Riang, Shanthal, Koki, Noatia, Lusai, Halam, Jamatia, Chakma etc.). They predominantly live in and around dense forest, and they depend upon the herbal treatment. The ethnomedicinal survey was conducted to study the use by different medicine men, *viz. Auchai* (Tripuri), *Kabiraj* (Bengali) and *Ozai* (Santhal). They posses very rich experiences about the diagnosis and treatment of several serious to minor diseases. The knowledge embodied in them are passed from generation to generation through oral tradition like *mantra* or song. However, much of traditional knowledge is secret with them. They collect their all plants from forest and surrounding *Jhum* land. Study shows that traditionally all these communities are using the different parts of plant live leaf, bark, root, flower, latex etc. for medicinal purpose. They use these various plants for wide range of diseases like curing kidney and urinary disorder (*Achyranthes aspera* L.), leucoderma (*Albizia lebbeck* Benth.), blood dysentery (*Clerodendrum viscosum* Vent.), blood cancer (*Dillenia indica*

L.) wounds healing (*Jasminum sambac* L.), sexual diseases (*Hibiscus rosa-sinensis* L.) etc. (Majumder *et al.*, 2006). In Meghalaya, different tribal community practices the knowledge regarding weed management and nutrient recycling. About 20 per cent of weed biomass left in the *Jhum* land to replenish nutrients, traditional eco-technology such as water harvesting system and drip irrigation through use of bamboo channels to retain moisture level of soils are few of the many TEK (Ramakrishnan, 1992). I would like to highlight another example from our neighbouring country. In Chittagong hill tract of Bangladesh, the natural resource management is done on the basis of TEK. This area is inhabited by different tribal communities', *viz.* Chakma, Tanchagaya, Marma, Murang, Bwam etc. On this basis different tribal communities have their own rights on community forest. They do selective harvesting for their domestic use only. Tree management in *Jhum* field is done by cutting the timber yielding tree like Gamar (*Gemelina arborea* Roxb.) and Teak (*Tectona grandis* L.) at about 1 metre above the ground before the spring. By doing so profuse coppices sprout from the stump gives 2-3 coppice, and the best one gives a healthy tree. For fuel and fire wood they go for selection of only those species which have slow, but consistent combustion property. They keep bark in teak log which protect it from insect and borer attack. The economy, culture and livelihood of the tribal people are well linked with and managed by TEK (Mohiuddin and Alam, 2011).

Indigenous Knowledge System (IKS)

According to Brundtland Commission Report, 1986, IKS has been emphasised as one of the strategies of sustainable resource management in order to achieve sustainable development. Before the world community realised the importance of indigenous knowledge in sustainable resource management, this knowledge system has been influencing resource management practices of traditional communities like the tribes for securing their sustainable livelihoods since time immemorial. Even today, these communities possess traditional knowledge, which has been recognised useful in eco-restoration. As a matter of fact, tribal communities in particular have been playing a vital role in preservation and management of natural resources within the frame of their indigenous knowledge, and it is not a surprise that about 80 per cent of the world's cultural and biological diversity have been reported in their inhabited regions. In this context it is imperative to explore the human nature relationship of tribal communities to understand the essence of conservation and sustainable ethics of resource use. This knowledge system is being increasingly utilised to identify useful species and methods for preservation, processing and application of those species. Growing popular unrest among indigenous communities because once bits of knowledge have been removed from the local in situ system, they lose control over information as mechanisms are not enough to protect this right. The potential of IK both for expanding scientific technical knowledge and for empowering its owners are overwhelming. The study of indigenous knowledge related to natural resources in academia over the last four or five decades falls into two broad categories: (1) ethnoscience and (2) human ecology. It involves a range of disciplines within the human and environmental sciences. Ethnoscience refers largely to local knowledge systems that relate ethnobotany, ethnozoology, ethnomedicine, ethnoveterinary and so on. IK is threatened from three sources, *viz.* (1) loss of indigenous people's base through the destruction of the rain forests and their displacements by government projects or through commercial user of natural resources, (2) the introduction of modern practices of farming, and (3) IK is increasingly endangered by misappropriation of this knowledge by outside researchers. Advocates of IK in development argue that we should aim to play off the different perspectives, the strengths and weaknesses, advantages and disadvantages of different knowledge traditions to improve our overall understanding of issues and problems by way of generating synergy between them. Perhaps the aim should be equitable negotiation, which is a central tenet of local knowledge in participatory development.

Many examples can be highlighted from North Eastern part of India. The Kuki tribes have a close relationship with the forests for the past centuries. Forests to them act as a culturally significant and multidimensionally appropriated space, and are meaningful in every religious, social and economic life. The indigenous knowledge are stored in people's memories and activities and is expressed in stories, songs, folklore, dances, myths, cultural values, beliefs, rituals, agricultural practices, and so on. The ecological landscape of the Kuki tribes demonstrates a close interconnection between their jhumming practice, religious beliefs and their social organisation. The Apatanis of Arunachal Pradesh, India, inhabiting in and around Ziro, under Lower Subansiri district at an altitude of 5500 feet. Haimendorf, an Anthropologist, through his first book (1962) made the world aware about the unique sustainable agro-ecosystem of the Apatanis, the knowledge of which transmitted orally from one generation to another. However, around 1960s, with the induced initiative, a new system of fish farming was introduced along with their traditional paddy cultivation for which they are now known even beyond the North East Region. They know how to preserve and introduce high yielding varieties of seeds, fertilisers etc. Life of an individual is concerned with 'health'. The main goal of traditional healers across the world is to cure sickness and maintain good health. The Lepchas, an indigenous community of Sikkim Himalayas and being an inhabitant to nature with their tangible knowledge utilises the natural biotic resources in one hand and prefer to undertake therapy by means of belief system to identify illness causation and its cure. To them, knowledge is warranted by direct experience based upon long term trial and error strategy. It is entirely concerned with a range of intellectual products what they always try to maintain from generation to generation. Accepting insects as food is part of integral traditional culture of several indigenous societies around the globe including the ethnic people of Arunachal Pradesh. Edible insects are nutritious being a good source of proteins, fats and other micronutrients and are comparable and or sometimes even better than the meat of other animals. However, the habit of insect eating is on gradual decline due to habitat degradation, and appreciation of Western attitude by these ethnic tribes. This may lead to the loss of a component of traditional knowledge among the ethnic tribes of Arunachal Pradesh which has been passed on from generation to generation without any written documents. Preservation of this ethno-biological knowledge and evaluation of its scientific basis may become a potential tool to ensure the food security on global basis and also may help in conservation.

Conclusions

When we go to find out the possible solution regarding the conservation of natural resources and to improve the women-environmental relationship then the major points comes to our mind are one or combination of the following aspects. Women must have rights to own and manage natural resources for betterment of their lives. A more holistic approach that incorporates poverty eradication, health awareness, education and women's economic empowerment in environmental conservation and management is the need of hour. Obstacle to further progress on women and their better relationship with environment like little participation of women in environment protection and management, insufficient numbers and inadequate influence of women in responsible positions and a male monopoly in the management of environmental resources must be removed from the system in such a manner that the participation of women must be ensured. The international community has recognised that without women's full participation, sustainable development cannot be achieved. Women are provided with the adequate knowledge and skills and their participation in environmental institutions, policy-making, decisions and initiatives must be acknowledged. There is need to integrate a gender perspective into all environmental policies, and agreements. A sense of ownership in terms of natural resources is a crucial factor in sustaining natural resources management and other initiatives in such a manner that they feel the confidence that the ruling government will not allot their dwelling areas for a particular developing project. The importance of women's knowledge in prevention and adaptation should be recognised, as they are able to map risks and vulnerabilities from their own standpoint and play an important role in early detection of environmental related obstacles. The privatisation of natural resources, such as water and energy (services), is another global development that should be watched consciously from a gender-perspective. Finally, it is important to underline that women should not be seen as just instruments for environmental conservation and management. The burden of environmental destruction can not be put on the shoulders of women alone. Women have a vital role in environmental management and development. Their full participation is, therefore, is essential to achieving sustainable development. TEK includes all specific knowledge that can be described as ecological or environmental, but it is much more than that. The future of TEK, ultimately, is related to the entrenchment of Indigenous rights. Indigenous knowledge cannot be separated meaningfully from the people who hold it. This means that, in order to protect TEK, the people themselves and their ways of life must be protected. There is an urgent need to have documented records and conservation initiative of TEK. TEK is always symbiotically favourable for nature. So, all effort related to conservation sustainable use must have participation of TEK. In those region where this system has not evolve, may be due to geographical barrier or presence of new knowledge, we should expend and motivate people for this. Although effort has been started, i.e. Department of AYUSH, Government of India has initiated many projects for the documentation of medicinal plant, but this effort should be extended to other areas like agriculture, food habit, NTFP, clothing etc. like importance of TEK in herbal medicinal practices we have to explore and preserve knowledge of all discipline like clothing, preservation, propagation, purification of natural resources etc. Advancement of technology in solving the environmental and ecological problems has some limitations and lacunae. That can only be solved by combination of modern science and traditional believes of local people and knowledge sharing. It would like to conclude here with the statement that "*recognition of gender and traditional based conservational effort for sustainable development is the outcome of lack or limitation of our present scientific understanding in solving the natural and cultural problems*."

REFERENCES

Agarwal, Bina, 1998. The Gender and Environment Debate. In: Leil Roger a.o. *Political Ecology: Global and Local*. Routledge, London-New York.

Johnson, M., ed., 1992, *Lore: Capturing Traditional Environmental Knowledge*. Ottawa, ON: Dene Cultural Institute and the International Development Research Centre, p. 190.

Lewis, H., "Traditional Ecological Knowledge: Some Definitions," *Traditional Ecological Knowledge: Wisdom for Sustainable Development*, N. Williams, and G. Baines, eds. Canberra, ACT: Centre for Resource and Environmental Studies, Australian National University, 1993, pp. 8-12.

Majumder, Koushik, Saha Reema, Datta, B.K. and Bhakta, T. (2006). Medicinal Plants prescribed by different tribal and non-tribal medicine men of Tripura state. *Indian Journal of Traditional Knowledge*, Vol.5(4), October 2006, pp. 559-562.

Mies, M. and Shiva, V., 1993. *Ecofeminism,* Zed Books, London.

Mirza, M.M.Q. (2003), "Climate Change and Extreme Weather Events," *Climate Policy*, 3:3.

Mohiuddin Mohammed and Alam M. Khairul (2011). Opportunities of Traditional Knowledge in Natural Resource Management Experiences from Chittagong Hill Tracts, Bangladesh. *Indian Journal of Traditional Knowledge*. Vol. 10 (3), July 2011, pp. 474-480.

Nakashima, D. "Astute Observers on the Sea Ice Edge: Inuit Knowledge as a Basis for Arctic Co-Management," *Traditional Ecological Knowledge: Concepts and Cases*, J. Inglis, ed. Ottawa, ON: International Programme on Traditional Ecological Knowledge and International Development Research Centre, 1993, pp. 99-110.

Plumwood, V. (1992), "Beyond the Dualistic Assumptions of Women, Men and Nature", *Ecologist*, vol. 22, No. 1.

Ramakrishnan, P.S., 1992. *Shifting Agriculture and Sustainable Development: An Interdisciplinary Study from North Eastern India*, UNESCO-MAB series Paris, Patheon Publ. Carnforth, Lames, UK, p. 424.

Shiva, Vandana (1989), *Staying Alive. Women, Ecology and Development*, London: Zed Books.

SECTION-IV

Entrepreneurship and Economic Development

26

Entrepreneurship

A Panacea to Socio-economic Problems of North Eastern Region

Deep Jyoti Gurung

Introduction

North Eastern states of india consist of eight states, namely Arunachal Pradesh, Assam, Meghalaya, Nagaland, Tripura, Mizoram, Manipur and Sikkim. These states have plentiful of untapped resources and according to 'Look East Policy' it is regarded as eastern gateway of the country. The North Eastern states are officially recognised under North Eastern Council (NEC), which was constituted in 1971 and is the acting agency for the development of the eight states. The Government of India has grouped the eight states under the Ministry of Development of North Eastern Region (MDONER) which was set up in September 2001. The North Eastern region is located between 89.46 degree to 97.30 degree east longitude and 21.57 degree to 29.30 degree north latitude and is spread over an area of 2,62,179 sq. km. The North Eastern region has remained underdeveloped in spite of being endowed with vast natural resources in terms of forests, biological diversity, hydro power etc.

Table 26.1: Glance of NER

Name of the States	*State Capital*	*Population of the State*	*Area (in sq. km.)*
Arunachal Pradesh	Itanagar	13,82,611	83,743
Assam	Dispur	3,11,69,272	78,438
Meghalaya	Shillong	29,64,001	22,429
Manipur	Imphal	27,21,756	22,327
Mizoram	Aizawl	10,91,014	21,081
Tripura	Agartala	36,71,032	10,486
Nagaland	Kohima	19,80,602	16,579
Sikkim	Gangtok	6,07,688	7,000

Source: Web Portal of MDONER.

Despite of tremendous resources and opportunities large percentage of the population is unemployed. Monthly per capita income of North Eastern region is also poor.

Table 26.2: Monthly per Capita Income of North Eastern States

Sl. No.	*States*	*Monthly Per Capita (Rs.)*	
		Rural	*Urban*
1.	Arunachal Pradesh	773.7	925.2
2.	Assam	691.7	871
3.	Manipur	871	955
4.	Meghalaya	686.9	989.8
5.	Mizoram	850	939.3
6.	Nagaland	1016.8	1147.6
7.	Sikkim	728.9	1035.2
8.	Tripura	663.4	782.7
9.	All India	972.8	859.6

Source: Web Portal of MDONER http://WWW.Mdoner.Gov.In/Content/Poverty-Estimates

From Table 26.2, it can be seen that most of the NE states have low monthly per capita income especially in rural areas. This also reflects uneven distribution of opportunities in NE states. The main reason behind is the lack of opportunities in rural areas and high dependency on government jobs which are saturating at a fast rate. The poverty ratios in Table 26.3 reflects deeper truth into the matter.

Table 26.3: Poverty Ratios of North East States and All India—Number and Percentage of Population Below Proverty Line by States–2009-10 (Tendulkar Methodology)

Sl. No.	*States/UTs.*	*Rural*		*Urban*		*Combined / Total*	
		% age of Persons	*No. of Persons (Lakhs)*	*% age of Persons*	*No. of Persons (Lakhs)*	*% age of Persons*	*No. of Persons (Lakhs)*
1.	Arunachal Pradesh	26.2	2.7	24.9	0.8	25.9	3.5
2.	Assam	39.9	105.3	26.1	11.2	37.9	116.4
3.	Manipur	47.4	8.8	46.4	3.7	47.1	12.5
4.	Meghalaya	15.3	3.5	24.1	1.4	17.1	4.9
5.	Mizoram	31.1	1.6	11.5	0.6	21.1	2.3
6.	Nagaland	19.3	2.8	25.0	1.4	20.9	4.1
7.	Sikkim	15.5	0.7	5.0	0.1	13.1	0.8
8.	Tripura	19.8	5.4	10.0	0.9	17.4	6.3
	All India	33.8	2782.1	20.9	764.7	29.8	3546.8

Source: Web Portal of MDONER. http://www.Mdoner.Gov.In/Content/Poverty-Estimates

It can be clearly seen that a huge population is still under poverty line in NE states. The socio-economic deprivation of NE states is also alarming.

Table 26.4: Levels of Socio-Economic Deprivation in India, 2001

Category	*Name of the States*
High	Rajasthan, Uttar Pradesh, Bihar and Madhya Pradesh
Medium	Jammu & Kashmir, Punjab, Uttarakhand, Haryana, *Arunachal Pradesh*, *Nagaland*, *Manipur*, *Tripura*, *Meghalaya*, *Assam*, West Bengal, *Sikkim*, Jharkhand, Odisha, Chhattisgarh, Gujarat, Maharashtra, Andhra Pradesh, Karnataka, Goa and Tamil Nadu
Low	Himachal Pradesh, *Mizoram* and Kerala

Source: Khan, J.H., Shamshad and Hassan, T., Unemployment and Levels of Socio-economic deprivation in India: A regional perspective, *British Journal of Humanities and Social Sciences*, January 2012, Vol. 3 (2).

From Table 26.4, it can be clearly seen that except Mizoram all other NE states are at alarming position in levels of socio-economic deprivation in India.

Table 26.5: Unemployment Rate of NE States

States	*Population (1000) Year 2004-05*	*Unemployment Rate (Per Thousand Persons In Labour Force) CDS*	*Population (1000) Year 2009-10*	*Unemployment Rate (Per Thousand Persons in Labour Force) CDS*
Arunchal Pradesh	736	14	843	12
Assam	22320	65	23747	66
Manipur	1426	16	1512	41
Meghalya	1763	4	1994	9
Mizoram	409	6	415	17
Nagaland	524	32	762	159
Sikkim	431	27	471	47
Tripura	2774	161	2742	141
All India	724346	82	741738	68

Source: DG, NSSO.

CDS—Current daily status gives the average level of unemployment on a day during the survey year.

The NE States is lagging behind rest of the country for various reasons such as dependency on agrarian economies, poor industrial base lack of infrastructure, political insurgency, violence and most importantly dependence on public sector employment.

Entrepreneurship A: A Panacea to Socio-Economic Problems

The NE states rely highly on national support for socio-economic development and thus have been lagging behind. According to endogenous growth theory the economic growth is primarily the result of endogenous and not external forces. Entrepreneurs are the persons who shift economic resources out of an area of lower productivity to an area of higher productivity and greater yield (Jean-Baptiste Say, 1803). Entrepreneur converts a source into a resource (Peter F. Drucker, 1964) entrepreneur are very important in developing economies (Kilby, 1971). According to David B. Autsrech (American Economist) entrepreneurs are the major drivers of economic development. North East states have plentiful resources of every kind from handicrafts, flora, fauna, places, minerals etc. The requirement is thus for potential entrepreneurs to be able to exploit the opportunities and enable development of the region. One important characteristics of entrepreneurship is that it turns entrepreneurs from job seekers into job creators, which is high need for ne states. Entrepreneurship creates job opportunities and thus enables the rise in per capita income of the people and supports socio-economic development.

The entrepreneurship mobilises idle savings of the people as an investment, which in turn generates profit. Establishment of entrepreneurial ventures also leads to development of education, health, transport etc. The gross national production and gross domestic product also increases and leads to growth of national economy. The standard of living also improves.

Various important resources are available in NE states, which if properly used can lead to improvement of socio-economic condition of North East states.

The geographical location and climatic condition of NE states offer vast potential for agriculture, horticulture and forestry products. There are many reasons which are holding it back from reaping the benefits of it such as lack of modern equipment and techniques, lack of implementation of research and development facilities, lack of education to the farmers, lack of proper marketing facilities etc. Though NE states accounts for total geographical area of 8 per cent of the country, only 3.4 per cent of this land is used for agriculture (Centre for Monitoring Indian Economy, 2007).

Table 26.6: Share of NE States in Production of Major Crops (2008-09)

States	*Rice Share (%)*	*Wheat Share (%)*	*Cereals Share (%)*	*Pulses Share (%)*	*Food Grains Share (%)*	*Oil Seeds Share (%)*
Arunachal Pradesh	0.17	0.01	0.19	0.06	0.11	0.11
Assam	4.04	0.07	0.04	0.44	1.77	0.50
Manipur	0.40	–	0.03	0.04	0.18	0.00
Meghalaya	0.21	0.00	0.07	0.03	0.10	0.03
Mizoram	0.05	–	0.02	0.02	0.03	0.01
Nagaland	0.35	0.00	0.32	0.27	0.22	0.26
Sikkim	0.02	0.01	0.17	0.08	0.05	0.03
Tripura	0.63	0.00	0.00	0.03	0.27	0.01
All India	100	100	100	100	100	100

Source: Agricultural Statistics at a Glance, Ministry of Agriculture, Government of India.

Some other agricultural and horticultural products of NE states are rubber (Tripura, Mizoram, and Assam), bamboo (Mizoram and other NE states), horticultural products (Arunachal Pradesh, Mizoram, Manipur, Assam etc.) such as kiwi, orange, apple, chillies, gingers, mustard seeds, pineapple, passion fruit, mushroom etc.

Table 26.7: Production of Major Horticultural Crops of NE States

(*In metric tonne*)

Sl. No.	*Crop*	*A.P Year (2004-2005)*	*Assam (2003-2004)*	*Megh-alaya (2004-2005)*	*Mani-pur (2003-2004)*	*Mizo-ram (2003-2004)*	*Naga-land (2003-2004)*	*Sikkim (2004-2005)*	*Trip-ura (2004-2005)*
(1)	(2)	(3)	(4)	(5)	(6)	(7)	(8)	(9)	(10)
1.	**Fruit**								
	Pineapple	36310	79889	92036	24000	2456	24800	–	105086
	Banana	14817	15308	67779		8059	5000	–	69330
	Papaya	–	21282	4484	5320	821	672	–	963
	Mango	–	997	–	–	1283	50	–	936
	Peach/Plum	–	3738	–	–	1431	–	–	–
	Guava	–	2298	–	–	1061	200	–	149
	Jack Fruit	–	3137	–	–	1065	–	–	254945
	Lime	–	7890	–	–	3037	–	–	10170
	Orange	–	5097	–	1962	18930	–	8350	17044
	Passion Fruit	–	15747	–	5300	2972	–	120	–
	Pomegranate	–	–	–	–	–	50	–	–
	Litchi	–	–	–	–	–	80	–	12449
	Grapes	–	–	–	–	–	115	–	–
	Citrus Fruits	27251	–	–	–	–	12500	–	–
	Satopa	–	–	–	–	–	–	–	124

(*Contd.*)

(1)	(2)	(3)	(4)	(5)	(6)	(7)	(8)	(9)	(10)
	Banana	14817	–	–	–	–	–	–	69330
	Kiwi	62	–	–	–	–	–	–	–
	Walnut	58	–	–	–	–	–	–	–
	Others	15362	12355	36805	–	2834	–	3740	12672
2.	**Vegetables**								
	Cauliflower	–	9658	–		–	108	–	–
	Cabbage	–	21033	–	2750	–	150	–	–
	Tomato	–	4632	–	–	–		–	–
	Pea	–	7686	–	–	–	255	–	–
	Radish	–	1762	–	–	–	–	–	–
	Carrot	–	1973	–	–	–	–	–	–
	French Bean	–	1994	–	–	–	–	–	–
	Lady's Finger	–	2802	–	–	–	–	–	–
	Brinjal	–	1481	–	–	–	158	–	–
	Knol-Khol	–	1081	–	–	–	–	–	–
	Bitter Gourd	–	273	–	–	–	–	–	–
	Bottle Gourd	–	468	–	–	–	–	–	–
	Others	–	2175	144180	–	10718	–	41401	271287
3.	**Spices**								
	Ginger	36666	12524	47138	–	29582	–	34710	2774
	Turmeric	–	4092	9242	–	2258	–	1735	3751
	Chillies	–	29296	1193	–	2307	–	–	16279
	Onion	–	5908	–	–	–	200	–	–
	Allium	–	295	–	–	–	–	–	–
	Corainder	–	493	–	–	–	–	3740	–
	Cardamom	572	–	–	–	–	–	–	–
	Others	133	182	–	16000	–	–	–	37
4.	**Tuber Crops**								
	Potato	–	160757	–	–	–	1750	33612	93472
	Sweet Potato	–	16172	–	–	–	86	–	–
	Tapioca	–	20644	–	–	–	2200	–	–
	Others	–	–	–	–	–	–	2242	–
5.	**Plantation**								
	Tea	–	3899	–	–	–	–	–	–
	Areca Nut	–	14294	–	–	5318	–	–	9042
	Cashew Nut	–	6837	–	–	–	–	–	1542
	Betelvine	–	–	–	–	446	–	–	–
	Tung	–	–	–	–	297	–	–	–
6.	**Flowers**								
	Cut/Pot	–	–	–	–	–	–	13994	–
	Plants/Bulbs	–	–	–	–	–	–	13700	–

Source: "Export Potential of Horticultural Products from NE States", Study Conducted by CMI Social Research Centre, October-November 2005.

Table clearly reflects the capacity of NE states to yield so many varieties of horticultural products. Most of them are not consumed completely.

Table 26.8: Surplus Quantities of Major Horticultural Produce in the North Eastern States

Commodity	*Arunachal Pradesh*	*Assam*	*Manipur*	*Meghalaya*	*Mizoram*	*Nagaland*	*Sikkim*	*Tripura*	*Total*
Citrus	18702	12000	1962	23000	5300	2000	1100	10500	74564
Banana	10168	85000	–	–	1200	–	–	–	96368
Pineapple	24919	29000	24000	70000	–	5400	–	31000	184319
Papaya	–	15000	5320	–	–	–	–	–	20320
Jackfruit	–	25000	–	–	–	–	–	93000	118000
Ginger	25163	42000	7045	35048	16500	–	24300	960	151016
Turmeric	–	–	–	6900	400	–	1300	1600	10200
Potato	–	–	–	117500	–	1750	32612	–	151862
Chillies	–	–	22200	–	424	–	–	11650	34274
Total	**78952**	**208000**	**60527**	**252448**	**23824**	**9150**	**59312**	**148710**	**840923**

Source: "Export Potential of Horticultural Products from NE States", Study conducted by CMI Social Research Centre, October November 2005.

Most of these products do not reach market because of lack of proper storage facilities, poor road connectivity, improper transportation facilities and lack of marketing channels and facilities. Entrepreneurs can use this opportunity to innovatemethods to market these products properly.

The NE States have some of the oldest oil refinery, coal mines and other important mineral resources. Some recent findings by Geological Survey of India (GSI) suggest that petroleum oil deposits were found in Mokokchung, Longleng and Tuensanj districts of Nagaland. Quartzite deposits are detected in Shillong basin. Sandstone and shale are found in barail range of lower Assam. Glass sand is found in Jiyajuri-Chapanala areas of Nogaon (Assam). Platinum Group of Elements (PGE) are found in Manipur. Umphyrnai and Pomlakrai are suspected to have metal copper. Chakung-jugdumareas of Sikkim are investigated for base metal and gold. Meghalaya has Phosphates, China clay, Dolomite, Silimanite, Carborundum, Uranium etc.

These rich deposits of minerals in NE states are opportunities, to be explored by the emerging entrepreneurs of NE states and promise a huge profit.

Apart from natural resources NE States of India have also great handicrafts and beautiful handlooms.

Table 26.9: Handlooms and Handicrafts of NE States of India

States	*Handicrafts and Handlooms*
Arunachal Pradesh	Carpet making, Masks, Painted Wood Vessels, Bamboo, Cane Crafts, Weaving, Woodcarvings, Jewellery, Pottery, Brass Cutting, Silver Works etc.
Assam	Handloom Weaving, Cane and Bamboo Works, Sitalpith, Brass and Bell Metal Works, Ivory, Woodwork, Sholapith, Pottery, Fiber Craft etc.
Manipur	Bell Metal Bowls, Cane and Bamboo Works, Spongy Reeds Mats, Gold and Gold Plated Jewellery, Dolls and Toys of Straw etc.
Meghalaya	Cane and Bamboo Works, Woodcarving, Artistic Textile Weaving, Silk Weaving of Endi Silk, Carpet Weaving, Pineapple Fibre etc.
Mizoram	Weaving, Bamboo and Cane Craft, Pipes, Musical Instruments etc.
Nagaland	Basketry, Woodwork, Jewellery Making, Products of Shell and Beads, Bird's Wings and Flowers, Pottery, Weaving, Wood-carvings etc.
Sikkim	Weaving, Thanka Paintings, Carpets, Handlooms, Wooden Carved and Painted Items, Wooden Masks, Cane and Bamboo Crafts, Traditional Hats and Caps etc.
Tripura	Stripe Handloom with Scattered Embroidery, Cane and Bamboo Craft, Lamp Stands, Tablemats, Sitalpati, Woodcarving, Silver Ornaments etc.

Source: Web Portal of Indira Gandhi National Centre for the Arts http://ignca.nic.in/craft004.html

The handlooms and handicrafts are unique, beautiful and are in demand in and outside NE states. Entrepreneurs can also play an important role in marketing the handlooms and handicrafts of NE states and also reap benefits out of it for themselves as well as the state.

NE states have many wonderful, historic, religious and adventurous places for tourism. There are many national tour and tourism agencies who are promoting tourism in NE states. Once blooming entrepreneurs of the state will realise the immense benefits of promoting tourism of NE states, it will be the backbone of the economy of the state (*see* Table 26.10).

The NE states of India thus offer a wide range of tourist interest places and experiences, which can be properly packaged by innovative entrepreneurs to improve tourism and generate huge revenue out of it.

Who will bell the cat? Despite having being blessed with immense resources of nature ne region is still lagging behind. One of the main reasons for this is lack of entrepreneurship in the region. Poor infrastructure is also adding fuel to the situation. Institutional support is also missing to a very large extent. Locational disadvantage with poor

Table 26.10: Places of Tourism Interest in NE India

States	*Places to Visit/Experience*
Arunachal Pradesh	Golden Namgyallhatse (Tawang Monastery), Parasuramkund, Malinithan, Itanagar City, Gyakarsinyi (Ganga Lake), Lake Paradise (Sela Lake) etc.
Assam	Kaziranga Wildlife Sanctuary, Talatalghar, Manas National Park, Sibsagar Town, Charaideo, Majuli, Sualkuchi Boat Race, Nameri National Park etc.
Manipur	Loktak Lake, Singda Dam, Imphal City, Govindajee Temple, Khwairamband Bazar etc.
Meghalaya	Living Root Bridge, Nokrek National Park, Mawlynnong Village, Nohsngithiang Waterfalls, Elephant Falls, Nohkalikai Falls, Jantia Hills, Mawkdokdympep Valley, Kyllang Rock, Mawsynram Village etc.
Mizoram	Thalfavangkut Festival, Lengteng Wildlife Sanctuary, Pukzing Cave, Milupuk, Palak Lake, Tamdil Lake, Phawngpui Mountain, Phulpui Grave, Tomb of Vanhimailian etc.
Nagaland	Hornbill Festival, Shillio Lake, Touphema Village, Japfu Peak Trek, Dzukou Valley etc.
Sikkim	Phọdọng Monastery, Goecha La Trek, Yumthang Valley, Ravangla Town, Yak Safari, Tsomgo Lake, Rumtek Monastery, Gurudongmar Lake, Nathula Pass etc.
Tripura	Neermahal, Unakoti Hills, Ujjayanta Palace, Sepahijala Wildlife Sanctuary, Tripura Sundari Temple, Unakoti, Pilak, Jampui Hills etc.

Source: http://www.thrillophilia.com/blog/things-to-do-in-North East-india/& state government web portals of the respective states.

connectivity with the potential markets is also hindering marketability of local products and due to this reason; local products are fetching very low prices leaving little incentives for the entrepreneurs. A mind set to get a government job is also a very big psychological barrier which needs to be broken. Need of the hour is to develop an integrated effort to develop entrepreneurship in the region, with the involvement of government's financial institutions and public. Tourism which is having high potential need to be developed and marketed globally to bring a turn-around in economy of NE region. Tourism related activities if carried out with inclusion of people at grassroots level can be a major differentiator for the region as North East offers ample opportunities for rural tourism, cultural tourism, adventure tourism, food tourism etc. A tendency to always look up to the government for help will have to be replaced with a mind-set of "help yourself".

With a more confident approach, necessary skill and more important strong will power to develop entrepreneurship in the region will only help to develop the economy of NE region.

REFERENCES

1. Sahu, P.P., *Employment Situation in North Eastern Region of India: Recent Trends and Emerging Challenges*, Nli Research Studies Series No. 096/ 2012.
2. Indian Chamber of Commerce, *India's North East Diversifying Growth Opportunities*.
3. Geological Survey of India, North Eastern Region (2012), *Base Document of CGPB Committee-VIII Geology and Mineral Resources of North Eastern Region*.
4. CMI Social Research Centre (October-November 2005), *Export Potential of Horticultural Products From NE States' Study*.
5. Ministry of Agriculture, Government of India, *Agricultural Statistics at a Glance*.
6. Khan, J.H., Shamshad and Hassan, T., Unemployment and Levels of Socio-Economic Deprivation in India: A Regional Perspective, *British Journal of Humanities and Social Sciences*, January 2012, Vol. 3 (2).

27

Trade and Economic Development through Look East Policy

Archana Mandal

Introduction

Ever since liberalisation of the Indian economy in 1990, a new orientation is sought to be given to India's foreign policy and trade by a thrust on South Asian and Southeast Asian countries. The then Prime Minister Manmohan Singh described India's LEP as "a strategic shift in our perspective" and further clarified that "the age old India-ASEAN linkages have been given a renewed thrust with the impressive growth of connectivity and the ever-increasing flows of tourism between India and ASEAN." In fact, ASEAN (Association of South-East Asian Nations) has reached 40 years of its existence in 2007. Recalling the recent events, Singh further said that "in the present phase of our Look East Policy, we in India seek to deepen our economic, integration by entering into free trade or comprehensive economic partnership agreements, both with ASEAN as a whole and with individual countries of the region". Considerable progress has been recorded in trade between India and the ASEAN countries in the past few years. The volume has risen from US $ 40 billion in 2007-08 to US $ 44 billion in 2009-10. A Free Trade Agreement (FTA) was signed between India and the ASEAN countries in Bangkok on 13th August, 2009. It is proposed to increase the trade volume to US $ 60 in seven years and to reduce the tariff rates drastically. The very first agreement in this field was the Indo-Myanmar Trade Agreement signed on 31st January, 1994. The agreement provided for "establishment of trade on the basis of equality and mutual benefit". The idea was to put in place a "signalling device to monitor the movement of commodities and people". Probably another objective was to provide "an insurance against the perceived threat of Chinese dominance of the region". A memorandum of understanding (MOU) was also signed between GOI and Myanmar on the same day. These two agreements were followed up by a delegation level talk on 10th June, 1994.

It is appropriate that the LEP first touched Myanmar. Myanmar has a common border of 1643 km with four of India's States, namely Arunachal Pradesh, Nagaland, Manipur and Mizoram. For trade with China and the South-East Asian countries by the land route, all movement has to be through Myanmar. It is true that Myanmar itself is poor. It does not have as much manufactured goods to offer as the other South-East Asian countries. But, it has vast natural resources which are yet to be tapped. In recent years the volume of trade between India and Myanmar has gone up to US $1.2 billion. At present India's imports include pulses, wood and wood products, fruits and nuts, natural rubber, paper and paper pulp. India exports drugs and pharmaceutical products, machinery and instruments, steel and transport equipments. Moreover, Myanmar's geo-strategic location cannot be ignored. That is why India is building the trans-Asian railway network through Myanmar to Singapore. The Asian road highway is also under construction through Myanmar. The ultimate idea is to link up the Indian Ocean with South China Sea. Besides, India has taken up several infrastructure projects in Myanmar. The Tatas are setting up a truck-manufacturing plant at Magway, the ESSAR group is joining in the attempt to build the multi-model Kaladan transpart project, the National Hydroelectric Power Corporation will build the Tamanthi power project, and GOI will help Myanmar to build a new part at Sittwe. All this effort to achieve closer Indo-Myanmarese relations reflected India's present pragmatism in matters relating to foreign policy. It may be recalled that writing about India's foreign policy in the Asian context, the former Indian Foreign Secretary, J.N. Dixit, had suggested that our trade relations with Myanmar should be normalised irrespective of the government that might be in power there because that country is geo-strategically important to India. Such close cooperation with Myanmar is also necessary in order that India may curb smuggling, border crimes, drug movement and insurgency (*The Sentinel*, 28th November, 2007).

The Look East Policy (LEP) has been one of the latest buzzwords in the context of economic development of the North Eastern Region of India, even though the policy was initiated by the then Prime Minister, Mr. P.V. Narasimha Rao in 1991, i.e. about two decades ago. The policy was inaugurated in 1992 when Dr. Manmohan Singh was the Finance Minister. Geographically, India is located in South Asia. However, the LEP is a turning point in India's focus towards East Asia, South-East Asia and the countries in the Pacific Region; although India's relationship with the countries of the Association of South-East Asian Nations (ASEAN) is said to be central to the LEP, with Thailand occupying a central place. The major objective of India's LEP is stated to develop economic relationship with the ASEAN. However, in the context of India's North Eastern Region, its primary objective is said to take advantage of the new opportunities in trade and investment by improving socio-economic and political relationship with the neighbouring countries. In the practical field, international trade has fostered the wealth of nations all along. In the tremendous economic development which has taken place in the six decades since the end of the Second World War, trade probably has played the most important role. It was in 1950 that General Issimo Chiang Kei Shek and his wife Sung Li fled to Taiwan (then called Formosa) after Mao Zedong's Red Army swept into power in mainland China. They started the process of Taiwan's economic development through trade. First they harvested and exported fish, then agricultural and agro-industrial goods and after that the products of village and small industries which included very large consignments of cheap readymade clothes. This continued for some time, when they started manufacturing and exporting computer hardware. Meanwhile, the entire young generation went through a sort of knowledge revolution which created a huge human resource base in a small country. Taiwan does not have many natural resources. But, it imported raw materials from different countries and transformed these into high-quality manufactured goods and exported the same.

This value addition became possible through its technically skilled and rich human resources. A number of countries including South Korea, Thailand, Singapore, Hong Kong, Malaysia and others followed more or less similar growth paths and became prosperous. Even Indonesia and the Philippines are going through the same process. To quote the Nobel Prize winning economist Joseph E. Stiglitz, "the most successful developing countries in the world have achieved their success through trade—through exports". But he has warned that "opening up markets in the developing countries to goods from the advanced industrial countries without full reciprocation" might not work. He quoted the case of Europe when in 2001 it "unilaterally opened up its markets to the poorest countries of the world" and "almost no trade followed". Stiglitz referred to the various trade agreements and opined that "even if trade agreements have been truly free and fair, not all countries would have benefited—or at least benefited much-and not all people, even in the countries that did benefit, would share in the gains. Even if trade barriers are brought down systematically, not everyone is equally in a position to take advantage of the new opportunities."

The LEP has passed two phases—the first phase from 1992 to October, 2003; while the second phase has started from November 2004. In the **first phase** India sought trade, political cooperation and institutional links with ASEAN (*viz.* Indonesia, Malaysia, Philippines, Singapore, Thailand, Brunei, Darussalam, Vietnam, Laos, Myanmar and Cambodia). In October 2002, the first India-ASEAN business summit was held at Delhi which was addressed by the then Prime Minister Atal Bihari Vajpayee. Since then, the summit became an annual affair. However, the policy could not make much headway during its first phase.

The second phase of LEP started with the India-ASEAN car rally (covering its nine countries other than Philippines) from Guwahati to Batam island in Indonesia covering about 8000 km road distance in 20 days during November-December 2004, aiming at promoting trade, investment and tourism and culture. The rally was ceremoniously flagged off by Prime Minister Dr. Manmohan Singh on 22nd November, 2004 at Guwahati. The rally has demonstrated not only the feasibility of direct physical connectivity, but also the keenness towards India as there were over 250 participants from the ASEAN countries and 3 teams from India. LEP was thus successful in its attraction. It is worthwhile to briefly take stock of some important milestones in regard to ASEAN since the start of second phase of LEP. These are:

1. Signing of first framework for bilateral Free Trade Agreement (FTA) with Thailand in October, 2003.
2. Comprehensive Economic Cooperation Agreement (CECA) with Malaysia during Prime Minister's visit to Malaysia in December 2004.
3. Strategic Partnership Agreement with Indonesia signed in November 2005.
4. Process of bilateral agreements with Myanmar since 2004.
5. CECA with Singapore signed on 29th June, 2005, came into force from 1st August, 2005.
6. India has constructed some major projects in Cambodia.
7. Several bilateral agreements with Laos.
8. A number of bilateral treaties and agreements with Vietnam.

Considerable progress has been recorded in trade between India and the ASEAN countries in the past few years. The volume has risen from

US $ 40 billion in 2007-08 to US $44 billion in 2009-10. A Free Trade Agreement (FTA) was signed between India and the ASEAN countries in Bangkok on August 13, 2009. It is proposed to increase the trade volume to us $ 60 in seven years and to reduce the tariff rates drastically.

India is now following a different policy towards the autocratic junta which controls Myanmar while at the same time supporting the world community's effort towards assisting the Nobel Laureate Aung San Su Ki's fight for democracy in her country. This is real politic. It is in pursuance of this real politic that India and Myanmar have exchanged high-level visits in recent times. The most important visit perhaps was that of the Myanmarese senior General Than Shwe, who as the "Chairman of the State Peace and Development Council of Myanmar" headed the autocratic government of that country. During his discussion with the Indian Prime Minister on July 27, 2010 India and Myanmar agreed a "close cooperation between the security forces of the two countries in tackling the pernicious problem of terrorism". Arrangements were also finalised for Indian participation in critical areas like medical science, education, telecom services and in major projects and manufacturing industries.

The objectives of this chapter are three-fold to analyse the emerging scenario of trade between India and China through LEP—1. It examines the trends of Trade Relations between India and China. 2. It seeks to find out why does India Look for East Asia? 3. Exportability and Potentialities of Border Trade Pertaining to India's North East Region and finally conclusion as follows.

1. India-China Trade Relations: An Overview

India-China trade relations are the most important part of bilateral relations between India and China. From a temporary decline in the influx of Chinese imports in the Indian markets, the scenario seems to have changed—India is enjoying a positive balance of trade with China. The India-China trade relations are regulated by the India-China JBC, which ensures a free exchange of products and services between the two nations. India and China signed a Trade Agreement in 1984, which provided for Most Favoured Nation Treatment and later in 1994, the two countries signed an agreement to avoid double taxation. The bilateral trade crossed US$13.6 billion in 2004 from US$ 4.8 billion in 2002, reaching $18.7 billion in 2005. The India-China trade relations have been further developed from 2006, with the initiation of the border trade between

Tibet, an autonomous region of China, and India through Nathu La Pass, reopened after 44 years. The leaders of both the countries have decided to enhance the bilateral trade to US$ 20 billion by 2008 and further to US$ 30 billion by 2010. According to the then Indian Commerce Minister, Kamal Nath, China would soon become India's largest trade partner within the next 2-3 years, after the US and Singapore.

Indian Export to China: Indian Exports to China is an integral part of the bilateral trade relations between the two Asian countries—India and China. Indian Exports to China focus on mainly primary products. In 1984, India and China signed a trade agreement, providing for Most Favoured Nation treatment, to foster greater cooperation between each other. Moreover, the year 2006 was celebrated as Friendship Year between India and China. The principal items of Indian exports to China are ores, slag and ash, iron and steel, plastics, organic chemicals, and cotton. In order to increase the extent of exporting Indian goods to China, however, there should be a special emphasis on investments and trade in services and knowledge-based sectors. At present, iron ore constitutes about 53 per cent of the total Indian exports to China. The other items that have potentials are marine products, oil seeds, salt, inorganic chemicals, plastic, rubber, optical and medical equipment, and dairy products. Not only this, great potential exists in areas like biotechnology, IT and ITES, health, education, tourism, and the financial sector—all of which will contribute to the services and knowledge based sectors. The need is to shift the focus from primary exports to the export of diverse range of high value added products, including—

- Auto engine components and automobiles
- Organic and inorganic products
- Pharmaceuticals
- Metal and metal based products like alloy steel bars and rods
- Agricultural products like grains, tobacco and oilseeds
- Engineering goods like diesel engines and compressors
- Marine foods
- Fresh and processed fruits and vegetables
- Medical and optical diagnostic equipment and laboratory equipment
- Consumer durables
- Textile yarns

Such diversification of Indian exports to China clearly indicates that there exists a steady demand for these products in the Chinese market.

Indian IT Exports to China is an integral part of the total Indian exports to China, with the bilateral trade between the two countries amounting to US $ 11.3 billion during the year 2005, which under joint efforts is to be increased to US$ 20 billion or higher by the year 2008. The bilateral trade has significant growth potential in areas like IT and ITES. Regarding the Indian IT Exports to China, the recent laws of China on restricting the foreign software companies selling software in China has been a set back for Indian software companies. The cordial bilateral trade relations however will soon ease out such tensions and there is a great possibility that Indian software companies will be allowed to sell software services to Chinese companies. Indian IT Exports to China has become a new bridge between the two countries facilitating the growth of bilateral trade and co-operation between the two countries. Not only software products, the Indian software companies also export IT-based know-how to the Chinese software firms. Chinese officials and executives of almost all major Chinese software companies travel to the Silicon Valley of India or the city of Bangalore in order to learn the essence of India's software industry. Many Indian software firms under the Confederation of Indian Industries signed a Memorandum of Understanding with the Shanghai-Pudong Software Park of China to promote Indian and Chinese co-operation in software. Moreover in order to accelerate the Indian IT Exports to China many Indian software firms have moved into the park. Some of the major Indian software houses like NIIT, Mphesis, Infosys, Satyam, and Tata Consultancy Services have been outsourcing in China. They on one hand in an advantageous position due to their superior traditional skills in terms of management compared to the weaknesses of Chinese developers. Moreover with the help of the local and language-specific expertise of Chinese professionals, the Indian firms can capture the Chinese domestic market as well as other ones in the far east Asian countries. Moreover, the conducive conditions of China like the upcoming opportunities in China, her economic growth, political stability, and human resources make China an ideal place for establishing a second global delivery centre for Indian software firms.

Impediments for Indian Exports to China: There are certain obstacles faced by Indian exporters in their attempts to capture the markets of China. Lack of information on customs procedures, imposition of excessive customs and other levies with frequent rate changes, complex customs valuation procedure, absence of a specified nodal agency, lack of transparency regarding technical standards, differentiated testing norms for imported and domestic products, unfamiliarity with regard to provincial rules and regulations, and frequent change in policies without any advance information on those changes are just some of those problems.

Potential for Indian Exports to China: In order to increase the level of Indian exports to China, there should be a continuous interaction through exchange of delegations, enhancing participation in each other's trade fairs and seminars and facilitating trade through positive initiatives.

Chinese Exports to India: Chinese exports to India focuses on resource based exports as well as the exports of manufactured products. China has emerged as a global manufacturing centre and India as the most lucrative market in the world. The main items that comprise Chinese exports to India are electrical machinery and equipment, cement, organic chemicals, nuclear reactors, boilers, machinery, silk, mineral fuels, and oils. Value added items like electrical machinery dominates Chinese exports to India. This exhibits that Chinese exports to India are fairly diversified and includes resource-based products, manufactured items, and low and medium technology products. It is said that if India is to capture the markets of China and enjoy profits, then it would have to discover new merchandise and branch out its exports to China. In 2004, the Chinese exports to India stood at US$ 5926.67 million. However, it industrialists in India were not in favour of China being given free access to the domestic markets. But bilateral trade relations between India and China have increased over the years, reaching US$18.7 billion in 2005 from US$ 4.8 billion in 2002. However, the bilateral trade is to be increased further to US$ 20 billion by 2008 and further to US$30 billion by 2010.

Recent Developments Regarding Chinese Exports to India: In the beginning, Chinese firms were keen on exporting cheap electronic items, garments, and toys to the Indian markets. But recently, Chinese exporters have been focusing on the cement market. Two Chinese cement companies, Yingde Dragon Mountain Cement Company Ltd. and Longkou Fanlin Cement Company have been authorised to sell cement in Indian market. The reasons behind the sudden interest of the Chinese cement companies in penetrating the Indian market are that China is the world's largest cement producer and that the per capita cement consumption is relatively low in India, around 150 kilogram per annum, less than one-third of China's per capita consumption, as in 2006. The prospects for Chinese exports to India have been enhanced from 2006, with the opening of the prospective Indo-China border trade. Trade has been initiated between Tibet, an autonomous region of China, and India through Nathu La Pass, reopened after 44 years. From then onwards, nearly 15 items are being exported from China to India.

2. India's Looking for East Asia

It may be mentioned that in the North East and East Asia, the major economies are China, Japan and Republic of Korea (ROK) and it would be worthwhile to glimpse at them also. The year 2006 was celebrated as the India-China Friendship Year. The state visited by Chinese President Hu Jintao during November 2006 was the highlight, in which a joint declaration was issued on strategic and co-operative partnership between India and China. Comprehensive economic engagement, bilateral investment protection and promotion agreement and the agreement to enhance trans-border connectivity and cooperation through expansion of border trade by strengthening of existing routes and exploring additional routes are major aspects of the declaration. In fact, border trade through Nathu La Pass was resumed during the year. India's relation with Japan to involve in the LEP has been one of its weaknesses. However, the relation got a fillip since the visit of India's Prime Minister to Japan during December 2006. The two countries agreed on Special Economic Partnership Initiative, which has Dedicated Freight Corridor and Delhi-Mumbai Industrial Corridor as its principal components.

Republic of Korea (ROK) is an important economic partner of India. India's relation with ROK acquired momentum after the visit of the then President of India, Dr. A.P.J. Abdul Kalam during February 2006 at the invitation of the President of ROK. This was the first ever visit of an Indian President of ROK. Four agreements were signed during Dr. Kalam's visit. A Comprehensive Economic Partnership Agreement (CEPA) between India and ROK has come into effect from the 1st January, 2010. In fact, South Korean President Mr. Lee Myung-bak was the Chief Guest at India's Republic Day celebration on 26th January, 2010. The then Prime Minister, Dr. Manmohan Singh and President Mr. Lee also agreed to enhance the bilateral relations between the two countries to a Strategic Partnership. It may be added that to the Indian Industry, ROK can provide an important gateway into the Asia-Pacific Economic Co-operation (APEC) region. It may also be noted that there has been a growing interest in East Asia in forming a broader grouping in the framework of ASEAN + 4 (*viz.* Japan, China, India and South Korea), i.e., extending to 14 countries comprising Japan, ten ASEAN countries, China, India and Korea Republic (JACIK).

India's LEP is an open economy policy. In this regard, it is necessary to test the 'openness' hypothesis. A simple measure to test this is by estimating the trade ratio (i.e. sum of exports and imports) of a country to its Gross Domestic Product (GDP). It has been estimated from World Bank Report data that in 2007, the degree of openness is 66.27 per cent for China, 48.49 per cent for Indonesia, 74.54 per cent for Philippines, 119.53 per cent for Thailand, and 30.91 per cent for India. India can gain more from the LEP but she has to open more, simultaneously. Thailand's global exports of $152,469 million in 2007 were more than India's figure of $145,228 million. Higher openness of East Asia's economy is also correlated with higher level of per capita income. The above countries are more industrialised than India. Share of industry in GDP in 2007 was 48 per cent in China, 47 per cent in Indonesia, 30 per cent in Philippines, 44 per cent in Thailand against India's share of 29 per cent. Agriculture accounted for 12 per cent in China, 14 per cent each in Indonesia and Philippines and 11 per cent in Thailand against India's share of 18 per cent. Higher industrialisation of East Asia is an opportunity to Indian importers though industrialists may consider otherwise.

It needs to be mentioned that in the recent decades, the East Asia has significantly increased its share of global GDP and trade. The centre of economic gravity in the world is now in East Asia. India's fortunes in trade and investment are now more linked with East Asia. Trade and transportation go hand in hand. Physical factors like infrastructure, transportation and their costs contribute to Industry's disadvantage in India's exports. As per a World Bank study (Ferranti, 2002), India suffers a cost disadvantage of about 9 per cent on account of transportation and freight related cost factors alone. On the other hand, as mentioned earlier, India's share of trade with neighbouring countries is, very low, at 9.9 per cent of her trade. In this respect, LEP is an optimal policy. It may be added that the combined population of East Asia and India (3224.93 million approx) accounts for 48.77 per cent of the world population, which is a huge market in terms of consumers. Since the region's GDP is growing fast, it has huge potentiality.

Who will be benefited more?: These are prophetic words with great potency. It is to examine whether the North Eastern Region (NE) of India is ready to participate fully in the Look East Policy (LEP) of the Government of India (GOI) and whether NE will actually gain from such a policy. Let me first lay down the expectations of the LEP in its historical perspective. The North East Region (NER) of India constitutes the states of Arunachal Pradesh, Assam, Manipur, Meghalaya, Mizoram, Nagaland, Sikkim and Tripura. Flanked by hills and with the mighty Brahmaputra river slashing a central path between its north and south, the NER is bounded mostly by the international boundaries near about 98 per cent.

Arunachal Pradesh lies to its north and Sikkim a little away in the north-west bordering China and Bhutan. Bangladesh and Myanmar lie to its south-west and east. The torrential Brahmaputra deposits its rich alluvial silt along the banks of the plains of Assam. Tropical rain forest, rich in flora and fauna, spread their arms across Arunachal Pradesh into Assam. The state of Assam is a land where Tea is the most powerful industry, handicrafts as a major occupation and martial arts a favoured sport. The western side of the North East is connected to the eastern part of the Indian subcontinent by a narrow land corridor, sometimes referred to as the Siliguri Neck or "Chicken's Neck" of only 22 kms. The eight states that comprise the region reflect ecological and cultural contrasts between the hills and the plains; there are also significant elements of continuity. The economy of NER has got its definite identity due to its peculiar physical, economic and socio-cultural characteristics. It is no doubt to say that the NER will be more benefited. *Now, question arises—do the people of NER want to be benefited? If so, how to? There are so many challenges.*

Challenges: To develop border trade there are so many barriers that should be overcome first. Some of these are given below. In recent times many countries have experienced upsurge among different groups. In NER the expenditure to control insurgency has been increasing day by day. But ironically along with the expenditure to control insurgency, insurgency has been increasing by leaps and bounds. Recently, in an NEC published paper a detailed account of expenditure is presented. This paper of expenditure is outside the budget of Defence Ministry and seven State Governments. After so much expenditure made for security purpose, bomb in Chief Minister's convoy, kidnapping of bureaucrats, bombs in buses are regular features. If anything serious happens, the Chief Ministers of this region make the lame excuse that is no sufficient Central forces in the region and also there may be a role of third party and the ISI. But, in the last six years, in NER, the Central Government spent an additional amount of ₹ 1,000 crore for deployment of police forces. After spending such huge amount of money, the condition of the region is no better.

Exploiting the socio-economic problems of the region, various divisive forces raised their ugly heads under the banner of regionalism to gain the support of the mass people. But sometimes their activities cause a serious threat to the unity and integrity of the nation. The problem becomes more serious as the governments of the concerned states of the NER had to spend huge sums of money, allotted for development activities. As a result, the economy of the region worsened further.

Expenditure to Control Insurgency: In NER the expenditure to control insurgency has been increasing day by day. But ironically along with the expenditure to control insurgency, insurgency has been increasing by leaps and bounds. Recently, in an NEC published paper a detailed account of expenditure is presented. This paper of expenditure is outside the budget of Defence Ministry and seven State Governments. In the last six years, in NER, the Central Government spent an additional amount of 1,000 crore for deployment of police forces. After spending such huge amount of money, the condition of the region is no-better.

Table 27.1: Expenditure in Security Arrangement of Police Force in North East Region

(Rs. in Crores)

Year *State*	*1997-98*	*1998-99*	*1999-00*	*2000-01*	*2001-02*	*2002-03*	*Total*
ANP	–	–	–	1.00	1.90	0.95	3.85
ASM	131.91	78.86	52.17	63.97	92.86	68.01	487.78
MNP	–	19.43	3.44	14.18	4.00	7.64	48.69
MGH	–	–	–	3.21	0.60	8.35	12.16
NGN	–	35.61	17.88	7.50	12.71	22.42	96.12
TRP	–	28.55	17.53	15.00	27.70	29.85	118.63

Source: *The Ananda Bazar Patrika*, 28th November, 2003.

During the period 1997-2003, the states of NER have sanctioned crores of rupees in their budget. Side by side an amount of Rs. 767 crores of (Table 27.1) they have spent for police security out of the enhanced amount of Rs. 1,000 crore sanctioned by the Central Government. Among these seven states, Assam having an expenditure amounting Rs. 487.8 crore, Tripura having Rs. 118 crore and Nagaland having Rs. 96 crore are at the top of the list. For the modernisation of police force another Rs. 278 crore has been spent. In this sphere also these three states top the list. The amounts spent are Rs. 103 crore, Rs. 46 crores and Rs. 39 crore respectively. Unless we bring back peace and security to the region, we shall stay far behind the rest of the country in the match towards development and prosperity.

In NER the expenditure to control insurgency has been increasing day by day. But ironically along with the expenditure to control insurgency, insurgency has been increasing by leaps and bounds. During the period of seven years (1997-2003) the states of NER have sanctioned crores of rupees in their budget. Side by side an amount of Rs. 767 crore they have spent for police security out of the enhanced amount of Rs. 1,000 crore sanctioned by the Central Government. Among these seven states, Assam having an expenditure amounting to Rs. 487.8 crore, Tripura having Rs. 118 crore and Nagaland having Rs. 96 crore are at the top of the list. For the modernisation of police force another Rs. 278 crore has been spent. In this sphere also Assam is on the top of the list along with the states of Tripura and Nagaland. The amounts spent for these states is Rs. 103 crore, Rs. 46 crore and Rs. 39 crore respectively. According to an official communiqué of the Home Ministry in the last 12 years only in the state of Assam, 1378 persons have been killed and 178 security personnel too have been murdered. This governmental information made it clear that despite the huge expenditure normalcy cannot be brought in the region. Here both the Central and the State Governments are a great failure (Dutta and Mandal, 2011) and ultimately affected the over all socio-economic development of the region.

Infrastructure: Inadequate and poor infrastructure, inhospitable terrain and a comparatively late start in the development process are some of the reasons for economic backwardness of the region. However, the NER has certain strengths in different angles to achieve economic development in easy way. From the geo-political angle, the NER is located in a strategic location as it is bounded by these several foreign countries. Naturally, it has got both advantages and disadvantages due to its location. So far advantages are concerned it is connected with the South-East Asian countries mainly China, Myanmar, Bhutan, Bangladesh, Malaysia, Thailand, Philippines, Cambodia and Indonesia etc. where almost half of the world's population live. There is no doubt that this vast population could have great advantage for establishing any kind of trade and commerce. But the vary geographical condition basically the rivers and mountains of the country stand as a barrier and create geo-political tensions which ultimately act as most disadvantageous factors in creating a conducive atmosphere in the path of developing trade relation among those countries. But in the recent developments in the field of communication and information technology, some visible changes are taking place. Now, the NER felt the need of the hour regarding the modern facilities of lives. They have realised that in order to develop the economy of the nation, the border trade could be an effective solution. Border trade would help to a great extent in the field of economic development and also the route between production points of India to the northern district of Myanmar *via* North East region is economically viable as it is much shorter than sea route.

Corruption and its Impact: In India, corruption attacks the fundamental values of human dignity and political equality of the people and hence there is a pressing need to formulate a fundamental human right to corruption-free service. Corruption affects India at all levels of governmental decision-making and in the distribution of state largesse. India is ranked 72nd out of 91 countries in the Corruption Perception Index, 2001, prepared by Transparency International (TI). India's experience with corruption has shown that laws, rules, regulations, procedures and methods of transaction of government business, however sound and excellent they are, cannot by themselves ensure effective and transparent administration if the political and administrative leadership that is entrusted with their enforcement fails to do so and abuses its powers for personal gain. The states of NER are no exception to it and badly affected by corruption in all spheres of life. Perhaps the corruption at all levels is the one of the main causes of the region's backwardness.

3. Exportability and Potentialities of Border of the North East India

The North Eastern Region (NER) is at the periphery of the National Geography but nearer to trans-border countries. The regional economy is embedded in the national economy. World Development Report, 2009 has documented that "openness and integration are most beneficial for smaller or landlocked countries, whose access to world markets depends on neighbouring countries." Land lock character of the NER is often cited as one of the causes of its underdevelopment. As a corollary to the above observation of the Report, it can be said that since a country embodies its backward areas, opening of such areas, *ipso facto*, would benefit from openness and integration. Hence LEP would benefit the NER in trade and development.

In this context, it may be worthwhile to see what the mainline trade theory says. Heckscher-Ohlin theorem is one such theory which predicts that with trade, a region would specialise in the production of those goods which uses its most abundant factor and export the same. Accordingly, there would be shift in factor employment in different industries that will ultimately lead to factor price equalisation across trading countries. As a corollary to this theorem, in the context of a country like India, it can be hypothesised that as a State engages more and more in foreign trade, its factors of production will tend to shift from the import competing activities where factor returns are lower to the export activity where it is higher. This will result in higher development of those states, which align their production structure to foreign demand. In other words, it is envisaged that greater the degree of openness of a State economy, the greater its level of development.

Trade takes place in space and time. Geographically, North Eastern Region is ideally and advantageously located between the East of India and East/South-East Asia as it offers shorter distance and time for international trade. With the internet breaking physical boundaries, this advantage can only increase. The ASEAN countries too are looking towards Indian economy for trade and investment.

It is to be kept in view that distance is also a function of quality of means and modes of transportation. Distance over space and time improves with the improvement of roads, railways, river/water transport, air service, telecommunications, terminal and handling facilities at ports/ depots, customs warehouse etc. There are also the factors which determine the degree of openness of Indian States to trade. This is a weak point in the geography of the NER, which needs to be eliminated or bring to an optimal level in order to enable the NER to reap the benefits to LEP and openness.

One may now ask a question—how much open is the NER? When geographical boundaries are aggravated by conflicts within the region or between India and bordering countries involving State action, economic transaction costs tend to rise because of insecurity and risk to life, property and investment, and jurisdictional and political uncertainly. Conflicts and territorial disputes reduce openness. Since such conflicts/disputes are not uncommon in the NER, to that extent it hampers openness.

If one asks a question on the major items of exports from the NER, historically the answer is tea and jute. Within NER, Assam is the only state that has got a long history of exports, particularly, of tea and jute. State-wise data on exports and imports are not readily available. However, as per data of the Directorate General of Commercial Intelligence & Satiations (DGCIS), Assam's share in total exports within India in 2002-03 has been 0.19 per cent of India's total exports (against highest Maharashtra's 21.55%), the year in which India's share itself in the world export was only 0.8 per cent. This data show that the NER is on the periphery in the export space, and Assam itself is uncompetitive in a globalised world. However, tea can be both exported and imported. As per a source, India accounted for 28 per cent of world tea output and 15 per cent of world tea trade till 2002. Given the NER's tea production accounts for over 50 per cent of all India, the above forecast has great significance for the NER's tea industry.

The Government of India libralised the Foreign Direct Investment

(FDI) regime in the tea sector by allowing 100 per cent FDI in it including tea plantation with effect from 5th July, 2002. It is worthwhile to suggest here that the tea industry in the NER should come forward with proposals to set up Special Economic Zone (SEZ) for tea sector to reap the advantages of economics of scale and global benefits. It has to reduce unit cost of production through productivity gains, capacity building of small growers, streamlining export marketing channels, propagating "organic tea benefits" for health, improving infrastructure etc. All this is feasible through SEZ. This would help not only in the rejuvenation of the tea industry but also in boosting exports. It may be mentioned that according to Chinese experts, tea is tipped to replace coffee and cocoa as the most popular and healthy drink of the 21st century. The Indian tea industry should capitalise on this. The region has potentiality in other agri-products also. According to some estimates, NER is going to be the strongest market, within next 5 to 6 years, for horticulture, passion fruits, organic food, floriculture, orchids, aromatics, medicinal plants and herbs, and fishery products in the South-East Asian region. This region should gear up for this opportunity. Nothing, however, is an unmixed blessing. Open trade is a two-way traffic. Some traditional industry like Muga Silk would face threat from Tassar Silk coming form China. The local industry has to undergo improvement in technology and productivity.

Case for entire NER as a SEZ: Given that geographically (boundary, topography and climate) and economically (in terms of backwardness) the states of the NER share common characteristics/identities and also given that some export base already exists and new capacity building is coming up, it would be advisable to bring the entire NER into a single mega Special Economic Zone (SEZ) to actualise the vision of LEP. This would offer economies of large scale, opportunities for specialisation, attract FDI, minimise risk and uncertainties, increase the chances of exports of the produce thereby turning the NER into an 'export hub', and giving a brand new image to the region. This would also be in line with inclusive growth in geographical sense. Such a concept is also justified from the following point. After the launching of liberalisation policy, the onus of attracting capital and job opportunities lies on each State Government of the Country. But the states of the NER are too poor to attract capital individually. In the absence of mega SEZ, it may be surmised that the region may turn up as an EXIM-corridor rather than as an export-hub.

The potentialities of growth in India's trade with the neighbouring countries are immense. The North Eastern region can also be a partner of this emerging trade scenario. The major impediment towards the growth of Border trade with India's Eastern neighbours is found to be the absence due to lack of strong and efficient transport and communication networks between India and the countries of BCIM because of their geographical proximity to each other. To achieve such benefits from Border trade, the physical linkages among the trading partners in the form of Trans-National Highways, Railways, Waterways and Airways, wherever possible, are essential. A huge amount of capital expenditure would be necessary to build such infrastructural facilities. It is possible only through financial assistance from international financial institutions and the participation of Multinational Corporation.

The prosperous East and South-East Asian countries are attractive destinations for Indian exports. ASEAN markets provide big opportunities for India. Most of ASEAN populations have similar cultural background as in India. Affinity in cultural background will make Indian products acceptable and saleable in ASEAN markets. By the end of the year 2000 Indian exports to Indonesia, Malaysia and Singapore increased impressively (87% increase to Indonesia; 47% to Malaysia and 39% to Singapore). Export figures to other countries of the region have also shown market increase. Seeing such export figures India realised that East and South-East Asian region offered attractive destination for exports. Accordingly, India decided to diversify its export direction towards the East. This is another aspect of India's Look East Policy. It is hoped that spectacular success would be achieved in this endeavour. The NER has following resources.

1. Importer of Food Grains: The NER continues to be a net importer of food grains even for its own consumption. In spite of covering 7.8 per cent of the country's total geographical area, NER produces only 4.0 per cent of the country's total food grain production (as per 2002-03) while agriculture provides livelihood support to 70 per cent of the population of NER. Poverty is one of the serious problems in India. About 82 per cent of the total poor live in the countryside. As a consequence, little attention has been given on the urban poor since independence. Urban Poverty is a complex and multidimensional problem—not only entangled in economic obscurities but also with social welfare facets, which are left neglected. If serious attention is not paid to this underprivileged section, it is likely to pose a severe threat to the urban future of our economy (Dutta and Mandal, 2011).

2. Tea Industry: Tea is indigenous to India and is an area where the country can take a lot of pride. This is mainly because of its pre-eminence as a foreign exchange earner and its contributions to the country's GNP. In all aspects of tea production, consumption and export, India has emerged to be the world leader, mainly because it accounts for 31 per cent of global production. It is perhaps the only industry where India has retained its leadership over the last 150 years. Since independence tea production has grown over 250 per cent, while land area has just grown by 40 per cent. There has been a considerable increase in export too in the past few years. Total net foreign exchange earned per annum is around Rs. 1847 crore. The labour intensive tea industry directly employs over 1.1 million workers and generates income for another 10 million people approximately. Women constitute 50 per cent of the workforce. The tea industry of NER is the world's largest tea growing region having 16 per cent shares, and is the largest producer and exporter of tea in India (share 55%). The production of tea in the state of Assam was of the tune of 438.9 thousand tonnes during the period 2002-03 which increased to 454.1 thousand tonnes in 2003-04 but decreased to 443.3 thousand tonnes in 2004-05. However, Indian tea producers suffered the most in terms of drop in average tea auction price compared with other auction centres around the world between January to October 2002 (*Business Standard-Saturday,* January 11, 2003). The following table shows the picture of Tea industry in NER (Annual export) during the 5 year period (2000-04).

Table 27.1: Picture of Tea Industry

	2000	2001	2002	2003	2004
Production	846	854	826	857	830
Imports	14	17	22	7	25
Exports	207	183	201	173	190
Consumption	653	673	685	697	710

Source: Report of the Meeting of the Committee on Financial Sector Plan for NER, March 2006.

The Assam Government has decided to offload a majority stake, and, along with it, management control of Assam Tea Corporation (ATC). It has already invited expression of interest for the move. The divestment of ATC could be either through outright sale of a 74 per cent stake in the company, or through long-term lease of individual gardens. The state government, however, is believed to prefer the option of leasing out its gardens on a long-term basis, to selling off a controlling stake in the company. The corporation, created by taking over sick tea gardens in the 1970s, has, by now acquired a total of 14 tea gardens scattered over the six districts of the Brahmaputra and Barrak valleys. The combined capacity of the 14 gardens is around 8 million kgs. The Corporation also has about 10 factories to process tea leaves to produce black tea. According to the ATC annual report, average production over the past five years was between 6 to 6.5 million kgs. (*The Telegraph*—Monday, November 5, 2001).

3. Forest and Horticulture Products: North East India is famous for its exotic flora and fauna. The North East is one of the few bio-diversity zones in the world. It has immense flora and fauna. The world's annual trade on medicinal and aromatic oil/plants is of amount, over $60 billion. North East only supplies the raw-materials for many of the industries inside and outside the country. Out of the 925 varieties of orchids available in India, as many as over 650 can be grown in the region due to the favourable climatic conditions. In fact approximately 200 varieties are unique to this region and 60 per cent of these are ornamental in nature with high demand at the international markets. It is also ideally situated to produce spices, fruit and vegetables, flowers and herbs. Therefore, the North East India can emerge as an exporter of orchids, flowers, apple, orange, pineapples, spices, herbs etc. Some of the best and rare quality fruits and vegetables are produced in North East region for example, pineapples produced in North East are considered to be of the highest quality. Moreover, the forests of North East offer a vast array of aromatic plants which can be used in the aromatic industry for the manufacture of perfumes, incenses etc. In fact, there is an increasing international trend towards natural perfumes and room fresheners, shifting the focus from chemical ones. With proper planning there exists scope for establishing aromatic industry in the region. The climate of North East is also suitable for wide range of agro-horticultural as well as exotic floricultural products. With support services like training, tissue culture laboratories, production, finance, marketing tie-ups and farm to market roads, the region can produce both for domestic market and international market.

4. Tourism: The North East India is well known for its bio-diversities and heritage sites. Tawang in Arunachal Pradesh, Majuli, Kaziranga, Manas, Pabitara etc. in Assam can be developed further as tourist spots attracting more tourists from Europe and America. The multi-ethnic culture coupled with snow capped mountains and mighty Brahmaputra provides ideal setting for development of tourism. The name Tawang was given by Mera Lama in the seventeenth century. Tawang Monastery popularly known as the 'Tawang Gompa' is the second oldest Monastery in Asia more than 460 years old and the largest Monastery in the Himalayan region constructed by Lama Lodre Gyatso in 1681 AD. Tawang is the birth place of the sixth Dalai Lama, the only Indian so far who rose to the highest position in Gelupa Sect of Buddhism. If modern transport and communication system between the ASEAN countries and India along with the requisite infrastructural facilities are developed, then tourists visiting the ASEAN countries are likely to extend their tour programmes to the North East India, a few hundred miles away, for visiting its exotic bio-diversity and heritage sites. In 1996, an internationally reputed consultancy firm, Coopers and Lybrand submitted a report to the Government of Assam, which state that if the vast tourism potentials of the North East India are fully tapped and developed, within 20 years the region will receive more tourists than Singapore or Bangkok. Because almost all the Western and Japanese tourists visiting South-East Asian region would fly or drive a few hundred kilometres more to enjoy the scenic and cultural beauties of the North Eastern Region. This alone can boost the economy of the entire North East. But for this, road and airways between the South-East Asian region and India have to be developed. All this is possible only when the region can attract foreign direct investment complemented with domestic investment.

Recently, the Madrid-based World Tourism Organisation has evinced interest in promoting tourism in North East India and already identified Nagaland and Sikkim as its priorities. These United Nations-affiliated organisations will assist initially Nagaland in preparing a suitable tourism development programme with emphasis on employment, especially for women and other disadvantaged groups. The World Tourism Organisation has advised the Union Tourism Ministry to constitute a panel of consultants for framing suitable tourism development programmes in Nagaland and Sikkim in the areas of rural tourism, eco-tourism, social-tourism, architecture-tourism and historical tourism.

5. Medical Tourism: Now-a-days, India is in a position to give world class medical treatment at a low cost in comparison to the developed countries. India has advantage due to low cost of treatment, large number and high quality of Indian health care professionals, world class corporate hospitals (Apollo, Escorts), presence in niche areas. It attracts the patients through out the world especially the African and Middle East countries. Presently, patients from developing and developed countries are coming to receive treatment in Indian hospitals. Health tourists from Middle East, CIS countries, neighbouring countries, Non-Resident Indians in developed countries, foreigners from some developed countries are coming every-day. It is observed that 1,30,000 international patients came to India (2003) from South Asia, Africa, Gulf mainly for treatment in India. Again, many foreign patients seek treatment in traditional and alternative medicine (Unani, Ayurvedic, Herbal Treatment). The North Eastern region is the home of Ayurvedic and Herbal medicine. Ninty per cent herbal medicine of India is seen in this Himalayas belt. The State like Arunachal Pradesh where almost all of herbals are available has a bright scope to attract health tourists to give treatment at a low cost.

The Central Council for Research in Ayurveda and Siddha, Department of Ayush, Ministry of Health and Family Welfare, Government of India has initiated research programmes in this state from the early seventies. Accordingly, it has taken up a special survey tour programme to study the traditions, culture, customs, folk medical practices and the extent of availability and the quality of the medicinal plants in the State. Consequently, the Council has also initiated other important research programmes, such as clinical research programme in the State and established Regional Research Centre at Itanagar in May 1979. The status of the centre has been upgraded to Regional Research Institute with effect from 9 September, 1999.

6. Hydroelectricity: Due to its geographical location and its hilly terrain, the North East Region has an immense hydel potential to use the power of water to produce electricity. The region is of turbulent perennial several rivers, big and small having high gradients which possess enormous hydro-electric generation potential. Arunachal Pradesh, which possessing a huge hydro power potential, may alone fulfil 30 per cent of the existing demand of the country if the potential is fully harnessed. The National Hydroelectric Power Corporation (NHPC) has already undertaken to construct several mega multipurpose hydropower projects in upper reaches of the Brahmaputra river in Arunachal Pradesh, estimated to generate 25,000 MW of power. The projects included Subansiri upper, lower and middle; Dihang, Dibang and Siang hydro projects. In near future Arunachal Pradesh is expected to be made a Power Surplus State so that after fulfilling the home demand it would earn much revenue by exporting power to rest of the country. The hydro-power potentialities of the major five rivers in Arunachal Pradesh are shown in Table 27.2.

Therefore, Arunachal Pradesh, having untapped estimated hydro-power potential of 49,000 MW, may alone emerge as Power House of India when this potential is fully harnessed. The power sector will herald a golden era for the region once its hydel potential is harnessed to make it the power house of the country. A major part of this power can be exported to neighbouring countries. But, the development of these power

Table 27.2: Major river basins and their potentials

Name of the River/Basin	*Probable Hydro Potentials (MW)*			*Name of Districts*
	ROR	*Storage*	*Total*	
Kameng	3799	847	4646	W&E/Kameng
Subansiri	10141	5050	15191	U&L/Subansiri/Kurung Kumey
Siang	3557	11700	15257	W&E/Siang U/Siang
Dibang	5946	1282	7228	U & L/Dibang Valley
Lohit	3594	3075	6669	Lohit
Total Potential	**27037**	**21954**	**48991**	

Source: Department of Power, Government of Arunachal Pradesh, Itanagar.

projects requires huge investment and technological support, which is possible only through foreign direct investment. The WTO regime has given an opportunity to develop these power potentialities of the region.

7. Oil and Gas: Assam alone has an estimated 1,300 million tonnes of oil and 156 billion cubic metres of natural gas. Not even 40 per cent area has been explored. Assam, Mizoram, Tripura, Nagaland, Arunachal Pradesh and even Brahmaputra river have a number of oil bearing strata, still to be explored. Other mineral resources like Thorium, Limestone etc. are available in huge quantities.

Remarks and Suggestion: Though the Look East Policy (LEP) was announced in the last decade of the twentieth Century, it virtually became visible in the North Eastern Region (NER) of India only from October, 2004 with the launching of India-ASEAN car rally from Guwahati to Batam Island in Indonesia. The test of success or otherwise of a policy can be assessed in terms of public response to some criteria or attributes of the policy in an ordinal way.

LEP is a paradigm shift in India's foreign policy. It is an inclusive, outward-looking and trade-creating model of trade and development. The policy offers new opportunities of market access, specialisation, economies of scale, transfer of state-of-the-art knowledge and technology, sharing of development experiences and strategies. LEP would attract East Asian investors and traders to consider NER as a short-cut window to access vast Indian market for trade and investment. LEP has been heralded as the harbinger of change and development. It would act as a mechanism to integrate the economy of the NER with the global economy. However, some shortcomings of LEP have been noticeable. These are failure to involve Japan and build economic relationship with it, slow progress of implementation, apprehension of some sections of Indian industry and their nervousness for cheaper imports competing with Indian products etc.

LEP recognises that major East Asian economies are significantly competitive global producers having complementary with Indian economy in resources, capabilities and policies. The centre of economic gravity is East Asia and India's future economic fortune lies in it. However, unless infrastructure and connectivity is improved, governance is responsive and other reforms are undertaken up-front, then Indian entrepreneurs would be unable to take on global competition on an equal term. The government policies must address these problems to enable the enterprises to complete at local, regional and global levels. To accelerate the forces of economic integration and reap optimal benefits from openness, the following are essential institutions of global standard, infrastructure (including information technology with state-of-the-art technology), intervention at the State Level to correct the deficits, incentives (in appropriate quantity) to propel up entrepreneurs, and inclusiveness.

In the context of integration of NER, launching of Look East Policy is, no doubt, a necessary condition but by itself cannot be a sufficient condition. Besides, the aforesaid general suggestions, the following are pertinent for the North East India:

- Under LEP, the government should focus on free border trade, long term investment, wider economic partnership, and promotion of mutual commercial interests, tourism and culture to get win-win outcome.
- To woo trade and investment, the governments have to be trade and investment friendly by creating optimal environment, drawing up roadmap, action plan.
- To speed up the process of integration and for outreach the concerned Ministries and Departments of the Government of India (like DONER, Home, Civil Aviation etc.) should show physical visibility in the NER through regional/field offices at the State Capitals.
- Connectivity through direct flights to the country's capitals in which India has not made presence so far is established.
- The Government of India should encourage foreign diplomatic missions to extend diplomatic/consular jurisdiction by setting up consular offices, branch embassies in the NER to facilitate issuance of Visa.
- Government should take proactive initiative in fostering

cooperation with ASEAN.

- Setting up of cross border facilities (including visas), mutual recognition of driving licence, vehicle permits etc.
- Ministry of Finance and the RBI should expand banking facility with foreign exchange dealings in all the custom points. Custom warehouses, testing facilities etc. should be setup/expanded for better trade facilitation. Foreign exchange dealers, currency changers (vendors) from local areas should be encouraged for due registration.
- Branches of EXIM Bank, Export Credit and Guarantee Corporation (ECGC) etc. should be set up in all the State Capitals.
- MNCs including Indian MNCs should be encouraged to widen and deepen their presence in the NER to avail emerging opportunities from LEP.
- All-India Trade & Commerce Associations should make their visibility by setting up their regional branches.
- Associations of Foreign exchange dealers, currency changers, exporters, importers, trans-border entrepreneurs should be encouraged.
- For entrepreneurial capacity building, trans-border entrepreneurial institutes should be set up. Asian language departments should be set up at the Universities/institutes of the NER and scholarships/stipends should be given to learn the same, also courses on Asian economy may be introduced.
- Overland road connectivity should be improved on both sides of the border.
- The entire NER should be recognised/served as a SEZ. Set up SEZ offices at the Indo-Myanmar border for resource-based industries like newsprint, wood and its products, agriculture and food processing.

NOTES

1. APJ Abdul Kalam, His Excellency the President of India, delivered the Convocation Address on the 2nd Convocation of Nagaland University, Kohima on Thursday, 15th March, 2007.
2. Office of the Economic Adviser (2006-07): *Handbook of Industrial Policy and Statistics*, Government of India, New Delhi.

3. *Arunachal Front*, Vol. 17, No. 1888, March 7, 2009.
4. *The Statesman*, 30th July, 2004, Kolkata.
5. *The Assam Tribune*, 26th October, 2004.
7. *The Ananda Bazar Patrika*, 28th November, 2003.
8. *www.economywatch.com/.../indo-china-trade-relations*

REFERENCES

Chattopadhyay, A. and Roy, T.K. (2005): "Are Urban Poor Doing Better than their Rural Counterpart in India? A Study of Fertility, Family Planning and Health", *Demography India*, Vol. 34(2): 299-312.

Dubey, Muchkund (2007): "SAARC and South Asian Economic Integration", *EPW*, Vol. XII, No. 14 April 7-13, Mumbai.

Dutta, P.C. and Mandal, R.K. (2011): *Growth, Inequality and Globalisation*, Kalpaz Publications, New Delhi.

Goswami, H. and J.K. Gogoi (2003): "Regional Cooperation between China, Myanmar, Bangladesh and India through bilateral Trade: Impact on North East India", *Assam Economic Journal,* Vol. XVI, Dibrugarh.

Government of India, Ministry of Commerce & Industry (Department of Commerce) *Annual Reports* (various years).

Jha, Veena (ed.) (2006): *India and Doha Work Programme: Opportunities and Challenges*, UNCTAD, MacMillan India Ltd.

Lama P. Mahendra (2003): "NE Region and South Asia Growth Quadrangles: Opportunities and Growth Prospects", in *Gangtok Times*, September 11. (Accessed from www.gangtoktimes .com)

Mandal, R.K. (2005): "Arunachal Pradesh as an Emerging Power House", *Journal of Global Economy*, Vol.1, No.4, October-December, Mumbai.

Majumdar, Chandrika Basu (2007): "Border Trade and Border Inhabitants with Special Reference to Tripura", *Journal of North East India Council for Social Science Research*, Vol. 31:1, April, Shillong.

28

Economic Integration between India and ASEAN through North Eastern Region

Issues and Challenges

Anjali Biswas

Introduction

The then President of India, Pranab Mukherjee, arriving to Arunachal Pradesh in his 2 days visit addressed the members in the State Assembly at Naharlagun in the special session today and said Arunachal Pradesh is an integral and important part of North East region of India and a core stakeholder in India's Look East foreign policy. India has long standing civilisation bonds with its neighbours in the South and South-East Asia as well as East Asia.

The North East of India provides a natural bridge between us and South-East Asia. The essential philosophy of our Look East Policy is that India must find its destiny by linking itself more and more with its Asian partners and the rest of the world. We seek to make our neighbours partners in our development.

We believe that India's future and our own best economic interests are served by closer integration with Asia. He also said, there is a little time to be lost. Considering the huge pool of natural resources and the quality of its human resources, the North East of India has the potential of being an important investment destination and a centre for trade and business.

We must harness the opportunities that are emerging from the rise of Asia and India's growing economic integration with the region. No longer should this State be considered remote. The Central and State Governments should together rapidly build the infrastructure linkage and connectivity with the rest of India that is required and this legislature and the people of Arunachal Pradesh should extend every assistance possible to this venture (*The Arunachal Pioneer*, Saturday, November 30, 2013, Vol. II, No. 092).

Though the Look East Policy (LEP) was announced in the last decade of the twentieth century, it virtually became visible in the North Eastern Region (NER) of India only from October 2004 with the launching of India-ASEAN car rally from Guwahati to Batam Island in Indonesia. The test of success or otherwise of a policy can be assessed in terms of public response to some criteria or attributes of the policy in an ordinal way.

LEP is a paradigm shift in India's foreign policy. It is an inclusive, outward-looking and trade-creating model of trade and development. The policy offers new opportunities of market access, specialisation, economies of scale, transfer of state-of-the-art knowledge and technology, sharing of development experiences and strategies. LEP would attract East Asian investors and traders to consider NER as a short-cut window to access vast Indian market for trade and investment. LEP has been heralded as the harbinger of change and development. It would act as a mechanism to integrate the economy of the NER with the global economy. However, some shortcomings of LEP have been noticeable. These are failure to involve Japan and build economic relationship with it, slow progress of implementation, apprehension of some sections of Indian industry and their nervousness for cheaper imports competing with Indian products etc.

LEP recognises that major East Asian economies are significantly competitive global producers having complementary with Indian economy in resources, capabilities and policies. The centre of economic gravity is East Asia and India's future economic fortune lies in it. However, unless infrastructure and connectivity is improved, governance is responsive and other reforms are undertaken up-front, then Indian entrepreneurs would be unable to take on global competition on an equal term. The government policies must address these problems to enable the enterprises to complete at local, regional and global levels. To accelerate the forces of economic integration and reap optimal benefits from openness, the followings are essential: institutions of global standard, infrastructure (including information technology with state-of-the-art technology), intervention at the State Level to correct the deficits, incentives (in appropriate quantity) to propel up entrepreneurs, and inclusiveness.

With the emergence of globalisation, the need for economic integration has been realised by the international communities and lately by the Less Developed Countries (LDCs). Most of the countries both developed and less developed, have reoriented their development strategies to improve their growth performance by integrating their economies with the world economy (Singh, 2008). In this process, India has experienced some significant changes and the country is identified as one of the fastest growing economies in the world. In this direction, India's Look East Policy is worth mentioning. Under this policy, India seeks economic cooperation with the ASEAN and its neighbouring countries through its North Eastern Region (NER). In this background, North East India (NEI) plays an important role and the region can serve as the bridge between the country's economy and the ASEAN due to racial affinity (Das and Thomas, 2005), cultural and social similarities (Mero, 2005), and more importantly geographical location. Since India's NER is in the strategic location to link the country with ASEAN, a reference of this region is of utmost importance while studying India's economic integration with the ASEAN. The LEP has passed two phases, the first phase from 1992 to October 2003; while the second phase has started from November 2004. In **the first phase** India sought trade, political cooperation and institutional links with ASEAN (*viz.* Indonesia, Malaysia, Philippines, Singapore, Thailand, Brunei, Darussalam, Vietnam, Laos, Myanmar and Cambodia). In October 2002, the first India-ASEAN business summit was held at Delhi, which was addressed by the then Prime Minister Atal Bihari Vajpayee. Since then, the summit became an annual affair. However, the policy could not make much head way during its first phase.

The second phase of LEP started with the India-ASEAN car rally (covering its nine countries other than Philippines) from Guwahati to Batam island in Indonesia covering about 8,000 km. road distance in 20 days during November-December 2004, aiming at promoting trade, investment and tourism and culture. The rally was ceremoniously flagged off by Prime Minister Dr. Manmohan Singh on 22nd November, 2004 at Guwahati. The rally has demonstrated not only the feasibility of direct physical connectivity but also the keenness towards India as there were over 250 participants from the ASEAN countries and 3 teams from India. LEP was thus successful in its attraction. It is worthwhile to briefly take stock of some important milestones in regard to ASEAN since the start of second phase of LEP. These are:

1. Signing of first framework for bilateral Free Trade Agreement (FTA) with Thailand in October 2003.
2. Comprehensive Economic Cooperation Agreement (CECA) with

Malaysia during Prime Minister's visit to Malaysia in December 2004.

3. Strategic Partnership Agreement with Indonesia signed in November 2005.
4. Process of bilateral agreements with Myanmar since 2004.
5. CECA with Singapore signed on 29th June, 2005, came into force from 1st August, 2005.
6. India has constructed some major projects in Cambodia.
7. Several bilateral agreements with Laos.
8. A number of bilateral treaties and agreements with Vietnam.

Little Descriptions about NER: The North East Region (NER) of India constitutes the states of Arunachal Pradesh, Assam, Manipur, Meghalaya, Mizoram, Nagaland, Sikkim and Tripura. Flanked by hills and with the mighty Brahmaputra river slashing a central path between its north and south, the NER is bounded by mostly by the international boundaries. Arunachal Pradesh lies to its north and Sikkim a little away in the North West bordering China and Bhutan. Bangladesh and Myanmar lie to its south-west and east. The torrential Brahmaputra river deposits its rich alluvial silt along the banks of the plains of Assam. Tropical rain forest, rich in flora and fauna, spread their arms across Arunachal Pradesh into Assam. The state of Assam is a land where Tea is the most powerful industry, handicrafts as a major occupation and martial arts a favoured sport. The Western side of the North East is connected to the eastern part of the Indian subcontinent by a narrow land corridor, only 22 kms, sometimes referred to as the Siliguri Neck or "Chicken's Neck". The eight states that comprise the region reflect ecological and cultural contrasts between the hills and the plains; there are also significant elements of continuity. The economy of NER has got its definite identity due to its peculiar physical, economic and socio-cultural characteristics. The map of NER is shown in Map 28.1.

Again the length of border with neighbouring countries are shown in Table 28.1.

This chapter tries to attempt (1) to focus on economic integration through the border trade of NER in view of the need to forge closer diplomatic and economic ties with the larger markets in the fast developing ASEAN economies, (2) to analyse the role of NER in the integration process highlighting its challenges that might hinder this integration process and suggestions with conclusion follows.

Map 28.1: India—North East Zone Map.

Economic Integration Through the Border Trade of NER

Association of South-East Asian Nations (ASEAN) and its neighbouring countries have become the largest market and one of the fastest growing economies in the world. The significant proportion of India's foreign trade is with the ASEAN nations and the country still can get benefit more by integrating with region. The very necessity to have trade relations with this region is realised in the recent past.

Back Ground of the Study

When we talk of the economic development in any region, the trade and commerce appear first in the scene. An effort to economic development without the growth of trade is an illusive agenda in the era of globalisation and at the same time, globalisation emanates as cross-border trade.

Table 28.1: Length of the Border Land Share between NEI and Neighbouring Countries

Border	*With States*	*kms*	*Total*
NEI-Myanmar	Mizoram	368	1450
	Manipur	352	
	Nagaland	280	
	Arunachal Pradesh	450	
NEI-China	Arunachal Pradesh	1000	*1000
	Sikkim	–	
NEI-Bhutan	Arunachal Pradesh	200	*650
	Assam	450	
	Sikkim	–	
NEI-Bangladesh	Assam	350	1500
	Meghalaya	400	
	Tripura	400	
	Mizoram	350	
NEI-Nepal	Sikkim	–	–
Grand Total		–	***4600**

* The area in kms is excluded from Sikkim's share Including Sikkim boundary share with five foreign countries is approximately 5000 kms.

Source: Yojana, 2007, December.

Economic development does not satisfy only with the rich natural resources, it concerns mainly with the efficient and fuller utilisation of the resources. Very often we have talked a lot about the geographical isolation of the NEI, which has resulted in its economic backwardness and its alienation from the mainstream India (Singha and Patikar, 2008). Now, a time has come to turn this geographical isolation into an economic opportunity. Cross-border trade can become an engine to economic growth process in the country, particularly in this region.

With the launching of India's economic liberalisation programme in 1991, Association of South-East Asian Nations (ASEAN) came to be identified as being pivotal to India's policy in the Asia-Pacific region. ASEAN also decided to expand its membership to include all countries which are geographically part of South-East Asia. A quantum jump in Indo-ASEAN relations came with the effort to forge closer links with the South-East Asian countries after 1991. This period saw the beginning of its Look East Policy, which was intended to reach out to the countries of East and South-East Asia which had been neglected by India in spite of cultural, religious, geographical proximity and historical links (Wayfarer, 2007).

India's desire to cooperate with ASEAN is reflected in the Look East Policy. It began with the bilateral trade agreement between India and Myanmar through Moreh (Manipur) and Tamu (Myanmar), which was signed on 21st January, 1994. The actual follow up action of trade was formally opened by signing a Memorandum of Understanding (MoU) between the Minister of State of Commerce, Government of India, P. Chidambaram and Myanmar counterpart Lt. General Tunkyi, the Minister of Trade, Government of Myanmar (Khathing, 2005). It is the first step of India's long cherished Look East Policy particularly for NEI, and this route (Moreh-Tamu) is the most convenient for the purpose. It logically signifies the route through Nagaland, i.e. National Highway 39 (NH 39), which goes from Dimapur to Moreh. Of all the individual countries in ASEAN, Myanmar is the only country that shares 1450 km (Singha and Patikar, 2008) long border with North Eastern part of India. In fact, the NEI shares boundary with Myanmar, the only member country of ASEAN.

Most of the things coming through formal and informal trade from Myanmar are the third country origin like, Thailand, Singapore, China, Malaysia, Korea, Japan, Hong Kong etc. (Das, 2000; Bezbaruah, 2007) and basically smuggled-in at large scale (Das, 2000). The same view point was also being advocated by several other scholars in the past, *e.g.* (Sen, *et al.*, 2004; Mero, 2005; Das and Thomas, 2005; Singh, 2007; Singh, 2008; Singha and Patikar, 2008). Myanmar is strategically an important country in the overall Indo-ASEAN relationship and can serve as a gateway to ASEAN. Likewise, we can say that the border trade with ASEAN through NER has a significant role in the Indo-ASEAN trade relation. The scope and density of relations between India and ASEAN has been steadily rising (Sen *et al.,* 2004). The social, cultural, religious and ethnic similarities among the populations of NER across the border can make strong ties between India and ASEAN countries. In this respect, it can be said that Nagaland has the privilege and enjoys special status in the cross border trade despite of being a smaller state and sharing lowest international boundary with Myanmar. Nagaland is either directly or indirectly an important contributor to border trade hype with Myanmar and other ASEAN countries. This is mainly because of its comparative advantage earned from its geographical location and other human and natural resources.

The Bilateral trade between India and Myanmar in 2007-08 was registered $1 billion, which has grown nearly eight-fold in recent years. In the imports from Myanmar, natural gas, teak woods, beams are main items while India exports to that the pharmaceutical products, cereals, electronic and electrical equipments and automobiles etc. (Koppuzha, 2008). Above all there exists, a brisk trading in narcotics like heroine, brown sugar, raw opium, charas etc., and high value low weight contrabands like gold, silver, rubies, jade, etc., which are smuggled in all along the Myanmar borders (Das, 2000).

Informal Trade: Almost the entire informal export from Indian side originates from Uttar Pradesh, Delhi, Haryana, Punjab region, and ends up in different parts of Myanmar extending to as far as Yangon. Cotton yams, which used to be exported through both formal and informal channels, travelled further as this item originated from Gujarat in western India and ended up not just in Myanmar but even in China. As for informal imports, excepting the farm products such as animals, beans and pulses and precious stones such as jade and ruby which originates in Myanmar, everything else comes from a third country which is either China or some ASEAN Countries or South Korea or Japan. While the imported precious stones usually go well beyond the North Eastern region to markets in the rest of India, the other items are more or less absorbed by consumers in the region. A few items like Chinese and Korean blankets find their way to markets in the neighbouring state of West Bengal tool. All the trade between NEI and Myanmar mainly flows through unofficial channels. Big operators from Aizawl, Imphal, Kohima, Silchar, Guwahati and Shillong work through the local agents at the different trade centres like Moreh, Champhai, Lungwa etc., along the Myanmar borders of the region (Das, 2000).

Need and Scope of Economic Integration: The so-called restrictive regime in 1930s created a situation in the international business world whereby export and import was restricted due to the tariff war. Such countries imposed tariff on its imports and retaliatory tariff imposed by other countries reduced their exports (Singha and Patikar, 2008). This process led to a situation where no country was in the position to reduce the tariff unilaterally and thereby free movement of capital, equipment, technology, resources etc. across the nations were strictly prohibited. This situation was not to the benefit of any nation and hindered their economic integration progress.

Aftermath of restrictive tariff regime (1930s), there was a need for multilateral tariff cut for the international business to restart and such idea ultimately materialised in the form of globalisation emerged with the establishment of GATT and subsequently WTO in 1995.[2] The economic integration has been adopted as a strategy for development in different parts of the world in the 1980s following the formation of single market by the European Union and NAFTA by the North American Countries (Mukhopadhyay *et al.*, 2008). As a result of which every country gets a scope to trade internationally and can be mutually benefited by matching of the complementarities in their resource bases. In this sense, economic integration or cooperation amongst the nations becomes indispensable and India is no exception to this (Singha and Patikar, 2008). By and large, the process of global economic integration has proved to be beneficial for most countries and the countries that have failed to integrate appear to have been left behind (Bezbaruah, 2007).

Why the Economic Integration: Market integration leads to both **trade creation** i.e., the emergence of new trade and industry, and **trade destruction**, i.e. the exit of inefficient activities due to competition from more efficient competitors from the integrating countries. This process stimulates specialisation depending on the respective regions' comparative advantage and eventually higher growth and welfare through economies of scale resulting from a larger market linkage (Sarma, 2007). As a result of which, the Indo-ASEAN two-way trade grew 30 per cent from $ 7.6 billion in 1999 to $ 10 billion in 2002. ASEAN's trade to India is still at a very low level, accounting for only 0.9 per cent of ASEAN's global trade in 2002, while India's trade to ASEAN countries still hovers around 7 per cent of its global trade. The volume of trade is still small, considering the vast potential for trade that exists among the countries of over 1.5 billion people, and it is hoped the target of $ 30 billion will be reached by 2010 (Mero, 2005).

In the regional integration, the growth dynamics of different countries reinforces one another, and a conspicuous process of integration of production, trade and investment takes place among the member countries. For example, though it is not from the same bloc, economic strength of the four Asian Tigers (Taiwan, South Korea, Hong Kong and Singapore) and China on the one hand may attract production, markets and demand for labour force from the neighbouring countries. While, on the other hand, the swift rise in those countries' imports and exports may lead to growth in trade and investment as well as in wage and welfare in the neighbouring countries. China is likely to be the largest trading partner of India replacing USA. Bilateral trade between India and China was around $ 30 billion in the year 2007 and expected to be $ 60 billion in 2010. In the words of Yumnam (2005), the time has now come for a genuine Regional Trading Arrangements (RTA), genuine from the angle of economies and not security, for a real trans-border trading relationship with South-East Asia.

India is now one of the four summit level partners of ASEAN, the other three being China, Japan, South Korea (ASEAN + 4). It has signed a free trade agreement (FTA) each with Thailand and Singapore. There are plans to do so with Indonesia, Malaysia and Brunei by 2011 and with the remaining ASEAN countries—the Philippines, Cambodia, Laos, Myanmar and Vietnam by 2016. Furthermore, Former Prime Minister Dr. Manmohan Singh made a proposal at the third ASEAN-India Summit for an Asia economic community including ASEAN + 4 (Sarma, 2007). The real drivers of economic integration, however, are the emergence of new markets, the erosion of old markets, shifts in public policies that reduce barriers of exchange, trends in corporate strategy and industrial organisation, the ongoing improvement of transportation and communications infrastructure, and technological change.

The economic liberalisation has provided a better scope for sustaining and accelerating growth. In the recent past, India has recorded impressive economic growth. As a matter of fact, India ranks the fourth largest economy in the world now, It is also estimated by the World Investment Report 2000, that by 2020, the six largest world economies will be US plus five Asian; namely China, Japan, India, Indonesia and North Korea. In order to build-up on its economic growth, Government of India has specified some targets which are to be accomplished by the year 2020. The targets are:

(a) a targeted approach to bring millions of families above the poverty line;
(b) generation of nearly ten millions of new employment opportunities per annum, especially for those in the lower income groups;
(c) massive investment in power generation, telecommunication, and other physical and social infrastructure;
(d) accelerate the acquisition of technology capabilities to raise the productivity in agriculture, industry and services; and
(e) to become more important player in the world economy in terms of both trade and investment.

These targets cannot be fulfilled without linking India's economy with the global market. It is the liberalisation of trade which will open up new vistas for export of goods, while increasing pressures on India's domestic industry to cope with competition from imports, especially from China. Future opportunities for manufactured exports will be focused on the high end of the technology chain, computerised, customised manufacturing processes and sophisticated engineering and capital goods, areas in which India has not yet strongly positioned itself internationally. Global trade in agricultural products is expected to grow rapidly in near future. And, India has the ability to become a major exporter of agricultural commodities. But this will depend most on its ability to improve crop quality and productivity, while lowering costs to international levels, and that is possible through import of much needed sophisticated tools, equipments, and machineries.

To make India's Vision 2020 a reality, the country needs to widen further the market for domestic businesses as well as import must needed capital equipment and technical know-how through economic cooperation with other countries in general and ASEAN nations in particular. The region-wise India's foreign trade evident from the (Table 28.2) below also clearly justified the economic significance of India's trade tie with the ASEAN.

Table 28.2: Direction of India's Foreign Trade

Import	*Export*
By Region % Share	By Region % Share
1. Asia and ASEAN 35.22	1. Asia and ASEAN 48.46
2. Europe 21.17	2. Europe 24.06
3. America 7.78	3. America 20.61

Source: Chronicle, April Issue 2008, Vol. XVII, No.10.

It is revealed from Table 28.2 that India's export and import to Asian and ASEAN region accounts for 48.46 and 35.22 per cent respectively as against the 24.06 and 21.17 per cent respectively with European region. While, India's trade with American region represents only 20.61 and 7.78 per cent export and import respectively. This clearly shows that Indo-ASEAN trade occupies higher status and has become the focal point.

Challenges for Economic Integration through NER

(i) Stumbling Economic Sustainability: Unfortunately, many of the institutions for administering border trade are located outside the state of trading points, where the cross border trade does not operate. Two paradigms dominated in the Government of India's policy, *One,* relates to overstress on security/strategic consideration rather than on development efforts. The *other* relates to minimum intervention in traditional systems and institutions of the hill economy, which is what has led to their non-compatibility with the functioning of market system (Sarma, 2007). In the same manner, Yumnam (2005) observes that the Government of India sees the region (NEI) as a "Signaling Device" to monitor the movement of commodities and people, and an insurance against the perceived threat of Chinese dominance of the region.

India is seen as a good investment destination by Thai enterprises. Thailand ranks the third largest investor in India among ASEAN countries, after Singapore and Malaysia. Unfortunately, neither the Indian Government nor its diplomatic mission in Bangkok seems to be truly invested in projecting the country and its business and cultural interests in Thailand through strong visible programmes and sustained campaigns as done by the other big countries in the Asia-Pacific region.

Second, the ongoing authorised bilateral trade (Indo-Myanmar) between the two countries is mostly en-routed through Kolkata port and Chennai particularly for exporting conmmodities to Myanmar *via* Singapore and Thailand. The route is quite long and uneconomical. But this trade arrangement between the countries to and from Kolkata port and Chennai does not serve the interest of NEI. It is noting here that in the total volume of Indo-Myanmar international trade, formal border trade across the North East is virtually negligible. For instance, in 2002-03 formal border trade across the North East constituted only 1.05 per cent of India's export, 0.71 per cent of import and 0.79 per cent of volume of trade with Myanmar. As percentage of combined domestic income of the seven states of the North Eastern Region also this trade is virtually negligible (Bezbaruah, 2007). This idea of India's economic integration with ASEAN countries does not seem to serve the purpose of long cherished Look East Policy. In the real sense, the attempts and initiatives taken up so far for the region in the name of "Look East Policy" are slightly slipped off from the main track.

Again, besides conventional aged-old problems like basic physical infrastructures including road and communications, the development initiatives in the region lacks a well-articulated policy framework. Neither the State Governments of this region nor the people here are the keen enough to become a part of the broad national programme of the free movement of people and goods. The sense of isolation and regionalism (tribalism and separatist movement) retards the smooth flow of both people and goods to and from the region. The possible threat to culture and identity of the region is yet another barrier to free trade. The curiosity to preserve bio-diversities at any cost restricts the development of infrastructural facilities and other amenities necessary for the border trade to grow. The insurgency problem in the state has created an atmosphere of fear and anxiety in the minds of businessmen and potential investors, which in turn add as a restraining force to business growth and thereby the state opportunity is ceased.

More importantly, India's foreign trade policy towards Myanmar was driven by four motivations (Koppuzha, 2008). They are: (1) access to natural resources; (2) desire to expand Indian influence in South-East Asia; (3) combat insurgencies in NEI; and (4) balance against growing Chinese influence. The prevailing system of trade (Singh, 2007; Singh, 2008) between India and Myanmar does not make any significant headway towards the cross-border trade and the region's economy. It rather helps to smuggling and informal trade, not to the over all development of the NE India. It does not favour cross-border trade at all. Potential trading points at the Myanmar border have not been opened up. Even if we cannot assess the exact volume of trade with ASEAN through the border trade points, informal trade or smuggling has been taking place. Thus, while informal trade continues to be the mainstream of exchange of goods across Indo-Myanmar border, the formal trade has practically dried up. The reason for the slow volume of cross-border trade between India and Myanmar appears to lay in the similarity of resource base and production structure across the border (Das and Thomas, 2005).

(ii) Economic Sustainability by Informal Trade: It is estimated that the volume of informal trade is many times more than the formal trade and may exceed 5 per cent of the total GDP of all NE States combined. Most of the goods travel from Myanmar to India is through this hill region. Most of the manufactured and 269 consumer goods are also the products from China, Korea, Japan, and ASEAN countries (third countries). This process increases social welfare of the state and other NE sister states, but the situation is not so in case of the formal trade, or so called "Look East Policy". A brief sketch of informal trade coming through the trade points of North East states is also depicted in Table 28.3.

In the study of border trade, whether it is reciprocal or transit trade, the kind of trade being promoted is important. For instance, border trade benefits would accrue to the NEI from storage, customs and tourism,

Table 28.3: Informal Imports to North Eastern States from Myanmar in 1996

Items	*% of Total Value of Import*
Textiles (including blankets and garments)	19.87
Food and Beverages (including alcohol)	19.02
Animals (pigs to Mizoram)	2.40
Electronic Goods	9.79
Precious Stones and Gold	43.09
Miscellaneous	5.83
Total	**100.00**

Note: Narcotics and small arms etc. have not been taken into account although these are known to be traded across the border.

Source: Baruah (2000).

which are typical for such transit state (Singh, 2007). According to the study conducted by the Indian Institute of Foreign Trade (1995), it is estimated that the annual volume of cross-border trade took place in the North East India at three border towns of Moreh (Manipur), Champhai (Mizoram) and Lungwa-Yangyong (Nagaland). It is at around Rs. 2,200 crore, of which Moreh contributed the largest share of around Rs. 1,600 crore followed by Champhai around Rs. 500 crore and Lungwa around Rs. 100 crore (Singh, 2007). The volume of trade with Myanmar is likely to go up with the setting up of four border trade points at Pangsha, Avakhung, Mimi, Mollem in Nagaland. Kohima (the capital town of Nagaland) to Pangsha in Tuensang is approximately 300 km. and slightly less distance is found between Kohima to Avakhung in Phek district. Though the distance between Kohima and Lungwa in Mon district (approximately 400 km) is quite far, it is an important place for border trade because the people on both sides of the border are same Konyak tribe of Nagaland and they speak same dialect. These routes are considered to be convenient enough for cross-border trade. However, volume of informal trade bypassing these trade centres will still sustain and grow following the complexities of legal formalities to be observed while trading through those border trade points.

Have we assessed sustainable development in this process in this region? Even if we cannot ascertain exact quantity of trade volume, it is cleared from the above analysis that the volume of informal trade is much higher than the formal trade. Formal trade does not create any social welfare of the region because only 22 items have been included in the present trade agreement (Indo-Myanmar). More interestingly, the commodities included in the agreement are more or less available on the both side of the borders. Greater the stringent of legal trade formalities, higher will the volume of informal trade in this region. There is positive correlation between the informal trade and economic sustainability in this hill region. For example, if we purchase the commodities used in day-to-day life through informal trade are much cheaper than the Indian counterpart. This compels the people of this region to go for informal trade (formal trade is unnecessarily stringent) and generates sustainability. So, cross-border trade (informal trade) brought about by the globalisation creates social welfare of this hill region.

From the above discussion to find out the economic viability of trade through NER, we have to calculate some trade indices. Trade indices are used to measure different aspects of a country's participation in the world trade. Such indices are Trade Openness Index (TOI) measuring the degree of openness of a country, Commodity Concentration Index (CCI) and Revealed Comparative Advantage (RCA) measuring diversity and competitiveness of a country's export basket. However, each index being a summary measure has its own limitation and specific use. One must, therefore, be extremely careful in drawing policy conclusions from the values of these indices obtained in context of a given data set at hand.

For any developing country for which international trade is a critical element of its long term development strategy, or for a country entering international trade after long periods of protectionism almost isolation from the rest of the world, one important question that needs to address is, what should be the desirable pattern and composition of trade. The answer, of course, may vary depending upon the immediate target that the country under consideration wants to achieve through exports, in particular, and international trade in general. For example, if the top priority of a country to promote exports is to earn foreign exchange to finance imports of necessary intermediate goods, it is desirable to gain competitiveness and specialise in those manufacturing exports that are relatively less import intensive, so that net foreign exchange earned by them is relatively large. A point in case is India's comparative advantage in exports of gems and jewels. For decades, the shares of these goods in India's manufacturing exports have been quite high. But these exports, being import intensive, contribute relatively quite small amount to India's foreign exchange kitty. Thus, the market-driven efficient allocation of resources may not be a desirable one as far as the net foreign exchange earned through such resource allocation is concerned.

Suppose, the competitiveness of exports, however, can more systematically be captured through the Revealed Competitive Advantage

(RCA) defined by Balassa (1989). Construction of RCA involves two steps. First is the calculation of the Penetration Ratio (PR^k) for export of product-k by country-i's (India's) to destination-j defined as:

$$PR^k = \frac{\text{Country-i's (or India's) export of commodity-k to destination-j}}{\text{Total import of commodity-k by destination-j}} \qquad \ldots (1)$$

This ratio indicates how important for country-j is the country-i as a source of supply of product-k.

Then the RCA is calculated as: $RCA^k = \dfrac{PR^k}{X_i / X_{jw}}$ ... (2)

Where,

X_i = Country-i's total export to destination-j
X_{jw} = destination-j's total import from the world

Essentially, the denominator of (2) is the total market share of country-i across all export commodities in country-j.

Therefore, every index depends upon the availability and reliability of data obtained at hand. But in case of NER where the volume of export and import done in illegal way is greater than that in legal way. If the data is managed but it will be poor qualitative. As a result, it is not so easy to remark that how much benefit may be achieved from international trade through NER.

(iii) Impact of Bandh and Blockades on Trade and Commerce in NEI: Major National Highways, 39 and 53, have been ordered to be of four lanes. Rail linked are to be extended from Jiribam (bordering Silchar of Assam) to Imphal. Further, it is likely to be connected with Myanmar through Moreh (Manipur's border town) as a part of Trans Asian Rail to connect 28 nations. Unfortunately, these developmental activities are getting delayed, and even some are not being materialised because of insurgency problems and negligence from government's side too. These result to *bandh* and blockade in the region. These are the economic losses termed as social costs. This is nothing but a negative impacts generated by the *bandh* and violence. These problems are more or less same in all the states of NE India.

It is a matter of deep concern that despite *bandh* being declared as unconstitutional and illegal by the Supreme Court in 1997 and it is also supported by various High Courts including Gauhati High Court; the whole North East continues to suffer from this syndrome. Still, all the states have become the highest victim of bandh in the country. Bandh affects directly trade and commerce, daily wage earners and business establishments, and indirectly the development of the region in the long run.

A total amount of Rs. 1319.96 crore has been lost in Manipur between April 1, 2004 and January 31, 2007 due to *Bandhs* and Blockades.

In the case of Assam, from April 2001 to March 2002, there were nine statewide *bandhs*, 13 regional *bandhs*, and 36 district *bandhs*, according to an official source it is said that Assam state government losses an estimate of Rs. 900 crore annually because of *bandhs*.

There is an urgent need for more creative thinking on how to design for an inclusive growth along with stable and conflict free society. It is learnt that the security related violence is the most important problem at present and leads to most of the *bandh* and blockades in the region. An investor needs two basic things; they are feeling of security and profit from their investments. This can be perceived only when the law and order situation in the region is maintained.

Now, the question that arises in front of us is: how far the implementing agencies are sincere and honest. Why does *bandh* come up frequently in the region? Do governments, both Central and State work intentionally? Do the civil organisations, general public including undergrounds work with sincerity in their mind and activities? These are the some formulae for peace and progress in the region.

The law and order problem or *bandh* in the state cannot be solved unless the two Institutions, i.e., Government and general public work together sincerely. Many government employees are taking advantage of *bandh*, and their contribution to the economy is very minimal in the real sense. Ministers are rearing underground. Bureaucrats are putting their barrel on undergrounds, and undergrounds are blaming the government. The question of insurgency movement in NEI is only a political melodrama and exaggerated issue.

The amount of money spent on security of individuals like politicians, bureaucrats, both serving and retired compel the government to shift the limited resources which tantamount to heavy losses on the social security front related to health care, education etc. This is the cost of misplaced emphasis on "Politics of Fear". India as a while, insurgency has become a constant source of expenditure. The total amount of money spent merely on relief and rehabilitation, on the special paramilitary forces deployed for anti-insurgency operations in the country crosses Rs. 45,000 crore. This is at the opportunity cost forgone in the villages in terms of development of electricity and power, health care and education and availability of roads etc.

It has become a tradition of calling on bandh or strike for any reason, whether it is genuine or not. Joining hands with the undergrounds becomes an avenue in the region. Contract works and developmental projects in the region are being sold out to undergrounds by the Ministers and the bureaucrats. Civil societies, student organisations, and NGOs are being used as frontal organisation by the anti-social elements in the region. There are also a lot of inter-community conflicts and differences within the region itself due to various differences, and it leads to various *bandh* and strikes. More importantly, the violent attitude towards outsiders and the mentality of chasing outsiders out from the region create more unstable situation in the region now.

Development of road and communication should be taken as priority job for the government. The attitude of wait and watch policy should be avoided. By and large, *bandh* or blockade ultimately affects the region in the developmental process and directly affects to the daily wage earner.

(iv) Chhitmahal Problem: 'Chhitmahal' means the piece of land containing village(s) of a country stands inside in another country. India has 111 numbers Chhitmahals in Bangladesh and Bangladesh has 56 Chhitmahals in India. The inhabitants of the Chittmahals can freely move both the countries the rules and regulations whatever may be. The Nehru Agreement in 1958 and the Indira-Mujib Agreement in 1974 could not solve the Chhitmahal problems. The inhabitants can carry goods of the both countries, for which both the governments do not get the custom duty. This no doubt hampers the border trade.

Conclusion and Suggestions

On the critical issue of limiting free trade and economic growth, we find that globalisation and sustainable development are not polar opposites, as frequently depicted. Rather, both discourses share many common positions, notably, in relation to the role for business, nation states, and the acceptance of the diffusion of market relations around the world. At least the globalisation recognises the need for economic sustainability, and most proponents of sustainable development accept the essential rationale of the expanding global economy. In this sense, globalisation and sustainable development have evolved as two sides of a common vision of our future. Border trade agreement between India and Myanmar through NER was not accompanied by domestic economic reforms on the Indian side as expected in a normal Regional Trading Arrangements. India has also initiated and agreed to finance the entire Kaladan Multi-model Project, which aims to develop the Sittwe Port in Myanmar's south-west as well as waterways and highways along the Kaladan river to receive goods from India (Koppuzha, 2008). But, this project is basically meant for trading through the sea port connecting Kolkata and Sittwe in Myanmar, not for NER. Mostly the exports are shipped through the port of Kolkata and, and a large amount of Indian goods are en-routed to Myanmar *via* Singapore and Thailand (Singh and Goswami, 2000). It is also evident that some consumer durable items produced by India, *e.g.* readymade garments, ladies shawl are imported from the Tamu (Myanmar) by the North Eastern Sister States. These are brought through Kolkata and Chennai port by the Tamil traders of Moreh and Tamu. So, the development of region through border trade with ASEAN (Myanmar) needs institutional change to fit the global environment of cross-border trade. Economic sustainability will be there only when the trade policies like "Look East Policy" are framed with a definite vision.

It is evident from the above discussion that the border trade with ASEAN has not been in the right direction. As a matter of fact, the effort puts is disproportionate to the volume of trade. Under these circumstances, border trade cannot flourish on the desired lines. The existing policies and initiatives have not been very effective. It is urgently required to re-orient and re-look in to the existing policy framework. The government is required to have a strategic planning for making border trade a reality. NER being a key player in the border trade process has to be an integral component in the border trade planning process.

NEI can derive much benefit from India's Look East Policy but at the same time the region has to adopt proactive measure to boost up India's trade with ASEAN nations. In the NEI market rigidities should be removed by the individual state or collectively within each constituent and between them (Sarma, 2007). The mind set of the people needs to be changed in favour of free movement of people, goods and services not only within the country but also across the border. Last but not the least it can be said that the good fruits of border trade cannot be achieved without locating the challenges and its solutions.

NOTES

1. ASEAN is a union of South-East Asian Nations. Indonesia, Philippines, Malaysia, Singapore and Thailand constituted this association on 8th August, 1967. Brunei and Vietnam joined this association in 1984 and 1995 respectively. Laos and Myanmar joined in the same year in 1997. On 30th April, 1999 Cambodia also joined the association. At present, 10 countries are the members of ASEAN.
2. During the great depression in 1930s, the International trade was badly affected and various countries imposed import restrictions for safeguarding their economies. This resulted in a sharp decline in the world trade. In 1945, USA put forward many proposals for extending International trade and employment. On 30th October, 1947, 23 countries at Geneva signed an agreement related to tariffs imposed on trade. This agreement is known as General Agreement on Tariffs and Trade (GATT). It came into force on 1st January, 1948. On 12th December, 1995, GATT was abolished and replaced by World Trade Organisation (WTO), which came into existence on 1st January, 1996. India signed Dunkel Proposal on 15th April, 1994. The very proposal was signed by 124 countries and gave birth to WTO in 1995.

REFERENCES

Baruah, M.P. (2007): "Indo-Myanmar Border Trade: The Stakes for North East India", *Dialogue*, July-September, Vol. 9, No. 1 [Accessed on October 3, 2008 (file:///D:/www/index.shtml)]

Baruah, Srinath (2000): "Certain Observations on Informal Border Trade with Neighbouring Countries and Economic Prospect of North Eastern Region", Akanksha Publishing House, New Delhi.

Bryan, L. and. Farrell, D: (1996): *Market Unbound: Unleashing Global Capitalism*, John Wiley, New York.

Byrne, John and Glover, Leigh (2002): "A Common Future or Towards a Future Commons: Globalisation and Sustainable Development since UNCED", *International Review for Environmental Strategies*, 3 (1):5-25.

Chattopadhyay, A. and Roy, T.K. (2005): "Are Urban Poor Doing Better than their Rural Counterpart in India? A Study of Fertility, Family Planning and Health", *Demography India*, Vol. 34(2): 299-312.

Das, Gurudas (2000): "Trade Between the North Eastern Region and Neighbouring Countries: Status and Implications for Development", in Das, Gurudas and Purkayastha, R.K. (eds.), *Border Trade: North East India and Neighbouring Countries*, Akanksha Publishing House, New Delhi.

Das, Gurudas and Thomas, C.J. (2005), "Economy of Myanmar: Trends, Structure and Implications or Border Trade with India's North East", in Das, Gurudas *et al.* (eds.) *Indo-Myanmar Border Trade: Status, Problems and Potentials*, Akanksha Publishing House, New Delhi.

Dubey, Muchkund (2007): "SAARC and South Asian Economic Integration", *EPW*, Vol. XII, No. 14, April 7-13, Mumbai.

Dutta, P.C. and Mandal, R.K. (2011): *Growth, Inequality and Globalisation*, Kalpaz Publications, New Delhi.

Goswami, H. and J.K. Gogoi,(2003): "Regional Cooperation between China, Myanmar, Bangladesh and India through bilateral Trade: Impact on North East India", *Assam Economic Journal*, Vol. XVI, Dibrugarh.

Government of India, Ministry of Commerce & Industry (Department of Commerce) *Annual Reports* (various years).

Jha, Veena (ed.) (2006): *India and Doha Work Programme: Opportunities and Challenges*, UNCTAD, MacMillan India Ltd.

Khathing, J.S.R. (2005): "Indo-Myanmar Border Trade", in Das, Gurudas *et al.* (eds.) *Indo-Myanmar Border Trade: Status, Problems and Potentials*, Akanksha Publishing House, New Delhi.

Koppuzha, Ann (2008): "India's Myanmar Policy for Alternative Roadmap", *The Morung Express*, 29/08/09, Dimapur.

Lama, P. Mahendra (2003): "NE Region and South Asia Growth Quadrangles: Opportunities and Growth Prospects", in *Gangtok Times*, September 11. (Accessed from www.gangtoktimes.com)

Majumdar, Chandrika Basu (2007): "Border Trade and Border Inhabitants with Special Reference to Tripura", *Journal of North East India Council for Social Science Research*, Vol. 31:1, April, Shillong.

Mandal, R.K. (2005): "Arunachal Pradesh as an Emerging Power House", *Journal of Global Economy*, Vol. 1, No. 4, October-December, Mumbai.

Mero, M.K. (2005): "Indo-Myanmar Border Trade in the Light of India's Look East Policy", in Das, Gurudas *et al.* (eds.) *Indo-Myanmar Border Trade: Status, Problems and Potentials*, Akanksha Publishing House, New Delhi.

Ohmae, K. (1990): *The Borderless World: Power and Strategy in the Interlinked Economy*, Harper Business, New York.

Ohmae, K. (1995): *The End of the Nation State: The Rise of the Regional Economies*, Free Press, New York.

Sarma, Atul (2007): *North East as a Gateway to South-East Asia: Big Dream and Home Truths* in Borbora, S. and Gogoi, J.K. (eds.), *Development Issues in the North East in the Turn of the Century*, Papyrus Books, Guwahati.

Sen, Rahul, *et al.* (2004): "ASEAN-India Economic Relations: Current Status and Future Prospects," *Economic and Political Weekly*, Vol. XXXIX, No. 29, July 17-23.

Singh, S.B. and Goswami, S.N. (2000): "Potentiality of Border Trade between India and Myanmar", in Das, Gurudas and Purkayastha, R.K. (eds.), "*Border Trade: North East India and Neighbouring Countries*", Akanksha Publishing House, New Delhi.

Singh, T.B. (2007): "India's Border Trade with Its Neighbouring Countries with Special Reference to Myanmar", *Margin The Journal of Applied Economic Research*, 1(4).

—— (2008): "Indo-Myanmar Border Trade: Issues and Opportunities", in Singh, E.B. and Singh, K.J. (eds.), *Challenges to Economic Policy in Manipur,* Akanksha Publishing House, New Delhi.

Singha, Komol (2009): *Bandh* Syndrome and Its Impact on Trade Commerce in North East India, *Journal of Global Economy*, Vol. 5, No. 2, April-June, Mumbai.

The Arunachal Pioneer, Saturday, November 30, 2013, Vol. II, No. 092.

Thurow, L.C. (1999): "Building Wealth: The New Rules for Individuals, Companies, and Nations in a Knowledge-based Economy", Harper Information, New York.

Wayfarer, C.J. (2007): "Indo-ASEAN Relations on the Upswing", November 12, [Accessed on October 3, 2008 (http://w\vw.mernews.com/catFull.jsp.?articlelD=127680)]

Wildavsky, A. (1995): "But is it true? A Citizen's Guide to Environmental Health and Safety Issues", Harvard University Press, Cambridge, MA.

Yumnam, Amar (2005): "Indo-Myanmar Trade through Moreh: Status and Assessment in India", in Das, Gurudas *et al.* (eds.), *Indo-Myanmar Border Trade: Status, Problems and Potentials*, Akanksha Publishing House, New Delhi.

Index

365-days tourism destinations, 122–23

Above Poverty Line (APL), 179, 244, 266
Adult education, 334
Adult suffrage, 185, 187, 196
African Development Bank, 26
Agricultural
 activities, 190, 192
 commodities, 418
 development, 359
 labourers, 235, 267
 land, 190, 246
Agriculture University, 57
All India Anna Dravida Munnetra Kazhagam (AIADMK), 326
Allied activities, 11–12
All-India Trade & Commerce Associations, 406
Anaemia, 330, 357
Anchal Samitis, 43–44
Annual Credit Plans, 55
Apatani Plateau, 11, 13
Appropriate Technology, 17, 21–22
Aquaculture practices, 12
Aquatic resources, 3
Aqua-tourism, 12–13, 108
Architecture-tourism, 402
Arunachal Tourism Information Counters, 125
ASEAN countries, 383, 386–87, 391, 397, 402, 410, 414–17, 419–20
ASEAN Tourist Summit, 108
ASEAN-India Summit, 417
Asian economy, 406
Asia-Pacific Economic Co-operation, 391
Asia-Pacific region, 413, 419
Assam Co-operative Societies Act, 187
Assam Tea Corporation (ATC), 400–401
Assam Tribune, 30
Assessment tools, 202–3
Association of South-East Asian Nations (ASEAN), 383, 385–86, 391, 406, 408, 410, 412–14, 416–18, 420, 426
ATM facilities, 158
Autonomy, 154, 157, 235, 290
Awareness
 campaign, 21
 camps, 152, 167
 creation, 244, 282

Bad economics, 253
Balance of power, 243, 266
Bangladeshi migration, 36
Bank credit, 234, 281
Banking constraints, 202
Bargaining power, 46
 collective, 151
 intra-household, 271
Batadrava Development Block, 168
Below Poverty Line (BPL), 30, 32, 55, 57, 179–80, 191–92, 196, 261, 264
Beneficiaries, 4, 43, 56, 63, 83–89, 130, 132, 135, 199, 337
 abled, 84
 disabled, 86

earning, 86
forwarded, 43
panchayat, 43
real, 179
respondent, 134
target, 130

Bilateral
agreements, 18, 386, 411
trade, 387–90, 414, 416

Biodiversity, 63–64, 362
Bishnoi community, 361–62
Block Development, 170
Bokajan LAMPS, 187
Border Area Development Programmes (BADP), 54
Border trade, 387, 391, 393, 395, 399, 411, 414, 418–21, 425–26
agreement, 426
benefits, 420
formal, 419
free, 405
Indo-China, 390

Brahmaputra Valley land, 286
Brundtland Commission Report, 366
Business
activities, 214–15, 281
enterprises, 21, 320

Capabilities, 36, 84–85, 165, 167, 170, 254, 260, 267–68, 331, 405, 409
advocacy, 271
approach, 165
credit absorption, 203
improving local, 19
women's, 150

Capacities
collective self-help, 244, 268
combined, 401
generating, 107
poor decision-making, 167
problem-solving, 162
soil water retention, 62

Cash crops, profitable, 61
Central Board of Secondary Education (CBSE), 71
Centre for Appropriate Technology and Rural Development (CATRD), 17, 19, 21–24, 26–28
Centre for Monitoring Indian Economy, 376
Centre for Women Policy Studies, 302
Child health, 167, 179
Child population forms, 50
Child Sex-Ratio, 49–50
Children care, 309
Children park, 13
Chinese
carps, 4–5, 8
exporters, 390

Chittagong hill tract of Bangladesh, 366
CIS countries, 402
Civic development, 290
Civil processes, 82
Climate change, 20, 357, 364
Clinical research programme, 403
CMI Social Research Centre, 379
Collaborative programme, 21
Collective decisions, 206, 210
Commercial banks, 58, 200, 269
Commercial cultivation of rubber in India, 61
Commodity Concentration Index (CCI), 422
Common carp, 4–5, 7
Common conceptual frameworks, 165
Common fund, 151, 211–12, 269–70
Common interest groups, 270
Communication skills, 22, 180, 225, 227–28, 232
Communities
academic, 18
affordable, 25
economic, 417
indigenous, 367–68
international, 149, 369, 409
local, 22, 101, 104–5, 107
rural, 40, 235, 289
student, 20, 24
traditional, 366
village, 71

Community
development, 41–42, 162, 275
Information Centre, 22
organisation, 185, 194–97
processing centre, 63

Comparative advantage, 95, 414, 416, 422
Competitive factors, 185, 196–97
Competitiveness, 422
Composite Carp Farming Technology, 3, 6

Comprehensive Economic Cooperation Agreement (CECA), 386, 410–11
Comprehensive Economic Partnership Agreement (CEPA), 383, 391
Conceptual Framework, 69, 322
Conceptual meaning, 129
Confederation of Indian Industries, 389
Conservation movement, 362
Constitution of India, 82, 321–22, 325
Constraint analysis, 345
Contaminated water, 356
Contraception, 358
Contraceptives, 312
Convergence Resource Group Meeting, 27
Co-operative
  leaders, 184
  leadership, 185
  movement, 183–85, 194, 196–97
  society, 183, 186
Co-operative Societies Acts, 184
Coordinated development, 294
Corruption Perception Index, 396
Cost of planting, 67
Cottage industries, 310, 347
CPWAI, 134–35
Create computer Service Centre (CSC), 22
Credit
  accessing, 234
  activities, 251
  augmenting, 57
  composite, 152
  co-operatives, 315
  culture, 58
  delivery, 53–54, 56, 152
  dispensation, 57
  micro, 268
  organisation, 151
  reforms, 46
  rural, 23, 201
  source, 200
  support, 55, 270
Creditworthiness, 203
Cultivated region, 61
Cultivation, 61, 193, 335
Cultural
  background, 142, 399
  degradation, 139–40
  ecofeminism, 360
Currency changers, 406
Dairy development, 261
Dairy farming, 217
Decision-making, 136, 149–50, 154, 162, 164, 168, 176–77, 179, 201, 210, 218, 223, 262, 276–77, 323
Defence Ministry, 393–94
Degraded environments, 357
Democracy, 129, 166, 184–85, 284, 387
Democratic economics, 44
Democratic leadership, 184–85
Demographic information, 300
Demonstration programmes, 4
Design-Build-Own-Operate (DBOO), 124
Destination branding, 110
Destination market place, 110–11
Destruction of nature, 104
Developing tourism, 96, 108, 120
Development
  activities, 152, 282, 345–46, 423
  constraints, 296
  facilities, 376
  organisation, 201, 270
Dipshikha, 129–35, 137
Directorate of Tourism, 120
Disabilities Act, 82
Disadvantaged groups, 18, 261, 402
Disbursement of bank loan, 230–31
Discrimination, 82, 242, 263, 289, 294, 321, 323–24, 359
Disseminate information, 82
Disseminate knowledge, 26
Distribution
  occupational, 193
  telephone line, 311
District Autonomous Council, 193
District Rural Development Agency (DRDA), 42, 44, 192
Dokmoka LAMPS and Lumbajong LAMPS, 187
Domestic markets, 66, 389–90, 401
Domestic violence, 159, 302, 308, 345–46
Don Bosco Mission Schools, 73
Draught Prone Area Programme (DPAP), 54
Drinking water, 86, 282, 329, 363
Dropout rate, 299, 324

Earthquake, 10, 20, 66, 357
Ecofeminism, 359–61
Ecological landscape, 367

E-commerce, 109, 111
Economic/Economy
activities, 89, 122, 167, 206, 215, 255, 271, 296
agrarian, 375
benefits, 97, 113–14, 166, 202
compulsions, 320
condition, 174, 220, 334, 363
constraints, 293
cooperation, 410, 418
disparities, 261
emancipation, 129
empowerment, 159, 173–74, 177, 199, 244, 253, 269, 271, 276, 322, 324, 368
expenditure, 138
factors, 291
fastest growing, 410, 412
formal, 302
fortune, 405, 409
free market, 162
gravity, 392, 405, 409
growth, 15, 17–18, 40, 82, 150, 284, 290, 376, 389, 417, 425
hill, 419
hub, 10
impact, 97, 201, 220
indicators, 218
informal, 162, 261
integration, 405, 408–12, 415–19
interest, 162
largest, 31, 417
life, 165, 294, 327, 367
local, 293
losses, 423
obscurities, 399
progress, 262
regional, 396
rural, 167, 295
security, 37
settlement programme, 63
solvency, 150
standing, 254
supremacy, 123
survey report, 31
sustainability, 420, 422, 425–26
transaction cost, 397
viability, 422
Ecosystem, 11–12, 14, 20, 355
Eco-tourism, 53, 58, 113, 402
Education
co-operative, 197
female, 291–92
formal, 284, 291, 334
gender disparities, 306
good, 129
growth of, 70, 73, 75
mass, 129
matric level, 196
modern, 71
non-formal, 264, 351–52
quality of, 74, 77
sex/health, 291
social, 262
status, 143
Educational
attainment, 68–69, 185, 194, 259, 285
choices, 285
opportunities, 284, 289–90
planning, 290
Effective empowerment, 352
Efficient Marketing, 124
Electrical machinery, 390
Elementary education, 71, 75
E-marketing, 125
Employment
foreign, 299
generation, 55, 85, 96
part-time, 65
public sector, 376
Empowerment
approach, 253, 262
defined, 165, 244
female, 325
political, 167, 177–78, 244, 259, 262, 276, 353
proper, 35
social, 129, 158–59, 166, 199, 251
socioeconomic, 153
Entrepreneurship development, 24
Environment/Environmental
activism, 361
awareness, 356
changes, 360, 364
conservation, 368–69
crisis, 365
cultural, 320
damage, 357
degradation, 356
destruction, 358, 362, 369

free, 103
global, 426
healthy, 362
informal, 188
information, 362
issues, 357
mountain, 357, 363
natural, 3, 123, 356
optimal, 405
perturbations, 356
problem solving, 19
rural, 259
single-crop, 64
ESSAR group, 384
Ethnic groups, 330, 365, 368
Ethnobotany, 365, 367
Ethnoscience, 367
Ethnozoology, 365, 367
E-tourism, 109
Export Credit and Guarantee Corporation (ECGC), 406
Family Development Approach (FDA), 130–32, 134
Family
planning, 37, 139, 156, 177, 255, 277, 282, 291, 300, 312, 352
pressure, 350
welfare, 150, 242, 267, 403
Female
literacy, 36, 47–50, 290
participation, 291–94
Feminism, 325, 359
Financial assets, 254
Financial decisions, 211
Financial resources, 243, 266, 287, 351
Financial transactions, 210–11
Fish
diseases, 14
production, 3, 10
seeds, 4–5, 14
Focused Group Discussions (FGD), 170
Food grains, 245, 399
Foreign
direct investment, 397, 402, 404
exchange, 96, 107, 400, 422
tourists, 94, 97–99, 101–4, 121, 125
trade, 396, 412, 418, 421
Formal credit agencies, 199
Free mobility of women, 156
Free Trade Agreement (FTA), 383, 386–87, 410, 417
Gender
awareness, 234
biases, 293, 296
equality, 242–43, 282, 285, 322, 327, 359, 362
gaps, 276–77, 285
Geographical isolation, 413
Geological Survey of India (GSI), 379
Global manufacturing centre, 390
Government aid, 147
Gram Panchayats, 43–44, 139, 141–42, 168
Grass carp, 4–5, 7, 14
Gross Domestic Product (GDP), 107, 122, 376, 392
Group-based approach, 130–32, 134
Group-based model, 200
Group cohesiveness, 166
Group development, 56, 200
Group funds, 152
Group leaders, 210, 212, 214, 229–32, 341
Group management, 231
Growing awareness, 73

Handlooms, 113, 380
Health centres, 353
Helplessness, 349–50
Herbal medicine, 403
Hill region, 4, 420, 422
Holistic concept, 243
Homogeneity, 206–7
Honey bee farming, 65
Horticultural products, 379
Human resource development, 237, 284

Implementation process, 54, 56
Income-earning power, 46
Income Generating Activities, 310
Income generation, 4, 55, 108, 152, 173, 267, 363
Increasing awareness, 74
Incredible India campaign, 108, 110
Incubation Centre, 26
Indecent Representation of Women Act, 263
India Look for East Asia, 387
India-ASEAN linkages, 383
India-China Friendship Year, 391
India-China Trade Relations, 387
Indian Major Carps and Exotic Carps, 12

Indian National Congress Party, 325
Indian North East Region, 288, 290
Indigenous Knowledge System (IKS), 366
Indigenous knowledge, 366–67, 369
Indo-Myanmar bilateral trade, 419, 421
Informal groups, 268
Information centres, 104
Infrastructural development, 70
Inner Line Permit (ILP), 121, 125
Institutional climate, 165
Insurgency, control, 393–94
Integrated Rural Development Programme (IRDP), 42, 54
Intellectual development, 74
Inter-cropping, 61, 63–65
International Conference on Population and Development, 322
International Council of Women, 321
International markets, 20, 108, 401
International Organisation for Standardisation for Arunachal Pradesh State, 48
International Tourism Mart, 108
International Women's Conference, 329
Inter-state boundary, 47
ism, 93

Jawahar Rojgar Yojana, 42
Joint families, 190
JRY, 42–43

Khadi and Village Industries Commission (KVIC), 21–22, 24–25, 27–28, 65
Khadi Movement, 23

Labour Force Participation Rates, 257–58
Lack of Freedom, 348
Landholding pattern, 192–93
Language barrier, 344
Leadership
composition, 189, 196
development, 129
skills, 225, 228
Less Developed Countries (LDCs), 410
Libertarian concept, 163
Livelihood
generation, 81–82, 90
promotion, 82–83, 87
Living condition, unhygenic, 34, 86–87
Locomotor disabilities, 81
Look East Policy (LEP), 373, 383–87, 391–92, 396–99, 404–6, 408–10, 413–14, 419–20, 426

Mahatma Gandhi National Rural Employment Guarantee Act (MGNREGA), 43, 46, 246
Malnutrition, 34, 291, 328, 330
Management leaders, 184
Managing committee, 186, 192
Mandal Samkhya (MS), 270
Marginal farmers, 46, 193
Market centre, 56
Mass customisation, 111
Massive self-employment avenues, 113
Measurement of Participation in Women Empowerment Activities, 131
Micro-credit, 200–202, 234, 282
Micro-finance management, 203, 229
Micro-income, 245–46
Millennium Development Goals (MDGs), 162, 200, 218, 242
Million Wells Scheme (MWS), 54
Mineral resources, 404
Ministry of Development of North Eastern Region (MDONER), 373
Monitoring authority, 272
Multidisciplinary Training Centres, 17, 23, 26
Multiple responses, 337, 339, 341–43, 345–50
Mutually aided cooperative societies, 270
Mysore Resettlement and Development Agency (MYRADA), 166, 202, 269

Nakabaru Women's Society, 362
Nathu La Pass, 388, 390–91
National Bank for Agricultural and Rural Development (NABARD), 4, 23–24, 57, 65, 151, 202, 269
National Commission for Women Act, 323
National Council of Women in India, 322
National Hydroelectric Power Corporation (NHPC), 384, 403
National Rural Employment Guarantee Act (NREGA), 287
National Rural Health Mission (NRHM), 287
National Women's Commission, 323
Natural bridge, 408

Natural resource management, 366
Natural rubber, 60, 384
Negative development, 251
Nehru Rojgar Yojana (NRY), 55
Nehru, Jawaharlal, 325
Nokia Corporation, 326
Non-agricultural activities, 190
Non-Governmental Organisations (NGOs), 18, 37, 54, 57, 74, 78, 81–83, 89–90, 166–67, 179–80, 208–11, 235–36, 270–72, 293–95, 324
Non-official leaders, 184
North Eastern Council (NEC), 18, 373, 393–94
North Eastern Region (NER), 10, 17, 27, 70, 254, 287, 373–74, 384–85, 392–400, 402–6, 408–12, 414–15, 418–19, 422–23, 426
Nuclear families, 190, 196, 205

Obnoxious gases, 4–5
Organic chemicals, 388, 390

Packaged tour, 100–101
Panchayati Raj, 41–42, 44, 46
Panchayats activities, 179
Paradigm Shift of Women Empowerment, 266
Participatory development, 367
Penetration Ratio (PR), 423
People's Education and Development Organisation (PEDO), 201
Per Capita Income (PCI), 34, 287, 376, 392
Personal development, 316
Platinum Group of Elements (PGE), 379
Political awareness, 197
Political background, 185, 194–97
Political leaders, 110, 293
Polygamy, 308–9, 334
Positions of Power, Access to, 305
Poverty, 30–32, 34–37, 40, 47, 87, 101, 104, 165, 167–68, 261, 277, 289, 291, 328–29, 336–38
  alleviation, 46, 53–55, 152, 167, 199–200, 282
  disproportionate levels of, 173, 255
  extreme, 34, 260–61, 336, 351
  level, 31, 206, 357
  reduction, 26, 37, 82, 200, 218, 253, 299, 316
  rural, 23, 42, 162
  stricken families, 294
Power Surplus State, 403
Powerless groups, 243, 266
Premature deaths, 342
Prime Minister Integrated Urban Poverty Eradication Programme (PMIUPEP), 55
Prime Minister's Rojgar Yojana (PMRY), 55
Productive community assets, 42
Productive resources, 244, 268, 287
Protected Area Permit (PAP), 121, 125
Psychological impact, 220, 225, 229
Public Distribution System (PDS), 34, 245
Purchasing Power Parity (PPP), 32, 124

Random sampling, 204
Regional Research Centre, 403
Regional Rural Banks (RRBs), 151, 200, 202
Regional Trading Arrangements (RTA), 416, 426
Rehabilitation Council of India Act, 82
Religious factors, 292
Repayment performance, 209–10
Research questions, 272, 278
Reservation of women, 262
Residential areas, 156–57
Resource
  allocation, 422
  based industries, 406
  economic, 269, 307, 376
  forest, 365
  immense, 380
  increasing, 150
  informational, 258
  intellectual, 129, 243, 266
  material, 129
  necessary, 112, 166
  physical/material, 243, 266
  plentiful, 376
  rich, 57
  scarce, 89
Revealed Comparative Advantage (RCA), 422–23
Rio Declaration on Environment and Development, 364
Rubber
  Board, 63, 66–67

cultivation, 60–61, 63, 67
gardens, 63–64
plantations, 60–61, 63–67
trees, 60–62, 64–65
Rural industrialisation, 23, 25
Rural Landless Employment Guarantee Programme (RLEGP), 42
Rural manpower development, 21

SAARC Countries, 18
Sarva Shiksha Abhiyan (SSA), 75, 287
Saving habits, 58, 152, 174–75, 205, 273, 275
Science, Technology, Engineering, or Mathematics (STEM), 285
Secondary Education Board of Assam (SEBA), 70–71
Self-employment, 3, 18, 78, 81, 105, 150, 167–68, 324
Self-esteem, 165–66, 177, 352
Self-help Group (SHGs), 149–55, 166–80, 199–218, 220, 222–30, 232–37, 242–45, 251–52, 268–73, 276–78, 281–82, 329, 331, 340–45, 350–53
Silicon Valley of India, 389
Silver carp, 4, 7, 14
Singh, Manmohan, 384, 386, 410, 417
Skill development, 235
Skill Development Vocational Training, 25–26
Small farmers categories, 193
Social awareness, 223
Social constraints, 129
Social environments, 277, 359
Social inclusion, 312–13
Social obligation, 345–46
Social welfare, 17, 253, 420–22
Societal structured beliefs, 242
Socio-economic
activities, 170
background, 140, 150, 169–70, 185, 269
characteristic, 186
development, 20, 53, 55, 58, 147, 183, 186, 201, 253, 270, 298, 347, 376, 395
empowerment, 105, 149, 151–53, 201, 282
Socio-psychological empowerment, 244
Software industry, 389
Soil moisture, 62
Soil nutrients, 62, 64
South Asia Travel and Tourism Exchange (SATTE), 108
Special Economic Zone (SEZ), 398, 406
Special programmes, 46
Spurious development, 78
State Institute of Rural Development (SIRD), 21–22
State of Living Condition, 86
State Tribal Co-operative Development Corporation, 55
State-of-the-art technology, 405, 409
Sub-health centre, 312
Suitable calcification, 15
Superstitions, 139–40, 289, 353
Supply of Improved Toolkits to Rural Artisan (SITRA), 54
Sustainability, 9, 15, 88, 200, 202, 229–30, 233, 359–61, 422
Sustainable development, 43, 58, 69, 122–23, 149, 151–52, 200, 355, 364, 366, 369–70, 425
Sustainable resource management, 366
Swarnajayanti Gram Swarojgar Yojana (SGSY), 23, 54, 56, 152, 168, 204, 262
Swarnajayanti Shahari Rojgar Yojana (SJSRY), 55–56, 168
SWOT Analysis, 229

Talented intellectual assets, 57
Tea
gardens, 99, 102, 155, 400
industry, 398–400
producers, 400
tourism, 102, 113
Teacher-student ratio, 74–75, 79
Technical and Vocational Education and Training (TVET), 17, 27
Techno Scrutiny Committee (TSC), 27
Technology transfer, 18, 21, 23, 28
Tibeto-Burman groups, 307
Tourism
industry, 96–97, 102, 105, 107, 109–10, 112, 114
marketing, 109–11
resources, 122
satellite accounting, 108
Tourist
attractions, 95, 112

destinations, 94, 112, 120–23, 126
guideship, 122, 125
attraction, 13, 98
spots, 99, 103
Trade
agreements, 385, 387–88
centres, 415, 421
cross-border, 412–13, 420–22, 426
formal, 420–22
global, 416, 418
indices, 422
openness index, 422
unions, 303
Traditional Environment/Ecological Knowledge (TEK), 365–66, 369
Trafficking, 307
Training for Rural Youth for Self-Employment (TRYSEM), 54
Trans-border countries, 396
Transparency International (TI), 396
Tribal communities, 70, 187, 189, 195, 197, 328–29, 363, 366
Tribal cuisines, 126
Tribal families, 63

Unanimous decisions, 230
Underprivileged groups, 329
Unemployed groups, 159
United Nations Conference on Environment and Development (UNCED), 149
United Nations Development Fund for Women, 255
United Nations Development Programme (UNDP), 18, 31–32, 34, 81, 255, 323
Urban Basic Services for the Poor (UBSP), 55
US Centre for Disease Control, 301

Vegetable cultivation, 58
Vegetable Oil Industry, 13
Vegetable wastes, 5, 7
Village Development Committee (VDCs), 300, 308–9, 311
Village Organisations (VO), 270
Vocational education, 291, 293, 295
Vulnerabilities, 143, 291, 324, 347, 349, 369
Vulnerable groups, 161, 296

Water bodies, 9–11, 14–15, 95
Water Quality Testing, 23, 27
Water resources, 3
Weak-Links, 55–56
Weaving, 154, 159, 217, 363
Woman
advancement of, 255, 322
contribution of, 242, 267, 277, 361
control decisions, 150
destitute, 261
earning, 144
empowerment, 161
farmers, 299, 356
fish vending business, 228
legislators, 260
literacy, 334
pregnant, 356
refugee camps exposes, 358
rural uneducated, 324
self-help groups, 151
unemployed, 155, 159
victimized, 142
Women's Reservation Bill, 262
Work participation rates, 77, 254, 257
World Bank, 26, 32, 63, 82, 165, 244, 331
World Health Organisation, 302, 357
World Heritage Site, 95
World Summit on Social Development (WSSD), 149
World Tourism Mart, 108
World Tourism Organisation (WTO), 93, 402, 415
World Travel and Tourism Council (WTTC), 107–8

Yingde Dragon Mountain Cement Company Ltd, 390
Youth welfare, 195
Yunus, Mohammed, 269

Zilla Parishads, 260